THE

SOCIALIST REGISTER 1978

THE
SOCIALIST REGISTER
1978

EDITED BY

RALPH MILIBAND

and

JOHN SAVILLE

Merlin Book Club

THE MERLIN PRESS
LONDON

First published in 1978
by The Merlin Press Ltd.
3 Manchester Road,
London, E.14.

Printed by A. Wheaton & Co. Ltd., Exeter

SBN 85036234 2   cloth edition
    85036235 0   paperback edition

TABLE OF CONTENTS

ACKNOWLEDGEMENTS

This is the fifteenth issue of *The Socialist Register* and we express once again our thanks for their help to our contributors; to Martin Eve and David Musson of Merlin Press; and to Paul Edmunson and Günter Minnerup for their translation of Rudolf Bahro's article.

The essays in this volume deal with many different subjects, and do so in different ways. But they nevertheless suggest and exemplify a common concern: with the socialist critique of Soviet-type and late capitalist regimes; and with the theoretical, programmatic and organisational problems that need to be tackled in order to reach coherent and adequate socialist positions. We will continue to explore these themes in future volumes. The essay by Colin Leys stands on its own here; but it is a further contribution to the interpretation of contemporary African experience which has been a continuing feature of the *Register*.

To speak of a common concern is not to suggest that we all necessarily agree with each other's views; and it may be as well to make the point explicitly.

August 1978   R.M.
                                                                      J.S.

RUDOLF BAHRO—AN INTRODUCTION

Günter Minnerup

"I have always believed in the power of the idea and the word, and that it matters whether one is convinced of oneself and one's cause and doesn't shrink back deep down inside when the decision has to be made." When, after ten years of work on his book *The Alternative. A Critique of Socialism as it Actually Exists,* Rudolf Bahro made his decision to come out into the open by having his work published in West Germany, his belief in the power of the idea and the word was immediately confirmed by his arrest—on the rather ludicrous charge of "espionage"—and imprisonment in the German Democratic Republic.

That was in August 1977. At the time of writing[1] Bahro is still in gaol, cut off from all communication with the outside world, awaiting a secret trial. But while they could arrest the author, the East Germany authority's fears concerning the powerful impact of *The Alternative* have been more than justified. Not only has the book reached the top ten of the West German bestselling list for several months, and been translated into several major Western languages,[2] but in the German Democratic Republic itself, where several hundred copies are estimated to circulate clandestinely, Bahro's work has immediately become a central point of reference for the socialist opposition.[3]

The significance of Rudolf Bahro lies not so much in the fact that yet again an Eastern European dissident has been hit by state repression; nor even in the fact that Bahro is an avowed communist and Marxist. In the GDR, at least, the publicly articulated voices of the opposition have always been from the left, from Wolfgang Harich to Wolf Biermann. The real importance of Bahro's *Alternative* lies in its theoretical achievement: not since the 1920s, when the Left Opposition was silenced in the Soviet Union, has such a powerful and original, comprehensive critique of the bureaucratic regime that calls itself "socialist" emerged from within its own sphere. Without, of course, dissociating himself from the struggle for human rights and democratic freedoms in Eastern Europe, Bahro puts the socialist opposition back into the offensive ideologically: Socialism, he asserts, is not merely the gradual democratic reform of the existing system; Socialism as conceived by Marx, Engels and Lenin requires what he calls a "Cultural Revolution", a comprehensive re-orientation that goes beyond the political, institutional, and includes the daily life-style of the

1

masses, a radical change in both individual and collective habits and mentalities—in short, the consciously planned creation of a "new man." Yet Bahro cannot be dismissed as a utopian dreamer: he is not content simply to counterpose his conception of "Socialism as it Should Be" to "Socialism as it Actually Exists", his analysis of East European society is highly concrete—with the detailed knowledge of the experienced party functionary he shows that, far from suffering mere "shortcomings", the socio-economic system of existing socialism is actually moving further and further away from the aim of a classless society; and with the keen historical awareness of the trained Marxist intellect he seeks to offer a novel explanation of how it was that the high hopes of the Bolshevik revolution ended up in the creation of a totalitarian system of oppression.

Born in 1935, Rudolf Bahro is in many ways a typical representative of a whole generation of SED (Socialist Unity Party of Germany; the East German Communist Party) functionaries. He joined the Party in 1952, and after graduating in philosophy at the East Berlin Humboldt University in 1959, served the SED in a variety of functions: as an editor of party journals in the campaign to collectivise East German agriculture (1959-60), and at the University of Greifswald (1960-62), as an employee of the central trade union apparatus (1962-65), again as a journalist as deputy editor of *Forum,* the SED's student paper, and since 1967 as an economist concerned with the rationalisation of production in a large Berlin rubber factory. In his "Interview with Himself" Bahro names the experience of Czechoslovakia 1968 as the decisive turning point of his political evolution; and from all we know, we can assume that August 1968 had the effect of an ideological earthquake on many of his generation. There have, of course, been manifestations of dissent in East Germany before Bahro and before 1968: several splits within the ruling Politbureau during the 1950s, the uprising of 17th June 1953, the intellectual unrest following the XXth Party Congress of the CPSU, the dissident writers of the early 1960s. The reaction to 1968 was less spectacular than most of the previous occasions, the critical consciousness engendered by it still remains largely anonymous. But it must have touched the raw nerve of the bureaucratic system: the ranks of the party functionaries at a lower and medium level, and Bahro, as such a functionary, stepping out of anonymity and articulating the latent critical consciousness in conscious criticism, must represent a more formidable threat to Honecker's ruling clique than any number of poets, artists and singers. Hence the ferocious reaction.

The originality of Bahro's theses is, without any doubt, also going to establish *The Alternative* as an essential point of reference among Western Marxists discussing the nature of the East European societies. At least in the English-speaking area, two major traditions have dominated the debate for a long time: the orthodox Trotskyist formula of the "degenerated workers' states" and the "state capitalist" school in its

International Socialism or (in the US) Maoist varieties. Within the narrow framework of this alternative, Bahro certainly has more affinity with the Trotskyist tradition. He rejects the notion that the East European regimes are in any way capitalist, and much of his terminology—such as the reference to a ruling "bureaucracy" and the need for a "political revolution"—is clearly more reminiscent of Trotsky than of Tony Cliff. But these similarities are largely superficial. In fact Bahro explicitly polemicises against the Trotskyist analysis: "I strongly believe that it is high time for revolutionary Marxists to abandon all theories of 'deformation', and call a halt to the old anger about the distortion and 'betrayal' of socialism, understandable as this at one time was. . . We cannot learn the path to follow from that opposition which lost the fight against the rise of Stalinism. Every revolutionary communist since 1917 has had Trotskyist feelings at a certain stage in the move away from domination by the apparatus. But this position really does lack historical prospects. We do not want to re-establish old norms, but to create new ones."[4] His essential difference with the Trotskyist tradition concerns the different assessments of the historical role of Stalinism and its relation to the Bolshevik October revolution. For Bahro, the victory of Stalin over the Left Opposition was inevitable and even historically progressive: "The opening of the gap between material progress and social and political emancipation. . . was unavoidable. The rapid technical and cultural qualification of the masses first had to create the preconditions for socialist relations of productions. But one must not forget that this is a justification of the kind given by Marx to the revolutionary practice of the bourgeoisie. It applies to an antagonistic reality in which 'the higher development of individuality is only acquired through a historical process in which the individuals are sacrificed'."[5] Despite Lenin's revolutionary genius and integrity, the Russian revolution could not but lead the backward country into a prolonged phase of "despotic industrialisation", albeit on a non-capitalist road, and "Lenin's Bolshevik Party. . . was to a large extent the extraordinary representative of the expelled capitalist exploiting class (without, however, taking the place of this class), which had not been deeply rooted enough in the economic life of a gigantic peasant country."[6]

But now that the historically necessary transformation from a predominantly agricultural to a predominantly industrial society had taken place even in Russia and the more backward East European countries, and given that the German Democratic Republic and Czechoslovakia had not, after 1945, fallen into the same category anyway, the Stalinist despotism has definitely outlasted its historical role and become an obstacle towards any further progress. Bahro devotes the central part of *The Alternative* to a highly original analysis of the motor forces of the coming "Cultural Revolution." He rejects the traditional concept of "working class" as outdated, and substitutes for it a broad alliance of all the bearers of what he terms "surplus consciousness," "the energetic and creative elements in all strata and areas of society, of all people in whose individuality the emancipatory interests predominate."[7] Bahro calls for the formation of a loosely-organised, new "League of Communists" to assemble all these elements, and proceeds to outline a concrete programme of action for the communist opposition thus constituted.

It is impossible within the confines of this short introduction to highlight the many novel ideas and concepts Bahro introduces into the Marxist discussion of Eastern Europe: his use of psycho-analytical concepts, his discussion of ecological and cultural restraints on quantitative economic growth, his vision of the future communist society. These are certainly many aspects of Bahro's *Alternative* that will meet with widespread criticism: quite apart from his views on the October revolution and the inevitability of Stalinism, his insistence that there should only be *one* party under socialism and certain passages with what could be described as "intellectual-elitist" overtones seem highly questionable. Such a necessary discussion of Bahro's theories, however, requires that the author be free to clarify ambiguities, to reply to critics, and defend his views against misrepresentation. As long as Rudolf Bahro continues to be imprisoned, as long as he is denied the freedom to publish and openly debate his views in the country he chooses to live and work in, the German Democratic Republic, all socialists, whether they agree with *The Alternative* or not, have the responsibility to do their utmost to support Bahro's struggle unconditionally. Believing that the power of the bureaucratic apparatus "must be undermined *ideologically* before it can fall materially", Bahro wrote *The Alternative* primarily as a weapon to be used in this ideological struggle against late Stalinism. It is as such, in its unquestionable superiority over everything else that emerged from the ranks of the socialist opposition in Eastern Europe for decades, that the importance of Rudolf Bahro's work must be judged.

NOTES

1. June, 1978.
2. The British edition, published by New Left Books and translated by David Fernbach, is due to appear in October, 1978.
3. Cf. the "Manifesto of the SED Opposition" published in *Der Spiegel* in January, 1978.
4. Rudolf Bahro, *The Alternative in Eastern Europe*; in: *New Left Review* 106, p. 6 and 33.
5. *Die Alternative*, German original, p. 137, my own translation.
6. NLR, p. 10.
7. NLR, p. 19.

RUDOLF BAHRO INTERVIEWS HIMSELF

Q. By the time we broadcast today's discussion your book "Contribution to a Critique of Socialism as it actually exists" will already have been published under the title of *The Alternative*. Does the new title not express your message more accurately than the original formula? Because of course you put forward proposals for an alternative political praxis for East European Communism. You make these proposals as a Marxist, as an East German (GDR) Communist, as an insider, so to speak.

A. What I wanted to provide was in effect not primarily a political polemic but the outline of a comprehensive political and economic analysis and alternative. My book is only polemical in as much as it destroys the Party's official self-portrait of socialism as it actually exists and discusses the situation as it really is. There is a widespread feeling here in the GDR that socialism as it exists and the socialism of Marx are two very different, substantially different things. I prove that this is so. I don't denounce it; I *explain* it as an historical fact. I analyse and criticise socialism as it actually exists as a *social formation of a specific type*, just as Marx understood capitalism as a social formation. I have gone back a long way in history, right back to the ancient Asiatic mode of production in order to show clearly the genesis of our present system, by which I mean of course in Russia and the Soviet Union. In East Germany or in Czechoslovakia socialism, as everyone knows, is a derived and not an original phenomenon. Here it is not something that can be explained in terms of itself.

Q. That is then your starting point. And what are your aims and objectives?

A. The main questions which my book raises and which I try to answer are these: What would the total emancipation of man— because of course that was Marx's most original aim—what would this total emancipation mean today? What barriers would it have to overcome? How could and ought a Communist praxis to look under

5

the conditions of socialism as it actually exists? Who would see this praxis through, and from what forces would its agents be recruited? And how ought the new league of Communists to be organised? And on the basis of what kind of political and economic action programme?

What's more, I pose these questions in such a way that they ought to be of interest to Western Communists and Socialists. For example, it seems questionable to me whether a united left, such as the one in France, should include as one of its essential programmatic points the raising of steel production and an injection of more investment—just a further dose of the same old medicine. In the short term many a thing can be correct, even a financial boost for the steel industry. But what kind of new civilisation is the PCF really anticipating? What has it really learnt since May 1968?

Q. Yes, of course, these are problems which are not only of interest to Communists today. Unfortunately it is idle to ask why your book has not been published in great numbers in East Germany where you live. But what will happen if you are forced to appeal to the public outside this country? Will people in the GDR be able to read your book at all?

A. Several hundred copies will of course find their way back here, and then a few thousand people will read it. I have also condensed the substance of the book into a series of lectures which will undoubtedly reach us via the radio. Besides, I have also circulated the book in the GDR, if only in the form of a small, unprofessionally produced edition, due to the limitations imposed on me. I am confident that the essential ideas will become well-known.

Q. How will the SED leadership react to the fact that yet another citizen, yet another Party member—because you have been one for almost 25 years—openly adopts a dissident position? Your book employs merciless logic and is quite uncompromising in its arguments. It could, in the long run, exert an influence in undermining the prevailing power structure.

A. I hope so. I am intervening in a process which has been underway for a long time. The original idea has been eroded away. The Party can be compared to the Papal Church prior to Luther's Reformation, with agnosticism deeply penetrating even its own ranks. Perplexity right up to the Politburo. No positive idea amongst broad layers. All means of mass mobilisation, especially in the economic sphere, are worn out and threadbare. Bewilderment wherever one turns. No discussion any more.

I wanted to provide the new layers with a theoretical basis for the struggle for the liquidation of the Stalinist social system to which they are heirs. This system must be done away with because it stifles life, because it is unproductive, because it hinders subjective motivation and paralyses and consumes it in competition with the West, a competition which we could never hope to win in this way.

Q. Do you think the SED will take issue with your book?

A. Who is "the SED"? Let us deal first of all with the Party apparatus. Because this is what you had in mind. Initially the apparatus will of course respond with the usual defence mechanisms. Not only will it brand my book as revisionist but also as counter-revolutionary. It will speak of some paymaster or other. In this connection it will exploit every attention I pay to non- or anti-Communist circles (recently it has even included a certain Santiago Carillo in this category). That has long been routine. The servile creatures hardly need to think about the procedure any more. Of course it requires no skill to snatch a couple of isolated sentences from their context. The apparatus *has to* distort all criticism. It *must not* be true that it stems from within its own ranks, that it has a broad and emotional layer of support at home, even, and in particular, among the Party rank and file. They will endeavour at all costs to avoid any debate with my *arguments* and *conclusions*.

In any case, the book will be read, even officially, so to speak. And now we come to the matter of real importance. Almost everyone who reads it—whether instructed to do so or not—will have thoughts different from those which he can or must subsequently express in public. I believe I have written a book against which the political police will be powerless, because it still appeals to the most loyal beings—in as far as they are prepared to think at all. At least as far as my analysis and characterisation of the existing situation are concerned, even members of the Politburo will sit in front of the pages and say to themselves from time to time: Yes, that's just what it's like. This disarms you psychologically. I build directly on the gulf that exists between the official position and the inner psychological process at work in the political individuals. Whenever I speak of the apparatus then I am always referring to a reactionary power structure, and not necessarily to the individuals who are connected to it at various nodal points. They could of course step out of this jungle tomorrow.

Q. And what about the rest of the East German public?

A.   Well, of course, my book is addressed not least to the many semi-loyal Party members and indeed to those people who associate themselves critically with the GDR. Most of these only continue their involvement because to them any prospect of a change seems to be out of the question. It is not a new historical phenomenon that a particular generation experiences a collective feeling that it "just won't work." For many here in this country nothing you care to mention "works", be it from the inside or the outside. Resignation rules. It's purely psychological. Ossification has set in, a tendency which the individuals must resist. The wheels of history have of course continued to turn. Suddenly it does "work" after all, it's just that in the meantime many have opted out. What I resolutely attack is the residual loyalty to the *apparatus* which has for a long time worked to the detriment of the non-capitalist foundations of the GDR. The reality is such that every Party intellectual in particular must ask himself whether he is dominated by the apparatchik—because to a certain extent that is what he is—or by the Communist in him. Nobody can evade this inner subjective dilemma.

And finally my book addresses itself to the real forces of opposition. I want to encourage them to adopt an optimistic and constructive position. Don't take the road of defeatism and despair, but the road of organised opposition! Be prepared, if necessary, to give up your present existence to this end, for instance, your particular role as a salaried intellectual.

Q.   Then you believe that your work will alter the situation in the GDR?

A.   Yes, especially the ideological situation. For this I am not counting on the immediate sensational impact. On the contrary, there will be a variety of emotionally determined reactions—all the more so since ordinary people won't be able to read the book at once. But I have provided theory. And that I certainly am relying on. I am relying on the long-term effect of every thought which really goes to the very heart of these problems. I have approached it with absolute seriousness, in all sincerity and consistency. I have staked not only my intellect but also my civic livelihood on it. That is sure to have its effect.

I am only speaking about myself here as an example. Of course I am not the first to have risked something. Personal examples can now have a tremendous effect. Full use must be made of the situation that has arisen since Helsinki, and even more so since the Berlin Conference, since the emergence of Eurocommunism, in order to drive the apparatus ideologically into a corner. If possible, don't allow them a minute's peace or any breathing space in the ideological battle. One appearance should immediately be followed by the next. I call that getting the apparatus used to having to look open opposition in the face. The aim of the exercise is finally to force it to take up the ideological battle in public in its own country and in all the so-called Socialist countries. This is the end towards which we must work. And for this the opposition needs a *comprehensive* counter-position and not merely fragmentary proposals. It must put a plan for an *alternative overall policy* on the agenda. Such aspects as the question of human rights must be found a place within a larger constructive framework. And I am absolutely certain that under socialism as it actually exists there is no alternative to the rule of the apparatus which could be implemented without or in opposition to the Communists. We need only step boldly out of the late Stalinist power structure of the apparatus and put our political experience, our Marxist method, at the disposal of *society*. That goes for each of our countries and, at the same time, for all of them put together, and first and foremost for the Soviet Union itself.

Q.   What consequences do you envisage for yourself personally? What do you suppose will happen?

A.   I could not afford to attach too much importance to this question. If one begins to speculate in a situation like this, one is not free to choose such a position. I am prepared for every conceivable reaction. I had time to prepare myself for the hour of truth. Of course, I won't be the victim; I'm the one who is doing the attacking. I was fortunate in being able to determine the hour myself.

Q.   You will of course be expelled from the Party.

A.   Yes, with the utmost speed and without any fuss. That will merely be normal procedure. It is clear from this book that I have been breaking the rules which the apparatus laid down for the Party for a long time, at least since August 21st, 1968. What is not so normal, but nevertheless typical of the system, is that I will lose my present job. Strong emphasis is being laid at present in the official propaganda of the GDR on the human right to work. Therefore I shall just have to wait and see how it applies to me.

Q.   And is that all you fear?

A.   Whether or not I shall be arrested depends on the international, and particularly the Communist public. That there are legal clauses in existence which I had to contravene in order to proceed at all, is indicative of the nature of our political system. It requires laws which are, as a precaution, designed in such a way that anyone who wants to disseminate dissident views—if he does not wish to disseminate them then he is not political at all—must contravene them. Under the new penal code—depending on the interpretation— I face from the outset between 2 and 10 years, if it is decided to classify my critique of the political superstructure as subversive agitation. But it begins much earlier than that. For example, I would have had to submit my book on time to the state copyright office, along with a request for it to be released for printing abroad. I pursued this course of action for my relatively harmless, and altogether acceptably designed dissertation after it had been turned down both by the university in Leuna—Merseburg and by the Dietz publishing house. I was told that there was no way that I would get the necessary permission.

In short, every alternative political conception and position becomes a criminal offence at the very first hurdle, namely as soon as it is made public. Publicity is not legally attainable at all. For Europe this is a very anachronistic state of affairs.

Q.   And you won't be expelled from the country? As you know, in recent years that has become an essential ingredient in the practice against oppositionists.

A.   It is possible that the apparatus will demonstrate its utter bankruptcy in this way. But it won't be able to exile the contents of my book in the same way. As far as I myself am concerned, my battleground is here, although I don't foresee any great difficulty in finding my place in the revolutionary ranks somewhere else. I have based my thinking on this premise. My entire development has made me, so to speak, into a product of the GDR through and through. Here at home I am co-responsible. I particularly don't want this point to be mis-understood. Since the age of 15 I have never stood on the outside; since 1950, i.e. from very early on, I have been one of the activists contributing to our present circumstances. I am thoroughly familiar with the terrain, not only theoretically but also in practice. And not only with regard to ideology and art etc.; I have done everything under the sun, in agriculture, in science and in higher education, and, during the last decade, in industry. People like myself must quite simply try to change the course of things *here at home* if they want to remain true to their origins. I never had the slightest inclination to leave the field of battle. On the contrary, when I had to quit regimented political life 10 years ago I launched myself all the more deeply into politics, into theory in the first place, but then entirely on my own account.

Q. Perhaps you can describe in a little more detail how you gained your experience and go through some of the stages in your development.

A. On the face of it, my biography follows the normal GDR pattern. One or two conflicts I could tell you about are typical for thousands of characters like myself, and not all of them have emerged from them as relatively unscathed psychologically as I have.

After completing my studies in philosophy, that was in 1959, the afterpains of my crisis of 1956/7 (the 20th Party Congress of the CPSU, Hungary, Poland) made me drift into the Oderburch area to an agricultural machinery and tractor station. There I was editor of a village newspaper for an area consisting of 7 or 8 communities. And I arrived just at the right time for the campaign for the full collectivisation of agriculture in 1960. I have been at home with farming all my life, thanks to my father. I come from a farming background. Collective farming is perhaps the greatest economic success in the GDR.

I subsequently spent two years at Greifswald University, not as a student, but again as an editor. There I edited the university newspaper which the Party leadership published. It was there that I became familiar with the academic atmosphere, and of course much more intimately than from a student angle. Because it was a small provincial university it was much easier to obtain an overall view.

From Greifswald the Science Department of the Central Committee of the SED brought me to Berlin, to the Central Executive of the Scientists' Trade Union. There I was, among other things, an adviser to the Chairman.

In 1965 I went to *Forum* as deputy editor. *Forum* addresses itself to students and the young intelligentsia. In 1963 a youth communiqué was put out by the Politburo; it was the green light for a certain amount of criticism on the bureaucratic apparatus by the younger generation. Then, in mid-1965, I was not aware that this line was about to be overturned. I had arrived too late.

During my years at the trade union and at *Forum* I lost my political naiveté, if initially in a very naive way. I didn't like the postures, the bureaucratic rules of the game. I never really fitted in. Then at *Forum* I gradually and consciously pursued a definite course and eventually tried to put forward topics for discussion which were not supposed to have been discussed. "Put the contradictions on the table instead of in the drawer" was my motto. I firstly had to undergo the experience that as a small cog in an ideological power machine one cannot move in a straight line. There was a debate on poetry. I didn't realise that I was starting a provocation against the poets when I set this debate in motion. The intended discussion was cut short. I myself had written from a rather strident, so-called "leftist" position, especially against Günter Kunert. At that time I thought the way that I wrote. But then the poets could not write what *they* thought, and in as far as they did still write it I was no longer allowed to print it. In the end the whole affair only proved harmful. When I realised that forces other than my personal convictions stood behind my typewriter, I abandoned my post there in spirit and decided to take a chance. The last straw was the printing of Volker Braun's "Kipper Paul Bauch", for which I was responsible. That must have been in the spring of 1966.

A few months later I landed up in industry, and, I must emphasise, it was a soft landing. On the whole I was always very lucky to be treated so well, even after my dismissal from *Forum*. I have never been made to feel personally angry or bitter.

Q. But what about the future? What will become of your family? You do have a family, don't you?

A. I did have a family until 4 years ago. My children are now aged 20, 15 and 13. Our circumstances are, however, arranged in such a way that one must eventually go it alone if one wants to act as I am doing now.

Q. And were you not afraid during all those years?

A. Yes, I was afraid too, but not so much of the consequences that I might have to contend with one day. I was afraid of not being able to cope with my work, and above all I was afraid of not finishing it, of being found out too soon, and of not reaching the public. But, for all that, I can assure that I slept soundly most nights. That's simply a question of temperament.

Q. But you are not trying to say that your situation was largely unproblematic, are you?

A. I was still faced with *one* problem above all. It is not easy to keep silent to the rest of the world about the consequences one is really living towards. I would much rather have come out into the open. It is actually the very "normal", conformist existence, which one is forced to lead publicly, which is the real nuisance. You cannot begin to imagine how pleased I am that for me the game of hide and seek is now at last over, that I can at last show my true face to society, or rather to those who know me. That has not often been the case since 1968. But I am confident that it will be absolutely clear to most of them that I had to behave as I did, if I was really serious about writing this book. The very nature of the operation meant that I simply led the double life of a law breaker. It was not directed against my colleagues and comrades, but against the machinery, which after all forces one to adopt this form of struggle. The best prophylaxis against inner tension is the writing of an important work itself. As you can imagine, my time was fully occupied. In this respect more than any other, I lived a double life, even if at the same time it was naturally somewhat one-sided.

Q.   Nevertheless, your book must now appear to many people who have worked with you day after day and who believed they knew you well like a bolt out of the blue.

A.   Yes, of course it will. Besides, those people who knew me somewhat better will only be so utterly taken aback for a brief moment. People could always speak reasonably openly with me, as long as it remained within the limits. It might even appear as if I had less to hide than others. Because, of course, it goes without saying that all political people in the GDR hold views different from those they can express at work etc. Of course, in private you do make yourself understood, more so to some than others. If often only needs a few words, only quite a small hint, and one's position is already recognisable. Anyone who has the courage to reveal his true identity earns a good deal of confidence, if his partner does not happen to be of a generally anxious disposition. Much more communication is possible than many people imagine. People, who have not the slightest reason to be, are still afraid of one another.

Q.   And how did you manage to find the *time* or the necessary *peace and quiet* to write this book in addition to a doctorate—and as a "side-line" at that—and apparently still maintain good health? You don't appear to have ever held a post in an academic institution.

A.   Still, I did study philosophy for 5 years at the Humboldt University in the fifties. You know, if I had subsequently ended up in the academic field, in our official academic field—it grinds you down. I would perhaps have got round to writing thicker manuscripts, but probably not this book. This may sound strange, but I needed better conditions in which to write it, and I found them too. Time is not the only thing one needs in a case like this.

When I hand it over to the public now, I can truthfully say that

I have not missed a single day's work in industry because of it, not one. But at least until 1975 circumstances there were relatively favourable. I was not in management, but was dealing with organisational and technical matters in an engineering office practising a sort of management consultancy for a certain branch of industry. The immediate contact with industrial and economic practice proved positively favourable for my purpose.

For my preliminary research my free time was sufficient. But then I needed a couple of consecutive months for the first draft. Here I had luck on my side. I got the chance to do an unscheduled doctor's degree. It meant that from 1972 to 1974 I was released from the firm for three months each year. 5 out of the entire 9 months were put on one side, and by the summer of 1973 the first draft was completed; even at that stage it was a thick book of over 300 typed sheets.

I then wrote the dissertation by the summer of 1975. In it I analyse quite concretely how the relations of production under socialism as it actually exists hinder the development of the subjective forces of production which are embodied in the growing number of university and technical college cadres in our industry. Of course, the actual conclusions are cut from or concealed in this text, and stylistically it keeps within the prescribed phraseology, albeit with a certain amount of difficulty. But the work aroused so much suspicion and uneasiness, particularly the appendix—an uncensored record of almost 50 interviews with industrial cadres—that the University eventually informed me that they had to reject it, ostensibly because it failed to meet the necessary academic requirements.

Q.   It astonishes me how much importance you have obviously attached to doing your job properly in the normal manner, despite and during your work on this revolutionary book, which has since been published.

A.   First of all one could say that that was simply the easiest approach. But apart from that—I have always found it difficult, in every respect, to do a botched job. One doesn't harm the apparatus so much as all those people who go about their normal business. One upsets the flow of communication. It quite simply shows a lack of solidarity. And it also impairs one's own ability to work.

It is generally a very important rule for the political struggle in our conditions *not* to spread any additional disorganisation—the level is already high enough!—but to articulate and qualify the anger at the prevailing disorganisation, in order to solidarise with those who want to do a proper job at their place of work. Never confuse the individuals with the apparatus, not even the functionaries. They are not infrequently the first to suffer from the faults of the system.

And I was concerned about something else too. Our conditions have deprived more than a few critical and thinking people of their productivity and have driven them into unhappy isolation and made them adopt some eccentric positions or other. I have proved that I can function even within the existing system. I was, as I said, a journalist. I was a trade union functionary in the central apparatus. I have taken part as a specialist in technological and organisational rationalisation projects. At the present time I am still in charge of production and production norms. . .

Q. With production norms, too?

A. Yes, with production norms too. Otherwise I would not know as precisely, as I describe in my book, why or to what extent they must be abolished. Even in the dissertation I was anxious to prove that it is possible to take on the dominant reactionary tendency in a constructive way. I didn't quite succeed. But when I think that firstly I gained the opportunity for concentrated theoretical work, and that secondly there were initially three favourable verdicts, and that it was only later, after an altogether scandalous episode, that two more negative opinions had to be procured in order to substantiate a rejection in the University's Academic Council. . . The rest is better forgotten.

Q. Up to now we have been discussing the external circumstances. But what was your inner motivation? If I understood correctly, you have been working in this direction since 1968.

A. It certainly isn't a book which emerged overnight. The story begins much earlier, even if I did only start to write definitively in the early seventies.

The incubation period lies between the two notorious August days of 1961 and 1968. I was one of the many, mainly young Communists in the GDR who associated the illusion that, in the new situation, the Party would make a radical attempt to win over the majority of the population to socialism with the, at that stage unavoidable, shutting off of the borders. It was, as one could say with hindsight, the hope for something like a Prague spring in Prussia, Saxony and Mecklenburg. The leadership yielded to this widespread sentiment with the "Youth Communiqué" of 1963, which I have already mentioned. But it was already clear by the mid-sixties that it was merely a question of tactical manoeuvring, and that, apart from a move towards a technocratic orientation, occasioned by the development of the productive forces on an international scale, it didn't intend to introduce anything new.

Around that time it became clear to me that it would be necessary to begin a systematic struggle against the conservative elements in the Party. I thought it would be possible to dislodge them step by step from their positions of power. One needed only to equip oneself better in order to be able to beat them in an inner-Party trench war. At that time I had no idea of the nature of this opponent and its sources of strength and constant self-reproduction. Because the apparatus as such, which guarantees the continuance of reactionary policies, still didn't present any problem for me. Only on this assumption was I able to place my hopes on a process of rejuvenating the cadre—because, in the final analysis, that is what I was concerned about. In reality, the suitable and selected cadres are integrated and absorbed by the apparatus according to a regular pattern. Exceptions only prove the rule.

Q.   How then did you apply this attitude to your work?

A.   At first I undertook a kind of global preparation, without any clear direction. I began to study Marx afresh and to uncover the true history of the CPSU and the Soviet Union. Trotskyist studies. I am particularly indebted to Isaac Deutscher for a lot of indispensable insights. At the same time I was interested in the Yugoslavian experiment, the Chinese road and the nature of the conflict between Mao-tse-Tung and Khrushchev. The mere fact of the breach between Peking and Moscow was of great significance because at last it drew Marxist principles back into the discussion again. Of course I then devoured the Togliatti memorandum, and I still have that cutting from the *Neues Deutschland* today.

In December 1967 I wrote a letter to Ulbricht on the basis of my initial experiences at my new job in industry. I raised the question of socialist democracy and workers' self-management within the framework of our economic organisation, in—as people call it here—a positive way. The reply was brought to me six months later, in May 1968, when the reform movement in Czechoslovakia was about to reach its climax, by an employee of the Central Committee: just a verbal warning. Nothing followed, not even after August 21st, although I had expressed my support for the experiment publicly to the end. They didn't seek out dissidents at the time and don't do that now, just as long as one doesn't draw attention to oneself publicly.

Q. The invasion of Czechoslovakia obviously played a crucial role in making up your mind. What was it like in 1968, what kind of feelings did it arouse in people here?

A. There was genuine and profound excitement, which had already been mounting since January, and then on August 21st, you could read something on the faces of many people. Disappointment, humiliation, downcast eyes.

For me 1967/68 were the years filled with the most intense hope. At that time, that was about 1967, I saw in China the great attempt to spare the most heavily populated country on earth the march through the depths of bureaucratic Stalinism. Then in Czechoslovakia the very same enemy, the Stalinist bureaucracy, which blocks all socialist progress in our part of the world, suffered a wound that has not healed to this day. The students and young workers of Paris for several weeks outmanoeuvred the conservative party functionaries and took the struggle against state monopoly capitalism forward to the beginnings of revolutionary dual power. The Vietnamese people inflicted a strategic defeat on US imperialism with their magnificent Tet offensive. . . I am not speaking here of my theoretical work, which for example, despite the use of the term "cultural revolution", is hardly inspired by Maoism, at least not in the sense of those West European groups strutting around so defiantly in their borrowed garments. I am speaking of my motivation.

Q. You spoke earlier of illusions after August 13th, 1961, and then of hopes prior to August 21st, 1968. One senses an ideal there towards which these illusions and hopes were directed. But what kind of impetus was really behind it? What was it, purely personally, that communists were so dissatisfied with?

A. I don't know whether I can make that fully clear to you. Why do people feel themselves moved to political action? In my book I mention the experience of the ancient Greek philosopher Plato, of whom it is said that he never found the state that suited him. Perhaps as a reference to an experience made here in the GDR by, I would say, hundreds of thousands of people who have joined the SED in their youth during the last thirty years.

I too have undergone this experience. I was 16 when I became a candidate member in 1952. Now we in the SED have preserved an old and disreputable German custom. Every society has to have its own badge. And so it is with the party. But if you walk through our streets today you will only come across a few people wearing the party badge, and they will almost exclusively be those who *must* wear it because of their public role. Yet there are 1.6 million party members in this small country.

At the time when I became a candidate and then a full member it was generally quite different. You'll find it difficult to imagine how proud we were then, I and countless other young comrades, to wear this party badge with the intertwined hands set against the red flag in the background. And now I ask myself and I ask all those young comrades from those thirty years: How has it come about that today we are ashamed to pin on this badge? The essence of the matter is that we have learned quite gradually to be ashamed of the party to which we belong, this party which enjoys the notorious distrust of the people, which holds people in political tutelage day in and day out, and which still feels obliged to lie about the most ridiculous trivialities, when everyone knows better, and in such a way that it brings a blush to the faces of all those who belong to it.

The longer one has been a member, the less one can tolerate, in the long run, how the party is destroying and exposing to ridicule the idea which was once sacred. As a rule it strikes one dumb. Most of the comrades no longer know what to say. But anyone who is equipped with the insight, with the tools and with the capacity to see through what has been happening, and what is still going on today; that here we have a new system of domination instead of socialist freedom and equality for all workers—anyone who sees through all this, and doesn't want to lose his self-respect, *must* quite simply seek an alternative, a chance to live in harmony with himself again. That was the secret behind the great hope of 1968, which attracted a wide range of support amongst the people of the GDR, too.

Whilst I had still been content with criticising the apparatus internally prior to the intervention, I now had to jump. Morally speaking I had no choice any longer. The invasion was a blow which struck me personally as deeply as any of the most heavily involved Czechoslovak participants. At that time I was drafting my letter of resignation from the party—and I was certainly not alone in this. Then I realised that this gesture, morally necessary as it was, would fall flat as soon as our rebellion had been suppressed. I could and had to find a better and more incisive course of action.

I do not know whether those responsible thought at the time that they would not have to pay for August 21st. It cannot do any harm for them to know where the intransigence which will cut across their political schemes all the more frequently in the future comes from. The struggle will not end until the source of such reactionary acts of violence as 1968, until the late Stalinist leadership of the apparatus has been removed. In the first hours and days after the intervention something in me changed for ever. In any case I now only wanted to provide them with a reply against which they would be as powerless as we had been against their tanks. I am convinced that this ideological impotence is more disastrous than the material one.

Q.   That doesn't really sound particularly Marxist.

A.   I don't mind what it sounds like. And after all Marx did say: "The idea becomes a material force. . ." I have shown that the apparatus is coagulated knowledge, consciousness, organised into a ruling power. Its dominance must be undermined *ideologically* before it can fall materially. This is precisely the lesson of the events leading up to the Prague spring. I have always believed in the power of the idea and the word, and that it matters whether one is convinced of oneself and one's cause and doesn't shrink back deep down inside when the decision has to be made. Marx himself is unthinkable without this conviction. The new truth need not even be proclaimed particularly loudly. It will still make headway, and will always provide the necessary courage.

Q.   Your book really comes across as much more objective than one would expect from the motivation which you reveal here.

A.   I can now reveal this motivation because, through my writing and revising, through the consumption of energy, I was gradually able to tear myself free from what was merely frustrated protest. I decided to suppress the first draft of the summer 1973. It contained—apart from the general weakness of the entire final section—too much resentment and subjective wishful thinking.

One has to get the better of all self-destructive bitterness. I see it as a weakness when many dissidents tend to resent the course of history if it doesn't fit in with their own immediate intentions. Anyone who allows himself to be made ill is normally lost to the cause of reform.

After the intervention, as soon as I had regained my composure, I studied Marx for the third time, and Leninism for the first time critically, I mean of course in the historical-analytical sense. Because the revolutionary integrity and world-historical greatness of Lenin are for me, now as before, beyond doubt.

And, in order to understand socialism as it actually exists, I have acquired my own picture of world history, i.e. of the multitude and variety of primarily the non-European civilisations and the unity of their general structural problems. Then, in 1971, I began writing.

Q. Whilst you were already employed in industry, that is.

A. Yes. And since 1975 I have revised the first draft as thoroughly as was possible in the time available to me, with, by the way, the exception of the first four chapters. There I have only made very few stylistic corrections, although originally I wanted to change more even here. But then I received a copy of Rudi Dutschke's book *An Attempt to Put Lenin Back on His Feet.* He had written his work at exactly the same time as I was writing these four chapters. My third and fourth chapters in particular refer to the same sources, and in the case of Lenin, partly the same quotes. But Rudi Dutschke arrives at a rather different assessment. Now I wanted to avoid that the certainly interesting contrast of positions should be obscured by extensive polemics, and therefore I left everything as it was.

The intervening dissertation stood me in good stead for the amendments and changes in parts two and three. I am now even more concrete concerning the economic practice of existing socialism.

Section Three in particular is for the most part new; the entire theory of general emancipation and the chapter on the economics of the cultural revolution were missing completely before.

Section Three is now the most important one for me, essential as the preceding analysis is and likely as it is to find more confirmation than the concept of the alternative. Analysis is not sufficient. Theory must halt before its practical political consequences. It is a question of drawing up a programme for which people who do not want to continue in the same way can be mobilised. I would like my book to initiate broader self-clarification and more co-operation for the struggle for a new perspective within socialism as it actually exists today.

(Translated from German by Paul Edmunson
and Günter Minnerup)

VOICES OF DISSENT

Tamara Deutscher

1978 may be a good vantage point from which to survey the development of dissent and opposition in the countries within the Soviet orbit. The blunder the Russians had committed by engineering the invasion of Czechoslovakia by the Warsaw Pact countries ten years ago produced in the whole of Eastern Europe an effect opposite to that intended. One of the aims of the utterly unimaginative men in the Kremlin was to stamp out once and for all the ferment of ideas which produced the Prague Spring. The shock of the invasion was at first stunning. Then, ostensibly, "normalization" followed, with the old orthodoxy once more imposed from above. And yet the ferment which the Russians had dreaded remained. Moreover, it has spread well beyond Czechoslovakia and has been in various degrees affecting the very depths of post-capitalist societies, now and again sending tremors up to the surface.

In East Germany it was perhaps Rudolf Bahro who most emotionally expressed the impact the events of 1968 had on him: ". . . the tanks, the intervention against this attempt to give socialism a new face—this changed something in me, irrevocably, fundamentally; from that moment on I became hard, intransigent." (West German TV interview, 23.7.77)

In Poland students demonstrated in the streets of Warsaw shouting rhythmically: "The whole of Poland awaits her Dubcek!"[1] In the Soviet Union the invasion politicized the Samizdat until then preoccupied mostly with freedom of artistic and literary expression. V. Turchin, the eminent theoretical physicist, exclaimed: "I cannot go on studying the flow of neutrons while in my country human rights are violated and while Soviet troops invade Czechoslovakia.[2] A year after the invasion a call for the withdrawal of Soviet troops was addressed to the Soviet government by Gen. Grigorenko and I. Yakhimovich and widely circulated in Samizdat clandestinity. True, this action involved only a handful of people, but it is a fact that in the Soviet Union articulate dissent, let alone active opposition, is the business of individuals or at best very small groups only.

During the past decade the movement of opposition to the Soviet model of socialism has become widely differentiated. Various tendencies compete with each other. Closer contacts have been established with the West and an enormous literature by the dissenters and about dissent is being

21

published in Munich, Frankfurt, Paris and London.

In the present essay I shall have to limit myself to surveying the developments of the last decade in a few countries only. I shall also confine myself to considering the problems which preoccupy those groups of oppositionists who may be described, somewhat vaguely, as the "broad left"; that is those who, though rejecting the "Soviet model" do not reject socialism. Among many others, two main questions determine the tactics and the strategy of the opposition: which class or which layer of society should be regarded as the main "agent of change" of the so-called "existing socialism" and what role in the process of this change is likely to be played by the established Communist Parties. Nowhere, of course, can clear-cut and definite answers be given to these questions. But the perspective in which they are viewed in different countries and the emphases which underlie the discussions are interesting and significant.

I

The awakening and the activity of the Polish working class placed Poland in the centre of attention in 1970-71, during the wave of strikes which began in the Baltic ports and ended with the removal of Gomulka, and again, in 1976, when the striking workers within 24 hours forced the government to annul the decreed rise in prices of consumer goods. This demonstration of workers' power was not yet, as some wishful thinkers in the West declared, the death-knell of the bureaucracy. Nor was it, of course, just an outburst of "destructive hooliganism" as the "Workers' State" in its humiliation had at first tried to claim.

Although both in 1970 and in 1976 the revolt was sparked off by purely economic demands, it could not be classified as pure economism. In the course of the strikes new political and social factors influenced the struggle. The contradiction between the very idea of socialism and everyday reality became even more blatant than before. The proletariat, solemnly assured day in and day out of its "leading role", realized that it had absolutely no say in matters affecting its very life and that, far from "leading" anything, it had been led into conditions in which the ordinary workers could not make ends meet.

> "About social justice, about equal distribution of the national income. . . can talk highly placed members of the party, pseudo-activists of trade unions, functionaries, militiamen, or members of the army, scientists and artists, who without any limitations can avail themselves of all material, cultural and social values. This narrow social layer, having no idea how the worker lives, has every reason to support the policy of the party and the government, because these people have been provided with nearly everything."[3]

Thus wrote a group of industrial workers from Poland. The sense of injustice and the frustrations are all the greater as the worker feels helpless. With the state as the only employer and with the "pseudo-activists" of unions which have a corporate character and which embrace all employees, from the top directors to cleaners, the worker feels that his particular interests are not given due weight. In the heat of the strike he becomes ever more aware of social inequalities.

In June 1976 in the industrial town of Lodz the strikers demanded an application of new methods of wage and salary increases by absolute figures, which would narrow differentials, and not calculated by percentages which give greater advantage to higher paid earners. On another occasion voices were raised for a limitation of salaries paid to functionaries of party and state. Some sort of "Part-maximum", decreed by Lenin but long since forgotten, which would equalize the pay of the official with the average worker's pay, was loudly demanded. The call for egalitarianism was unmistakably heard.

Discouraged from showing any initiative at the factory bench—any improvement in production is the concern of technical and scientific staff—deprived of any say in the running of "their" factory, the workers demonstrated during the strike a surprising, hitherto unseen, capacity for organization. The setting-up of workers' councils, of strike committees, liaison and coordination of action between groups and factories were achieved with speed and efficiency; all democratic processes were also duly observed during debates on policy plans and in decision making. This common action, in which the workers became conscious of their own power and ability, increased their resentment at the shabby and disdainful way they had been treated by the high-ups. Together with economic demands and those for free trade unions—"our own"—indignant protests were also heard against the authorities' insulting language: "The government should react differently" the leaflet of one factory said, while in another tools were downed in protest against lack of information or plain misinformation by the national press.

If so much dignity, inventiveness and resourcefulness became released among the workers during their strike activity, how much more of it would come to the fore if it were directed towards positive aims, towards a truly socialist and democratic organization of labour by a free association of producers.

S. Horton, a Polish oppositionist whose Samizdat essay has been circulating in Poland since the beginning of 1977, characterized the events of 1970-71 as a "revolution of hope" and those of 1976 as a "revolution of hopelessness." How is it that so much courage and ability on the part of the workers, so many sacrifices and even bloodshed, brought only meagre results and blighted hope? Both strike waves involved considerable numbers, both frightened the rulers and shook the fabric of society; they were "won" in so far as some of the economic demands were met. In

1970-71 one discredited leader made his exit and was replaced by a new one whose fate may, in the end, be similar. But the essence of the regime with its rigid hierarchical structure, with centralized decision making at the top and orders executed without question at the bottom of the social ladder, remained unchanged.

If one looks into the history of the Polish workers' movement since the end of the war, one can see that much more was achieved in the first major confrontation way back during the exhilarating "Polish October" of 1956. Numerically the industrial working class was then weaker—it has nearly doubled within the last 22 years. But—as Horton rightly remarks—at that time in its striving for fundamental reform it had its allies in the anti-Stalinist faction of the party: the power bloc at the top was split, and the socialist urban intelligentsia was from the beginning providing active support and assisting in the formulation of a programme of political action.

In 1968 the government succeeded not only in isolating the workers from the intelligentsia, but even in turning them against the students in revolt; in 1970-71 the dockers and textile workers acted on their own, deprived of any allies; in 1976 the intelligentsia came to the rescue of the strikers after the main battles had been fought. The chief merit of the Workers' Defence Committee (KOR) lay precisely in breaking down the barriers separating "brawn" from "brain." It was a defensive organization, quite effective in protecting the strikers from the worst excesses of police terror and a vengeful judiciary, but it was too heterogeneous a body to provide a political framework which could, in competition with the official ideology, oppose successfully the socio-political control monopolized by party and state.

In the course of the year 1977-78 the Workers' Defence Committee transformed itself into a Committee for Social Self-Defence and has become an unstructured vanguard of intellectuals. It is from among these, mostly young writers and academics, that the staff of the so-called "flying universities" come—irregular, unofficial and much harassed groups, meeting in private homes and listening to lectures conducted outside normal and approved educational channels. Needless to say, the curriculum would not have met with the approval of the Ministry of Education.

The tradition of this kind of activity is still very strong in Poland and it goes back to the times of the struggle for national independence when it contributed to the preservation of Polish culture against the attempts at Russification and Germanization. Adam Michnik, the well-known historian and KOR activist and one of the most irrepressible of the founders of the "universities" explicitly refers to this national tradition. The students of the "universities" with some exceptions are said to belong to the working class, but, says Michnik, "It is the intellectuals who create independent public opinion and develop non-conformist attitudes.[4]

The Committee acts as a pressure group and by various half-legal means tries to expose the violations of legality by the government and its agencies. The "violation of legality" and not only the "law" on censorship preoccupied also the last Congress of the Union of Writers. The President of the Union was charged with bringing to the attention of the Party Secretary, Edward Gierek, certain "irregularities" in the application of the law.

The law itself and the "irregularities" brought a result as paradoxical as it was unwelcome to the authorities. More and more writers whose works cannot pass through the eye of the censorship needle have recourse to the Samizdat. More of less ephemeral publications, like *Zapis*, *Puls* or *Opinia* contain writings which were never submitted to the censor and were not even meant to appear openly. Some of them have that freshness and spontaneity that comes with freedom from self-imposed constraint. Others reached readers after having languished for months or years in the drawers of the censors. Much of this Samizdat is only half-clandestine. In some cases the editors' names and addresses are provided and authors' names are concealed behind very transparent pseudonyms.

*   *   *

Trotsky once wrote that "without a guiding organization the energy of the masses would dissipate like steam not enclosed in a piston box. But nevertheless what moves things is not the piston, but the steam."

What organization could play the role of the piston box? Could the Communist Party perhaps fulfil that task? To this question the answer of the main currents of Polish opposition is negative, though there are differences in emphasis in the treatment of the problem.

In Poland, perhaps more than in any other country of the Soviet bloc, the line between socialist opposition and opposition to socialism is blurred. ". . . the new opposition does not refer any more to 'true' or 'good' or 'democratic' socialism. It seems rather to turn towards certain traditions and towards the rights of man and citizen, rights which have already been won in many European countries" states in the preface the editor of *La Pologne: une société en dissidence,* referred to before.

The Polish intelligentsia on the whole resents not so much the counterfeit brand of socialism imposed on their country as the violation of the country's sovereignty by the traditionally despised Moscovites, and the opposition, even on the left, has a strong nationalistic edge. Jacek Kuron (co-author with K. Modzelewski of the famous 1965 letter to the party), a co-founder of KOR whose courage is undiminished in spite of two longlish spells in prison, is introduced in the book quoted above, as representing an extreme left Marxist tendency. In his draft of the Common Platform of the Opposition (p. 113) he stresses that he attaches equal weight to the struggle for independence as to that against totalitarianism. His language is curiously reminiscent of the old all too familiar verbiage of the pre-war Polish establishment. We are reminded of the "substantial Polish contribution" to European democracy in the XV and XVI and XVIII centuries and "especially of the Constitution of 1791." We are also assured of the "congenital independence" of the Polish Catholic Church, the great defender of individual freedom which is a "fundamental concept of Christianity and our whole civilization." The "congenital independence" of the Polish Catholic Church is a myth, nor does it have much of a tradition in defending individual freedom in the pre-war Poland of Piłsudski and the Colonels. In a country which used to be described in pre-war history books as "the bulwark of Christianity", the Church has always stood for law and order. Since the war it has acquired new weight as the only tolerated centre of opposition. Some of this influence is undoubtedly due to the spiritual comfort it gives to people sorely tried by the horrors of war, by persecution, poverty and oppression.

The Church has, in these new circumstances, changed its tactics. Straight anti-communist tirades against the godless regime have been replaced by sermons about the rights of man, freedom of conscience and human dignity. This most hierarchical institution has come to speak in sociological terms about the working class and its right to strike. But when it comes to practical issues of, say, divorce, contraception or abortion, the Church remains as retrograde as ever. It is indeed difficult to understand Kuron's great trust in the genuine metamorphosis of this most immutable and dogmatic of institutions.

Adam Michnik in his programmatic statement "For a Strategy of the Polish Opposition",[5] speaks much less about the Church. He acknowledges the merits of the Catholic intelligentsia in the struggle for a greater degree of political and economic independence from the Soviet Union and in winning for the Church quite a considerable measure of tolerance and freedom. But, he says, the leaders of the Catholic Organization *Znak* have abandoned their own political line in exchange for an "entente" with the Party and thus brought their movement into disrepute. Michnik maintains that there can be no "entente" with the Party which has "deleted this very word from its political vocabulary." He is also of the opinion that the time when the opposition could, with any hope of success, address itself to the Party or to the ruling group and thereby influence it, has long passed. Those who had believed in the possibility of "humanizing and demo-cratizing the system" by acting "within the framework of the party and the Marxist doctrine" had achieved nothing and would achieve nothing. Now, he says, it is time to speak not to the rulers but to the ruled. "Instead of suggesting to the power bloc how it can 'improve itself'," the opposition must teach society "how to act."

Two critics of the regime who belong to the older generation,

W. Bienkowski and E. Lipinski, represent those who still want to "speak to the Party" and see the party as the main agent of the change.

Bienkowski had been a member of the Communist Party in pre-war Poland. After the Polish October of 1956, in Gomulka's best days, he became a member of his government. Now under a cloud and in opposition he analyses the tensions in post-capitalist societies labouring under the ossified "Soviet model" and hopes for the inner regeneration of the system. Couched in semi-Marxist terms, but published only abroad, Bienkowski's writings somewhat disprove Michnik's contention that "in present-day Poland Marxist-Leninist doctrine is nothing but an empty discourse, an official ritual." Bienkowski detects in the Party enough dynamism to reform itself and to resolve existing social contradictions which, he fears, threaten the very premises of socialism.

Professor E. Lipinski, an old Socialist, joined the Polish United Workers Party in 1949. His popularity and prestige in the country was considerably enhanced when he acted as co-founder and main spokesman of KOR. As an economist he calls for a loosening of economic structures and the introduction of some reforms on the line of the Russian NEP. In his Open Letter to Gierek he tries to persuade the Party Secretary that "the replacement of the conveyor belt by team work in a Volvo factory" is "more important for the building of socialism than would be the nationalization of that factory."[6] In the name of social peace, in the name of progress, he appeals to the party to admit plurality of views and plurality of parties. Unchanelled and unguided, social discontent may endanger the friendly relations with the USSR which her geographic position imposes on Poland. In his disarming naiveté, Professor Lipinski does not seem to fear that precisely "plurality of parties" may endanger this friendship.

Underneath the wish to preserve "friendly relations" with the Soviet Union is the anxiety common to the party and the opposition lest Poland suffer the lot of Czechoslovakia.

*   *   *

Is the party then a "dead loss" which should be written off or are there still in it forces capable of embarking on the road of fundamental changes? Michnik does not deny that the party hierarchy is not monolithic, but contains various tendencies, often contradictory ones. But, he maintains, even its most progressive elements have no interest in democratizing the system or admitting a plurality of parties or any degree of self-management into the life of society. If they seem "progressive", it is only because in their pragmatic way they understand that a measure of collaboration with the democratic forces may be more effectual than brute repression. These "progressive" pragmatists, concludes Michnik, can therefore never become the "allies" of the democratic opposition, though they "may become its partners." The precise difference between "allies" and "partners" is not quite clear.

At the beginning of 1978 an unusual document came to light, a document testifying to the existence of "liberalizing" elements (or at least wishing to appear as such). The semi-clandestine *Opinia* circulated an Open Letter to Gierek insisting that this had been done without the consent of the signatories all of whom are well known public figures. Albrecht, Matwin, and Morawski were prominent Gomulka supporters in 1956; Ochab, at one time described as a Stalinist, had been the General Secretary of the Party, then became Head of State. He resigned in protest against the antisemitic drive of the late 1960s. The Letter is a plea for a "dialogue with the citizen", for democracy within the party and outside it. "The sources of our major difficulties are largely political. . . To them belong the undemocratic form of government and, first and foremost, the lack of a democratic exchange of opinions. . ." says the Letter demanding "the activation of healthy forces in the party" stifled by bureaucratic control of the machine. Conditions must be created for the re-establishment of workers' councils, as well as for the "independence of the existing political parties" with their own "authentic positions" in parliament and local institutions.[7]

This admirable "Platform of the 14" has not had much effect on the party. It was easy to dismiss it as the grumblings of a group removed from power at the time of the exit of their leader. It was even easier to recall that in their time of office not much was done either to "re-activate the healthy forces" or to "re-establish workers' councils" or enter into a "dialogue with the citizen." Now the citizens do not see any reasons to enter into a dialogue with relics of a not too glorious past. The "Platform" is known all over Poland, but it is so innocuous that no attempt has been made to penalize those who signed or circulated it. This kind of semi-institutionalized opposition has not found an echo in society. But this does not preclude the appearance of a more trustworthy splinter group whose appeal may meet with some success.

II

Returning to Trotsky's metaphor, one could rightly say that what "moved things" in Czechoslovakia in 1968 was the "steam" enclosed in the "piston box" of the Communist Party. Only brutal intervention from outside stopped the process. Should one count on remaking the existing piston box or aim at building a new one on a different pattern? Much of the discussion among the present day opponents of Husak centres on this problem.

Though the trends in the Czech resistance are varied, the hard core is undoubtedly socialist. One might say that in fact there are two Communist Parties in existence: one the ruling official party of Husak, and the other, diffuse, with hardly any organization and subject to persecution and harassment—the Party of the Expelled. It is a considerable force as it consists of half a million members of the CP who were deprived of their party cards after the 1968 invasion. If some of them, weary and disillusioned, fell by the roadside, the Party of the Expelled was strengthened by the influx of new and younger cadres.

The first major political act of the Czechoslovak resistance was to draw up the Manifesto of 28 October 1970 which in the form of leaflets was distributed all over the country. Formulated by representatives of various regions, groups and trends which managed to come together under cover of clandestinity, the Manifesto, with the Short Action Programme which followed later, was a basic programmatic statement of the Socialist Opposition. At that time, after two years of occupation, it became clear that not much could be salvaged from the reforms achieved during the Prague Spring. And yet the view that "the Party remains in spite of everything the forum from which the struggle for a renewal of socialism must be waged" was not completely abandoned.[8] The adherents of this view could argue convincingly that the very initiative for the Prague Spring came from within the official party in spite of its murky past, in spite of the purges and mock trials. (Might not a sense of guilt and shame for these crimes have also helped in the spring awakening?) However, by 1970 opposition within the official party was wellnigh impossible, although by no means all of the one million card carrying and vetted members were enthusiastic supporters of the regime. Nor is the apparatus and leadership immune from conflicts which may lead to a new crisis.

The Manifesto was proclaimed not on behalf of a new *party*, but on behalf of the Socialist *Movement* of Czechoslovak Citizens. The distinction is significant. The Movement is not a structured organization but a "political trend" with its roots in the socialist consciousness of society. It has "an intellectual centre determining the general political line and taking practical initiatives", but leaves a great deal of autonomy to socialist resistance groups which were spontaneously springing up among various layers of the population. The authors of the Manifesto explicitly renounced the setting up of any structure, any formal hierarchy with directives "from above", but placed reliance on loose links between groups which, within the common programme, would act according to local conditions.

Is there then a danger that the "energy of the masses will dissipate like steam"? This objection which, say the Czechoslovak socialists, is in principle correct, cannot be automatically applied in all cases. The "intellectual centre" anticipated that in the process of the struggle the "loose groups" would acquire a degree of stability and gradually develop into parties or organizations with a clear and viable structure.

In Czechoslovakia, much more than in Poland or in the Soviet Union, an "intellectual centre" is able to address itself and speak directly to the people. The barriers between the intelligentsia and the working class, if they exist at all, are easy to cross. The Czechoslovak workers are to a high degree class conscious; the memories of social struggles as well as those for democratic rights in the pre-war Republic are still alive; and, last but not least, communism had been much more of an organic growth than an order imposed by the foreign conqueror as it was elsewhere. Also the fact that the core of the resistance is formed by the Party of the Expelled assures it a firm base among the rank and file. True, among the expelled there are more intellectuals than workers, but the Party of the Expelled has been able to preserve its former links and its influence in factories and plants. Even if the Czech workers cannot afford openly to register their disapproval of "normalization", they remain passively discontented. Independent trade unions and factory councils, which played a considerable role in management and in social life, were re-activated after the exit of Novotny and became a notable feature of the Prague Spring. Of such gains no advanced working class can easily be deprived especially by taskmasters who rule in the name of socialism, and were put in power with the support of foreign tanks.

Could the debâcle of 1968 have been prevented? The "errors" of the Prague Spring are still issues which agitate all the oppositionists in their search for a new political strategy. How to steer a safe course between the Scylla of the repugnant "Soviet model" of socialism and the Charybdis of an anti-Soviet bourgeois democracy with its ugly face of capitalism? In this search the Czech socialists see themselves as a vanguard of other forces in the Soviet bloc. "Ten years after the Prague Spring", says Jiri Pelikan, "the main questions are these: Could the Soviet intervention have been avoided? And how? These are not academic questions because the answers will be useful to oppositionists and dissidents in Prague, Warsaw, Budapest and Berlin... The answer should be of interest to all those in the West who seek a socialist alternative... They should have no illusions: Any attempt to introduce 'a different socialism...' will meet the same hostility of the Kremlin's ruling group."[9]

What are then the lessons of 1968? Had the leaders been unduly compliant *vis à vis* the Russians? Should they have mobilized the population instead of bargaining with the invaders? Should they have sent urgent SOS messages to Belgrade, Bucarest and Peking asking for support against the Russian tanks? The answer to these questions affects the character of Czechoslovak resistance and determines various trends within it.

While the Socialist Movement of Czechoslovak Citizens expressed a definite political tendency, the movement for the Charter 77 was more diffuse and heterogeneous. Charter 77 was animated by the Helsinki spirit and geared to the abortive Belgrade conference on Human Rights. The signatories represented nearly all left groups from the Radical Socialist Opposition (Peter Uhl) to Havel's National Democrats and Vaculic's Christian Democrats. The government was quick to condemn the Charter outright. It also tried to present it as a whimsical act of a handful of disgruntled intellectuals. But here it did not succeed. At huge meetings called in factories, workers refused to endorse the condemnation of a document they were not given a chance to read. In the event, the whole feverish campaign had to be called off, but only after the news about the Charter had spread far and wide and the authorities realized that they had acted as unwitting publicity agents for a "subversive" movement they were determined to extirpate. The courageous stand of the signatories evoked a considerable response; it caused embarrassment not only to Husak but to his fellow bureaucrats in the Eastern bloc as well as to the bosses in Moscow. It stimulated the demand for the observance of Human Rights among oppositionists in other countries with whom the Chartists succeeded in establishing contacts. They themselves condemned violation of these rights not only in the Soviet orbit, but also in the West, when they expressed solidarity with the victims of *Berufsverbot* in West Germany and defended Heinrich Böll against the witch-hunt of the German Establishment. They stirred the consciences of Western Communist Parties and enlisted the support of Western Trade Unions.

However, by the very fact of being al.-embracing, the Chartist movement contained centrifugal forces which grew stronger with the disillusionment brought about by the fiasco of the Belgrade meeting. Even at the very inception of the movement there were some activists whose courage and genuine socialist credentials could not be doubted, but who refused to sign the Charter. To these belonged for instance Karel Kosik, a Marxist sociologist, the author of *The Dialectic of the Concrete,* who, in 1968 had opposed all concessions to the Russians. It was not that people like Kosik did not have Human Rights at heart, but they feared that by eschewing political issues, the Chartists would contribute to the depolitization of the opposition, blunting thereby its combative edge. As the Human Rights campaign began to fade, these arguments acquired new cogency. However, if the solidarity of the Chartists has not been impaired, this was due perhaps more to the persecution by Husak's police which welded them even closer together than to the intrinsic cohesiveness of the movement.

Within the Socialist Opposition attempts were made to steer the Charter towards a more distinctly political and radical outlook. The pressure came mainly from the younger generation of dissidents. Many of them are grouped around Peter Uhl and his banned Revolutionary Socialist Workers' Party. This movement dates from before 1968 when it was widespread among university students. Many among these "children of the Prague Spring" were later denied the possibility to continue their studies as punishment for the sins of their parents who now belong to the Party of the Expelled. Often "proletarianized", they have close links with educated older workers as well as with apprentices now entering factories and political life.

Peter Uhl, a former research student, was tried for oppositional activities in 1971 and spent four years in prison. His prestige among all shades of socialist opinion had been growing through the years of occupation. This was so not only because of his undaunted courage and the firm ideological stand with which he faced his judges, but also because the past decade had shown how correct was the criticism of the "Dubcek solution" of the 1968 drama Uhl made at the time. Even those who did not approve of Uhl's "extremism" acknowledge that he gave proof of greater perspicacity than older and more experienced politicians. Uhl had no illusions about the good faith of the Soviet "negotiators." They, like Stalin before them, did not have the interests of socialism at heart, but were motivated only by their own *raison d'état*. Uhl saw the fall of Novotny as a palace revolution: would it not have been better if his successors had the courage to take this revolution out of the "palace" or party headquarters, into the streets, schools, and factories. Why were Smrkovsky and Dubcek shy of proclaiming a general strike although a million metal workers had promised their support? The Czech leaders, argues Uhl, should have freed themselves further from their own Stalinist deformations, shed their distrust of the masses and aroused the whole population to action.

Peter Uhl, not having gone through the Communist Party School, has preserved the ability to speak in a bold and undiplomatic language. He openly describes himself as a Trotskyist (or "better still—a revolutionary Marxist") and, as an avowed member of the Fourth International, commits in the eyes of the authorities the double sin of heresy and insubordination. Addressing himself to the Western Revolutionary Left he rejects the "parliamentary and other junk of bourgeois democracy." He treats Euro-communism as the "latest component" of reformism and believes that only revolution not gradual piecemeal democratization will bring about socialism.

To-day Uhl and his friends represent the left wing of the Chartist movement. Without in any way weakening their bonds of solidarity, they are critical of its a-political character. Uhl has, however, no patience with the pseudo-radical in the bourgeois democratic West which often displays "an aversion to the defence of civil rights and democratic freedoms" even when it flows "from the often justified opposition to reformism." It is against this "aversion" that he defends the Chartists: "Charter 77" he explains, "is not a political opposition nor does it wish to become one. . . It is nonetheless the most significant movement in this country. . . and has had significant resonance amongst the workers. It expresses their interests, even if not fully or directly."[10] It is, however, true that within the last year or so the movement has not expanded or developed. It may have become just a little more "politicized" and this is reflected in the changes in the leadership: last October Vaclav Havel, who represented the National Democratic opposition, resigned as the main spokesman; his successor, Jiri Hajek, resigned from this position for reasons for health in April this year. The present chief spokesman, Jaroslav Sabata, Uhl's close friend and father in law, stands somewhat further to the left than his predecessors.

The more moderate wing of the movement came to the fore in the early spring of 1978 when it circulated a commemorative statement on "A Hundred Years of Czech Socialism." It is indeed difficult to see what objections the authorities could possibly have had to such a publication, except perhaps that it showed how far away from socialism Dr. Husak's government had taken the country. The statement or Manifesto was signed by 23 socialists, non-party activists and Church leaders, as well as by Fr. Kriegel and Jaroslav Sabata, the two party members who had most vigorously protested against Dubcek's conciliatory policy. Two letters with a desperate "cry for help" for the persecuted authors of the Manifesto were sent to Western leaders with whom they felt the greatest political affinity: Jiri Muller, the student leader who had already spent quite a few years behind bars, addressed himself to the Socialist International, while Rudolf Battèk, a representative of the "Committed non-party members" appealed to W. Brandt, Kreisky and Palme.[11] The authors of the Manifesto, though all or most of them are also signatories of the Charter, asserted in this manner their own socialist and non-party current within the general movement. Its more radical wing would not in any way disagree with a document which did nothing more than "declare its allegiance to the century old traditions of the early Czech workers. . .", but it would probably not address its appeal to the leaders of the Socialist International.

All activists are persecuted, harassed, intimidated, arrested, released and re-arrested again. It would be invidious in this context to mention some names and omit others. Uhl and Kriegel, for instance, are under constant police surveillance and uniformed sleuths spend sleepless nights and boring days on checking all their visitors. However, in an amazing way both are from time to time able to evade controls. An Austrian journalist managed to interview Uhl, while *Mundo Obrero*, the organ of the Spanish Communist Party has published a conversation with Kriegel. On the occasion of Kriegel's seventieth birthday a spate of congratulatory telegrams arrived at his home. One was from the Spanish Party with which Kriegel has special ties dating from the time of his participation in the Spanish civil war. There was even an invitation to a dinner in Madrid to celebrate the occasion. What other mail did Kriegel find in his letterbox full of sincere good wishes? A few messages from Bohemia, of which one read: "We wish

you all the worst and spit on you, dirty Jew." Signed: "Patriots".[12]
Are these "patriots" Husak's allies or friends?

An Italian journalist succeeded in arranging a secret meeting with an
unnamed oppositionist. To evade the police, he was led by a round about
way to the place of the meeting by a friendly but rather taciturn guide:
"Why don't you try to emigrate from your country where the conditions
are so hard. . .?" asked the Italian. "My place is here", answered the guide.
"And also did you notice that this morning we had snow and now a warm
sun is shining. Here everything may change suddenly as it did ten years
ago. . . in the Spring. . . All is not yet lost."[13]

III

The deeply felt isolation of the intellectual in a society of the Soviet type
is poignantly expressed in a book which came from Hungary. *Le Marxisme
face aux pays de l'Est*, by an author who signs himself Marc Racovski, contains a welter of ideas, only half clarified, and brilliant flashes, which seem
to have been put down on paper as if breathlessly and in great haste.[14]
Racovski, who is a Marxist, tries to come to grips with the much debated
question of the nature of the Soviet state. He sees it as neither socialist nor
capitalist, nor a transitional mixture of both, but quite a new type of class
society *sui generis* in which the party is the "dominant class." The fact
which he himself recognizes, namely that the party itself is an "inter-class"
organization containing a large section of the working class as well as various
layers of bureaucracy in no way affects his analysis. Racovski does not say
what proportion of workers constitute the "dominant class" in Hungary;
in the Polish party, for instance, nearly 40 per cent are workers, according
to the latest statistics.[15]

This conglomerate of classes which is also according to Racovski, the
"dominant class", is subordinated to the political elite vested with a
monopoly of power. In such a type of society all institutions are integrated
into a rigid hierarchical administrative structure which does not permit of
organized expression of social contradictions or conflicting interests. Any
liberalization of the regime can, therefore, be only very superficial and
cannot go beyond the limits imposed by the "dominant class." True,
changes may occur when a "crisis of maladjustment" breaks the unity of
the party. This happened, for example, when Stalinist terror hit the party
itself and a segment of the ruling bureaucracy, in order to defend itself,
was ready to seek support of the masses. But the mere potentialities of
such an alliance provoked a revolutionary ferment among the rank and file
threatening the very foundations of the power of the "dominant class"
and had to be brought under control by military means.

Racovski sees the situation in the East as completely static. The "new
type of class society" is there to stay: no autonomous organizations

expressing conflicting aspirations and needs can come into being to challenge the monopoly of power of the single party, of the "dominant class", whose character remains, in the author's conception, extremely elusive.

The working class is apathetic, worn down by the struggle for existence and hardly conscious of its own interests. It is also internally divided. This division is graphically described by another Hungarian writer Miklos Haraszti in *A Worker in a Worker's State*. Its original title *Piece Work* was perhaps more correct, as many aspects of piece work are as common in a "workers' state" as elsewhere. But there are also significant differences. Haraszti, who himself worked at the bench in a tractor factory, affords us a glimpse into the state of mind and behaviour of the factory crew. The main effort goes into straining every nerve to beat the invidious incentive system, but illusory victory turns into defeat as this results only in periodic increases of the "norm" which wipe out the hoped for gain.

> "Everyone is on his own. Alone he pursued a daily battle against machines and time. Defeat cannot be shared: how could we want a common success?"
> ". . . a brigade is not composed of workers involved with a single type of machine, but includes an assortment of borers, millers, and turners. This most effectively prevents members of a brigade from discussing anything in common, or from regulating the level of production to defend themselves against revisions of the norm—even if this were possible."[16]

There are also the setters, the rate fixers, the engineers, the quality inspectors who "are not there to make life easier for you." There are "good" jobs and "bad" ones, and the foreman decides who gets them. "The slightest suspicion of a secret understanding between two individuals, and his disapproval would at once be reflected in their pay packets."[17].The net result is that "Football, beer, motor cycles, the house and TV programmes regain their rightful place. Other subjects. . . merit at most a few words now and then—but aren't worth an argument."

Haraszti, born in 1945, belongs to the same post-Stalinist generation as Racovski. A rebellious poet and song writer, twice jailed and released after a hunger strike, he was commissioned by the authorities to write about factory conditions. His assignment gave him an extraordinary opportunity to earn his living in a large factory on equal terms with his fellow workers. His embarrassing sociological survey, never published in Hungary, seems to illustrate Racovski's theoretical assumption that the working class is unable—nor does it aspire—to act as a coherent social force. It may be too rash, however, to draw such a sweeping conclusion from a sociological survey limited in scope and time.

Racovsky's and Haraszti's, pessimism reflect perhaps the stagnant atmosphere of "Kadarized" Hungary. The highly sophisticated dissident philosophers of the so-called Budapest School like Agnes Heller, F. Feher,

M. & G. Markus and Mihaly Vaida have left Hungary, greatly to the relief of the pundits of the Politbureau. Somewhat younger rebels, Haraszti and Conrad are in West Berlin. Other critical intellectuals like Hegedus have been effectively deprived of any means of expressing their views in print, and completely "marginalized."

In which segment of society can any unorthodox ideas find an echo? According to Racovski, only among the numerically restricted members of the intelligentsia still young enough to delay the decision which they will soon have to face: either to remain on the margin of society or to join the "established intellectuals." This last category is, according to him, quite hopeless. In spite of their differences, they all, as he says, in a "polyphonic choir" reject any oppositionist activity. Their arguments vary: opposition needlessly provokes the authorities, makes any *modus vivendi* impossible and thereby endangers even further the progress of liberalization. Some go even so far as to denounce the protesters as "just bad writers", or resort to the time-honoured charge of all establishments and declare the critics to be "unbalanced" or "maladjusted."

It is of interest that Hungary is one of the few countries of the Soviet bloc where writers have not had recourse to Samizdat. It was only in September 1977 that two Samizdat volumes began to circulate from hand to hand. The first bears the title *Marx in the Fourth Decade*, edited by A. Kovacs. The second, *Profile*, a volume of 800 pages, apparently took ten years to prepare and consists of hitherto unpublished writings of 34 authors.

Officially there is no censorship in Hungary; though non-existent it nevertheless plays a cat and mouse game, and rejects manuscripts under all sorts of pretexts in such a way that an author only very rarely knows for certain that he has no chance to appear in print. The rejection formula is "Your MS does not fit our profile"—hence the title of the Samizdat—which does not deprive the author of the hope that perhaps, if he does behave, he might be more lucky with his next work or with another publisher.

Only a summary of the two Samizdat volumes has so far reached the West. *Marx in the Fourth Decade* contains answers to 21 sociologists between the ages of 30 and 35 to the question: "What is Marxism and what is your attitude to it?" and this makes a rather melancholy reading. The editor sums it up for us: "Not one of the contributors believes that any special advantage can be derived from thinking in Marxist terms as against any others. . ." and concludes: "What can be seen from the volume is the complete collapse of Marxism. . ."

Whether the 21 answers are representative of only one trend of thought, it is impossible to judge. The fact is that nearly all contributors now reject the "unofficial Marxism" which they had embraced some ten years before. There is also an aura of mysticism around their statements—a striking evidence of a search for the "purpose of life", for "human essence" and religion. This seems to apply also to Haraszti, who found that genuine religion is more satisfying than Marxism as "it is tied to the absolutes of existence" while "Marx's absolutes are merely tied to the social entity. . ." It has been reported that Haraszti, now in West Germany, is on the way to adopting a Zen Buddhist Weltanchauung.

Lenin was once asked what he thought of someone declaring: "Socialism is my religion." Lenin replied that much depended on who made the statement. If a religious person made it, he was saying in effect that he was abandoning religion for socialism; if someone who considered himself a Marxist claimed socialism as his religion, he was abandoning socialism for religion.

*   *   *

It must be admitted that the "Kadarization" of Hungary was more successful and more beneficial to the population at large than was Husak's "normalization" of Czechoslovakia. Kadar's "reign" is undoubtedly an improvement on that of his predecessor Rakosi, while Husak cannot but suffer badly when compared with the exhilarating though short-lived Dubcek experiment. Kadar's measure of economic decentralization has resulted in a rise in the standard of living and rendered everyday life somewhat easier. The authorities are aware of their "successes" and encourage the Hungarians to visit other countries of the Soviet bloc: even disgruntled citizens find that the comparison works in Hungary's favour.

For Racovski and his friends it can hardly be a consolation to learn that their fellow dissenters in Poland and Czechoslovakia consider the Hungarian situation so much better than their own. On the contrary, the awareness of the tremendous distance which separates other countries of the Soviet bloc as well as their own from genuine socialism can only deepen their sense of hopelessness. And yet Racovski's book should in itself be an antidote to his exaggerated pessimism. It is difficult to believe that his work is the only flower blooming in what he describes as an intellectual desert.

There is no doubt that the departure of the "Budapest school of philosophers" has impoverished the Hungarian scene even further. Not without a touch of hypocrisy Imre Pozsgay, the Minister of Culture, deplored the loss of these "intellectuals of the highest level." Why then did they have to leave? "Between us and them—he said—there arose a grave conflict over strategic aims—though. . . these aims were largely identical with those of the Party—and over tactical questions. . . We did not demand unconditional surrender. We looked for a solution by way of a discussion. But this was not to be."[18]

No, the authorities did not demand an "unconditional surrender"; they were even generous enough to allow them to publish *abroad* so long as these books did not deal with Hungary or with the "Soviet model" of socialism. A dialogue was indeed hardly possible. These writers, complains Pozsgay, "offend against the political and ideological foundations of the system." Agnes Heller openly admits: "I do not criticize the leaders; I criticize the system itself", the system which does not allow "political pluralism, pluralistic democracy which are an integral part of socialism", such as is proposed by the Italian Communists and which she admires.

Agnes Heller and her friends do not see themselves as "emigrés of the traditional type." After a three years' spell abroad they plan to return to Budapest in the hope that some dialogue will become possible. In the meantime many changes at the top may occur. Perhaps after three years of intellectual stagnation even the most dogmatic apparatchiks may feel the need for a refreshing breeze of new ideas.

IV

The survey of the Soviet opposition has been placed at the end of this essay. This is not accidental. Hard as it is to part with preconceived ideas—and illusions—one has to face the fact that the movement of dissent with the Soviet Union is in a deep crisis. And the reasons for this are not far to seek.

First of all there is, of course, the relentless persecution by the state. Non-conformists and protesters are put out of the way, placed in psychiatric "hospitals", prisons and camps. According to some conservative estimates, two to four thousand restless souls are under lock and key. The threat of punishment hangs over many, many more and creates what V. Turchin aptly called "Inertia of Fear" which renders all activity practically impossible.

Besides, the method of disposing of the critics by sending them more or less forcibly abroad brought a double or even a triple benefit to "the system." While more savage persecution created martyrs, evoked compassion and spread disaffection even wider, those who left the country, even under strong pressure, were regarded with less sympathy, and, sometimes even with a shade of disapproval. The exodus of over 130,000 Jews, of whom many were either active or at least potential dissenters, has also weakened the movement. Incidentally, it helped Brezhnev to pacify somewhat public opinion in the West. Moreover, the "freedom to emigrate", so dear to American Senators, is not very high on the list of freedoms for which an ordinary Soviet citizen would be prepared to fall foul of the authorities. Nor can Amnesty International and the Human Rights groups have a wide appeal. Courageous as their few leaders are, their aims are narrowly circumscribed; they too have been weakened by trials, arrests, exile, internal splits and emigration. By transferring the opposition abroad, the government has rendered it to a large extent harmless. It is significant that Boris Weil, a "veteran of Marxist opposition", who after years of prison and forced labour recently reached Denmark, avoids using the term "Soviet opposition", but speaks of the "movement of dissent." "We have found", he says, "a form of political existence... without organization, without programme, without statutes, and which somehow survives." It does, however, to a certain degree "destroy itself" by the sheer fact of emigration. On the other hand, adds Weil hopefully, the movement is "like a living chain of relationships: the authorities destroy some links but ever new ones seem to grow."[19]

The most profound source of the weakness of the opposition should perhaps be seen in the fact that it proved unable to provide, even in the subterranean life of society, any ideology, broad, comprehensive and powerful enough to stir peoples' mind and emotions and to compete with the established and ruling orthodoxy.

One cannot gauge from London or Paris the numerical strength of active opponents of the regime. According to Roy Medvedev, who is on the spot, while at the beginning of the 1970s they could still be counted by the hundreds, now, towards the end of the decade, their number has declined to no more than one hundred. The opposition reached its high peak at the end of the 1960s. This was the period when, within the party and outside it, the opposition was mobilized by surreptitious or even open attempts at the rehabilitation of Stalin coming from the die-hards in the hierarchy. These attempts failed to a large extent, and the anti-Stalinist movement subsided. But these rather discouraging figures do not by any means allow one confidently to assess how widespread is the mood of dissent. The few who are active have around them sympathizers, co-thinkers and passive supporters; those who are languishing in prisons have left behind them a trail of sorrow, and their families and friends, though intimidated, are future potential subverters.

A great volume of literature of "dissent" appears now in the West and comes from the pens of political emigrés. Although it may possibly shed light on the state of mind of those who have stayed behind, it cannot serve as a reliable guide or an undisputable source of information. The emigrés are often confused by the sudden confrontation with the unfamiliar bourgeois democratic order which they tend to romanticize; sometimes they are moved by an unconscious desire to ease their transition into a new milieu and effect a degree of osmosis with the prevalent opinion. Much of their energy goes into bitter polemics with fellow emigrés.

One of the prominent dissenters who remains in Russia and whose writings are available in the West is Roy Medvedev. Moreover, he is also one of the very few who has remained firm in his socialist convictions. He has often been described—not without reason—by the Western Left as a 'Fabian', a social democratic reformist, distrustful of the masses and inclined to place too much hope in the possibility of the inner regeneration of the Soviet party. However, the information that he provides seems accurate and his judgment so far has proved sober. It seems therefore that a few more words about his work and opinions would not be out of place here.

Judging the present situation not propitious for strictly political opposition, Medvedev uses his time and freedom for educational work. From his prolific Samizdat writings those who want to know can learn how tortuous and dramatic was the road which led from the high ideals of 1917 to the horrors of Stalinism, and, if they are not too traumatized by the Gulag revelations, they can also discover how profoundly wrong is the identification of Stalinism with socialism which Stalin so successfully imposed within Russia and outside it. Many Marxists in the West cannot always agree with his interpretation of Soviet history; many, whose anti-Stalinist credentials were established as early as the 1920s or 1930s must take issue with his evaluation of those Oppositions which preceded today's dissenters. All the same, for Soviet readers brought up in the Stalin school of falsification, the truth, which he reveals, even if somewhat slanted, is of immense importance.

In his view, the present dominant position of the CPSU is not generally contested. Though the "system" is not based on active consensus, it is given passive assent, tinged with resignation and apathy, by the overwhelming majority of the population. Moreover, "in the perpetuation of this system are also interested millions of party and State functionaries, managers, and a large part of the intelligentsia in the service of the State. For them it is simpler to live as before. A more pluralistic system would create too many problems."[20] Medvedev does not, however, see the situation as completely static and believes that the fear of "too many problems" will not in the long run prevent the development of a pluralistic society.

Medvedev is above all anxious to assure a smooth transformation of the present regime into a modern democratic socialist state. His evolutionary temperament and Weltanschauung make him look to the party, and to think that if only it were to reform itself—and this is a big "if" indeed—it could still contribute to such a transformation. "In this struggle [for democratization] the political pressures from 'below' do not a priori exclude a direction 'from above'. . . . a correct control over the process of democratization by the supreme organs of the Communist Party and the State could even guarantee that the struggle would be conducted with a minimum of disorder and within the framework of legality."[21]

The dangers threatening the process of democratization come from two quarters: from the still powerful Stalinist forces entrenched in society as well as in the hierarchy "above" and from the pent-up discontent and anger of the masses which may burst out and destroy the existing social structures without being able to replace them with new ones. This "fear of the masses" can be detected in the writings of many oppositionists, even those who adopt a much more radical stand than Medvedev.

In the supreme organs of the Party, the die-hards of Stalinism are still quite strong. And, what is perhaps worse, the Stalinist frame of mind still persists among a considerable layer of the intelligentsia. Ominous echoes of undisguised Stalinism were heard at the end of 1977, when the notorious Union of Soviet Writers organized a great public literary meeting. From the platform paeons of praise were lavished on the "authentically" Russian literature of the late 1930s and 1940s. It was stressed with a great deal of satisfaction that the promotion of this "authentic Russian" literature had put a stop to the despicable *avant garde* of the earlier period when, due to excessive intellectual freedom, all kinds of "non-Russian elements", decadents, cheats, and frauds like Meyerhold and Babel, had flourished. When Efros, the much harassed theatre producer, rose to defend the memory of Meyerhold, he was prevented from speaking, attacked for his "impudence" in busying himself with Chekhov and Gogol, the truly Russian classics, and advised to create his own "national", that is Jewish theatre.

It was not an accident that the meeting took place on 21 December, the date of Stalin's birthday.[22]

*   *   *

The working class of the Soviet Union still remains the great unknown. But all observers, no matter what their political complexion, agree that it is largely "dormant." "There is no workers movement in the Soviet Union" states with unusual bluntness Leonid Plyushch.[23]

It is a sad paradox that in the country which was the first to accomplish a proletarian revolution, the tradition of class struggles has by now been largely forgotten. Collective memories are short. The history of the Great October in its Stalinist version, not only outrageously falsified, but also decked out in turgid bureaucratic verbiage, can hardly act as an inspiration for a new revolt against autocracy. The very concept of a strike as a legitimate weapon of working class defence has been largely erased from the mind of the Soviet proletariat.

The strikes which do break out in various parts of the country are sporadic and uncoordinated, and the authorities, not hesitating to use troops and firearms, all too swiftly succeed in crushing them. V. Belotserkovsky, who had, as a labour correspondent of the Soviet press, more contacts with the workers than perhaps any other member of the Soviet intelligentsia, recalls some incidents in which desperate courage was followed by heartbreaking helplessness. The lack of safety precautions in many industries, the social injustices, the incompetence and bungling of the management with its complete disregard of the human factor—all this drives people to desperation. In their anger, they resort to violent acts, the results of which are quite out of proportion to the sacrifice involved. A wave of strikes broke out in 1962 in Novocherkask where a real insurrection occurred. The troops refused to fire and for two days the town was in the hands of the rebels. Other strikes took place in Tula, Odessa, Vladivostok, Dniepropetrovsk and other centres. All were crushed under the iron heel.[24]

The initiative of V. Klebanov and his comrades was, at the beginning of 1978, greeted in the West—somewhat prematurely—as a sign of the awakening of the Soviet proletariat. Klebanov, a former coal miner, collected a number of signatures under a protest against corruption and unfair dismissals from among workers who had met accidentally in the waiting rooms of one of the governmental "Complaints Offices." They could, of course, obtain no satisfaction from their officials, and so launched a moving appeal to the West "for moral and material support" in face of repression: "On the one hand, the Party and Government call upon citizens to correct violations wherever they occur: in industry and in the life of society. On the other hand, the authorities come down with special brutality on those who respond. . . by speaking out in the interests of the enterprise"—they remark. Confronted day in and day out with this "organized hypocrisy", Klebanov and his group applied to the International Labour Organisation with a request that it should recognize the group as a "free trade union." For this they claimed the support of some 200 workers from places as far apart as Kiev, Chelyabinsk, Odessa, the Caucasus and Moscow.

It was reported that at one stage Klebanov turned to Academician Sakharov for help in publicizing the protest. Sakharov apparently refused to get involved because he feared that the signatories "did not understand the risks of open dissent."[25] Incidentally, this warning seemed gratuitous, because Klebanov had already spent considerable time in a psychiatric "hospital" for his previous activity. Sakharov's refusal may be seen as another instance of the gulf that separates the intellectuals from the workers. Even the most courageous of the former show no concern for the most vital preoccupations of the latter.

At the time of writing most members of the "free trade union" are confined to prisons and psychiatric establishments. Could there be a more tragically ironic diagnosis: one of the patients is said to be "suffering from nervous exhaustion brought on by her quests for justice."[26] What an indictment of a system in which "quests for justice" lead into a psychiatric ward!

*   *   *

Depressing as the Soviet scene seems to be to-day, there will undoubtedly come a moment when the ruled will not be able to live as before and the rulers will not be able to rule as before. The present Soviet leadership cannot for much longer cling to power. The average age of those on top is well over three score and ten. Changes must come. The party's monolith is a thing of the past, yet it still presents to the country and to the outside world a façade of unanimity; the various strains within it are prevented from coming to the fore. But any crisis at the top may crack this façade further and release forces more susceptible to the pressures from below and less able to withstand them. And this must considerably affect all societies within the Soviet orbit.

NOTES

1. *La Pologne: une société en dissidence,* ed. Z. Erard & G.M. Zygier, (Maspero, Paris, 1978), p. 102.
2. Roy Medvedev, *Intervista sul dissenso in URSS,* P. Ostellino, (Laterza, Rome, 1977), p. 8.
3. Quoted in *Na Lewo,* published by Polish revolutionary Marxists, no. 6, February 1978, (Paris).
4. *La Pologne,* op. cit., p. 111.
5. Ibid., pp. 99-111.
6. Ibid., p. 169.
7. Reproduced in *Labour Focus,* Vol. 2, no. 1. A Socialist Defence Bulletin on Eastern Europe and the USSR, which contains a great deal of information about opposition movements.
8. J. Pelikan, *Socialist Opposition in Eastern Europe,* (Allison & Busby, London, 1976), p. 41.
9. J. Pelikan, Interview in *Espresso,* 22nd April, 1978.
10. *Labour Focus,* Vol. 1, no. 2.
11. Rudolf Battěk, *Open Letter to W. Brandt, Kreisky and Palme,* (Palach Press Ltd., London).
12. *Le Monde,* 17th January, 1978.
13. *Espresso,* 22nd April, 1978.
14. Marc Racovski, *Le Marxisme face aux pays de l'Est,* (Savelli, Paris, 1977).
15. Quoted by K. Pomian, *Les Temps Modernes, Vivre à l'Est,* November-December, 1977, p. 959.
16. Miklos Haraszti, *A Worker in a Worker's State,* (Pelican Books in association with New Left Review, London, 1977), pp. 66-67.
17. Ibid., p. 66.
18. *Wiener Tagebuch,* (Vienna), 4th April, 1978.
19. Il Manifesto, *Pouvoir et opposition dans les sociétés post-révolutionnaires,* (Seuil, Paris, 1978), p. 109.
20. *Intervista sul dissenso in URSS,* op. cit., p. 76.
21. Roy Medvedev, *De la deomocratie socialiste,* (Grasset, Paris, 1972), p. 360.
22. *Le Monde,* 9th February, 1978.
23. *Pouvoir et opposition dans les sociétés post-révolutionnaires,* op. cit., p. 44.
24. V. Belotserkovskii, *Svoboda, Vlast i Sobstvennost,* (Ize. Achberg, 1977), p. 50.
25. *New York Times,* 20th December, 1977.
26. Amnesty International, *Psychiatric Abuses documented by the workers' group in the USSR,* 1st March, 1978.

NICOLAI IVANOVICH BUKHARIN 1888–1938*

Ken Coates

1978 marks a macabre anniversary. Forty years ago, in March 1938, there took place in Moscow the last of the great show Trials.[1] Previously there had already been two earlier public trials of former Bolshevik leaders, mowing down among others, Zinoviev, Kamenev, Piatakov and Radek.[2] A closed court-martial involving foremost Red Army commanders like Tukhachevsky, Yakir and Kork had also preceded this last trial,[3] which was to involve Bukharin, Rykov, Krestinsky, Yagoda, Rakovsky and sixteen others.

The third great trial was in one sense the keystone in a horrendous arch: all the charges which were brought in its forerunners were calculated to prove that Trotsky, from exile, was organizing with a selection of foreign powers to bring about the downfall of the Soviet Government, and that the internal opposition was not only disloyal, but criminally implicated in a vast terrorist conspiracy. By extending the web of this plot to implicate Bukharin and Rykov, a final amalgamation was thus charged against former oppositions of both Right and Left, and the effect was to establish that henceforth no "loyal" opposition was in fact possible. The Soviet political structure still manifestly suffers the ill-effects of this tragic decision, which would have been baleful even if the absurdly implausible charges in the trials had all been true, and was simply paralysing in the actual event, that they were all deliberately fabricated.

Rykov was, after all, a former prime minister, and Bukharin had been not only editor of Isvestia, and long-standing politbureau member, but, from 1926 onwards, chairman of the Communist International. His popular exposition (co-authored with Preobrazhensky) on *The ABC of Communism* was the primer of the world-wide communist movement during the 'twenties, while his scholarly works on imperialism and on the doctrines of marginalism were certainly among the most creative works of the marxist school of his time. Yet his distinctive political contribution had been his unrelenting support of the continuation of the New Economic Policy throughout the 1920s, in pursuit of which he had formed his alliance with Stalin during the crucial days in which the various

---

*A booklet on *The Care of Nikolai Bukharin* (Spokesman Books, 1978) argues this case at greater length than is possible in a short article.

oppositionists of the left were defeated. Without this alliance, Stalin could not have prevailed. All the more shattering, then, was the decision to "arrest, try, shoot" the man upon whose support Stalin had at one time so evidently depended.

Of course, the deaths of Bukharin and Rykov were completely un-remarkable in the given context. Most other leading veterans of the October Revolution also perished, whether in trials or not. So, too, did vast numbers of lesser known communists: in the wake of each trial in turn there were vast numbers of arrests and summary executions, deportations and imprisonments.[4] The veritable bloodstorm among Soviet communists had been initiated after the assassination of S.M. Kirov in 1934, but it was not the first crop of purge trials: before the destruction of the cadre of old Bolsheviks there had been a major show trial involving Menshevik leaders in 1930.[5]

Much light has been thrown on these terrible events in the literature of samizdat, the "self-published" circulation of essays, memoirs and interviews by critics of the present Soviet government, which has burgeoned since the fall of Khrushchev and the partial restoration of Stalin's badly damaged political image.[6] In fact, since Khrushchev's famous "secret speech" of 1956, it has been more than obvious to any critical student of the verbatim records of the widely publicised major trials, that these were all complete travesties of justice. We shall briefly consider the evidence on this matter in due course, but it is sufficient at this point to say that when, in 1957, the year after the XX Congress, Khrushchev posthumously rehabilitated the military leaders who perished with Tukhachevsky, and when the leading Polish communists who were executed without trial at about the same time were proclaimed to have been innocent, so seriously punctured were the official charges against Bukharin and many of his colleagues that in any normal democracy there would have been an instant move to re-examine the proceedings which had brought about their deaths.

Khrushchev himself was thoroughly aware of the significance of his own remarks at the XX Congress, and of his further onslaught at the XXII Congress a few years later, in 1961.

"Just before the Twentieth Party Congress I summoned the State Prosecutor, Comrade Rudenko, who has been involved in many of the cases during the purges of the thirties. I asked him, 'Comrade Rudenko, I'm interested in the open trials. Tell me, how much basis in actual fact was there for the accusations made against Bukharin, Rykov, Syrtsov, Lominadze, Krestlinsky, and many, many other people well known to the Central Committee, to the Orgbureau, and to the Politbureau'?

Comrade Rudenko answered that from the standpoint of judicial norms, there was no evidence whatsoever for condemning or even trying those men. The case for prosecuting them had been based on personal confessions beaten out of them under physical and psychological torture, and confessions extracted by such means are unacceptable as a legitimate basis for bringing someone to trial.

Nevertheless, we decided not to say anything about the open trials in my speech to the Twentieth Party Congress. There was a certain ambiguity in our conduct here. The reason for our decision was that there had been representatives of the fraternal Communist parties present when Rykov, Bukharin, and other leaders of the people were tried and sentenced. These representatives had then gone home and testified in their own countries to the justice of the sentences. We didn't want to discredit the fraternal Party representatives who had attended the open trials, so we indefinitely postponed the rehabilitation of Bukharin, Zinoviev, Rykov, and the rest. I can see now that our decision was a mistake. It would have been better to tell everything. Murder will always out. You can't keep things like that a secret for long."[7]

This is a most interesting explanation. Khrushchev was right, of course. Foreign communists (and non-communists) had played a major role in whitewashing the Trials. Writing within hours of Bukharin's execution, Harry Pollitt said:

"The trial of the 21 political and moral degenerates in Moscow is a mighty demonstration to the world of the power and strength of the Soviet Union. . .

All the groups within the Soviet Union who doubted the capacity of the Government to construct Socialism, groups who lost faith and could go no further in the hard fight to overcome difficulties, groups defeated in political struggles as to which policy should be followed by the Soviet Government all tended to draw together, and by their infamous activities conspired to hinder or destroy the great structure that millions were devoting their lives to build.

When fascism rose to power in Germany, and the militarist fascist regime in Japan gained strength—these two countries were assisted by Britain to develop into 'bulwarks against Bolshevism in the East and West.'

And then, inevitably, the wreckers inside the Soviet Union made a common front with Germany and Japan. The gigantic conspiracy is being unfolded in the present trial. The threads of the previous trials are being drawn together. No need here to amplify or explain the evidence—it speaks for itself.

The roots of the cancer are being ruthlessly plucked out. We must, however, appreciate one point clearly—there is a lot of talk about 'confessions'—it is not a question of confessions which bring to light the deeds of these criminals. These people have been forced to admissions when faced with the facts produced by the judicial authorities. They can no longer hide the truth.

You will remember how Zinoviev and Kamenev grovelled when faced with the death sentence and cried out that they had revealed everything. The facts show they had told nothing in comparison with what they were still hiding. The evidence of *Yagoda* is conclusive on this point. The full facts only come to light now through the patient and painstaking work of the Soviet authorities."[8]

Of course, any careful reading of the trial script would have shown that Bukharin made very few tangible specific "admissions" at all, and was confronted with no material evidence outside the "confessions" of others.[9] Indeed, at one point in his final plea, he insisted that "confessions are a medieval principle of jurisprudence."[10] What Bukharin did plead was his "guilt" in some overall moral-political sense, detached from any particular criminal action. It is nowadays widely believed that this abstract plea was the price of the lives of his young wife, Larina, and their baby son. But Pollitt had scarcely had time to familiarise himself with the trial record, since his copy had to be in *Inprecor* which actually appeared on the 19th March, only days after the conclusion of the event upon which he was commenting. Such was Pollitt's faith in the Soviet Government at that time that one might easily believe that no conceivable villainy on its part would call forth a protest from him. Indeed, in the same article, he speaks enthusiastically of "the Stalins, Molotovs, Kaganovitchs, Yezhovs, these are the men of steel. . ."[11]

By contrast, Khrushchev tells us:

"Beria didn't create Stalin. Stalin created Beria. And before him, Stalin created Yezhov. 'The Blackberry' and 'the Mailed Fist'—these were Stalin's nicknames for Yezhov. And before Yezhov, there was Yagoda. Stalin created Yagoda, too. One by one they made their entrances and exits. The rapid turnover among the main characters created by Stalin was very much part of Stalin's logic. He used henchmen to destroy honest men who he knew perfectly well were guiltless in the eyes of the Party and the people. Then Stalin stood above it all while the terror consumed its own executors. When one band of thugs got too embroiled in the terror, he simply replaced it with another. That's how the three echelons came about: first Yagoda, then Yezhov, then Beria. . ."[12]

To do him justice, Pollitt never contested the downfall of any of these monsters, after it had been accomplished. But until it became an accomplished fact, each in turn was "a man of steel."

Englishmen should not believe that Pollitt was exceptionally gullible or corrupt. Hardly any major Comintern leader escaped the relentless pressure to endorse these trials in similar terms. Dimitrov, considering the Zinoviev trial, had set the framework of the official communist reaction:

"The trial of the terrorists, who are agents of Fascism, is an integral part of the struggle of the international working class against fascism."[13]

That Dimitrov himself was the hero of the Reichstag Trial in Hitler's Germany was, for any in Western Europe who were not agnostic, a material guarantee of the soundness of this judgement. Writing in the journal *Communist International,* Togliatti spoke of "bandits" plotting "sacrilegious crimes", and identified the 1936 opening trial as "a touchstone of our class vigilance."[14] Years later, in an interview given on 16th June 1956, Togliatti still hankered after some foundation in fact for all the Trials, if rather more tentatively than had been his earlier wont:

"It is still not clear to us whether the current denunciations of the violation of legality and application of illegitimate and morally repugnant prosecuting methods extend to the entire period of the trials, or only to a given period, more recent than that to which I have referred. . .

I repeat, with respect to the initial trials—which we were able to consider, the later trials for the most part not being public—my opinion today is that there existed simultaneously two elements: the conspiratorial attempts of the opponents against the regime to commit terrorist acts; and the application of illegal prosecuting methods, censurable on a moral basis. The first, naturally, does not minimize the gravity of the second."[15]

To give him his due, Togliatti apparently assumed that some effort would be made, following Khrushchev's revelations, to determine the extent to which such a mixture had really existed, and to reassess the verdicts of at any rate the "later" trials. No such limited concern for justice can be found in the memoirs of D.N. Pritt, who was one of the most prominent fellow travellers to justify the first trial, in a veritable rash of articles and pamphlets, and to dignify a Left Book Club account of the second trial with an approving foreword.[16] At the end of a boastful account of his attendance at the 1936 Trial, he appends a short note about contemporary Soviet attitudes:

"What their views of the case now are, after the revelations made at the Twentieth Congress. . . of the tragic abuses of the Stalin period, I do not know. I have thought it best to leave unchanged my account of the trial. . ."[17]

Curiosity was not a consuming passion of Mr. Pritt, nor for a whole number of more distinguished commentators on the same themes.

No-one should think that uncritical acceptance of the official view in the USSR was confined to communists: not only Churchill[18] and Ambassador Davies[19] of the United States tended to accept that "wreckers" had indeed been at work, but far more plausible socialist voices lent support to the conspiracy theory. Notably, the Webbs swallowed the package whole, and were widely quoted in support of the necessity of repression.[20] By contrast, since 1956, some prominent Western communists have already made clear and sometimes moving statements repudiating their witness of the 'thirties. Foremost among these is perhaps Ernst Fischer, the Austrian marxist writer, who wrote a heart-breakingly honest account of his unwitting complicity in what he later came to regard as judicial murder.[21] The British Communist review, *Marxism Today,* published a favourable appreciation of the life and work of Bukharin early in 1978. More weighty action is to be taken by the Italian Communist publishing house, which has commissioned a work by Roy Medvedev on this subject.

For all that, the communist and socialist movements outside the Soviet Union can still do a great deal more to help set straight the record on this painful matter. It is vain to plead that this is an internal Soviet affair, because at the time that the victims were being shot, it was regarded as no such thing. Enormous publicity was given to the prosecution's fabrications in the communist and socialist presses of every European country, and a small library of apologetic literature was generated. After the second world war, a similar flow of misrepresentation accompanied the not dissimilar programme of trials in Eastern Europe, each of which aimed at discrediting President Tito of Yugoslavia, in precisely the same manner that the earlier scripts had been calculated to isolate and defame Leon Trotsky.[22] The proceedings against Laslo Rajk and others in Budapest, against Traicho Kostov and others in Sofia, and against Slansky, Sling and their colleagues in Prague each had their specific targets, but all formed parts of the strategy to contain any influence that might have been exerted by events in Yugoslavia on communists in East or West Europe. But although Western Communists had joined in this reprehensible campaign with as much energy as they could muster for it, it was not left to them to make restitution for its evil effects. On the contrary, the Hungarian and Bulgarian communists were encouraged by the Soviet authorities themselves to revise and repudiate these trials, and to "rehabilitate" (most often posthumously) their victims: this was necessary in order to normalise Soviet state relations with Yugoslavia, and because, unlike Trotsky, Tito had not been a victim of the murderous attention of the overseas desk of the NKVD, and remained alive: a force still to be reckoned with. Thus, Western communists faced the rehabilitation of Rajk and Kostov as a given fact to be explained, rather than as a just cause to be campaigned for.

By contrast, in 1978, the Soviet Trials have still not been revised, and their most grisly inventions have only been repudiated by implication. 1978 is not only the 40th anniversary of Bukharin's execution, but it is the 90th anniversary of his birth. One fears, however, that a more weighty anniversary preoccupies the Soviet leadership: 1979 will be Stalin's Centenary. Should anyone intend to dig up the dictator's bones, or even some of them, it seems clear that it would be impolitic to have previously exonerated Bukharin. Are we wrong to assume that this conjunction of dates partially explains the following samizdat document?

"Early in June, 1977, an official of the Central Committee, Klimov, phoned at the apartment of A.M. Larina (N.I. Bukharin's widow) and asked that she get in touch with him. On June 9, since A.M. Larina was out of Moscow, Yu. N. Larin, her son and son of N.I. Bukharin, called the number indicated by Klimov and asked him hadn't he phoned in connection with the letters sent by Bukharin's son and widow on the eve of the 25th Congress (of the Communist Party of the Soviet Union) to the Congress itself, to the Presidium of the Congress, to the Politburo of the Central Committee of the Communist Party of the Soviet Union, and personally to the General Secretary of the CC, CPSU, L.I. Brezhnev, appealing for Bukharin's rehabilitation. Klimov confirmed that his call was connected with this matter and said the following:

"I have been instructed to inform you that your appeal to have Bukharin reinstated in the Party and restored to full membership in the Academy of Sciences of the USSR cannot be granted since the guilty verdicts pertaining to the criminal offences for which he was tried have not been set aside."

Yu. N. Larin replied that many of Bukharin's co-defendants have been rehabilitated; for example, Krestinsky, Ikramov, and Khodzhaev.

Klimov answered that obviously Larin didn't know that the majority of the accused at the trial had not been rehabilitated. Yu. N. Larin asked, 'Do you really believe that Nikolai Ivanovich (Bukharin) murdered Gorky?' Klimov answered: 'That question falls under the jurisdiction of the courts and the procurator's office.' Yu. N. Larin asked: 'Does that mean that you think I should turn to these bodies?' To this Klimov answered: 'That's your right', but made it clear he oughtn't do that at the present time. 'You should know how complicated the situation is now.'

A.M. Larina and Yu. N. Larin first appealed for N.I. Bukharin's rehabilitation in 1961. Thus the rejection came 16 years after the first request and a year and a half after the last. (V.I. Lenin's friends, E.D. Stasova and V.A. Karpinsky, having made an analogous appeal in 1956 died and consequently never got an answer.)

Having received the foregoing statement, Yu. N. Larin addressed a petition for Bukharin's rehabilitation to the Chairman of the Supreme Court of the USSR on June 11, 1977."[23]

Whether or not this remarkably obtuse official reaction can be explained by a hankering to forgive Stalin on the part of some section of the Central Committee of the CPSU, it is tragically plain that Larin and his mother have, since June 11, 1977, got precisely nowhere in their efforts to secure justice for Bukharin.

This explains why Larin felt it necessary to appeal to Enrico Berlinguer for help, in an extraordinary letter which brings the bygone atmosphere of the late 'thirties menacingly back to life:

Respected Comrade Berlinguer,

I am writing this letter to you on the eve of the 40th Anniversary of the tragic death of my father, Nikolai Ivanovich Bukharin. At that time I was only two years old and naturally was unable to remember my father. But my mother, who had spent many years in Stalin's prisons and camps, miraculously survived and told me the truth about my father. Later G.M. Krzhizhanovsky, one of V.I. Lenin's closest friends, and Old Bolsheviks, who had lived through the terror and who had known Nikolai Ivanovich in one circumstance or another, told me about him. In addition I read many Bolshevist books (which are banned in our country even today and have been preserved only by chance by certain Old Bolsheviks) including books by Nikolai Ivanovich himself and the works of foreign researchers. The information which I obtained in this way helped me to fully appreciate the character and the social and political activity of my father. I understood the enormity of Stalin's crimes, the extent to which he had falsified the history of the Party, the absurdity and stupidity of the accusations levelled against my father at the Plenum of the Central Committee of February/March 1937 and the trial of the so-called "Right-Trotskyist Bloc." However, on the basis of these absurd charges (espionage, treason, sabotage and murder), my father was expelled from the Central Committee and from the Party and condemned to death.

Beginning in 1961 my mother A.M. Larina and then I myself persistently raised with the highest Party-State organs of the country the question of the withdrawal of the monstrous allegations against N.I. Bukharin and his restoration to Party membership. This question was also raised with the Party leadership by the most senior of the Old Bolsheviks led by the former secretary of the Central Committee of the Party, E.D. Staseva. They died some time ago without receiving an answer and it was only last summer (1977) that we at last received some response in the form of a telephone call. An official of the Commission of Party Control of the Central Committee of the CPSU informed us by telephone that the accusations made at the trial of Bukharin had not been withdrawn as the process of examining the documents relating to the trial had not been completed; the question of the restoration of his Party membership could not, therefore, yet be resolved. This means that 40 years after the execution of my father we have received an answer, which, in effect, confirms the monstrous charges of Stalin. My approach to the Courts (the Supreme Court of the USSR) has been fruitless: the simple truth is they don't answer me.

In a country where the greater part of the population has been brought up on the mendacious "Short Course" there are many who still consider my father as a traitor and a hireling-of-Hitler although in reality the truth is that he was an outstanding fighter against fascism and in his last years he devoted all his energies to the exposure of fascism and to warnings against the growing fascist threat.

Leaving home for the last time for the Plenum of February/March 1937 (from which he never returned) my father said to my mother "don't become embittered: there are sad errors in history. I want my son to grow up as a Bolshevik." He looked on the events which had occurred as tragic but transient; he believed in the ultimate victory of the forces of socialism.

I am not a member of the Party but for my father the word 'Bolshevik' undoubtedly meant a fighter for social justice. And we are unable to obtain such justice in our country for a man whom Lenin before his death called "the favourite of the whole Party." For my mother, who lived through the horrors of Stalin's camps, who knew many of Lenin's comrades-in-arms, representatives of the old Bolshevik Party—people about whom she preserves in her memory the happiest recollections and of whom she always speaks with tenderness and love—life in such a situation is becoming more and more intolerable. It is inconceivable that people who still carry on their shoulders the burden of Stalin's crimes and have not cast it into the dustbin of history can fight for high ideals.

I am approaching you, Comrade Berlinguer, not only because you are the leader of the largest communist party of western Europe and have thrown off this burden but also because N.I. Bukharin was a Communist-Internationalist, an active member of the International Workers' Movement. He was known to Communists of many countries: they always recalled him with warmth. Some of them are still living and are working in the ranks of the Italian Communist Party. I particularly have in mind Comrade Umberto Terracini.

I am approaching you to ask you to participate in the campaign for the rehabilitation of my father, in whatever form seems to you to be the most appropriate.

Not long before his death Nikolai Ivanovich wrote a letter "to the future generation of leaders of the Party" in which he appealed to them "to unravel the monstrous tangle of crimes." My mother learnt the text of this letter by heart in the dark days after her rehabilitation she passed it on to the Central Committee of the Party. This letter ended with the words:

"KNOW COMRADES THAT ON THE BANNER WHICH YOU WILL CARRY IN YOUR VICTORIOUS MARCH TOWARDS COMMUNISM THERE IS A DROP OF MY BLOOD."

Yours sincerely, Yu. Larin (Bukharin).   12.3.78

The Russel Foundation, having received this message, circulated it in many countries for endorsement, and secured a very wide response. But it remains all too apparent that in the one country that matters, it will fall upon ears which will rest studiedly and impassively deaf.

For this reason, socialists outside the USSR must surely take a hand. The case for revising the Bukharin trial, like its forerunners, is morally overwhelming.

We may summarise it very simply.

First, of the 21 defendants charged in 1938, at least seven have been fully rehabilitated: these include Krestinsky, Ivanov, Chernov, Grinko, Zelensky, Ikramov and Khodzayev. All the charges were, however, interwoven, since what was alleged against the accused was a great conspiracy, in which all were said to have been parties.

Second, at an "all-union Conference of Historians in 1964, the Central Committee Secretary Pospelov said, in reply to a question, that neither Bukharin nor Rykov were spies or wreckers."[24]

Third, as we have pointed out, the 1957 rehabilitations of Tukhachevsky and the military leaders, and of the executed Polish communists, sank without trace a key part of the Bukharin indictment.

Fourth, Goloded and Cherviakov, the Byelorussian communists, have been completely rehabilitated, although at the trial Sharangovich confessed that they were Polish spies. Ikramov, mentioned above, was supposed, according to the Trial script, to have been trying to make over Soviet Central Asia to the British.

Fifth, Rudzutak and Yenukidze have both been rehabilitated, although the Trial "proved" their complicity in the plots.

Sixth, Gorky's secretary has been rehabilitated, whatever the truth about Gorky's alleged "murder."[25]

Seventh, the identical format of the East European trials in Hungary, Bulgaria and Czechoslovakia reveals the existence of the technology and expertise of witchcraft trials: more, the scripts of pre- and post-war trials were to some degree interlinked.[26]

Eighth, we know beyond doubt that Stalin was guilty of the mass-murder of communists outside the quasi-judicial legitimation of the trials: we know that the security forces were completely lawless and vicious in their operation, and we know that every head of the security service from Yagoda to Beria perished in total infamy.

And yet the Trial as a whole remains unrevised, and Bukharin and Rykov are still victims of continuing slander. It is only possible to murder a man once, but it is possible to lie about him repeatedly. If the Soviet authorities are unwilling to make amends, will no-one else? As a one-time leader of the Communist International, has not Bukharin the right to call in aid his former disciples and their pupils? It is greatly to be hoped that we shall not have to ask these questions much longer.

Afterword

At the time this essay was finished, the response to the Russell Foundation's appeal for support for Larin's request for the rehabilitation of his father was not yet clear. It soon became evident, however, that there really was widespread support for it.

The reply from the Italian Communists, when it came, was dramatic and completely unambiguous. On Friday, June 16th, the Party newspaper, *Unita* published a long statement by Paolo Spriano, who had already privately endorsed the appeal. It began with the injunction

> "the need to do justice to this eminent representative of the international communist movement, as well as to the other victims of the trials of the '30s, is not merely a problem concerning their historical merit, but a moral and political necessity."

A week later, the text of the Larin letter was published in the independent newspaper, *La Repubblica,* together with another strong interview with Spriano, and a statement from Aldo Tortorella, the PCI's main official spokesman on cultural affairs. Subsequently, *Rinascita,* the Party's cultural weekly, featured a long article. Meantime, the signatures of the appeal were flooding in: French Communists Althusser and Balibar, the international secretary of the French Socialists, Robert Pontillon, Claude Bourdet of the radical Unified Socialist Party, and Simone de Beauvoir; the secretary of the Greek Communists, the Spanish historian Claudin, and the leader of the Fourth International Ernest Mandel; from the USA, Noam Chomsky, Corliss Lamont, Joe Hansen and Robert Cohen, Bukharin's biographer; the Australian Communist Party, which sent a heartwarming letter of complete solidarity; and Pierre Joye, the veteran Belgian Communist leader.

In England, a number of Labour MPs and several members of the Party Executive endorsed the appeal. The Labour Party newspaper, *Labour Weekly,* carried a full report:

> A worldwide campaign has been launched on behalf of a long-dead victim of the Stalin purges.
> Labour MPs have joined socialists in 15 countries to urge the Soviet Union to rehabilitate Nikolai Bukharin. . .
> In Britain it is backed by Labour Party chairman Joan Lestor and seven other Labour MPs—Ian Mikardo, Norman Buchan, Geoff Edge, Martin Flannery, Eric Heffer, Stan Newens and Audrey Wise. Playwrights Tom Stoppard, Trevor Griffiths and Howard Brenton, and members of the Bertrand Russell Peace Foundation which is co-ordinating the British appeal, are also among those who have signed.
> They are demanding that the Soviet Union gives a "full explanation to the circumstances which led to Bukharin's wrongful conviction. . ."

Liverpool Walton MP Eric Heffer, who has signed the appeal, says: "Undoubtedly the charges against him were part and parcel of Stalinism.

"If the Soviet Union is to get back to a democratic type of regime, which it had for only a short time after the revolution, it will have to accept that there were fundamental and vicious policies which they will have to totally repudiate.

"Bukharin was a great political leader and one of the early Bolsheviks, a man of tremendous intellectual ability."

The first batch of signatures has been sent forward to the Soviet authorities, and we await their reply.

NOTES

1. Cf. *Report of Court Proceedings in the Case of the Anti-Soviet "Bloc of Rights and Trotskyites."* Moscow, March 2-13, 1938. Moscow 1938. This "trial" involved Bukharin, Rykov, Yagoda, Krestinsky, Rakovsky, Rosenglotz, Ivanov, Chernov, Grinko, Zelensky, Bessonov, Ikramov, Khodjayer, Sharangovich, Zubarev, Bulanov, Levin, Pletnev, Kazakov, Maximov-Dikovsky, Kryuchkov. Bukharin and Rykov were shot two days after the end of the hearing.
2. Cf. *The Case of the Trotskyite-Zinovievite Terrorist Centre,* Moscow 1936, and *Report of the Court Proceedings in the Case of the Anti-Soviet Trotskyite Centre,* Moscow 1937. Both these trials were carefully examined by the Dewey Commission, whose report was published under the title: *Not Guilty: the Case of Leon Trotsky,* London, Secker and Warburg, 1938.
3. Cf. Medvedev: *Let History Judge,* Nottingham, Spokesman 1977, pp. 209 et seq. For accounts by military eyewitnesses, Bialer: *Stalin and His Generals,* London, Souvenir Press, 1970, pp. 63-86.
4. "All the former members of the various defunct opposition groups numbered no more than twenty to thirty thousand people, and most of them had been jailed or shot by the beginning of 1937. That was a painful loss to the Party, but it was only the beginning. Throughout 1937 and 1938 the flood of repression rose, carrying away the basic core of Party leadership. This well-planned, pitiless destruction of the people who had done the main work of the Revolution from the days of the underground struggle, through the insurrection and the Civil War, the restoration of the shattered economy and the great up-building of the early thirties, was the most frightful act in the tragedy of the thirties."
   Medvedev, op. cit., p. 192.
5. *Wreckers on Trial,* edited Andrew Rothstein, London, Modern Books, 1931.
6. Cf. notably Medvedev, op. cit., which quotes from an extraordinary clandestine documentation and displays a remarkable objectivity and scrupulousness in evaluating the most dreadful evidence.
7. *Khrushchev Remembers,* London, Andre Deutsch, 1971, p. 352-3. This book was repudiated by Khrushchev when the first volume appeared in the USA: but the second (subsequent) volume contained explanatory evidence about the circumstances of its publication which validate it as his work, at any rate in large measure. The book was prepared from tapes which Khrushchev dictated from memory, so that there is room for double error: it could be mistakenly edited in transcription, and it could be wrong because of Khrushchev's faulty recollection and the absence of necessary documentation. There is, however, no room in this particular passage for errors of either sort, and therefore we can take it that this actually was what Khrushchev said.

8. Pollitt: *The Crushing of the Traitors—a Triumph for Peace and Socialism*: International Press Correspondence, No. 14, 19th March 1938, p. 309 et. seq. A similar view was put forward in a British Communist Party pamphlet published in May 1938: R. Page Arnot and Tim Buck: *Fascist Agents Exposed in the Moscow Trials*. Tim Buck was, of course, spokesman of the Canadian Communists.

9. Cf. notably Katkov: *The Trial of Bukharin*, London, Batsford, 1969, and Stephen F. Cohen's exhaustively comprehensive biography: *Bukharin and the Bolshevik Revolution*, London, Wildwood House, 1974. Fitzroy Maclean, who attended the trial, gives an eyewitness account which emphasises this view in *Eastern Approaches*, London Pan Books, 1956, pp. 55 et. seq.

10. *Report of Court Proceedings*, p. 778.

11. Pollitt, op. cit., p. 309, col. II.

12. Khrushchev, op. cit., p. 352.

13. *The Communist International*, Vol. XIII, No. 10, Nov.-Dec. 1936, p. 641.

14. M. Ercoli: *The Lessons of the Trial of the Trotsky-Zinovievist Terrorist Centre*, Communist International, XIII, 10, pp. 341-51.

15. Togliatti: *Answers to Nine Questions*. In C. Wright Mills, *The Marxists*, London, Penguin Books, 1963, pp. 372-3.

16. Eg. Article in *News Chronicle: The Moscow Trial War Fair*, reprinted in "Russia Today" pamphlet, n.d. (1936?) and foreword to *Soviet Justice at the Trial of Radek and Others*, by Dudley Collard: Left Book Club (Gollancz) 1937.

17. *Autobiography of D.N. Pritt*: Vol. 1, From Right to Left. London, Lawrence and Wishart, 1965, p. 112. Pritt has the gall to continue ". . . industrious anti-Soviet propagandists in the West—those who sought to find a basis for their stories instead of just inventing them—eagerly studied the transcript, believed they had found a certain number of errors of fact in it which would help discredit the trial, and published the errors broadcast. I and others then, naturally, studied the allegations, and found that they were not in fact errors, although they looked as if they might be." (p. 113)

18. *The Second World War*: I. 1948, London, Cassell, pp. 288-9.

19. Cf. Sayers and Kahn: *The Great Conspiracy*, New York, Boni and Gaer, pp. 111 et. seq.

20. This is apparent not only from the relevant afterthoughts added to their book *Soviet Communism*, but also from the Correspondence, edited by Norman Mackenzie, and published by Cambridge University Press in 1978. (See especially Volume III), For a comprehensive discussion of a pathetic literature on this matter, see David Caute: *The Fellow Travellers*, London, Quartet, 1977.

21. *An Opposing Man*, London, Allen Lane, the Penguin Press, 1974, pp. 304 et. seq.

22. It is tedious to list all these tracts since the record has now been clearly established. But notably, in England, there was Derek Kartun: *Tito's Plot Against Europe* and James Klugman: *From Trotsky to Tito*. Both books were published by Lawrence and Wishart.

23. *In These Times*, November 16-22, 1977, p. 13. See also the useful article in the same journal, by Louis Menashe.

24. Roy Medvedev: *Bukharin's Last Two Years*, New Left Review 109, 1978. I am grateful to the editors of NLR for sending me a pre-publication proof of this important article.

25. For further evidence see *Let History Judge*, pp. 179 et. seq.

26. See, notably, Artur London: *The Confession*, New York, Ballantine Books, 1971: and Eugene Loebl: *Sentenced and Tried*, London, Elek, 1969.

THE "ENEMY WITHIN": THE CASE OF *BERUFSVERBOT*

Claudia von Braunmühl

The first half of the year 1978 saw two events carefully demarcated from each other, both, however, concerned with the same issue: the practice of "Berufsverbot" (professional ban) in West Germany in the 70's. In early April, the Third International Russell Tribunal on the situation of human rights in the Federal Republic of Germany commenced its proceedings. The sole topic under investigation for the first session—another one will follow at the beginning of next year—was the question: "Is the right to practise their professions denied to citizens of the Federal Republic of Germany?" This central question was dealt with under the following three aspects:

1. Does the practice of Berufsverbot constitute a serious danger to human rights?
2. Is the practice of Berufsverbot against people who hold certain political opinions applied in a discriminatory way?
3. Does the practice of Berufsverbot relate to discriminatory practices of other institutions, particularly trade unions, professional organisations and churches?

A week before the Russell Tribunal met, a group of liberal journalists, authors and a couple of members of the SPD announced the launching of the "Gustav Heinemann initiative" (Gustav Heinemann was the third president of the FRG, highly esteemed for his liberal thought), which had its founding congress at the end of May. Within the last ten years, the founding declaration states, "liberty in the Federal Republic of Germany became increasingly endangered by fear, apathy and resignation. Intimidation and self-censorship constrict the space for free debate and drive young people to the margin of society." It was argued with great emphasis that first and foremost the "Decree on Radicals" needs to be abolished, "because the practice of Berufsverbot lies at the root of the apathy."

The two bodies, distinctly different in political orientation with a careful demarcation line drawn by the latter towards the former, nonetheless find themselves united in their concern over the practice of what is referred to as "Berufsverbot."

The word stands for the refusal to access to or exercise of employment in the public sector, which includes the whole educational system, social services, and most of the infrastructure services (railroads, post office, etc).

Somewhat more than 15% of the working population of the FRG are employed in the civil service. A declaration of war on the "enemy within", considered to be radical democrats and socialists, has become the basis for refusing admission into the civil service. The practice of the Berufsverbot has given birth to its own apparatus and has long since proliferated into the private sector.

The Russell Tribunal concludes in its intermediate report:

> "The extent of the violation of human rights by the practice of Berufsverbot and the resulting consequences have to be judged as extraordinarily grave. The responsible authorities pose increasing requirements for the assessment of 'constitutional loyalty' (Verfassungstreue) and for the demanded proof thereof. The difference between loyalty towards the Constitution and loyalty towards the state, and loyalty towards those administering the state, tends to disappear. Special branch (Verfassungsschutz) authorities are continually enlarged and develop an ever increasing dynamic of their own as does any bureaucracy."

When did this dynamic start? Political repression is not altogether new in West Germany. In 1950, the newly founded republic found it appropriate (Adenauer-Erlass) to eliminate communists and so-called fellow-travellers from the civil service, even before the Communist Party was declared to be "hostile to the Constitution" (verfassungsfeindlich) and therefore illegal by a Constitutional Court ruling in 1956. Since that particular court is the only agency authorized legally to pass judgements on questions of constitutionality, it was thus legalizing a hitherto constitutionally highly doubtful practice.

In 1968 at the suggestion and decisive encouragement of the SPD, the Communist Party was refounded with a new abbreviation, DKP instead of KPD (which nowadays is used by a maoist-oriented communist group) and a new programme impeccable in terms of constitutional loyalty. The constitutionality of the DKP as well as that of any other communist organisation has not been challenged by Constitutional Court ruling.

The professed hope and calculation of the SPD, born out of a narrow-minded, organisation-bound notion of politics, proved to be quite out of line with reality. Neither did the DKP remain all that insignificant, nor did it channel sufficiently those located left of the SPD into its organisational framework. When in 1969 the Grand Coalition of CDU/CSU and SPD gave way to a social democratic-liberal government, the boom following the economic and political crisis of 1967/68 was accompanied by a short period of liberalisation, which grew to be associated with the name of Chancellor Willy Brandt. Little more than a year later, however, with the student movement generation applying for jobs, the winds of change blew drastically backwards. With the legality of all communist organisations maintained, in January 1972, in the absence of Federal competence, the Conference of Prime Ministers of the constituent Länder agreed on

"Principles on the question of the forces hostile to the Constitution in the civil service", which came to be known as the "Decree on Radicals." Because this decree is often referred to but hardly ever cited completely it is worthwhile to quote its exact wording.

> "According to Federal and Land legislation pertaining to the civil service
> —only those persons are eligible for the civil service (Beamtenverhältnis) who can guarantee that they will at any time actively support the free democratic fundamental order (freiheitlich demokratische Grundordnung) in the sense of the Constitution.
> —civil servants are obliged, on duty as well as off duty, actively to strive for the preservation of that fundamental order. These are binding regulations. Each individual case has to be investigated and decided upon its own merits. The following principles have to be applied:
> Applicants: an applicant who exhibits activities hostile to the Constitution, will not be employed in the civil service. Membership in an organisation that pursues goals hostile to the Constitution, constitutes doubt, whether the applicant will support the free democratic fundamental order at any time. As a rule this doubt will justify refusal of the application.
> Civil servant (Beamter): In the case of a civil servant who through his activities or through membership in an organisation pursuing goals hostile to the Constitution does not meet the requirements of §35 of the general legislation on the civil service (Beamtenrechtsrahmengesetz), on the basis of which he is obliged to identify (sich bekennen) with the free democratic fundamental order in the sense of the Constitution by his total conduct and to support its preservation, the employer (Dienstherr) will have to take necessary consequences based on investigated facts. He in particular has to evaluate whether the removal of the civil servant from the service is to be sought.
> The same principles apply to workers and employees in the civil service within the framework of the respective wage agreements."

By 1978, on the basis of this "Decree on Radicals", 1.3 million applicants for the civil service have been screened, 15,000 have been called to an interview because of "doubts" that arose out of special branch "findings" (Erkenntnisse), and roughly 1,000 have been refused access to the civil service.

Before filling these apparently meagre figures with a description of the socio-political life they entail, an analysis of the "Decree on Radicals" itself will prove quite revealing about its political implications. Four features are particularly noteworthy.

1. "Civil Service" is given an extraordinarily broad meaning independent of sensitivity of the job and/or status. The notion of "obligation of political allegiance" (politische Treuepflicht), in itself highly doubtful because of its pre-democratic origin, its ample use under fascism and its closeness to an obligation of uncritical allegiance to those in power, was originally valid only for civil servants (Beamte) in the narrower sense of the word. It now proliferates generously into the rank and file of cleaning personnel and locomotive engine drivers.

By now there has been ample jurisdiction on the matter on the part of the higher courts, affirming this extended version of "civil service"—and throwing a most telling light on its intention. In the case of Sibylle Plogstedt, who was refused a one-year assistantship at the Free University of Berlin, the highest court of appeal for citizens of West Berlin in December 1974 gave reason for this proliferation. It was not that the expected results of her research activities might be influenced by her belonging to the Fourth International; but rather that while pusuing her research obligations she could communicate with members of the university and in that way might exert influence. Sibylle Plogstedt's presence in the university was considered to be unacceptable. In addition, the court reasons: "As she can vote and is eligible, she might try, further-more, to misuse the institutions of the university for her political goals."

The implication that political organisations held to be hostile towards the Constitution by their very nature misuse the rules and institutions a democratic system provides is not even considered worthwhile to elaborate upon. And, equally important, the court establishes what came to be known as the "taboo of association" (Berührungstabu) and even "guilt by association" (Berührungsschuld). In this ruling, it is the court which "protects" the members of the university from the suspected devastating effects of contact and communication with a communist. Subsequently, to an increasing extent, citizens have been held liable for their contacts with left-wing ideas, be it through people or through books. Marriage, flat-sharing, attendance of left wing electoral campaign meetings, subscription to left-wing papers, etc., all are included under "contact", likely to cast doubts on one's constitutional loyalty.

2. One of the historic achievements of capitalist liberal democracy as opposed to feudalism was the differentiation between public and private. Even though this entails alienation and a rift between private and public speech, creed and morals, it does, when contrasted with the totality of domination in pre-capitalist political systems, constitute an historical achievement, one to be defended at all costs as long as a totality of liberation is not in reach.

The "Decree on Radicals" and subsequent administrative action, legislation and jurisdiction mark a decisive step in the abolition of that difference, so crucial to liberal democracy. No longer are particular qualifications and correct job performance considered to be sufficient, but the whole of the 24 hour conduct of a person is taken as a basis of assess-ment of constitutional loyalty. To put it in official phrasing, it is the "total conduct" (Gesamtverhalten) and the "total personality" (Gesamtpersönlichkeit) that is under scrutiny.

Ironically, it is the very article of the Constitution that originally was designed and formulated to guarantee that liberal democratic differentia-tion of private and public life with precisely the experience of a totalitarian political system still fresh in people's minds, that has come to serve as an instrument for the implementation of exactly the reverse of its original intention. Article 33, §2 reads as follows:

> "Every German has equal access to the public sector according to his suitability, competence and professional performance. Nobody should be disadvantaged for his affiliation to a denomination or political conviction."

Up to the early seventies this clause of the Constitution was read and reaffirmed by the courts as a guarantee for free access to the civil service irrespective of private political and religious convictions. The last case to that effect was a 1973 Constitutional Court ruling on a neo-fascist teacher, whose activities were deemed to be private and in no evident way affecting his professional performance. Furthermore, since the NPD has not been declared unconstitutional by the only institution entitled to do so, which is the Constitutional Court itself, the court saw absolutely no basis for depriving the teacher in question of his job.

The issue, however, seems to appear in a completely different light, when the question of the "total personality" of men and women suspected of left-wing "deviation" is at stake. "Inner commitment" is demanded and is to be proved; it is made an inherent part of "suitability."

The by now classic formulation of the central Constitutional Court ruling on the Berufsverbot in February 1975 read as follows:

> "The obligation of political allegiance demands more than merely a formally correct but, for the rest, disinterested, cool, internally distanced attitude towards the state and the Constitution; it demands in particular from the civil servant that he distance himself unequivocally from groups and aspirations that attack, fight and denounce this state, its constitutional organs and the valid constitutional order. It is expected from the civil servant that he realize and appreciate this state and its Constitution as a high positive value on whose behalf it is worthwhile to intervene. The obligation of political allegiance is tested in times of crisis and in serious situations of conflict in which the state relies on the civil servant taking its side. The state—and that is more concretely, each constitutional government and the citizens—must be able to rely on the civil servant in his administration to be willing to hold responsibility for this state, for 'his' state, that in this state which he is supposed to serve, he will feel at home—now and at any time and not only after aspired changes have been brought about through respective changes in the Constitution."

In that interpretation the notion of "suitability" extends to the most intimate feelings and inclinations of a person. This is necessary, reasons the court, because a teacher e.g. "would at least unconsciously run the danger of influencing students in a way which might not be compatible with the liberal democratic fundamental order." The existence of that most private conviction and its firm rootedness in the unconscious has to be convincingly, positively demonstrated.

"Doubts have not been removed whether the plaintiff will at any time support the free democratic fundamental order inasmuch as the plaintiff did not exhibit a sufficiently clearcut attitude towards communist goals. He does indeed maintain that he will not want the governing principles of the free democratic fundamental order to be touched. . . When, however, on repeated questioning he clearly responded that he considers communists to be democrats, this indicates that he will find it difficult to perceive that communist aspirations which aim at the elimination of the free democratic fundamental order are directed against the Constitution and as a civil servant to react accordingly. It cannot be excluded that the plaintiff might not recognize these aims and might therefore be unable actively to support the free democratic fundamental order when it is in danger. He might then find himself pushed into the situation of a man, who witnesses the course of events perplexed, to be sure, without actively participating in the overthrow of the free democratic fundamental order, but also in no condition to oppose that overthrow through his own active behaviour. The plaintiff therefore is not to be labelled an enemy of the Constitution. . . He is not one of those. The refusal of acceptance to the civil service is not only justified in case of the applicant actively fighting the free democratic fundamental order, but also when his attitude towards it is indifferent." (Regional court in rejecting the claim of a conscientious objector.)

In fact and not surprisingly, in an increasing number of cases, "inner commitment", "positive", "total conduct" have become the dominant and decisive criteria for "suitability". Remuneration was refused an author who had contracted with a governmental institution for a manuscript that was accepted and already in print, when months later the author signed an electoral proclamation in favour of the KPD. The article, argued the court in favour of the institution, was without fault on its own merits, but "has been made useless afterwards by her conduct." The author therefore not only did not get remunerated but was required to pay the institute compensation as it had to find and pay another author.

3. A third feature, nowadays often taken to be an expression of a misconceived understanding of the Decree on Radicals, is actually an integral and decisive part of it: the difference implicit in the phrase "free democratic fundamental order in the sense of the Constitution."

Two frameworks of reference are mentioned: the one, the free democratic fundamental order clearly constituting a narrower version, as the phrase "in the sense of" indicates, of the larger framework—the Constitution. Indeed, as the above cited quotations, taken from the central and decisive ruling of the Constitutional Court indicate, "the prevailing constitutional order as it stands today" is nothing else but the socio-political status quo in the interpretation of the present government. Perfectly legal but not realized policies and possibilities of the Constitution, i.e. everything the "prevailing" state of the nation leaves to be desired, is placed in the realm of radicalism, whose proponents are not suitable for any kind of job in the civil service.

4. Fourthly and consequently, the notion of what precisely is "hostile to the Constitution" (verfassungsfeindlich) or who is actually an enemy of the Constitution (Verfassungsfeind) remains legally obscure, while its political content becomes frighteningly transparent.

As already indicated, according to the Constitution, it is only for the Constitutional Court to pass judgements on the constitutionality of political parties. This privilege has not been made use of since the prohibition of the Communist Party in 1956. Therefore, any left wing political party can exist legally, can take part in elections on all levels, can publish, hold meetings, etc., and indeed does so. In order to justify discrimination against left-wing citizens, including those organized in political parties, the construction of "unconstitutional goals" has been introduced. Unconstitutional goals are taken as quite self-evident. Phrases like "as everybody knows", "according to general knowledge" serve as proof— where proof is still held necessary. Even in the highest court rulings it is by now sufficient to charge a person with the fact that he or she joined the DKP "although they knew that the present federal government as well as its predecessors made it clear that the Communist Party pursues unconstitutional goals."

In the routine procedure of Berufsverbot it is just taken as a matter of fact that certain memberships, activities, reading habits, social environments *are* "hostile to the Constitution." It is for the applicant or the job-holder to give evidence to the contrary, to prove that in his or her particular case the assumption does not hold true. The burden of proof is reversed.

The matter to be proved is something quite intangible: inner commitment, total conduct, total personality. The matter to be affected by the proof is something even more intangible: doubts. Doubts are defined by the Constitutional Court.

> "That the one responsible for the hiring at the time of his decision is not convinced that the applicant has given sufficient guarantee that he will support the free democratic fundamental order at any time. This conviction is based on an appraisal that at the time implies a prognosis. . . It is a prognostic judgement of the applicant's personality, not merely the ascertainment of individual elements of appearance."

Subsequently, the court reasons, legal action cannot be taken against doubts. The courts may call for reconsideration of the case, but they may not pass judgements on the material content of the doubts and consequently they cannot enforce the reversal of decisions the public employer has made on the basis of "doubts."

As the right to work in the civil service in most cases is identical with exercising one's profession (e.g. for a teacher) or even having a chance to work at all, it is absolutely crucial for the future or actual civil servant to disperse doubts once they arise. But how is one to reason against a prognosis on the basis of contemporary evidence? How is one to give proof of the inadequateness of a prognosis? How is one to disperse "doubts" that may not in the least wish to be dispersed?

Indeed, the reasons given for job refusal are quite often as irrational as is the point of reference, constitutional commitment. Answers that leave nothing to be criticized are rejected as "mere pretext", "not convincing", "camouflage." One teacher was charged with unduly stressing those parts of the Constitution "that most Communists tend to stress" while neglecting to list the rest.

Another was refused tenure, "because as he is intelligent and self-confident he is capable of keeping his communist attitude under control and covered for quite some time. This is perfectly in line with communist tactics."

In what way do doubts emerge and how do they articulate themselves?

"Doubts" actually is a discrete paraphrase for what more precisely would have to be called "findings" of the Special Branch (Verfassungsschutz) that are passed on to the employer. In fact public employers are obliged to check with the Special Branch before filling vacancies; private ones are urged to, or are "offered" findings. Thus the Special Branch has grown to be an integral part of the hiring and firing system.

On the basis of legislation also passed in 1972, the same year as the Decree on Radicals, under the SPD/FDP administration, the various intelligence services intensified their cooperation, irrespective of their field of activities, coordinated their ways and means of collecting "findings", and particularly expanded enormously in manpower. The latter holds particularly true of the Special Branch which, originally set up for counter-intelligence, expanded into a horrifying apparatus to keep the "enemy within" under control—with exactly the same and much more refined methods that originally were designed to cope with foreign intelligence activities. These methods range from infiltrating particular groups with agents, to illegal methods like tapping phones, bugging, breaking into houses, etc. Terrorism served and serves as a handy pretext, ready to be used at simply any time for large scale raids to fill the files.

The everyday work of the Special Branch, however, is considerably less spectacular—and possibly much more dangerous. Any electoral campaign or other political activity of left-wing groups, community action, women's movement, youth groups, etc. will be carefully documented. Leaflets, petitions, lists of signatures, registration and attendance at meetings, demonstrations, publications are carefully registered, filmed, reported upon. Supported by a wide network of new legislation which obliges citizens to report on their employees, students, teachers, and neighbours, and technically supported by a highly developed computer system that centrally collects all kinds of data a highly bureaucratized society will ask of its citizens, the Special Branch uses all opportunities to collect information: public libraries reports on reading habits, border crossings are taken as an opportunity to check on friends, destinations, books and journals taken along, etc.

"Detrimental to the state" (staatsabträglich) serves as a classification and excuse for such large-scale observation which leaves fairly little private space that is not snooped into. Indeed, given the fact that it is not legality or illegality of action that serves as legal criteria but rather qualities of mind, feeling and conviction, it is only logical to broaden the undefined notion of "hostile to the Constitution" into the even more diffuse one of "detrimental to the state" (which incidentally originated with the Gestapo) to safeguard "inner security" (innere Sicherheit)—which is the headline title for repressive activity—in carefully taking cognisance of all non-conforming movements and aspirations that might possibly endanger the "prevailing order." This affects the nature of the Special Branch insofar as it broadens the scope of its activities to collecting "findings" on anything that might serve as an indicator for deviant thought and to produce classifications and judgements on the degree of possible dangerousness of the citizen.

Critics call this "snooping into one's conscience" (Gesinnungsschnüffelei). To refer to Special Branch activities in that way, however, is enough to raise doubts as to constitutional commitment. Doubts, in fact, are quite easily aroused. The following list of causes to doubt is a random sample taken from copies of letters summoning people to interviews in order to elaborate upon their relation to Constitution and state.

Candidature or support for any communist party on any level—in schools, universities, trade union organisations, parliaments—legal registering of an anti-Vietnam War demonstration in 1965, legal registering of a demonstration organized by Amnesty International, activities for a self-organized youth centre, publicly reflecting on the possibility of joining the DKP, distribution of a leaflet amongst whose signatories was a radical party member, living or having lived in the same flat with "members of the new left", activity in a left student group, candidature for a student parliament on a radical list, even one that at the time was the official student organisation of the SPD, parking near the Communist Party office when a meeting was being held, signing a petition against the closing down of a hospital, participation in the movement against nuclear power plants or dumping grounds, working in any organisation like a prisoners aid committee, neighbourhood organisations or community action in which members of radical parties are working, visiting someone who has been arrested for alleged sympathies with anarchists, selling leftist pamphlets, criticism of the practice of Berufsverbot as "snooping into one's conscience", being on the mailing list of a left publishing house, signing a resolution against Berufsverbot, sticking up posters for a radical party, asking for information and forms for a course run by the DKP, protest against the pro Vietnam War film "The Green Berets", participation in anti-Vietnam War demonstrations, parking one's car near a demonstration, conscientious objection, donating money to any organisation in which there is a communist working, visiting a political prisoner, informing the public in leaflets and meetings of one's own pending Berufsverbot, contributing a painting to an exhibition of political art organised by a group of artists supposedly close to the DKP, being the wife of a lawyer of a person accused of anarchist affiliations, being the wife of a teacher dismissed by Berufsverbot, having passed on in class the address of a lawyer defending an alleged anarchist, inviting a political theatre group to play in school, etc.

These and similar data and information are collected by the Special Branch and passed on to the public employer who gives notice of his doubts in a letter.

> "The investigation of your allegiance to the Constitution in connection with your lectureship has given reason for doubts. The Land Office of the special branch branch (Landesamt für Verfassungsschutz) has given us the following information on you." (Written in March 1978 to a Frankfurt academic active in the DKP student organisation.)

The person thus addressed is then asked to appear for an interview, whose proceedings are handled differently in different constituent Länder, particularly as concerns the right of minutes and of legal assistance. In any case legal assistance is strictly confined to procedural questions. (There is, incidentally, *no* significant difference in the number of persons screened, interviewed, and struck by Berufsverbot between the various Länder, regardless of whether they are run by CDU or SPD governments).

It is within the discretion of the employing institution whether or not to inform the applicant about the "findings." The questioning is done either by a centralized interview commission, particularly set up for that very purpose, or by the immediate employing institution. In case the findings are communicated, this may be done in writing with the summoned person asked either to answer in writing or to appear for an interview. Alternatively, the institution may choose to confront the applicant with their doubts directly. In either case, the person is obliged to give answers.

> "I have to point out to you, that in connection with the examination of your constitutional suitability it will be to your constitutional disadvantage, if you should not answer the questions concerning your membership in the above mentioned organisation." (Same letter as above.)

Usually the interrogation will start with a reference to the findings concerning the particular person under scrutiny and will then be broadened to general questions on the applicant's attitude towards the "free democratic fundamental order." The practice of the interview itself gives ample evidence of the crude identification of the political opinion of the interviewer with "constitutionality" and of how far indeed it is "snooping into one's conscience."

The following questions are taken as random samples from documented interviews:

"Do you often visit the German Democratic Republic?

Do you think the Decree on Radicals is unconstitutional?

Are you prepared to take my view, that the SEW (DKP branch of West Berlin) pursues aims hostile to the Constitution as binding for yourself and to adjust your conduct on and off duty respecting that opinion?

Have you ever referred to the FRG as an imperialist country?

What do you know about concentration camps in the eastern bloc? For instance Brandenburg, GDR?

Have you read Solzhenitsyn? Is the GDR not much worse than the Third Reich?

Do you hold a revolutionary development in the FRG to be desirable?

Have you read leaflets of the Fourth International?

Have they been discussed in your flat?

What in general do you think of flat-sharing?"

It would be quite misleading to take the figures on formally carried out Berufsverbot and on preceding interviews at face value. They are only the tip of the iceberg. Underneath, given a tightening job market and growing unemployment, is an unknown number of persons who will be denied jobs without ever getting to know whether Special Branch intervention was involved. It became known that in West Berlin, school authorities were told not to inform applicants that Special Branch investigation was the reason for job refusal or delay of employment. The very process of investigation can be decisive, where candidates who are beyond the shadow of "doubts" are immediately available to fill vacancies. Furthermore, the employing institution more often than not will prefer to avoid conflicts with the authorities on behalf of a candidate who may be perfectly qualified and acceptable but unfortunately is "in doubt."

Below the level of institutions of any kind, even below the level of the very effective fear created by the knowledge of an ever-sprawling, ever-present repressive state apparatus, the Berufsverbot has a devastating effect on the social psychology of the ordinary citizen and his/her everyday life.

No political opinion that touches on not altogether superficial differences with those in power is safe from being drawn into the proximity of hostility towards the Constitution. The consequences are fear, intimidation and political apathy. The taboo of contact, in addition to its destructive effect on particular persons, not only isolates the person who is labelled "enemy of the Constitution" or "sympathizer of terrorists", but isolates the citizen from any but officially prescribed thought. Thoughts, feelings, attitudes will not be the result of information, communication and reflection but of sheer fear and conformist acquiescence. Most disconcerting in itself and absolutely detrimental to anything that could possibly deserve the name of free democratic order, the transformation of opinions, thoughts and convictions into legal facts and their subsequent utilisation against individuals actually produces not only apathy but potentially violence, both of them twins in a political system that leaves no room for peaceful change and public discourse.

The political mechanism of Berufsverbot has penetrated into all features and realms of society. Aided by a history of state orientation in social thought and attitude in Germany, Berufsverbot has had the active support of a legislature that provides a broad network of legislation authorizing political repression, of a judiciary that is frighteningly cooperative and pliant, and, most alarming, of a trade union movement, that with only few exceptions collaborates to the point of—admitted and documented—"cooperation" with the Special Branch.

> "It is correct that in the above mentioned shop stewards meeting, I quoted information from the Special Branch pertaining to members that have already been expelled from our organisation due to conduct detrimental to the union or pertaining to those against whom procedures of expulsion have been initiated. I did so, because sympathizers of these colleagues repeatedly maintained the assertion that none of the colleagues in question were members of a left wing radical organisation or were supporting them and that there was no evidence to that effect.
> I declared that the reports of the Special Branch have been asked for in order to gain the greatest possible security in the judgement.
> I had already said in the last shop stewards meeting that I have not passed on information to the Special Branch. I would, however, have to think over whether that should be maintained in the future." (Letter dated 4.1.74 from the Berlin Branch to the central headquarters of the Union for chemical, paper and ceramics industries.)

In 1973 the DGB, umbrella organisation of all trade unions, passed the so-called "incompatibility decisions" (Unvereinbarkeitsbeschlüsse) that neither in wording nor in spirit differ considerably from the Decree on Radicals—with the—important—exception that in practice they more or less exempt the DKP. Indeed, alarmingly often, it is trade union expulsion that accompanies, if not introduces, a Berufsverbot.

Following are some random samples of letters sent to trade union members, all of them expelled and subsequently struck by Berufsverbot.

19.10.1976 GEW (teachers trade union)

"At the parliamentary election to the Bundestag on the 3.10.1976 you were a candidate in district 69 (Cologne) for the Communist League of West Germany (KBW). According to the decision of the DGB federal executive of 3.10.1973. . . this political activity is incompatible with membership of any DGB trade union. Therefore your expulsion has been initiated by the president of our union."

14.4.1975 GEW

"You are active for the KPD and you support this organisation through your support of the 'Initiative against Berufsverbot and incompatibility decisions.' According to the decision of the DGB executive of 3.10.1973. . . this is incompatible with membership of the DGB. The executive of our union therefore has initiated your expulsion."

24.1.1975 ÖTV (Civil service, transport and traffic)

"In a letter of January 1975, several colleagues of the firm Hadeler objected to the expulsion of colleague Sandermeier.

You have been present as a member of the executive at the procedure of expulsion. Therefore you should know, that S. is a member of the KBW or supports that organisation. According to the decisions of 3.10.1973 and 25/26.10.1973 members belonging to a left or right wing extremist organisation or are active for it, have been expelled.

Although you knew this you identified yourself with your signature and as a member of the executive you have disregarded a decision of the ÖTV.

As a member and particularly as a member of the executive you are expected to support union interests internally and externally and to respect and adhere to union decisions.

In both cases [the other was editorship of a critical shop floor journal] you have acted in ways detrimental to the union (gewerkschaftsschädigend), so that I had to initiate a procedure of expulsion against you."

The whole West Berlin branch of the GEW was expelled for not adopting the incompatibility decisions.

The entire procedure—charges, findings, letters for interviews, etc.—is disconcertingly similar to that of state institutions. In fact, the similarity goes decisively further, as, given the system of united unions (Einheitsgewerkschaft), i.e. one union for one industrial branch, trade union expulsion indeed does imply a Berufsverbot not only in the public but in the private sector. The names of the expelled are passed on to the union branch, which has to agree to hirings. Quite frequently, they are even published in the union papers.

Possibly even more important than the absence of active political support for those struck by Berufsverbot on the part of the trade unions is their voluntary synchronization of thought and speech and public debate, which allow these dubious criteria of civil service recruitment to penetrate into all strata of social and political life. For instance, as happened in June 1978 in a small town in Hesse and as happens all over the country without appearing in the news, a youth group of the society of conscientious objectors was denied entrance to the local youth centre on the grounds that they pursue aims hostile to the Constitution. It is not only predictable that the social conduct of these youngsters stands a good chance of deteriorating rapidly, but it has absolutely nothing to do with the alleged aim of the Decree on Radicals. It becomes quite clear, that the search for the "enemy within" serves the purpose of a large scale social witch-hunt and class struggle from above rather than the maintenance of pro-constitutional security within the state apparatus.

There has been opposition to the practice of Berufsverbot ever since 1972: local and regional committees (of various political composition) against Berufsverbot, legal advisory groups for those summoned to an interview and the like. In particular instances, unease even reached the major political parties, e.g. when in May 1975 François Mitterand in France announced the founding of a commission to investigate Berufsverbot—or when in CDU-run Länder SPD members were struck. Highly attended congresses have taken place, most recently the one mentioned earlier. So far none of these has had enough impact actually to turn the scales.

In the daily struggle against Berufsverbot the state has ample means of fighting against efforts of this kind. Civil servants or applicants for the civil service are required to observe "due moderation" and not to take—what has been made a legal offence—"refuge in publicity (Flucht in die Öffentlichkeit). This amounts to saying that any publicizing of a case still in process will be sufficient to definitely decide against the candidate on a legal basis. The use of the very word "Berufsverbot" has been forbidden: rather one is to say "means to eliminate enemies of the Constitution from the civil service" or the like. Statements to the contrary may easily be prone to prosecution for "slander of the FRG and its constitutional institutions" (Verunglimpung der BRD und ihrer verfassungsmässigen Organe). In some instances, the flat of an applicant was raided under the pretext that the published minutes of her interview were taken with the aid of a tape-recorder. Her private employer was informed about subsequent legal action taken against her and she was dismissed. Frequently, "breach of confidence" has been claimed in cases of publicising a pending Berufsverbot, again with the consequence of job refusal on that ground, rather than the grounds of the validity of the original "doubts." It is remarkable, however, that no case is known where the authorities have challenged the truth of what has been published.

Needless to say, anybody active in the struggle against Berufsverbot is a safe candidate for Special Branch files.

In recent weeks and months, one hears and reads of increasing public concern with the practice of Berufsverbot, particularly on the part of SPD and FDP. New regulations for a less extensive use of the Decree on Radicals are being drafted. However, this is due less to the opposition within the FRG than to international concern over Berufsverbot, which threatens to be particularly embarrasing with the European elections ahead. The SPD in particular is anxious not to represent the right-wing of a European social democratic organisation, which might in the long run harm its dominant role. If this proves to be unavoidable due to its general political positions, it would at least want to be a respectable right-wing.

As a less rigorous handling of the Decree on Radicals becomes a possibility, a problem, which so far has gained little attention becomes more evident. The last years have seen an enormous increase of the repressive state apparatus, particularly in the form of the police and the Special Branch. It is still a totally unsolved question how that expanded apparatus can be kept under control. It has been set up, expanded, every single employee has been recruited with "constitutional suitability" to keep track of the "enemy within." Little would be gained if only the rather formal side of having "doubts", calling for an interview, etc., were to be curtailed, while the smoothly functioning mechanism of collecting information and passing it on could be maintained—with growing unemployment substituting for the more formal and in that respect at least tangible interview. This is a problem the democratic movement in West Germany has as yet hardly dealt with.

SOCIAL POLICY AND CLASS INEQUALITY
Some notes on welfare state limits

John Westergaard

I

Whether capitalism is still capitalism—that old dog of a controversy whose very refusal to lie down and die suggests that its object remains no less alive—hangs in large part on the answers to two questions about the state: its role in production and its role in distribution. Of course the two cannot, in the end, be kept apart; they are intertwined because capitalism as a mode of production is also a mode of exploitation. But my concern here will be, in essence, only with the second question: with the distributional impact of government social policy, the effects of the "welfare state" on class inequality. I have misgivings about treading on ground much of which is already well-trodden. But there are patches of that ground which still look rather desolate—in between the large and flat acres of practical description of welfare provisions; the smaller though widening and bumpy strips of general theorising about the philosophical premises, formative socio-political contexts and ideological orientations of social policy; and the tracks marked out by cartographers of poverty. There are, in particular, questions left open about the limits of state action as a means to modify the patterns of exploitation—of "differential reward", to use another vocabulary—set by the property and market mechanisms of a capitalist economy.

To some pragmatic social-democratic ways of thought, perhaps, the notion of such limits may appear an elusive abstraction: the road may be seen as open to a progressive intermingling of distribution according to need with acquisition according to ownership and market strength, through a succession of reforms in which at no particular and identifiable point will the interests behind the latter criteria either decisively dictate a stop or be equally decisively set aside. Both right and left, however, realistically acknowledge that there must be limits: the right when they claim to see before them already a creeping erosion of profit and pay incentives through misguided state benevolence; the left when they characterise the same benevolence as a set of only marginal concessions, designed to sustain the long-run viability of private capital against its self-engendered exposure to the twin risks of inefficiency and popular dis-

71

loyalty. But if there are, and must be, limits beyond which public welfare provision would wreck the engines of a capitalist economy, whereabouts do they lie? If the amelioration embodied in state social policy involves only marginal concessions, what are the margins implied; and what hypothetical transformations of policy would take it beyond them?

I have no magic formula to propose in reply. In that sense I shall end, as I start, with question marks. But I hope nevertheless to be able to do something to clarify the issues against which these stand: to explore the ways in which state policy does and does not modify class inequality; to identify, if sketchily, the points on which it fits within, and also those on which it may reach out across, the distributional principles of a capitalist economy. To do that I must begin by setting out those principles. There are two.

The first principle is that property gives its owner a recognised claim to a share in resource output. That it also, with well-known exceptions, gives owners a claim to share directly or indirectly in resource management is crucially important in general, but relevant here only for one reason. The rationale for the right of owners to consume merely by virtue of their ownership is that the return to capital constitutes the primus motor of economic enterprise: so, if private profit is to drive the wheels of production, it and the property from which it derives must constitute a means of private consumption. There are significant corollaries to the principle. First, the right of owners to a share of societal income is unconditional: it stands with no questions asked about either their "contribution" or their "need." Second, therefore, it is in inherent contradiction to the criteria which otherwise govern distribution, for these require of income recipients either a contribution, through work; or some demonstration of need, whether directly or through membership of a population category recognised as in need. Third, because property rights invariably include some right to transmit ownership to others by inheritance (or gift), they legally entrench a contradiction also to the notion—familiar as a diffusely formulated ideal to which tribute is paid in contemporary capitalist societies—that the individual's place in the socio-economic order should reflect his/her own "merits" without avoidable influence of his/her circumstances of origin. When sociologists proclaim a triumph of "achievement" over "ascription" as the predominant criterion by which, in principle, individuals are placed in the hierarchies of modern western societies, they rarely note the blatant incompatibility of that, not just with hard social facts tenaciously resistant to policy, but with the law's endorsement of inheritance as a right attached to property. Fourth, because property which yields substantial income—property in productive assets—is highly concentrated, only a small minority enjoy the prime benefits of the property principle; but their privilege contributes sizeably to the overall inequality of distribution.

The second principle is, of course, that the majority who do not own substantial income-yielding property must rely for their livelihood in the first instance on the labour market: they have either to hire out their own labour or to depend on others—usually related members of their own household—who do the same. There are again several significant features associated with this principle. First, labour market earnings are governed largely by capital's considerations of long-run profit optimisation. Except when a category of labour can maintain control over its own sectional market, collective labour organisation by itself seems to have had little impact on the broad pattern of income inequalities; more on the extent to which workers can exercise some control over their jobs in the everyday work situation. Moreover, even though the state is now commonly the largest single employer, terms of employment in the public sector have not been—and arguably cannot be—detached to any considerable degree from those in the private sector; and government attempts to manipulate labour market earnings through its responsibility for payments to one employee in four (to cite the British case) have been directed to holding back wage pressures rather than to boosting low earnings and cutting down high earnings on any more, at least, than an occasional basis. Second, different kinds of labour power are in effect hired out in different markets on very different terms: in some cases at high premiums because the earner-group in question—an established "profession", for example, occasionally a group of skilled manual craftsmen or technicians—have achieved collective control over their own corner of the labour market, notably over admission to the corner. Third, top management in private enterprise occupy a position on which much confusion has centred. Nominally "labour", in so far as their incomes derive from salaries, honoraria and perks in return for the "jobs" they do, in fact they acquire their "earnings" from their command over capital, in a manner akin to profit extraction. That, for one thing, makes it difficult to assess the significance of such shift as has occurred in the statistically recorded distribution of aggregate personal income between property income and employment income. For another, the generally very high—though characteristically also individually variant—levels of emolument for directors and other top managers set correspondingly high standards both for managerial pay on the rungs a little further down the control hierarchies of private business and, at one remove, for management salaries in the public sector. Fourth, for all these reasons, the range of labour market earnings—especially by nominal definitions of "labour", but also by more real ones—is very wide. Superimposed on the dichotomous inequality between property income and employment income, therefore, there is a very visible pattern of multiple inequalities which both generates conflicts of immediate interest among different categories of labour and veils the conceptual simplicity of the two contrasting principles of capitalist income distribution: acquisition by right of ownership and allocation according to labour market "contribution." Fifth, just because the majority live by the second principle, while the minority who live by the first are not readily visible, the common dependency on the labour market as a fact of life is easily translated into popular acceptance of an "ethic of work", notwithstanding the immunity from that ethic conferred by property on its owners.

Two points need to be added to this schematic account of the principles of distribution implicit in a capitalist economy. One, a point of elaboration, is that for all their mutual contradiction the two principles together mean that "incentives" are institutionalised in monetary form. There are, of course, subsidiary institutionalised incentives in non-monetary form; but neither officially awarded "honours" nor diffusely recognised patterns of "social status" operate in general as alternatives to the hierarchy of monetary rewards: they follow with financial advantage, rather than compensate for its absence. The other, a point of qualification, is that— even apart from "welfare state" interventions—the money incomes set by the workings of property and labour markets are not the sole, though they are the prime, determinants of consumption power. Effective access to the means of livelihood is influenced also by the workings of consumer markets and by differential capacity to obtain credit. Here again, however, inequalities of access in consumer markets, and to credit, generally favour the wealthy and impede the poor: their effect is to reinforce the initial inequalities of income.

State provision—direct provision through benefits in cash and kind, indirect provision in so far as taxation and a multitude of other government activities modify the impact of property and market mechanisms— adds a third source of "livelihood" to those constituted by ownership and labour hire. Do then the distributional principles and effects of state provision clash with those associated with ownership and labour hire, or merely complement them without subverting them?

II

Because they are in part inexplicit, the distributional principles of state provision cannot be fully identified without reference to effects. So it makes some sense to start with effects and defer consideration of principles: to take results before objectives, roundabout though that may seem. In fact, some recent information makes it possible to get a little closer to an assessment of the impact of "welfare state" measures on real income distribution, in the case of Britain, than was feasible earlier. Using these data, for 1976, we can take off from estimates of the spread of incomes for households of different composition, before the state intervenes to extract taxes and allocate benefits; and go on to trace the estimated effects, first of taxes and then of benefits, on households at different levels of the "original income" hierarchies.[1]

Of course the data—primarily from sample survey information about household incomes and expenditure—are deficient for the purpose. Money incomes before taxes and benefits cannot be equated with incomes as they would be in the hypothetical absence of any state activity. Even apart from the facts of public sector employment, whatever their significance, public policy may bend the contours of income distribution by means other than tax deduction and benefit bestowal—though the apparent relative stability of broad patterns of overall and employment income inequality, in this and many other countries since the 1950s, suggests that the net effects of increased state activity during that period have not been to shift the contours substantially, or much more than to neutralise possibly countervailing tendencies. Reported incomes may differ from true incomes; and under-counting in the upper reaches of the hierarchy could compress the recorded range of inequality. Taxes and benefits, in kind as well as cash, are brought into the estimates only to the extent that assessment of their allocation among individual households was judged feasible by the statisticians responsible for the exercise—the taxes so taken into account making up 60 per cent of government revenue in 1976, the benefits in the balance sheet 44 per cent of government expenditure. Their allocation even within those limits, moreover, required assumptions in some respects open to question—in the case of public health and education services, for example, an assumption of equal effective use among all individuals of a particular category (of given age and sex, or in a given type of school or college) which is bound to be significantly at odds with a reality in which privilege and disadvantage are known to be cumulative. Omission and distortion on these scores are inevitable. For all that, this material takes us closer than before to a picture of how far the "welfare state" reshapes inequalities of livelihood, and of the mechanisms by which it does so—and does not.

Inequalities are *not* reshaped by taxation. This is stale news to those familiar with relevant research over the last fifteen years or so. But it is essential to hammer the point home; and the new information available does so most emphatically. In the case of households comprising two adults and one to four children, for example, taxes of all allocable kinds (including national insurance contributions) took away 36 per cent from the "original incomes" of the initially richest ten per cent in 1976; and much the same fraction (or just a little more) from all but the poorest ten per cent, whose total tax bill—direct and indirect—came to 44 per cent of original income.[2] The pattern was similar, but carried still more of a sting for the very poor, among "non-retired" households of other kinds: commonly more or less flat rates of aggregate taxation (around 40 per cent of original income) from the rich down to the near-poor, with the rate rising at the very bottom of the scale—for the poorest ten per cent—to 63 per cent in the case of poor two-adult households, and to totals actually well in excess of original income (income before receipt of state cash benefits) in the case of the very poor among single non-retired people living on their own and a heterogeneous category of "other" households. Regression in the incidence of tax relative to original income was still more evident among "retired" households, for whom the rates rose steadily step by step down the scale from the top, to reach figures well above the negligible initial incomes of the many households in these categories more or less totally dependent on state support.

The mechanics behind these patterns of flat-to-regressive rates of total taxation may also be familiar; but they can bear repetition, though elaboration of detail is unnecessary here. Direct taxes are progressive: they take proportionately more from the rich than the poor. Even so, however, their progression is confined in large part to the range from poverty to median income. Rates of direct taxation rise most up the steps which separate the gradations of working class low income in or out of employment from the more solid incomes of the "middle mass" derived, for example, from one man's wage packet of skilled manual size or from two smaller wage packets in conjunction. But above that level, increments in the effective rate of direct tax taper off: among both households with children and "non-retired" childless households of two adults in 1976, for example, the richest ten per cent had to pay out only 3-5 per cent more of their original incomes in direct tax than did households of similar composition in the fifth decile group from the bottom, with incomes little more than two-fifths those of the richest. Indirect taxes—moreover—and here's the main rub—are consistently regressive. Add the two together—direct plus indirect—and the rich are then seen to pay no larger a share of their original incomes into the state cash box than others; and the very poor in fact to pay more *pro rata*—in some cases, very much more.

It makes full sense in the present context to calculate rates of taxation as I have just done—in relation to *"original"* incomes. For my purpose is to trace through the steps by which income distribution in its "pristine" shape—in abstraction from the activities of public authorities to raise money in taxes and in turn disburse much of it as benefits—is subsequently recast by precisely these state activities. The impact on initial income distribution of what is logically the first step in those activities—the raising of revenue—proves then to be nil or worse: to maintain the pattern of inequality as it was, and indeed somewhat to accentuate it. But there may be objections raised to this mode of calculation as unrealistic. Taxes, it may be said, are in fact extracted from *gross* incomes which include cash benefits from the state. To describe the poorest tenth of households with children as taxed at a rate of 44 per cent—still more the poorest tenth of some other types of household as taxed at rates well over 100 per cent—is patently mis-leading (so the argument may run), when these people can pay so much in tax only because their very initial poverty leads to relatively substantial augmentation of their original incomes by cash from the state: calculated in relation to their "real" money incomes, including cash benefits, their tax rates will be a good deal lower. There is obvious point to the objection. But it is valid only for a purpose different from mine: to describe the incidence of taxation, taken by itself; not, as is my concern here, to identify its contribution to a process of income redistribution by state action in which logically it is the "first" step, while the "second" step is state allocation of benefits from the money raised by taxation.[3]

Let me nevertheless go along with the objection, briefly, and try to re-describe the incidence of taxation as it appears when calculated in relation to "gross" money incomes, in which cash benefits from the state are added to "original" incomes. The 1976 material used before will not serve for this purpose: it does not set out the relevant household hierarchies, from rich to poor, by reference to gross incomes. But by minor adjustment of some other information—similarly originating in household expenditure survey data—it is possible to do the exercise demanded for two broad types of household in the preceding year, 1975.[4] The results, of course, look somewhat different; but not markedly so. In the case of households with one to three children, rates of aggregate tax—direct and indirect together—varied hardly at all relative to gross money income: 38 per cent for the top ten per cent, 37 per cent for the bottom ten per cent, 35-36 per cent for the decile groups between the richest and the poorest. There was more variation, and some progression, in the case of the other group for which the analysis can be made: households comprising one or more adults only, but excluding those mainly dependent on state pensions. Here tax rates relative to gross income ranged from 40 per cent at the top to 25 per cent at the bottom. In fact, however, the progression which this indicates was almost entirely confined to the lower rungs of the ladder. From the quarter of money incomes paid out in direct and indirect taxes by the poorest ten per cent (no negligible fraction itself for people so hard up), the rate rose stepwise to over one third (36 per cent) for the fourth decile group up the scale; but beyond that point—for the 60 per cent of these households with better incomes—the further increments up to the top decile group's rate of 40 per cent were self-evidently very small. So, for the majority of non-pensioner households without children—whether quite modestly placed or very wealthy—the effective incidence of tax relative to money income showed essentially the same pattern as for all households with children: an almost flat rate of some 35-40 per cent, varying only minimally if at all according to financial capacity.

In short, even a descriptive mode of calculation favourable to the case provides no more than the flimsiest support for the common view that taxes bear proportionately heaviest on the strongest shoulders. And, to revert to the earlier mode of calculation relevant to my analytical purpose, far from diminishing initial income inequality the "welfare state's" tax-raising activities actually add to it. It follows that, in so far as state intervention nevertheless makes for some reduction of inequality in the end, this can only be by means of the second step in the process: through a pattern of benefit distribution sufficiently progressive to outweigh the net regression characteristic of tax incidence. This is indeed what happens, to a degree. Take the case of households with one or more children in 1976. All of these, to repeat, eventually lost about two fifths of their original incomes in tax payments of one kind and another, the poorest rather more and the very rich marginally least. But all in turn gained from state benefits in cash and kind; and this countervailing boost to original incomes was at rates which were high at the bottom of the scale and successively tapered off up its steps: amounting to some 130 per cent of original income for the poorest tenth but only 11 per cent for the richest tenth. On balance, most households lost more on the swings of taxation than they gained on the roundabouts of state benefits; and this follows from the point, made earlier, that a higher proportion of government revenue than of government expenditure is incorporated into the estimates as capable of allocation to individual households. But net swings-versus-roundabout losses were proportionately greatest for the richest; while the very poorest actually gained on balance, and quite substantially so measured against their initial incomes.

So, in the event, there was redistribution from top to bottom, notwithstanding the tendency of taxation by itself in the opposite direction. Sheer logic of arithmetic, indeed, would make it difficult to conceive of any other outcome. Just because the poor start with little or nothing, the relative value of the benefits they obtain is very high measured against original incomes; and the indirect taxes which make up the bulk of their tax bills, while charged at high effective rates, are still limited by the low purchasing power of the poor even when cash benefits are added to their negligible initial incomes. The wealthy, by contrast, receive only small sums in *cash* benefit; and although in absolute terms they get roughly as much as the poor—sometimes more—out of state benefits in *kind,* their high initial incomes receive only a relatively small boost on that score. That boost, naturally enough, is more than outweighed by their payments of tax which, though at favourable rates in proportionate terms, involve substantial sums of money just because they are extracted from very substantial incomes.

The extent of this process of redistribution, its incidence and its limits, need more precise statement. That is the purpose of the table below, which summarises the estimated outcome of "welfare state intervention", in 1976, for households of varying type according to their original incomes. Figures above 100 indicate net gains—benefit values exceeded tax payments—and figures below 100 conversely net losses. It is clear that there was a transfer

The combined impact of taxation and state benefits on households of different type at different levels of original income in 1976: average final income expressed as a percentage of average original income.

Decile of original income within each household type	Households of following type, comprising:					
	Non-retired		2 adults and 1-4 children	Other except retired	Retired	
	1 adult	2 adults			1 adult	2 adults
Highest decile	56	62	75	70	107	86
9th decile	62	64	79	73	154	138
8th decile	60	65	81	75	231	186
7th decile	67	65	83	77	329	245
6th decile	67	68	86	81	469	336
5th decile	72	70	87	89	792	437
4th decile	89	77	92	101	)	572
3rd decile	120	86	97	116	)	)
2nd decile	195	107	103	161	) 7788	) 2476
Lowest decile	1086	252	188	789	)	)
All households of stated type	75	73	87	88	303	221
Percentage of all households accounted for by each type	9	23	26	21	12	9

Explanatory notes:
  (i)   Within each household type, households are ranked in ten-per-cent bands (deciles) according to their original incomes: highest decile = initially richest 10 per cent, lowest decile = initially poorest 10 per cent.
  (ii) "Retired" households are those in which the combined income of members aged 60 years plus, who described themselves as retired or unoccupied, accounted for at least half the gross household income.
  (iii) "Original" income = income before any payment of tax and any receipt of benefit.
        "Final" income = income after deduction of all allocated taxes (direct and indirect) and after addition of all state benefits in cash and of allocated state benefits in kind (including subsidies) at estimated money value. The figures shown are to be read thus (for example): among "non-retired" households of one adult, the initially richest ten percent ended up with estimated "final" incomes amounting to 56 per cent of the "original" incomes.

Source: The calculations were made from the data in appendix table 3 of the source referred to in note 1 to the text.

of resources within each income hierarchy, downwards to those initially worst off: among all household types, not just among those with children singled out for attention above as an example. It is also clear that, household type for type, the pattern was fairly consistently progressive: where there were net gains, they were proportionately larger the poorer the households in question according to original income; where there were net losses, they increased in proportionate magnitude more or less step by step up the scale of initial income.

That said, however, there are three mutually connected points to be made in major qualification. First, net gains of substance were confined to households of two kinds: to "retired" households; and, among all other households, to the very poor only (the lowest, sometimes the two lowest, decile groups). Second, and in elaboration of that, there were very substantial transfers of resources "horizontally" between household types. "Retired" households registered net gains at every level of original income except the very top. Households of every other type registered net losses en bloc—proportionately heaviest in the case of "non-retired" households of one or two adults—with only the poor and near-poor here exempt from contributing to a flow of funds moving on balance towards the old.

Third, and not least, the progression in the contributions of the "non-retired" to the flow showed a pattern somewhat akin to that of progression in direct tax: fairly steep increases up to around median income level, smaller increases in the higher reaches of original income. Take the case of "non-retired" households of two adults: from the cut-off point turning gains into losses between second and third lowest deciles, proportionate net losses rose sharply to about 30 per cent for the fifth and sixth deciles, but by only a small number of further points (to 38 per cent) all the way up the rest of the scale. The pattern was similar for "non-retired" households of one adult, though their wealthiest decile group did sustain a noticeable further loss by comparison with the next wealthiest. Among households with children—overall smaller contributors to the flow of funds—net losses rose to nearly 15 per cent up the four steps from cut-off point to sixth decile, but increased by only another 11 per cent up the remaining four steps to the top. In consequence, to pursue this last example, families with initial annual incomes of around £4,000 (then equivalent to a well-paid male manual worker's earnings, only a fifth of male manual workers having more before tax) lost almost 15 per cent of that on the swings and roundabouts of "welfare state" activity; families with initial incomes over twice as high (more than £9,000, in the top decile) lost only another 10 or 11 per cent more. So, too, among two-adult "non-retired" households: roundabout 30 per cent net losses for those with the equivalent of good manual-work incomes; not even 10 per cent more by way of net loss for those at the top of the scale, in this case with average incomes of nearly £10,000.

In summary, the picture which emerges from the new and more comprehensive material drawn on here is in sharper focus than the sketches available from earlier information; but it is not radically different. The massive and complex series of government operations which enter into these balance sheets produce some significant redistribution of effective income. As already suggested by other data from the past fifteen years or so, however—and in diametrical opposition to fond conventional belief—taxation by itself makes only a negative contribution to that process. The point stands out starkly: when indirect are added to direct taxes, they cut down the incomes generated by property and labour market mechanisms by much the same share (around 40 per cent in 1976) at all decile-levels—except among the very poor, who lose more by the same measure. Taxation plays a part in eventual redistribution to the opposite effect only because it provides the funds from which benefits are paid; and because the progressive pattern of benefit allocation outweighs the regressive pattern of tax extraction.

Much of the positive redistribution which does occur in the end is "horizontal." It involves transfers between households of different composition, in effect between people at different stages of life, irrespective of place in the economic hierarchy: transfers especially from childless adults of working age; to a lesser extent from families with children, because children attract countervailing benefits in cash and not least in kind; to elderly people who have reached retirement. None of that "horizontal" redistribution on its own alters aggregate inequality between classes. Detached from any concomitant "vertical" redistribution, it would constitute only a massive system of infra-class collective insurance: workers' welfare funded entirely from the wage packets of workers in active employment. Even so, to the extent that the "welfare state" is just that, it is still significant for the detailed configuration of class inequality. State provision of "age-directed" benefits (as of unemployment and sickness benefit) has modified the character of the "proletarian condition", because it has helped to reduce those fluctuations of life cycle experience which have traditionally exposed people of the wage earning class to a special risk of poverty in childhood, parenthood and old age (as also in unemployment and in sickness).

In any case, the "welfare state" is not exclusively such a system of state-sponsored self-protection for the working class. Coupled with extensive "horizontal" redistribution, there is also "vertical" redistribution to a degree, and within limits, more clearly identifiable from these than from earlier estimates. Ordinary wage earning households, except those on very low incomes, certainly contribute substantially to the "welfare state"; and it is striking that the progression in net contributions—in the balance of taxes paid over benefits received, as these have been allocated and valued in the accounts for 1976—tapers down rather than steps up once the level of income equivalent to a well-paid male manual worker's earnings is reached. Nevertheless, slower though it becomes, there is some continued progression above that point. Not because they put more into the state kitty relative to the high incomes with which they start, but because they take less out by the same measure, the rich do in effect contribute proportionately more than others to the "welfare state." It would take a taxation system of a steeply—not, as it is, of a marginally—regressive character to save the rich from that. The end result is, as the table below indicates, to raise the real incomes of the poor especially by cutting the real incomes of the rich. In the case of all household types in 1976, the initially wealthiest fifth still had around 30 per cent of total real income in their hands in the end; but even disregarding the special case of the retired, this was some 4-9 percentage points below their share in total income at the outset.

The impact of "welfare state" intervention on the initially rich and the initially poor, 1976.

Highest and lowest quintile groups according to original income	Households of following type, comprising:											
	Non-retired				2 adults 1-4 children		Other except retired		Retired			
	1 adult		2 adults						1 adult		2 adults	
	O	F	O	F	O	F	O	F	O	F	O	F
Initially richest 20%	42	33	37	32	34	30	38	31	68	27	63	29
Initially poorest 20%	3	14	7	13	9	14	4	12	*		*	

O = "Original" income, F = "Final" income.

* Figures cannot be presented for the initially poorest 20% among the "retired", because incomes here were so low to start with that calculations only for the poorest 40% and 30% respectively were practicable. In the case of one-adult "retired" households, the initially poorest 40% received 1% of aggregate original income for this category of households as a whole, but 36% of aggregate final income for the category. In the case of two-adult "retired" households, the corresponding figures for the initially poorest 30% were 2% "before" and 25% "after." This striking compression of initially highly unequal income hierarchies among the retired reflects, of course, the general net flow of state funds to the elderly, the majority of whom (retired from manual and lower rung non-manual jobs) have little if any means of livelihood other than support from the state.

For other notes, see text and also previous table.

Overall post-welfare-state-activity income distribution is not in fact compressed as much by comparison with original property- and market-generated income distribution as this might suggest. Some of the initially richest and poorest households are replaced in those positions by others, precisely in consequence of the complex pattern of transfer payments which occurs. While the data used here do not allow a direct estimate of final income distribution by itself, without reference to original incomes, extrapolation of calculations from similar raw material for the previous year makes a reasonable indirect estimate possible.[5] Taking all households together, irrespective of type, the initially richest fifth in 1976 had 44 per cent of all income in their hands before taxes and benefits. The share of the same households in total income after taxes and benefits was down to 34 per cent. But as the result was also to remove some of these from the category of "richest fifth", with others taking their place, the share in final income of those households now constituting the richest fifth was about 38 per cent. This still indicates a compression of the range of inequality by comparison with the original "top quintile share" of 44 per cent; but not as much as suggested by figures of the kind shown above, which trace only what happens in consequence of "welfare state" activity to those who *start* at the top and the bottom of the range. For all that—and for all the reservations which are necessary about the accuracy of the basic figures both of "original" and "final" income—public policy clearly does to some degree mitigate class inequality.

III

So much, in a fairly crude quantitative manner, for "effects"; now to "principles." My purpose here is to take a step towards filling in what seems to be a gap in the literature on social policy: between detailed practical description of welfare measures on the one hand, very broad and general summary characterisations of alternative welfare ideologies on the other.[6] I shall try to identify, somewhat in catalogue form, the various kinds of objective with a bearing on class inequality which appear to be represented, in this or that combination, in the social policy packages of Britain and— to go by an occasional fleeting glance—some other contemporary western countries. By "objectives" I mean both aims which have found explicit expression, and also such strands of implicit purpose as can be read off from the character and operative mode of particular policy measures. These different "objectives" may each be said to incorporate at least an implicit conception of a kind, or degree, of equality which it is appropriate for policy to pursue—if only by inference from the kind, or degree, of inequality which policy in this or that form seeks to reduce.

There are significant limits to those various conceptions of "acceptable" equality embodied in present-day social policy. To make such limits stand out the more clearly, it may be as well first to sketch a conception of equality which goes well beyond them all: a set of hypothetical objectives nowhere represented in the reality of current social policy, by which the more readily to identify the points where those which are represented stop short. That imaginary alternative conception of equality I call *equality of condition*. I mean by it a state of affairs in which life circumstances and opportunities would be more or less the same for all, in so far as means to that end could be found; and with avoidable deviations only to the extent that such deviations could be specifically shown as required for the achievement of other specified ends of policy explicitly awarded higher priority. Inequalities would not be ruled out. But the burden of proof—for their justification as either inescapable or instrumentally necessary—would rest on public policy: the initial presumption would be against them; above all against cumulative inequality as distinct from discrete and particular inequalities. With that as a counterfoil, let me try to set out such class-relevant objectives (and associated more restricted conceptions of acceptable equality) which appear to figure in some mixture or other in actual current social policy. There are, as I see them, five.

General minimum

The objective to guarantee all citizens a minimum livelihood seems now to be an element in the welfare packages of all western countries. In Britain, as in a number of other places, there are two basic forms to this ostensible guarantee. In the first form certain contingencies in life—e.g., retirement in old age, illness, "involuntary" unemployment—are intended to give entitlement without individual demonstration of lack of alternative means. Even so, and significantly, entitlement requires demonstration of a record of "contributions" normally made in the course of previous employment. The second form was originally conceived only as subsidiary, "last resort" provision; but it has come to verge on "common resort" provision, its role as such inhibited only by inherent disincentives to application on the part of those nominally eligible. Here entitlement requires demonstration of need on the initiative of the needy—though one means sought to give more substance to the "guarantee" in this second form has sometimes (e.g., in Sweden) been to impose a formal obligation on the authorities to seek out potential applicants; another, to shift the balance within official assessment of "need" from exercise of discretion towards more application of standard and publicised rules.

There is no principled definition of the "minimum" to be guaranteed; and it is liable to vary both between, and under different sub-schemes within, the two forms of guarantee. But there are three implicit understandings associated with it, which give some body to the term "minimum." First, the level of fall-back livelihood offered is officially conceived as the minimum acceptable—to a generalised "public", if not to the poor themselves. Second, while precisely for this reason it can be and normally is stepped up from time to time—indeed, may be index-linked—it is set at all times well below the level of livelihood associated with current average labour market earnings. Third—in application especially to categories of recipient who otherwise arguably might be deterred from work, but by extension to others as well—it is intended to be so set as rarely, if ever, to equal the current level of low grade wage earnings.

In so far as any conception of equality as a goal of policy can be said to enter into provision of this kind—and such claims have been made for it[7]—it is that all citizens participate as "subscribers" and potential "beneficiaries" in a set of schemes guaranteeing to all a relatively small livelihood in need. In fact, of course, the risks of becoming dependent on the "minimum guarantee" continue to be highly unequal. Nevertheless, the institution of minimum provision across the board has modified class inequality to some degree. First, there is of arithmetical necessity at least a modest re-distributive effect, of which the preceding statistical analysis—though it concerned a welfare package with other ingredients as well—is a reminder. Some benefits (e.g., for unemployment, and those which are means-tested) will be concentrated on people in the lower reaches of the economic scale; others (e.g., basic pensions) will be spread more or less equally. But benefits of both kinds will add proportionately more, and—unless taxation is steeply regressive—counter taxes proportionately more, at low than at high levels of initial income. Second, even apart from such redistribution between classes, the large-scale transfers of resources involved "infra-class"—from workers in active employment to those unemployed, sick and old—have played a part in blunting the sharper edges of fluctuations in circumstances otherwise characteristic of wage-earning life. To that extent, "minimum guarantee" has helped to make the proletarian condition less distinctive than it was.

These, however, are hardly major modifications of class inequality. "Vertical" redistribution is kept to limited dimensions by heavy reliance on simultaneous "horizontal" redistribution (for which a prime means is taxation operating in overall effect on a near-flat-rate basis). And while some of the traditional uncertainties of working class life have been reduced, some new uncertainties have been added through the complexities facing claimants who wish to press their "welfare rights." These restrictions on class impact, incidentally, are in no way peculiar to Britain. Nor is the central point that the principles associated with minimum provision are, at a general level, in full accord with the basic distributive principles of a capitalist economy. They endorse the "work ethic", and the emphasis on monetary incentives, in three ways: by qualifying the "guarantee" through potential exclusion of the "work-shy" from full eligibility;[8] more generally, by making "contributions" during employment a condition of benefit without test of means; and by adjusting the "minimum" to the floor of labour market earnings.

This is not to say that "minimum guarantee" policy is safe against attack on the grounds that, at its margins, it may nevertheless subvert the operating mechanisms of a capitalist economy. However evenly spread in fact, taxation on any considerable scale is liable to be seen as a threat to profit and to pay incentives. More specifically, once provision for a minimum livelihood is introduced, it is difficult consistently to ensure a gap between it and the floor of labour market earnings. In all their wide range, the latter pay no regard to variations in household circumstances—to the number of dependent children, for example. But even the most niggardly conception of "need" incorporated in schemes of minimum provision is bound to do so. So in practice, in particular cases, the state's offer of livelihood may be at a level marginally exceeding a low wage; or it may be believed to be at such a level, even if it is not. The recurrence of socio-political tension on this score—of outcries against "scrounging"—is familiar; and the defensive character of the common "pro-welfare" response (that there is little if any real overlap) itself underlines the labour market orientation implicit in policy. In part from the perennial nature of this clash between considerations of "need" versus "work ethic", and from the pressures imposed by the latter considerations to keep any general minimum low, have come proposals and measures so to differentiate state provision that—without abandonment of monetary "work incentives"—not all potential recipients are held down to a level dictated by the lowest wage earnings of a strictly inhumane labour market.[9]

Equality of opportunity

To provide for "equality of opportunity"—or for means to reduce barriers to it—is now, like provision for minimum livelihood in some version or other, a basic and explicit objective of social policy, probably throughout the western world. Indeed, some welfare packages may go little beyond these twin aims—that, for example, of the United States. The notion of equal opportunity prescribes a removal (more weakly, a diminution) of "accidental" impediments to perfect competition among individuals for unequally rewarded places in the socio-economic structure. Success and failure in that competition, so it is postulated, should depend only on inherent individual "capacity" and "merit." The "accidental" impediments to be removed (or diminished) are those which stem—according to varying perceptions incorporated into policy—from socio-economic circumstances of birth and upbringing; from stigmatic "social labelling"; from territorial barriers and barriers to information. The notion prescribes, in the first instance, free mobility of individuals—economically, culturally, geographically. It also prescribes free access in consumer markets: the removal (or reduction), for example, of differentials in access to housing unrelated to monetary purchasing power.

This objective is most clearly represented in the formal gearing of public educational systems to "equal" selection for unequal destinations. But it is a main strand of purpose also in legislation—generally   more recent—to remove discrimination by colour and sex; in "poverty" pro-grammes developed in the United States from the 1960s, directed in considerable part to releasing children and young people from inherited poverty (whether the "trap" from which they are to be freed is described primarily in cultural terms or by reference to cumulative material dis-advantage); in "priority area" policies in Britain, similarly in part justified as means by which to break a "cycle of deprivation"; and again, though with less trumpet and flourish, in provision for mobility allowances, re-training and the like.

Some of the support which measures of this kind have attracted has, of course, had other ends in view besides "equality of opportunity"; ends reflecting broader conceptions of equality. The case for eradication of discrimination by colour and sex, for example, rests also on a demand for "equality of respect": on rejection of the elementary outrage to human dignity constituted by differential treatment of labelled categories of people irrespective of their individual qualities. Some proponents of educational reform designed in part to widen opportunities, again, have been inspired additionally by a concern to create foundations for a "common culture"; or, through increasing the supply of qualified labour, to diminish pay differentials between skilled and other work—thus to take a small step or two towards diminishing inequalities of condition as well as opportunity. None of these further aims, however, is in principled conflict with the rules of distributive justice implicit in a capitalist economy—though they are in conflict with a variety of entrenched particular interests, whose salience makes for a reality of imperfect competition very different from the model of perfect competition. The energy to drive the engines of public policy on these matters, moreover—to add practical political weight to minority pressures—has come primarily from the concern to provide "equal opportunity for equal talent" *tout court*. That concern—on grounds both of efficiency and of a notion of equity to which lip service has long been paid—is in no way antagonistic to the nominal rules of capitalist economic enterprise. Though it is new for the state to take major initiatives to that end on the scale now common, it is neither new nor a challenge to capitalist principle to seek to enhance circulation of "human resources."

So it may seem, at least; but only if the goal of equal opportunity is not pressed too hard. For even at the level of abstract general rules, it clashes—because capitalism's general rules are internally contradictory—with the right of inheritance attached to property in law. In hard fact, moreover, it clashes with the inescapable realities of class division. Whatever the law, socio-economic advantage and disadvantage tend to be transmitted from parents to children, although there is certainly no pattern of rigid inheritance. More significantly still, the privileged—and there are successive levels of subsidiary and minor privilege below the concentrated privilege at the economy's top—have a natural interest in protecting their own scope for such transmission. They will not now typically oppose the aim of equal opportunity, expressed as an ideal; but their resistance adds substantially to the inertia which dilutes the means adopted for its pursuit. That inertia is one which transforms the symmetry of movement inherent in the ideal into an assymetry which defeats its implementation. "Equality of opportunity" requires downward no less than upward movement. Few deny the case for upward movement according to "talent": it makes good general economic sense; and its morality is now commonly accepted as irreproachable. But the price of corresponding downward mobility—and of the radical policy measures which would be needed to ensure it—is very far from acceptable. So, by and large, increases in individual movement up the socio-economic scale in western countries, over many decades, have occurred only in so far as they could be accommodated without matching increases in downward movement—through shifts in occupational and industrial structure. And the major effect of widening access to the more rewarding forms of education has been to step up the thresholds of paper qualification required for entry to the more rewarding jobs, without substantially reducing the old inequalities of opportunity for entry to such jobs. In short, even the apparent consonance with capitalist principle of the goal of equal opportunity incorporated in so much contemporary social policy has failed to give it much impetus in practical effect.

Individually graduated "risk reduction"

As an alternative or significant supplement to provision of a general "guaranteed minimum" in need, western social policies have increasingly turned to provision of a graduated kind, which in effect incorporates a different objective: to make for greater continuity in the material conditions of individuals between periods of normal employment and periods when—by virtue of circumstances deemed to be wholly or largely outside their own control—they are out of work. Benefits are typically still tied to "contributions" made in the course of past employment, with corresponding symbolic endorsement of the "work ethic." Such contributions in turn are typically graduated at least over part of the range of employment earnings— if only to give provision in this form an illusory appearance of "insurance". But the essential feature of such schemes—irrespective of the modes of taxation nominally attached to them—is that benefits vary according to previous earnings in the labour market. The rationale is to prevent an "excessive", "intolerable" or "debilitating" drop in level of living when individuals face short-term crises of unemployment or illness, alternatively the long-lasting contingencies of old age or irremediable handicap: in short, to counter some of the common risks of dependence on the labour market, at rates which bear an individually differentiated relation to pickings in that market. The rates of "compensation" or "income maintenance" may still fall well short of past rates of earnings, as in Western Germany where graduated provision has long been predominant. But in Sweden and Denmark, for example, new schemes introduced within the last decade or so have provided for short-term benefit—in respect of unemployment or illness expected to be followed by resumption of work—at rates at least nominally up to 80 or 90 per cent of previous job earnings. There is here a conception of "equality" at work—not of course societally, between classes; but for individuals, over much of each span of life.

Such graduated provision, if only noticeably in the more generous versions towards which Scandinavian social policy has been edging, has a positive implication for reduction of class inequality in one respect. That is to extend the protection against sharp fluctuations in wage-earning life circumstances offered, on a very modest basis only, by "minimum guarantee" provision. It was indeed precisely this consideration—a demand to reduce the traditional element of "unpredictable risk" in proletarian life, to give manual workers more of the security otherwise reserved for non-manual employees—which social-democratic sponsors of the recent social security reforms in Scandinavia underlined among their arguments. And on that score, another set of legislative changes, in several countries including Britain, bear comparison with graduated benefit provision: changes in labour law which, to some degree, have extended to ordinary wage-earners protection against dismissal and redundancy previously limited by employers' discretion to "staff." Such statutorily enforced changes in contracts of employment, moreover, resemble graduated benefit provision also in offering, in effect, more protection for skilled workers than for unskilled workers, who are liable to change jobs frequently and thus not adequately to meet the conditions attached to legal protection.

But that is also as far as any significant softening of class inequality goes. No necessary transfer of resources follows between classes as aggregates. True, although graduated contributions are counteracted by graduated benefits, provision may still be made for some element of positive redistribution within the terms of such schemes, seen in isolation from the rest of the "welfare system." But the results of that cannot be assessed in isolation—without reference, in particular, to such encouragement as may simultaneously be offered to members of well-paid occupations to "opt out" into ostensibly private schemes, on more favourable terms in effect buttressed by the state through tax concessions. The new arrangements for graduated pensions passed with support from all major parties in Britain, for example, will need eventual detailed assessment precisely on that score. Graduated provision, moreover, positively endorses capitalist principles in two quite specific ways. First, one significant aim in meeting individual "crisis" by financial "compensation" is to avoid such debilitation or demoralisation through poverty as might prevent the individual from returning to work. It appears in fact to have been this "rehabilitation" argument—a concern to make the "work ethic" effective when it might otherwise be undermined by personal and family stress—which was more persuasive than the case in equity for manual-worker security, in swinging majority political opinion in Scandinavia behind generous rates of "income maintenance" in respect of unemployment and limited-term illness. (Even so, the balance between "rehabilitative" and "penal" approaches to enforcement of the "work ethic" is delicate; and 80-90 per cent compensation rates remain vulnerable, especially in periods of economic crisis, to the charge that they remove incentives to work rather than maintain a morale conducive to a return to the labour market.) Second, and very obviously, graduated provision sets an explicit stamp of approval—or at least of unalloyed acceptance—on the inequalities generated by market mechanisms. Far from endeavouring to detach income and its distribution outside working life from the forces which determine it in working life, it rigorously extends capitalist rules of distribution from work into non-work. The road to development by the state of any autonomous conception of economic justice is closed.

Selective equality of condition

Traces of a fourth specific objective can be identified in the social policy compendia of some western countries. To extract an "ideal type" from arrangements in reality never so clear cut, the aim here can be seen as that of insulating a particular area of life from control by the distributive principles of capitalism; and of seeking, within that area, equality of condition for all. The clearest, indeed the only, approximate example is that of provision for health and medical services; and there the British National Health Service, in the form in which it was enacted in 1946, remains the prime model—whittled down at its edges since then; but its scope as initially envisaged still not quite parallelled, for example, by later reforms in the same direction in Scandinavia. The essence involved was this. Public policy declared health an "essential" good: access to the medical and immediately associated institutional means for its protection or restoration an equal right of all citizens, irrespective of income or other circumstances apart from medical need. Any deviation from equality of service according to need would, in principle, be acceptable only in so far as it concerned what might be deemed "frills"—matters inessential for protection or restoration of health. Here was a conception of real "equality of citizenship"—not merely by virtue of nominal common participation in a scheme of national social "insurance";[10] but by virtue of a goal of substantive equality of condition, though to be sought only in this selected field.

It may be argued that the very restriction of the conception to this one field undermines my contention that the aim was "equality of condition" in respect of health. Equality of health could not and cannot be achieved without substantial reduction of the contextual socio-economic inequalities which influence morbidity and mortality: reduction on a scale well outside the ends and means of accompanying social policy either then or now. What was sought through the National Health Service, so this argument may run, was less equality of condition than equality of access to services—a goal similar to that of "equality of opportunity" set for the English system of public education in 1944; and there again effectively, and weakly, re-interpreted as "equality of access." There is much point to this argument, in so far as it identifies inherent contradictions in social policy: the tension between a radicalism of vision embodied in the original National Health Service Act and the reforming conservatism which characterised other social security legislation at the time. But there was, precisely, tension of that kind. Unrealistic though this was, the proponents of national health dreamed of equality of health; and they made larger plans for preventive, as well as curative, medicine to that purpose than in fact materialised. There is, moreover, little utility to an analogy with education. In both fields, it is true, equality of access has been postulated as an aim of policy—but to different ultimate ends: in education, for the sake principally (and at best) of equating opportunities for eventual inequality; in health, exceptionally, with a hope of approximating equality of condition.

The key word here is "exceptionally." Even within the field of health, the goal of substantive equality has receded into elusiveness, both as the pressures from the contextual inequalities of the larger society have made themselves felt; and as the institutional devices to secure equal access have proved inadequate or, in some respects indeed, have been stripped down. Still more noticeably, neither in Britain nor elsewhere has the implicit notion of "selective equality of condition" been extended from health to other possible spheres. Health, no doubt, is intrinsically the least contentious candidate for immunisation from market forces in this manner—though that in no way makes it an inevitable candidate, as especially the American record demonstrates. But a good case could be made for taking housing wholly or largely out of the market. To say that is not to deny that, even from a stance in favour of equality, there would be sizeable attendant problems in guaranteeing housing of good current standard as a citizen's right of all households: the risk especially of a concentration of effectively irresponsible power in the hands of bureaucratic agencies and "professionals", entrusted with assessment of need and allocation according to household circumstances. The striking point, however, is that such risks—to which in any case, of course, the predominantly wage-earning class tenants of public housing in one form or other are already selectively exposed—have never been weighed against counter-means and potential advantages, in serious consideration of possible adoption of such a policy. The option has in practice hardly figured on political agendas. The risk of usurpation of power on the part of "dispensing authorities", moreover, need hardly rise if the principle of "selective equality of condition" were extended to certain forms of provision in cash rather than in kind. It would be possible, by way of significant example, to provide "citizens' pensions" in old age at a standard set equally for all, by reference neither to general minimum wage earnings nor to individual past earnings, but on a par with the average level of living currently yielded by the economy. Indeed, unlike the more radical possibility of providing all households at whatever stage of life with a basic solid income, varying only by household composition, "average income citizens' pensions" would pose no direct threat to the "work ethic." Yet to practising politicians, such a proposal would be in the realm of fantasy.

Policy makers with their feet well on the ground would rule out any such extensions of "selective equality of condition" in the first instance, no doubt, merely by reference to cost. And on that score alone there would indeed be some challenge to the operating principles and mechanisms of a capitalist economy. The sheer quantity of funds required for transfer payment would sizeably step up overall levels of taxation and thus— whatever the incidence of the additional taxes—make for a further perceived threat to profit and pay incentives as economic regulators. More- over, for greater redistributive effect, measures to extend "selective equality of condition" would need to be coupled with more progression in the total tax system, in order to "claw back" from the wealthy the value of the citizens' benefits which they obtained initially on a par with others. But beyond all this, the absence of proposals to extend "selective equality of condition" beyond the field of health—even to ensure full application in that field—must be ascribed to the challenge of basic principle which this conception of social policy, quite unlike the three discussed earlier, poses to the rules which govern distribution in a capitalist economy. For what it entails is an overt and public denial of legitimacy to those rules: in the first instance, of course, only to their application in the field selected for "immunity", health and no more so far. But even that circumscribed denial of legitimacy sets the shadow of a question mark against the moral validity of capitalist distributive rules in other applications. Give substance to the shadow by also taking housing out of the market, for example, or by detaching livelihood in old age from all reference to labour market minima and differentials: and two intertwined consequences would follow. The spheres of life within which capitalist distribution has effect—and from which its potency to fuel the economic engine derives—would have been narrowed significantly, if still not so far as to bring the engine to a stop; and the prospect of further curtailment would loom larger, just because the question mark set in public policy against the legitimacy of property and market mechanisms would have acquired more body.

Diffuse redistribution

Each of the four objectives which I have so far tried to disentangle from the knot of contemporary social policies has a fairly clearly definable character, and a fairly readily recognisable place in relation to the twin principles of capitalist distribution from which I started. The first three are broadly compatible with the latter. The fourth is in essence at odds with tham: it incipiently echoes the conception of wholesale equality of condition which I sketched as a hypothetical counterfoil to the cumulative inequality of capitalism; and just for that reason it is represented in current social policy only within a strictly confined space. But the catalogue is incomplete without reference to a further class-relevant orientation in public policy: one which, by itself, has no such specific character and thrust. This is the gearing, actual or purported, of government measures to some mitigation of inequality, but in a manner that leaves the extent, purpose and boundaries of the redistribution to result undefined even by implication.

A "diffuse redistributive" objective of this kind is often one tacked onto policies in large part directed to other ends. An obvious example is direct taxation. The "other ends" of that, of course, are to raise revenue and, since World War II, to regulate levels of economic activity. There are evident ambiguities of purpose to its redistributive element: both because progression in the rates of direct tax is arranged and modified *ad hoc;* and, at root, because it remains unclear whether progression is intended only as a means to place the heavier revenue burdens on the stronger shoulders or, more positively, also as an active instrument to change the pattern of real income. Counter-inflationary "incomes policies", again, quite commonly now have attached to them some ostensible provision for priorities to favour the lower-paid—at least from time to time, but even then without specification of any target distributional outcome or of the norms of justice intended to be represented in it. Regional aid and employment creation programmes are in part, even primarily, directed to raising levels of economic activity and utilising wasted resources; but in the same breath therefore also to changing the balance of labour demand and supply with consequential, though rarely precisely designed, effects on income distribution. Provision for some redistribution to boost low incomes may again be built into schemes of social security principally tuned to other purposes. The new British pension scheme is both an example and, as emphasised earlier, a reminder that ultimate effects on inequality cannot be assessed by reference only to the public face of such a scheme in itself.

This last point is central when written large. Considered in the round, and in the context of associated measures, measures of "diffuse re-distribution" appear to have had little net impact on class inequality. Their potential is more or less neutralised by other ingredients of the packages in which they are wrapped up. Such progression as there is within direct taxation is countered by regression through indirect taxation: this general pattern seems to be repeated from country to country, as well as over time, though the precise balance between progression and regression is not unalterably fixed. And indirect taxation has much to make it palatable to policy makers. It yields large sums in revenue, at rates relatively simply adjustable from time to time, in an "invisible" form which cannot be decried as undermining pay incentives. The latter is a crucial consideration in economies where incentives in general are institutionalized in monetary form; and where the very steepness of initial inequalities, moreover, arguably requires very sizeable real increments as incentives to additional initiative or effort on the part of those—managers and directors especially— who are well placed to start with. In addition, while policy makers now cannot fail to know that regressive indirect tax counters progressive direct tax, the general public are likely to know this at best only hazily. The combination of the two forms of taxation therefore helps to subdue potential social conflict—so to smooth the way for continuity in policy— by maintaining an appearance of progressive equity in taxation while avoiding its risky substance.

"Incomes policies", too, seem at most to have made only marginal dents in class inequality. Even if the overall spread of incomes should have undergone some mild compression during the last decade or two—and the evidence for that as against broad overall stability is open to question— there are too many variables at work for any separate effects from govern-ment manipulation of restraints on pay, profits and dividends to have registered.[11] Nor is that surprising. When British governments, for example, have gone beyond mere rhetoric in coupling restrictions on monetary income growth with preferential treatment of the lower-paid, this has been limited to particular phases, ordinarily succeeded—as in prospect for 1978/79—by concessions to iron out "anomalies", restore "differentials" and re-establish an allegedly eroded hierarchy of incentives among higher management. Even within purportedly redistributive phases of incomes policy, moreover, loopholes proliferate for evasion: for the continued operation of labour market pressures through productivity bargaining and through "wages drift" by local settlement; for managerial incomes to grow *de facto* through unrecorded augmentation by new perks and allowances. Even in Sweden, where an ostensibly far firmer and more consistent policy towards inequality reduction has been tacked onto incomes control by government in association with unions and employers, "earnings drift" and pressures for the reassertion of differentials appear to have reduced the net effects to inconsiderable dimensions.[12]

Measures of "diffuse redistribution" have a potential quality of radicalism to them on two scores. First, they imply doubt about the moral validity of the pattern of distribution resulting from capitalist economic mechanisms; and just because the precise target of purported redistribution is left in the air, the boundaries of the doubt implied are similarly open. Perhaps only "poverty" is questioned, as it is in the philosophy of "minimum guarantee"; but perhaps—perhaps—also inequality across a wider range? Short as it is on substance, even the rhetoric of "diffuse redistribution"—recently magnified to accompany government restraints on pay—could help to bring the issue of inequality into clearer focus on political agendas. Second, policies of "diffuse redistribution" might conceivably be so sharpened and detached from countervailing measures as to be given real bite. But if it is possible to discern that sort of potential for radicalism, it is at the same time, so to speak, negated by its own inner self. No targets for redistribution are set, no alternative norms of economic justice are asserted in clear challenge to those which prevail; and there has been no real bite in fact to the policies actually implemented. The inference is pressing, if not proven, that they cannot acquire bite within the continuing context of a capitalist economy.

IV

So back, in summary, to the question of "welfare state limits." Among the five catalogued objectives of social policy—broadly defined to embrace measures such as incomes policies which play upon property and market incomes *ab initio,* as well as taxes and benefits which modify the initial pattern of incomes *post hoc*—three are not in central conflict with the distributive rules and economic mechanisms of capitalism. To say that is not to postulate that capitalism is served positively better by the presence of policies incorporating these objectives than it would be by their absence. Moderate as these objectives are, the growth of an elaborate state machinery to pursue them has in part been forced upon capitalist economies, both by direct pressure from collectively organized labour and by the need to contain indiscipline, disruption and potential subversion on the part of labour. But provision of a "minimum guarantee"; the state's emblazonment of "equal opportunity" on its banners and its institution of a variety of measures to lower barriers to that end; the proliferation of graduated benefits tuned to labour market differentials, with a reduction of old risks and uncertainties in wage earning life as both aim and effect— these can be accommodated within a capitalist economy fairly well. Not, certainly, without a price and without attendant tensions. They require large funds and so high levels of taxation, even if the consequent threat to profit and pay incentives is mitigated by effectively even rates of taxation across the board. They make for some redistribution of resources between—

not just within—classes, moderated though this is again by the way in which taxes fall. Both minimum and graduated benefits may—or may seem to—put maintenance of the "work ethic" marginally at risk, given the institutionalized emphasis on monetary incentives characteristic of a capitalist economy.[13] And for all the resources devoted to this, reduction of barriers to unequal opportunity cannot apparently be pushed far without adoption of measures, beyond that aim itself, to reduce substantive inequalities; and so it is not pushed far. Yet, in their essentials, these three objectives of social policy remain within the limits of capitalist rules and mechanisms.

Not so the objective of "selective equality of condition" represented—if rather raggedly—in British and now also Scandinavian health service policies. Nor again would a determined re-gearing of measures of "diffuse redistribution" to effective compression of the range of inequality in all likelihood be compatible with the complex of profit returns to capital and income inequalities in the labour market which turn the wheels of enterprise in capitalist economies. It is on an extension of those two orientations of social policy that any hopes of radical reform would have to rely. For only they at all significantly challenge the prevailing principles of distribution and the mechanisms associated with them. But just for that reason, it is hard to conceive that such reform could be taken far—without conversion into revolution.

This—a pessimistic conclusion for those who like myself see no signs of revolutionary impetus, now or round the corner—may be to assign rather more fixity to "welfare state limits" than is justified. If those limits have already here and there been marginally exceeded—as they have in health service provision—they might be exceeded again, by extension of the same principle to one or two other fields. The circumstances in which that might occur, and the cost still be counted as compatible with maintenance of the capitalist economic engine in running condition, seem no more easily predictable than was the British health service ten years before its institution. Nor is it possible to define in advance the precise point at which, say, a redistributive re-gearing of the entire bundle of taxation would put—or be seen to put—profit and pay incentives so far at risk that the only alternative to outright conversion of the economy to some socialist form would be retreat. But if on these grounds, the limits of welfare reform within a capitalist framework are not entirely fixed, there seems nevertheless little enough elasticity to them. Any hopes that they can be stretched very much further than to form a compound package of ingredients already present in some policies somewhere is likely to prove illusory.

NOTES

1. The data referred to appeared in G.A. Stephenson, "The effects of taxes and benefits on household income, 1976", *Economic Trends*, February 1978. The latest in an annual series of such reports, this differed from earlier ones in allowing analysis of tax and benefit effects to be traced consistently through each stage for decile groups (the richest 10 per cent, the next 10 per cent, etc.) according to "original" income, household type by type. Parallel material was presented for 1971, but I draw on that here for only one point (see note 11 below). All calculations which follow in the text and tables are my own, based on the material in Appendix Table 3 of the source. (Detailed definitions can be found in that paper.)

2. Throughout I have counted "subsidies" (to council housing and to reduce food prices to consumers) as "benefits", whereas in the summary analyses of the original source they were treated as a form of "negative indirect tax" to be deducted from indirect taxes proper.

3. In the more complex sequence of reality (with which analysis of material for a single year cannot cope), one year's benefits of course are financed in part from the preceding year's taxation.

4. The calculations which follow in this paragraph are based on the material (again from Central Statistical Office family expenditure survey data) presented in *Report no. 5* of the Royal Commission on the Distribution of Income and Wealth, 1977 (Cmnd. 6999), table 23, page 53. The figures presented by the Royal Commission do not allow direct addition of the respective incidences of direct and indirect taxes because, while direct taxes are related there to "original" income plus cash benefits, indirect taxes are related to such "gross" income *minus* direct taxes (i.e. to "disposable" income). The result is to understate the degree of regression in indirect taxation as it would appear (and as I estimate it here) in relation to "gross" income *before* deduction of direct taxes. (The adjustment I have made, in order to make my estimates, is to assume a ratio of indirect tax to net income in each decile group of gross income equivalent to the ratio shown in the Royal Commission's figures for the corresponding decile group of net income).

5. My extrapolation is from table 22, page 51 of Royal Commission *Report no. 5* (op. cit.), which in respect of all households in 1975 shows virtually the same share (44 per cent) of all "original" income in the hands of the initially richest 20 per cent as do the 1976 data; and 38 per cent of "final" income in the hands of what by then is the richest 20 per cent—a share which I assume likely to be roughly correct also for 1976.

6. This may sound as if I claim more for what follows than I intend or than is justified. I have drawn heavily on previous work, both detailed description and especially general characterisation, in my catalogue of social policy "objectives" relevant to class inequality. If there is any originality to it, it is in the attempt to classify specific policy measures according to the class-directed aims, and the implicit conceptions of acceptable equality (or unacceptable inequality), represented in them: thus to put a little more "policy flesh" into general characterisations of the "welfare state." Among the general characterisations and discussions on which I have drawn, the following especially deserve note: V. George and P. Wilding, *Ideology and Social Welfare*, 1975; J.C. Kincaid, *Poverty and Equality in Britain*, 1973; T.H. Marshall, *Citizenship and Social Class*, 1950 (chapter I); idem, *Social Policy*, 1970 (new ed. 1975). R. Mishra, *Society and Social Policy*, 1977; Julia Parker, *Social Policy and Citizenship*, 1975; R.M. Titmuss, "The social division of welfare" in his *Essays on the Welfare*

State, 1958; idem, *Social Policy,* 1974; Dorothy Wedderburn, "Facts and theories of the welfare state", *Socialist Register 1965;* with respect mainly to the USA, P. Marris and M. Rein, *Dilemmas of Social Reform,* 1967 (2nd ed. 1972); and with respect to Denmark and Sweden—B.R. Andersen, *Nyere målsaetninger i socialpolitikken,* 1966; idem, *Grundprincipper i socialpolitikken,* 1971; Socialutredningen, *Socialvården—mål och medel,* 1974 (Swedish official reports, SOU 1974: 39). I have also made some use of such comparative studies as A.J. Heidenheimer et. al., *Comparative Public Policy,* 1975; P.R. Kaim-Caudle, *Comparative Social Policy and Social Security,* 1973; B.N. Rodgers et. al., *Comparative Social Administration,* 1968 (2nd ed. 1971)—although their orientation did not on the whole match my purpose in this paper.

7. Cf. especially Marshall, op. cit., 1950.

8. This point and the general role of welfare provision in enforcement of labour discipline are underlined especially by Kincaid, op. cit.

9. The Family Income Supplement introduced in Britain by a Conservative govern-ment in the early 1970s, for example, stepped up benefits to children (on means test) without direct risk of the "work ethic", because it was made available only to households with an earning member. The new "child benefits" in Britain—to replace family allowances and tax allowances for children—will similarly constitute no threat to the work ethic, because they will be paid to all families with children (whether with or without earners) and will be free of tax. But by the same token they will, in themselves, be non-distributive except in adding proportionately more to low than to high incomes. The measures of "graduated provision" discussed later lift, and have been designed to lift, benefits for many above a "general minimum"—i.e., by reference to past earnings.

10. My use of the term "citizenship" here thus differs from Marshall's (op. cit., 1950), though the coinage is his. While National Health was part of the welfare state system discussed by Marshall, he saw a significant equality of status (citizenship) implicit even in the basic national insurance arrangements designed to provide only a "general minimum" in need.

11. The Royal Commission's tax-return based figures (op. cit., pp. 20-22) show a fairly continuous trend towards mild compression of income inequality, before as well as after income tax, over the period 1959-1975. But this might, not implausibly, conceal a possibly counteracting appropriation of real income by the relatively wealthy in the form of increases in fringe benefits and the like not recorded in the figures. Regardless of that possibility, data from the regular family expenditure surveys suggest, for the period 1961-70, an increase in inequality of "original" incomes barely neutralised by a simultaneous increase in state redistribution (J. Westergaard and H. Resler, *Class in a Capitalist Society,* 1975, pp. 44-49, 66-68). The parallel material on which I have drawn for Part II of this paper, moreover, suggests very little if any reduction of "original" income inequality over the later period 1971-1976, but again some slight stepping up of redistribution through state activity. Whatever the precise truth behind these discrepancies in the evidence, clearly no major shifts occurred—in either original or final income distributions. It is also worth noting that, fairly inelastic as the limits of "welfare state" activity arguably are, redistribution is sensitive at the margins to policy measures; and that, generally over the 1960s and 1970s, such redistribution increased a little—though if the family expenditure survey evidence can be trusted on this score, not quite enough to balance a countervailing increase in initial inequality during the 1960s; only thereafter with a mildly positive net effect on the trend of "final" income distribution.

12. Cf. R. Scase, *Social Democracy in Capitalist Society: Working-Class Politics*

in Britain and Sweden, 1977.

13. It is possible, of course, that a socialist economy adopting some version or other of my goal of "equality of condition" would decide to buttress an "ethic of work" by means of monetary incentives. Its options on this score, however, would be wider than in a capitalist economy, in which monetary incentives are highly institutionalized by the inherent logic of capitalist economic mechanisms. And whether or not a socialist economy used monetary incentives to deter total withdrawal from work, any monetary incentives to additional effort or to induce mobility of workers could be compressed within a much narrower range than in a capitalist economy, in that the base levels of income (shorn of any such incentives) would be equal.

Acknowledgements

I presented an early version of the major part of this paper (all except part II) to a large seminar at the Danish Institute for Social Research in Copenhagen in November 1977. I wish to thank the sponsors and audience of the seminar—among them, Iver Hornemann Møller, Henning Friis, Ole Høeg—both for this opportunity to put my ideas in draft and for comments and criticisms which allowed me to revise them. I wish also to thank my colleagues at Sheffield University, Eric Sainsbury, David Phillips and Alan Walker, for detailed and cogent comments on a translation of that seminar paper. I wish finally to thank Mr. E. Jones of the Royal Commission on Income and Wealth and Mr. G.A. Stephenson of the Central Statistical Office for guiding me to the latter's paper (see note 1 above), and the Swedish Institute in Stockholm for sending me much relevant Swedish material.

THE MAKING OF A PARTY?

The International Socialists 1965-1976

Martin Shaw

The history of organised marxist politics in Britain, for almost a century, is one of continuous marginality. The number of people involved in marxist parties and organisations of any description has never exceeded a few tens of thousands at any one time. The problem of creating a socialist organisation of real political weight, to the left of the Labour Party, might well seem insoluble. Many have concluded, indeed, that this is so; from the leadership of the Communist Party, with its desire for long-term merger with Labour, and the deep-entry trotskyists of *Militant* to the thousands of ex-Communists and revolutionary socialists who have joined the Labour Party as individuals.

The overall record of failure should not blind us, however, to the real opportunities which have been lost due to the inadequacies of the marxist left itself. To give only the most important example, early British marxism was dominated by a sectarian propagandist tradition, which greatly militated against its achieving any decisive influence, either in the formative period of the modern labour movement, or in the great industrial upheavals just before, during and after the 1914-18 war. Nor should this record allow us to assume that the underlying features of British working-class politics, which have made for the unique dominance of Labourist reformism in the last three-quarters of a century, will never change. On the contrary, there are reasons for believing that they have already begun to be transformed.

The 1945-51 period of Labour Government was, in fact, a watershed in working-class politics. After a quarter of a century, we can see that 1945 was the political culmination, for the British working class, of the entire experience of two generations. In the first, the mass labour movement which emerged at the end of the nineteenth century found it needed a political "wing". In the second, the defeats of the mass struggles in the 1920s, followed by the frustrations of the thirties and the war, combined to focus all the hopes of the working class on the election of a majority Labour Government. The disappointment of these hopes has had effects which have been profound, for all that they may have been slow to reveal themselves.

Labour has been in a long, gradual decline since 1951, in numbers of voters, members, and activists, and above all in the commitment and conviction of all three. The decline has stemmed from the failure of the state-dominated "mixed economy" to satisfy either the old hopes with which it was born, or the new aspirations which it has helped to create. In the 1950s and early '60s, the problem seemed to be that larger, socialist goals were "irrelevant", since liberal reform was more appropriate to a prosperous welfare state. But as the contradictions of state-managed capitalism began to appear, Labour was returned to the managerial role which, in a sense, belonged naturally to it. In presiding, as it has now done for ten of the last fourteen years, over a system whose failings and conflicts have become more and more apparent, Labour confirmed that its decline of the 1950s had not been accidental, but was a symptom of a deeper failure, of a particular version of working-class socialist politics.

Labour's failures and decline have offered opportunities of a new kind to the marxist left, to break out of its isolation and to begin to create a credible, alternative socialist organisation. The opportunities have been magnified, in that they have come after a long period in which the working class has grown in numbers, strength and willingness to fight for its interests. Labour's crisis has been a crisis of the capitalism it has tried to manage, and has brought it into conflict with a militant working class. In such a period, it would be surprising if alternatives to the left of Labour had not grown.

There was, of course, one force to the left of Labour which survived the long period of its dominance: the Communist Party. It had, however, its own great political disadvantages—not just the legacy of stalinism, but its close association with the Labour left, and indeed with a left-wing version of Labour's statist, reformist, parliamentary politics in general. Although the CP was the only sizeable organisation on the left in the 1950s, its paper membership was small (never more than 30,000), its vote tiny, and even its industrial strength, its most important feature, still patchy. The CP was therefore unable to pose, by sheer size alone, as the overwhelming focus for the left. Its membership stagnated, despite all the opportunities, as new groups grew up to challenge it.

The main organisational focus for a new growth of the left was, therefore, in the revolutionary marxist groups to the left of the CP. Although a large number of these groups emerged, and several of them have had some significance, the main beneficiary, by a sort of natural selection process, was the International Socialists. Indeed on 1st January 1977, IS renamed itself the Socialist Workers Party, and claimed that, while still small and weak, it had become the new revolutionary socialist party which the British working class required. At the same time, the number of its critics on the marxist left, including many former members, was growing. While the SWP had undoubtedly a sort of pre-eminence on the far left, it was by no means clear that it had really overcome the difficulties which had traditionally handicapped marxist groups in their attempt to form serious parties to the left of Labour.

The purpose of this article is to look at the development of the International Socialists in the decade of their real growth, from 1965 to 1976, up to the formation of the SWP. It is written by a participant, and the interpretation inevitably relies a great deal on my own experience and memory of the processes which I describe, as well as on documents of the period. The aim, however, is to ask two important questions. How far did IS realise the potential for a new socialist party which existed in this period? And to the extent that it has failed, what are the implications for socialists in Britain today?

I. THE EMERGENCE OF INTERNATIONAL SOCIALISM, 1965-68

The emergency of the "far left" is usually dated, in Britain as elsewhere, from 1968. But it is certainly not the case that new groups came from nowhere, out of the upheavals of that year. Throughout the world there had been a long process of disenchantment with the social-democratic and communist parties, the cold-war opposites that dominated the labour movements. Mass movements against the bomb, and then the Vietnam war, had mobilised new generations of activists, uncommitted to the dominant ideologies of the "old left." And as the editor of a recent compilation has pointed out, the 1956 crisis in the Communist Party had a particularly "critical impact" in Britain, "antedating the formation of an independent Left in other countries by some years."[1] In this "new left", as it was first called, the previously subterranean currents of trotskyism, the tradition of revolutionary opposition to stalinism and reformism, surfaced and took on new forms. The origins of International Socialism, as IS were known (it became "The International Socialists" only after 1968), were in this process. In the struggles of the years up to 1968, IS grew to the point where "take-off" was possible.

1. *In the shadow of "orthodoxy"—the early years of IS*

The history of IS before 1965 is essentially that of a propaganda group. This was, naturally enough in view of their tiny size and isolation, the main role of all the revolutionary groups in Britain between the late 1940s and mid-1960s, whether trotskyist, anarchist or (in the '60s) maoist. The success of one group or another was a function of the content, presentation and style of their ideas. Since the groups competed for influence in the same restricted milieux, a great deal depended on their mutual interaction. In the case of IS, its approach was greatly influenced—negatively—by the dominant form of trotskyism in Britain.

The Socialist Review Group, forerunner of IS, had been formed in 1950-51 after its founders were expelled from the British section of the

Fourth International, then pursuing entry work in the Labour Party under the leadership of Gerry Healy. This was a period in which the traditional trotskyist opposition to stalinism was being muted and replaced by optimism about its revolutionary role. Even Natalia Sedova Trotsky, widow of Leon Trotsky, came to denounce the leadership of the international movement her husband had founded.[2] The Fourth International's uncritical attitude to Tito was one source of conflict. The uncritical support given by Healy's group to the Russian bloc in Korea was, however, the final cause of the split.[3]

Underlying these political differences, of course, Socialist Review had a major theoretical difference with the mainstream of trotskyism. Its leader, Tony Cliff, argued that Russia and its eastern European satellites were not "degenerated workers' states", but bureaucratic state capitalist societies. Because the former view was held by Trotsky himself at his death, it was characterised as "orthodox": Cliff however saw it as involving revisions of basic marxist ideas. In his own work, as I demonstrate elsewhere, Cliff sought to apply the main categories of marxist orthodoxy to Russian society.[4]

This theoretically distinct stance enabled SR to survive as a tiny alternative to the larger trotskyist group led by Healy. The Hungarian Revolution apparently confirmed Cliff's analysis of a fundamental class struggle in Eastern Europe, and his perspective of a full social revolution. But it appears that, as Ian Birchall has written in his "official" history of IS. "Its small size prevented it from benefiting from the events of 1956."[5] The group had only 33 members at its foundation, and seems not to have been much larger six years later. Certainly it was Healy's group which gained an audience among the leftward-moving ex-Communists, workers and intellectuals, who left the Party in 1956 and 1957. Their new organisation, the Socialist Labour League, formed in 1958, and the looser movement of the "New Left", were the two main outgrowths of that crisis.

The late fifties were however a period of some growth for SR, which may have had around 100 members at the turn of the decade.[6] And they were important in two ways, neither of which Birchall really mentions. First, the emergence of an "independent left", open to discussion on an anti-stalinist basis, but unconvinced by "orthodox" trotskyism, certainly gave the group a wider audience. Second, and much more crucial, this was the period in which the group began to develop its theory beyond the orthodox, even fundamentalist basis of Cliff's *Russia,* and develop the basis for a distinctive approach to British politics. As I describe elsewhere, the theory of the "permanent arms economy", first developed by writers of the American trotskyist movement led by Max Shachtman (which had split from the Fourth International in 1940), was popularised by Cliff, and later developed by Michael Kidron, the group's most innovative writer.

Whatever our ultimate judgement of this theory as an explanation, it did give SR a perspective based on an understanding of two crucial points: that capitalism was not going to collapse into another 1929 crisis, and that state planning, by itself, had no inherently socialist quality, but was a means used by capital itself in its latest stage. In a striking series of theoretical articles and polemics in the late fifties and early sixties, Kidron filled out his analysis, and laid a distinctive economic basis for a perspective of "reformism from below." The period, he argued, was one in which reforms were increasingly won by sectional industrial action and other grass-roots struggles, not by parliamentary legislation or central bargaining. The revolutionaries of SR therefore presented themselves as the most consistent fighters for reforms.[7]

It was not until the mid-sixties that this perspective really came into its own, but at the end of the fifties it was one element which helped to mark off SR further as a realistic alternative to the "orthodox" trotskyism of Healy. The SLL degenerated swiftly from its fairly promising start: within a year or so of its foundation it had become profoundly bureaucratic, and many of its most talented members, workers and intellectuals, quickly left. It soon became the caricature of a trotskyist organisation for which it was well known throughout the 1960s. Heralding the collapse of capitalism at every turn, denouncing betrayal in every failure, constantly exorcising revisionist devils, it was in some ways clearly more stalinist than the Communist Party itself.[8] The SR group, which differed from orthodox trotskyism in general, came to represent the polar opposite to the SLL: realistic in economic perspectives, able to explain the failures of labour bureaucrats as well as to condemn them, non-sectarian towards other socialists, the champion of thorough working-class democracy in all areas of practice. This last point was emphasised by the publication in 1959 of Tony Cliff's study of Rosa Luxemburg, in which he suggested that Luxemburg's ideas of organisation, rather than Lenin's were the model for contemporary socialists. It was stressed again in 1961, in Cliff's attack on "substitutionism", the substitution of the revolutionary party for the working class, in which he advocated a party which discussed and decided quite openly in front of the workers.[9]

The SR group was the most coherent, open and thinking marxist alternative to the dominant "orthodoxy" of the SLL, and in the early sixties it began to grow, attracting refugees from the League (and the fading New Left), but more importantly a few young workers and students from CND and the Young Socialists. In 1962 the group took the name "International Socialism", from the journal launched two years previously, and with the slogan "Neither Washington nor Moscow but International Socialism", it appealed to the new activists more than other trotskyists with their defence of the Russian "workers' bomb." But despite opposition from IS and the forerunners of today's other main marxist groups (IMG, Militant), the larger SLL were still able to dominate the YS. In 1964, before the return of Labour to office, they prematurely led its main body out of the Labour Party, forming an independent YS which has led a shadowy existence ever since. The remaining official YS, eventually renamed "Labour Party YS", became a rump. The IS group had grown to around 200 members, perhaps half the strength of the SLL. It was by no means a massive expansion, but it represented a growth in numbers and experience to match the new ideas which Kidron and Cliff had developed, and placed IS in a good position for further advance.[10]

2. *In the "fragments" and the student movement—the first phase of rapid growth*

One paradox of IS's theory of "the shifting locus of reforms"—from parliament and union hierarchy to shop floor and grass roots—was that before 1964 it had to be combined with support for Labour's return to office. IS warned of the "managerialist" tendency of an incoming Labour government, but in 1963-65 there was a powerful tendency for the newly politicised activists to invest it with many of their hopes. Indeed, movements like CND and Anti-Apartheid had achieved most of what was possible through mere protest and pressure, while the YS had torn itself apart in factional strife. The idea of an end to "thirteen wasted years" captured many socialists and trade unionists at the time, and certainly there was no electoral alternative to Labour.

The shattering of illusions in the Labour Government, which began in 1965 with the Immigration White Paper and the failure to act over Rhodesia's UDI, and developed rapidly in 1966 because of the seamen's strike and the wage freeze, was therefore a crucial turning-point in working-class politics. It was the point at which the working-class "apathy" of the fifties, still evident in Labour's declining vote in 1964, began to turn into active opposition to the Labour leadership itself. But it was an opposition which was sectional and even fragmented—the seamen's "stage battle" was hardly typical of these years. What was happening, indeed, was that the short, shop- and factory-based unofficial strikes of the boom period were becoming more widespread as the contradictions of British capitalism came to the fore. Unlike the Communist Party, whose main thrust was to pressurise the left-wing MPs and union officials, or the SLL, who raised grandiose demands in order to expose these same people, IS recognised that the situation was one of grass-roots reformism in crisis. Patchily, in 1965-66, its members started to withdraw from activity in the Labour Party and the YS, and concentrated more on the small-scale "fragments" of grass-roots militancy. These included strikes to defend shop stewards and to gain union recognition, private tenants' struggles against racist landlords, and the council tenants' battles against rent rises forced by the government in 1967, in which IS made its largest intervention.

An extension of IS's analysis was very important to this change of direction. Cliff and Colin Barker concentrated attention, as marxists had not done in Britain since the 1920s, on the forms of organisation "at the point of production." They picked out the spread of shop stewards, particularly in engineering, as the key development of the post-war boom. They hypothesised, moreover, that the imposition of incomes policy, together with attempts to control shop stewards by law, would generalise the response of the stewards, and create a shop stewards movement for the first time since the first world war. This movement, in conflict with the union bureaucracies as well as the employers and the Government, would be the basis of a new revolutionary workers' movement.[11]

It is obvious in retrospect that this analysis was oversimplified, and that the paradox we have noted, in the theory of a "shifting locus" of the struggle for reforms, was to prove deeper. But in 1966-67, these ideas fitted well with the level of struggle. IS was still, moreover, very much under the sway of its thoroughgoing reaction to "orthodox" trotskyism, especially as represented by the SLL; it was more likely to minimise its own importance than to try to invent a pretentious machinery to fit its conceptions. The "struggle in the fragments" was practised empirically; indeed one of its dangers was, as Birchall rightly points out, that of syndicalism—adaptation to the narrow conditions of wage or rent struggles.[12]

Although the mass economic struggles of the working class were mainly confined to the sporadic strikes and protests which IS focused on, the most important struggles of this period were in fact elsewhere, in the growing student movement and movement against the Vietnam war. IS had, as Birchall points out, "no thought-out strategy for student work" before 1967; its student members, together with those of other marxist sects, had been active in the National Association of Labour Student Organisations which had been very strong in the period around the 1964 election. IS no more had a theory of students than did any other marxist group, but its ideas of the struggle at the "point of production" were rapidly translated into the student field. "Workers' control" became "student and staff control", and the opposition between militant students and the right-wing NUS machine easily fitted the general schema of grass roots versus bureaucracy. IS students were centrally involved in the movement at LSE, where student activism dated back to UDI in 1965, and effectively led the first sit-in in 1967. Starting here, IS members took part in most of the student actions of late 1967 and 1968. As the CP's student work was concentrated on the NUS, and the SLL idiotically counterposed its own organisation to the student actions, IS (although far from being generally dominant) was the largest single group in the new student left.

Closely linked with the student movement, but distinct from it, was the campaign against the Vietnam war, which took off with the mass demonstrations in October 1967, March 1968 and, of course, October 1968. This movement proved the vitality of the strand of mass political campaigning, essentially apart from the mass of the working class and their organisations, which had been apparent in CND. It also showed the political advance made in this sort of movement, and in the student left which composed much of it. While CND had been polarised between legal protest and direct action, the Vietnam movement was divided between the advocates of "peace" and of "victory to the NLF." By 1967, however, it was clear that the latter position, represented by the Vietnam Solidarity Campaign, held the initiative. Because the CP clung to the "peace" position, it was outflanked even more than in CND; the SLL was reduced to handing out leaflets proclaiming "Why we are not marching"; the effective leadership of the movement was in the hands of revolutionaries— "The Week" (forerunners of IMG) who started VSC in 1966, IS who were the main force in mobilising in the localities and colleges, and various maoists.

In one sense, therefore, IS's strategy of "work in the fragments" was being overtaken by events in 1967 and 1968. Certainly the great expansion of the group in those years—from a little over 200 in 1966 to 450 at the end of 1967 and a notional 1,000 in late 1968[13]—owed less to the proclaimed strategy than to IS's energetic, imaginative and flexible role in the student and Vietnam movements. Of course, it is probably true that the most serious of the new recruits were attracted to IS both because it always insisted that the main job was to win the working class, and because it had a realistic perspective on this task which stressed the modest level of workers' struggles by contrast with the revolutionary euphoria of VSC and the colleges. To that extent, IS got the balance right, more so than others such as New Left Review, some of whose leaders advocated the extravagant idea of universities as permanent "red bases" within capitalist society, or the infant IMG, who based themselves on the "new student vanguard" as its main upsurge subsided—let alone the CP or SLL.

But the events of 1967-68 were also, in ways which only later became apparent, beyond the understanding of the IS "old guard" itself. The central cadre of IS was formed in an orthodox—even, as I have suggested, fundamentalist—marxism, centred on the industrial working class. Its perspectives were firmly hitched to the traditional sectors, indeed to a large extent to the particular context of engineering. Some of the leaders, particularly Tony Cliff, were enthusiastic for the student movement while it lasted, and prepared to give the students their head; others less so. None of them, with the exception of Michael Kidron[14] who played little part in IS after 1968, seem to have understood the structural changes in capitalism which the student movement highlighted, and which were analysed by IS's own students. And even that analysis fudged the most critical issue, the extent to which the political period was changing beyond the framework of IS's perspectives.[15] The events of 1968 itself revealed the inevitable confusion into which IS was thrown by the whole unprecedented upheaval.

3. *Rites of passage?—the 1968 crisis in IS*

1968—that truly amazing year, in which so much was happening that it is difficult to sort out a pattern of events—was an obvious turning point for IS. If its modest perspectives and traditional style were strained by the upsurge in 1967, they were at breaking point by the summer and autumn of 1968. Crisis was piled upon crisis: the Tet offensive, Powell's speech, the May events, Czechoslovakia, the great October 27 demonstration, not to mention the flowering of sit-ins in the most unlikely colleges up and down Britain. From the international point of view, Britain's '68 may seem mild, even insipid, but for those involved the impact was overwhelming.[16]

For IS, Powell's speech, and the dockers' support for him, was a critical moment. Even Birchall, for whom IS's history is generally an extremely orderly progress, admits it was "a stunning shock for the left."[17] IS had been working around the London docks during the struggle over decasualisation. It responded well, with its slim resources, at the level of anti-Powell propaganda, but the reaction was stronger than that. IS issued a call, under the exaggerated heading "The Urgent Challenge of Fascism", for revolutionary unity around four basic points.[18] This call quickly took on greater significance, as the revolt across the Channel made clear the momentous changes which were taking place in the political prospects of revolutionaries. IS's unity proposal was not therefore a well thought-out "first step" on the road to a revolutionary part, but something of a panic response. It was however a vital initiative, and showed the healthy non-sectarian instincts which were deeply inbred in the group. The refusal of the SLL to take it up was predictable enough, but that of others, such as the semi-marxist "Solidarity" group (quite close to IS at the time), or the newly-formed International Marxist Group, was not automatically expected. The opportunity to form a united organisation, which would, for example, have been able to build much more solidly than any one group on the gains of VSC, was lost. The fault lay with groups such as IMG who were unwilling to risk their new political existence in a united project. The failure greatly strengthened IS's belief, well nourished by previous experience of the SLL, in the inherently sectarian character of "orthodox" trotskyism.

Of course, any united organisation, involving mainly the new student generation brought into revolutionary politics in 1968, would have faced enormous problems. Greater political agreement than that represented in IS's four points would undoubtedly have been needed for it to work: there was the danger of degeneration into sectarian squabbling which was the early fate of the Revolutionary Socialist Students Federation, a super-unitary body set up at the height of the euphoria of 1968. IS's failure to clarify the basis of unity sufficiently in advance did in fact lead to problems with the one tiny sect, Workers Fight (an orthodox trotskyist group previously expelled from both the SLL and Militant), which did accept the unity call. The position of this group, which operated its own organisation and discipline within IS, was to cause immense problems in the next three years, hardening many of the IS leaders against allowing any organised opposition in the group.

IS's problems in 1968, although they centred on organisational questions, were in fact political. Although they can be seen as the trials of transition, from a small group to an embryonic party, they also brought into question the theoretical and practical traditions of the group. IS's acknowledged leader, Tony Cliff, had been responsible for veering away from orthodox leninism, towards a looser conception of revolutionary organisation as the servant of the mass movement. As a reaction to the caricatural vanguardism of the SLL, this had been a valid response, and it had many positive aspects—the emphasis on open political discussion, before the class, for example. But the failure of the May events to lead to revolution, together with the confusion caused by rapid growth in IS itself, led Cliff to turn right back to Lenin. The lesson was the need for a revolutionary party, not substituting itself for the working class, but formed from its real vanguard, and fighting for leadership of the class.[19]

This lesson was so radical for IS that it eclipsed all the others which should have been drawn from the unique events of 1968. To understand how sharp the turn was, we can note the overwhelming rejection, in 1967, of the proposal merely to include the *aim* of building a revolutionary party in the list published in the group's paper. The paper itself was still called "Labour Worker" until the summer of 1968, which implied a continuing orientation to that party rather than the building of an independent revolutionary alternative. But after May, the idea of a party suddenly became viable. There was no pretence that IS was the party, or even its nucleus. But it could be built, and with the failure of the unity proposals IS came very gradually to treat itself as a *de facto* nucleus. The old federal structure of the group, with an Executive Committee based on delegates from branches and a loose conception of national discipline, was challenged by Cliff. Instead, he proposed the election of a National Committee by Conference on a political basis, with a smaller EC to run the group from day to day.

The proposals provoked a most intense debate, with several factions springing up. These ranged from "libertarians" opposed to the changes to "democratic centralists" who felt that their political basis should have been more clearly developed, since Cliff himself tended to explain them in practical rather than theoretical terms. The most coherent argument in favour of democratic centralism was made by Chris Harman, in a published article, arguing via Lenin and Gramsci for an organisation based on collective political appraisal of members' activity; but Harman like Cliff did not join or declare a faction.[20] The proposed changes were adopted, and gave IS both the forms and some of the substance of democratic centralism. Full rights of internal discussion were guaranteed, factions were freely allowed and possessed the right of representation on the NC (this was exercised by Workers Fight), and central discipline was understood tentatively, in the light of a two-way flow of experience and ideas (of which, indeed, there was a great deal in the next few years).

It is certain that the general political basis of the new "democratic centralist" constitution was not fully understood, either by many of the pre-1968 members on whom it was suddenly sprung, or by the new recruits whose first experience in IS had been the hectic six-month debate. More important, however, was the specific rationale for the new structure which Cliff in particular began to develop: the "turn to the class." It was the inexperience of the majority of the new members, especially the large number of students, which made a need for more central direction apparent. Cliff's central idea was the need to turn this new membership towards the working class, to use as a base for beginning to recruit workers themselves on a larger scale. The gap between the experience of the leadership and that of the "1968 levy" was to play an important part in the subsequent development of IS.

II. ON A RISING TIDE—BUILDING IN THE WORKING CLASS, 1969-1973

Very great opportunities for building a revolutionary organisation, which would represent a small but significant minority current in the working class, existed in Britain in the five years after 1968. For the first time since the 1920s, massive struggles erupted across a wide range of industries. Like those immediately after the 1914-18 war, they marked the onset of a serious crisis in the British economy. But the crisis did not develop so sharply and potentially disastrously, and it took new forms: unemployment moved steadily upward instead of shooting through the roof, and was for the first time accompanied by serious inflation. The working class, too, was stronger, with more workers in trade unions, and more established, confident shop-floor organisation. And there were other significant advantages for revolutionaries—the opposition between the rank and file and the trade union bureaucracy was well established in key industries; while the Labour Party was in decline and increasingly discredited.

These main features of the situation were ones which IS, more than any other force on the left, generally understood. What is more, there were a number of specific reasons why IS's position was promising at the end of 1968. It had grown to around 1,000 members, which gave it some sort of base in nearly every large city and many smaller towns; the membership was young and energetic; the results of the 1968 debate had generally been positive, giving the organisation more coherence, and few had left over the changes. The Communist Party, by contrast, despite its much larger paper membership, was partially paralysed by its close relationship to Labour's left and the new left-wing union leaders, and was convulsed by disagreements over Czechoslovakia. The SLL, although the daily paper and the "party" were still to come, was playing itself out as a serious force. The much smaller IMG had failed to recruit from VSC, and was still trying to gain an initial cadre from the student movement. Militant, in the Labour Party as always, could make very limited gains while the Labour Government continued not just to disillusion trade unionists and young people with itself, but to drive them away from the Party as well.

IS entered the period after 1968 with confidence, and to a real extent this bore fruit. Five years later the organisation was much larger, and much more working-class in composition. But problems had developed, and there was an unease among some of the more experienced members which was soon to erupt into open conflict. This period of great opportunities and considerable success must be the main focus of our history.

1. *Industrial struggle and emerging political dilemmas*

Just as disillusionment with the Labour Government had provided the greatest spur to IS's growth from 1965-68, so the experience of Tory government created the conditions for its even more dramatic expansion in 1970-73. The difference, however, was that whereas the first period had seen isolated, "fragmented" working-class struggles, the second was to be marked by great mass, often political struggles, in which class-wide generalisation was dramatically easier. And while the growth of IS in 1965-68 had not, by and large, actually occurred in the fragmented workers' struggles, but in the student and Vietnam movements—seen by the IS leadership as something of a "windfall"—in 1970-73 the main politicisation shifted to the arena IS had always seen as central, the industrial class struggle.

In one sense, therefore, IS was very well prepared for this new challenge. Its leaders knew well that the real test of the new upsurge would be when the political focus passed from the students to the industrial working class. They had highlighted the threat of laws to control shop stewards, three years before Labour's "In Place of Strife." They had observed the rising level of industrial conflict before it reached boiling point at the end of the 1960s, and had attempted to orient IS towards it. In 1968-70, they had particularly fought for IS, with its largely student composition, to make a "turn to the class." By the time the Tories were returned, IS members had considerable experience, if mainly from the outside, of the new wave of struggle: in the dustmen's strike, the textile strikes, and the battle at Pilkington's, to give some of the most important examples.

In these struggles, IS's politics had fitted well. At a most basic level, the "revolt of the lower paid" in 1969-70 conformed to the classic pattern of the struggles of the 1950s and '60s. They were spontaneous, unofficial actions, in which the union bureaucracy was the enemy as much as the employers themselves. What was new and exciting was the awakening of workers who had been passive for decades: their strikes were bigger, longer, less predictable, more politically provocative than the well-practised walk-outs in the engineering industry. They were more reminiscent of the mass strikes of May 1968, or indeed of Russia in 1905, than of the staid pattern of British trade unionism. In the argument about "In Place of Strife", too, it seemed that the difference between the TUC and Labour was over how to control the shop stewards, not whether they should be controlled. The rank and file opposition—May Day 1969 saw the first political strike for decades, and an unofficial one at that—was the crucial feature of the situation.

But for the same reasons that IS was politically well-prepared for the struggles of 1969-70, the change in the situation once the Tories were elected posed crucial problems. IS's whole analysis had stressed the convergence between Labour and Tory parties.[21] In the 1970 election, there was a strong "plague on both their houses" faction, and although the organisation as a whole called for a Labour vote "without illusions" (the case for IS candidates was perhaps too lightly dismissed), much of IS's propaganda was of the "Tweedledum-Tweedledee" variety. A sharp turn had therefore to be made, in understanding the importance that the change of government made, and launching into "anti-Tory" campaigning.

Even more important, the role of the trade union leaders changed with the Tories in power. The rising wage militancy and legal threats to union independence had already begun to force them to lead some struggles. The removal of the political loyalty which they owed to a Labour government gave this tendency a big impetus. The big strikes, like the postmen's in 1971 and the miners' in 1972, became official strikes. The political struggles, against the Industrial Relations Act and other Tory policies, were officially led by the union leaders. Of course, they did not develop the struggles as they might, strikes were sold out, and the political campaigns dampened down. The official leadership of some struggles did not rule out action by the rank and file—on the contrary it encouraged it, not just because a spur to the union leaders and a fight against betrayals were always needed, but also because rank and file initiative was all the more viable when some official backing would be forthcoming. It is easy to see the early '70s in terms of the stage battles of the big battalions, but there was a host of other struggles. The wave of closures and redundancies in 1971-72, accompanied by the rise of unemployment over the million mark, gave rise to the factory occupations, of which UCS was only the most famous. Here again industrial struggle went way beyond its "normal" methods.

To a large extent, IS's leadership was capable of adapting to the new conditions. The problems arose, again, from the speed with which changes had to be made. For not only did tactics have to be adapted; the previous one-sided political emphases, in which little distinction had been made between basic analysis and propaganda, had also to be corrected. The membership could be carried, obviously, to campaign to "Kill the Bill"; but not so easily for a Labour vote, or an anti-Common Market campaign. There was little inclination, moreover, among the leaders to produce the kind of generalised analysis of the new situation which it had made in the early sixties—although this might have given more coherence to the changes of line. The "permanent arms economy" remained the official explanation of modern capitalism, but it had the appearance of dogma, not living theory.[22]

The most important change of tactics was that away from independent, spontaneous rank and file action towards the conception of "rank and file movements", fighting within the unions as well as at the grass roots. IS as a whole never made the mistake of, for example, some of the Italian far left, of arguing for organisation outside the unions, nor did it support the idea of breakaway unions, raised by the Pilkington strike. IS was too well rooted both in the political traditions of Communism and in the experience of the British labour movement. From these, indeed, came the idea of an eventual national rank and file movement, modelled on the Minority Movement of the Communist Party in the 1920s.

There was also limited practical experience which could be generalised. Although the main body of IS students and white-collar workers had been engaged, in 1969-70, in a "turn to the class" which involved mainly regular factory leafleting from the outside, a few IS teachers founded a teachers' journal called "Rank and File" which within two or three years had a readership of several thousands. (They included very experienced activists such as Duncan Hallas, a founder member of Socialist Review who rejoined IS in 1968 after 14 years absence.) A supporters' group which was established involved hundreds of activists, the majority of them outside IS, and soon became the major left-wing force in the newly radicalised NUT. Rank and File played a leading role in teachers' strikes in London, and eventually had two of its members elected to the union's executive.

Early in 1970, IS's main industrial intervention was still around the plant-level "employers' offensive" of productivity deals, through the very effective propaganda of Tony Cliff's book, an impressive compilation based on contact with industrial workers up and down the country.[23] But by 1972, there was a serious attempt to set up rank and file papers and groups, consisting of non-members as well as an IS nucleus, not only in o ther white-collar unions like NALGO, ATTI and the CPSA, but also among hospital workers (NUPE and COHSE), miners, carworkers, and other manual workers. These groups were genuinely open, in some cases involving members of other small left-wing groups as well as Labour Party and even CP members. Although some collapsed quickly, a number won considerable minority support in their unions for several years. The main successes were, however, among white-collar workers; among manual workers the complexity of shop-floor and union organisation, the slower pace of radicalisation, and the strength of the Broad Left in the AUEW, all combined to weaken the impact.

The basis of the rank and file movements was the willingness of potential supporters to fight against the employers, the union bureaucracy and the government, rather than for any particular programme of demands. In practice, in this period of rising struggle, the demands tended to set themselves: for higher wages and against government controls; against anti-union laws; against unemployment (35-hour week, etc.); for union democracy; and (in the public sector especially) against cuts. Although the rank and file groups were supposed to have more limited programmes than the revolutionary organisation, IS itself propagated roughly the same demands: there seemed little need to go further. The demand for "a sliding scale of wages", i.e. index-linking against inflation, a classical slogan raised by "orthodox" trotskyists inside and outside IS, was particularly resisted.

The new rise of struggle under the Tories offered great opportunities to IS, but they also raised major questions. The size and scale of the industrial battles made it clear that even a rapidly growing IS could have only a slight influence on events. In the most decisive confrontations, such as the miners' strikes, IS—however much its solidarity work gained it the respect of the rank and file—remained basically an outside force. IS could grow in the groundswell, but the outcome of this phase of—highly political—class struggle would be determined independently of IS. What this outcome would be, what IS should say and do about it, raised deeper political questions than IS's leaders were willing to ask. In the end, they were to contribute to a major political crisis from which the organisation has still not recovered.

2. *New left or old?*

While IS's industrial strength advanced slowly, but nevertheless convincingly, in the early 1970s, in most other "areas" the group encountered increasing problems. Indeed, the segregation of the "industrial" from all other political questions, and the absolute priority given to it over all else, was the root of many of these. The IS leadership understood one key question, that a largely student and white-collar organisation, in a period of mounting workers' struggle, must attempt to root itself in the manual working class. But it is hardly unfair to say that they understood little else. This fundamentalism brought some definite gains, but it had its price, which was quite a serious one for IS, and was a major factor in the crisis to come.

We have already seen that the growth of IS before and during 1968 rested on the paradox, that it was not its central perspective, but factors distinctly secondary and even, in a sense, accidental to it, which were responsible. This remained true, although in different ways and not always so obviously, in the early 1970s. It was certainly the case that in the crucial moments of the class struggle, the traditionally militant sections of the working class played a decisive role. The engineers fought the Industrial Relations Act far more consistently than any other section of workers; the shipyard workers fought at UCS; the dockers, with the printers, freed the Pentonville 5; the miners brought down the Heath Government. To this extent IS's perspective was completely justified. But we have seen that behind these "stage battles" lay a much more diverse pattern of struggle. The "revolt" of the lower paid had not ended in 1970, but had merged into a general movement. Vast new sections of workers—white collar, women, service workers, as well as less militant workers in many manufacturing industries—were brought into the strikes and occupations of these years. Struggle outside the factory, over housing, rents, and services, continued to flourish. Students remained an active and occasionally explosive force. It was the involvement of all these sections which gave the battles against the Tories much of their mass character, and it was from them, rather than the traditionally militant unions, that most of IS's recruits came.

IS's leadership had, therefore, peculiarly contradictory attitudes to the majority of its members who were not male, manual workers in the traditionally militant industries. It was glad to have them, since without them the organisation would have looked very thin, and little of the necessary work could have been done. It promoted rank and file work among white collar workers, in particular. But politically, it dismissed them in all different degrees, and devalued their particular activity.

Similarly, the leadership refused to recognise the *other* lesson of 1968, that the struggle which was unfolding in the Western world was cultural, ideological, and political in the specific sense, as well as economic. Very many people continued to be drawn to IS for these sorts of reasons, and to raise these sorts of issue in the organisation. This was another source of major conflict.

A great deal of activity outside the "traditional" sectors of the industrial working class was actually carried on, since members would naturally work where they were or around issues they were particularly interested in. To a large extent, initiative was encouraged, or at least allowed to develop unhindered. But in a number of key areas a line was fostered or defended by the leadership, which directly restricted IS's intervention, and discredited its attempt to create a new socialist organisation.

Probably the most important single set of challenges to which IS failed to respond adequately were those posed by the women's movement and sexual politics in general.[24] The women's movement in Britain could trace itself back to the campaign of the Hull fishermen's wives, and the equal pay strike at Ford's Dagenham plant in 1968, both of which IS had naturally supported. But the movement as such, responding to similar movements in America and Germany, grew out of groups formed in 1969 by women around the student left, and really took off from a conference in Oxford in early 1970.[25] The issues were first raised at an IS Conference in March of that year: a motion supporting "independent women's organisations", calling for IS to be involved in women's liberation groups, for members to practice equality, and for a national sub-committee on the women question to be set up, provoked fierce opposition from the leadership, and was narrowly defeated. A more acceptable motion was passed, emphasising the militancy of women workers and avoiding the issue of support for the women's movement. But even the recommendation of this motion, for a coordinating committee to be set up, was not acted upon. By 1971, however, IS women were meeting among themselves, a newsletter was being published, and Conference gave its "general support to the women's liberation movement", as well as demanding that a women's committee functioned. "The official attitude in IS", Sheila Rowbotham noted, "has shifted from joking incredulity to grudging support."[26]

"Women's work", and the organisation of women involved in it both locally and nationally, were, however, to remain highly problematic. The underlying reason, not always recognised by women themselves in their desire to reconcile their activity with the line of the organisation, was that the basic political attitudes to women's liberation were never fully clarified. As David Widgery was to complain in 1975:

"For the last 5 years, we have been toing and froing in IS about our attitude to the Women's Liberation Movement, about how we organise women at work and at home, about the weight revolutionaries should put on questions of the family, marriage, children, homosexuality and the other non-industrial aspects of women's oppression."

The "EC's informal line for years" had included "complete isolation from the Women's Liberation Movement in all its forms" and "explicit rejection of work with housewives" (i.e. with women outside the work situation).[27] Politically, the leadership simply refused to recognise women's oppression in its totality. As Widgery recorded on another occasion, a leading member of IS "was responsible for the classic line 'I.S. does not have a line on what you call sexism and has not found it a phenomenon which exists in the working class.' "[28]

It was, in fact, the question of gay liberation which bared this political contradiction. It was possible to conceive of women's struggles in terms of the economic battle for equal pay, and indeed this was a vital part, but only one part, of any struggle for women's liberation. It was also possible to criticise the main women's movement for failing to involve itself actively with women in the workplace. These issues could be used to confuse the debate, and divert attention from the questions of sexual oppression as a whole and support for the women's movement as a movement against that oppression. On the gay question, there could be no such compromise with the workerist, economistic line of IS. The attempt to set up an IS Gay Group between 1972 and 1975 met, therefore, with consistent opposition from the leadership. Its harassed existence in those years makes "A Grim Tale", as one of the participants was later to describe it.[29]

IS women did do some good work among women workers, which few sections of the women's movement managed, although many others were of course working politically with working-class women over cuts, battering, abortion, etc. They maintained a paper in various forms and kept the issues alive in IS. But the general conclusion must be that there was an unnecessary divorce between IS, the main organised current of revolutionary socialism, and the women's movement, in a period which was crucial for them both. IS was certainly gravely weakened by its failure to relate successfully to what was, after the rank and file movement in industry, the most important social movement of the period. And the women's movement, too, reacted against the failures of IS (and other groups) by insulating itself against organised revolutionary socialism. Only recently has a strong "socialist feminist" current revived, in which revolutionary ideas have a real place.

In many cases, the failure of the left to respond to the women's movement might be put down simply to sexism, and of course that was not lacking in IS. But IS's failure raises other problems. The group had previously shown itself highly flexible and responsive to movements outside the framework of its theory and perspectives—particularly to the student movement of the late sixties, which had far less potential for working-class appeal than the women's movement. It was clearly the *particular* re-assertion, in this period, of a narrow and fundamentalist approach to socialist politics and the working class, which was responsible for the situation. Indeed IS's attitude to students also changed. The idea of support for a student movement, and intervention in it, was replaced, particularly in 1971-73, by the idea of recruiting individual students "to work at the factory gates." It was as if the late sixties had never happened: IS leaders took their ideas of students from Trotsky and ignored IS's own experience and analysis of more recent years.[30]

These trends did not represent just a strategic error, or a series of tactical misjudgements, but a political failure. It was a failure to recognise that the social crisis which was developing had more than economic and industrial dimensions. It was a failure to respond politically to the situation as a whole. A particularly crucial index of this weakness was IS's record of response to the situation in Ireland. When the civil rights movement first erupted, IS had responded with solidarity action, and in 1969 tried to develop a mass Irish Civil Rights Solidarity Campaign, which it saw as a successor to VSC and an important bridge to the Irish working class in Britain.[31] The escalation of the conflict in the North quickly led, however, to a situation in which "solidarity with civil rights" was overtaken. The border, it was soon clear, was still a crucial issue. The sending in of British troops, too, provoked a critical debate within and around IS: the organisation's reluctance to call immediately for their withdrawal—although based on a tactical case, and certainly not the betrayal of principles of which IS was accused by other trotskyists[32] — fuelled suspicions about IS's commitment to the struggle in the North. Certainly, after this early phase, IS's interest waned: its involvement in the various solidarity organisations, like that in VSC, was uneven, and even on a propaganda level IS often played down the issue. It is true that, particularly after the Provisionals' military methods came to dominate the struggle in the North, the possibilities of mass solidarity action diminished. No one has been able to develop a viable mass movement around Irish issues. But IS tended, in the early '70s, to see them as a diversion from the possibilities of industrial struggle, and abdicated much of its responsibility to maintain an opposition to Britain's war in the North.

IS's wider political weaknesses contributed to dissent and disillusionment among sections of the membership. But while IS continued to grow, these often appeared as isolated problems, and the oppositions which focused on them were tiny minorities. At the same time, it is important to note that the IMG, while lacking a serious approach to or experience of the industrial struggle, grew rapidly in the early 1970s largely because it developed a more principled political response to the issues of sexual politics, Ireland, etc. It grew, particularly among students, at the height of IS's "workerist" phase. In 1968, the only other far-left organisation of any size was the ultra-sectarian SLL; by 1972, the IMG was a noticeable rival to IS in some fields and localities.[33]

3. The organisation and its life

The years 1968-69 had seen a new pattern emerging in IS. It ceased to be "The International Socialism Group" and became "The International Socialists"; if not yet a party, it was no longer a mere group but a definite "organisation." For the first time IS had a weekly paper, *Socialist Worker*, which was expanded step-by-step from four pages to sixteen, between 1968 and 1972. For the first time it had a full-time staff, ludicrously small in 1968 but rapidly expanded in the following years. The new constitution, with the nationally elected political leadership, radically altered the shape of IS. Although there was no growth in membership until 1970, the year or so after 1968 saw a real consolidation of the enlarged membership and its activity. From this base, further rapid expansion took place under the Tories, to 2,351 in 1972 and 2,667 in 1973.[34] Within this membership, only a few dozen had experience from before the mid-sixties; the real core of the organisation was a couple of hundred or so activists recruited mainly in 1966-68. Many of these were, of course, ex-students; the contradictions between their experience and the demands of IS's industrial strategy, as defined by the leadership, were a critical factor in IS's development.

The "leadership" of IS, to which we have so far referred without explanation, was itself changing. Before 1968, there was no elected national leadership, but the group was informally led by Tony Cliff, whose ideas and initiatives were very much the basis of IS's success. The looseness and openness of the group had enabled its members to respond flexibly to events, and given IS's small size had posed little problem of political cohesion. Only in the two or three years of "working in the fragments" had some difficulties arisen, as fragmented activity led to some political divergences which were not always articulated.[35]

The changes of 1968 led, both formally and in practice, to a more collective leadership; not only in the National Committee of 40, which included quite diverse representatives of both the older and newer generations, but also on the Executive Committee, the sub-committee which effectively ran the group on a day-to-day basis. Although the EC was very much a working group, it included the effective political leadership. And even if Cliff was still the most important figure, he was now much more the first among equals, with other members of the older generation, particularly Duncan Hallas and Jim Higgins, playing key roles. On the EC and NC, these comrades, together with others such as Chris Harman (always a very close collaborator of Cliff), Roger Protz (editor of *Socialist Worker* from 1968 to 1974), and John Palmer, tended to provide a balanced leadership. Cliff's imagination, and his enthusiasm for a key project, together with his tendency to see matters in purely industrial rather than political terms, were often complemented and corrected by other members of the EC. This leadership was able to provide much of the positive direction the organisation needed for its decisive growth after 1968, despite the very serious weaknesses which we have noted.

The leadership was more stable than the rest of the membership of the NC, among whom many of the "late sixties" generation were replaced— sometimes rather arbitrarily—by the new industrial militants. And indeed, the organisation itself was in constant flux, mainly because its growth posed new problems all the time, but also because organisational solutions tended to be sought for political problems, at local even more than national level. A thorough-going anti-formalism was very powerful in IS, and was rooted in its rejection of "orthodox" trotskyism, with its tortuous concept of "the degenerated workers' state" and plethora of international apparatuses. (It also reflected the strong anti-authoritarianism of the student upsurge, and the rank and file rejection of bureaucratic procedures in the "official" labour movement.) The consequence, however, was not the rejection of organisational forms but a principle of constant flexibility. This belief in flexibility was strongly held by the leadership, particularly Cliff, and was to prove a useful means of controlling the membership.

The units of IS organisation were the local branches, but during the early seventies, with the growth of the industrial membership and of rank and file organisations, there was a serious attempt to construct a parallel system of industrial "Fractions". These consisted of all the members in a particular industry or union, and were generally organised on a national basis. Where, however, there were several members in a locality in the same union, industry or better still workplace, a cell would be formed within the local branch. Indeed as the branches in the larger cities often had over 50 or even 100 members by 1972-73, cell organisation became normal, even where branches divided. A cell would often consist of an industrial worker together with a few students, ex-students or white collar workers who were collaborating with him in working "around" a particular workplace or industry. Cells were rarely stable and were the focus of endless local reorganisations.

IS's rapid growth in 1971-73 was urged on by "membership campaigns", recruiting drives aimed mainly at workers, using big public meetings (Bernadette Devlin was a frequent speaker). These reflected the fear of the leadership, and particularly Cliff, that local branches led by the members recruited in the sixties and accustomed to the consolidation of the year or so after 1968, would be "conservative" in their attitude to the new generation of rank and file workers coming into the fight against the Tories. Aware of the real possibilities for growth inherent in the great industrial upheaval, Cliff's overriding worry was that the organisation would be insufficiently daring and imaginative to take advantage. In a sense he was right: but political imagination was lacking, as we have already seen, among the leadership as well as the members—indeed in his own approach. And the recruitment campaigns themselves, with the inevitable rapid turnover among new members, caused disillusionment among some of the membership who saw them as a diversion from the more serious, long-term tasks of building in the workplaces and unions. They led to what David Widgery later called the "supermarket mentality", a purely operational concept of "building the party." Those who criticised them or failed to show the necessary enthusiasm were called "conservative, backward-looking elements", and castigated for their "small-group mentality." Full-time organisers who were appointed in the major industrial areas were charged with stepping up the recruitment; many of them came on to the NC where they tended to reinforce the leadership's, and especially Cliff's, impatience. The organisers were generally ex-students, but frequently developed the worst "workerist" attitudes towards others from the same background.

It is clear in retrospect that the consolidation of the "apparatus"— the full-time leadership together with the network of local full-timers and the fast-expanding centre, based on a viable commercial printshop— posed serious dangers for IS. None of these developments were exceptional in themselves, and indeed they made big contributions to the effectiveness of IS's national intervention. But for them to play their proper part presupposed effective political control by the membership as a whole. This in turn required that the organisation, as Chris Harman had pointed out in his article on "Party and Class", should be based on a membership "willing to seriously and scientifically appraise their activity and that of the party generally."[36] This would have meant an organisation of "worker-intellectuals", trained not just scholastically but by the practice of constant debate, attempting to apply marxist analysis to problems of political practice. IS was failing, however, to create this sort of organisation. The reasons were not just the lack—which continues to this day—of any serious "formal" education in marxism, but a specific downgrading of serious political discussion.

When IS was a small propaganda group it had placed a good deal of emphasis on political ideas and discussion. In 1966-68 it had attracted to it, partly for this reason, large numbers of students (and others) who were educating themselves in marxism, both generally and through IS's ideas. In 1968 it had had the most varied political debate which, however inconclusive in some ways, was generally felt to have been a positive experience. There was, therefore, a developing tradition of internal discussion, and in the 1968 debate everyone took it for granted that this was an essential part of the life of the organisation. But five years later this tradition was somewhat soured, and it was soon to become clear that it could not be assumed.

There were certainly important specific disagreements within the leadership and the general membership of IS in this period—over wider political issues such as the attitude to Labour in the 1970 election, the Common Market, and women, as well as organisational and tactical issues such as factory branches (to which we shall return). By and large they were debated openly, with active involvement of the members. The tradition of branch resolutions, which were voted on by the NC, was strong for several years after 1968, NC and EC minutes were issued to all branches, and a more or less regular internal bulletin was maintained. But there was always a reluctance on the part of some of the leadership to commit themselves on paper to explain their ideas, the feeling being that articles in the paper for the outside world were far more important than purely internal documents. This division between public and internal discussion was in fact fairly strictly maintained—not by strict control of ideas but because part of IS's general reaction against sectarian trotskyism was the belief that workers were not interested in the often petty and obscure disagreements that occurred among revolutionaries. On occasion, however, articles reflecting the more political differences were published in *IS* journal, and this remained a constant aspiration.[37]

The general eschewing of public debate, while not seriously harmful in itself, was however indicative of a tendency to devalue discussion which was strengthening in this period. The belief was strong among many of the leadership and the local activists that the possibilities were great and the need was to "get on with the job." IS's theory, developed in the early sixties and before, was seen as a key which could now be used to open the door to the working class; there was no need to refine it further.[38] The theme was, "We've got the ideas, now let's get the worker-membership to put some flesh on them." Political discussion could easily be seen as an impediment to this task, particularly when criticism was general and wide-ranging, and where it was linked with a different theoretical tradition. This was the case with successive opposition factions, which were eventually expelled from IS. The leadership, and some of the members, complained of the "disproportionate" amount of time which was spent in discussing the differences. In the end, it was the effects of the conflicts on IS which were truly disproportionate to the significance of the particular oppositions.

There were two main factional battles before 1973. The first concerned Workers Fight, the tiny trotskyist group who had fused with IS (it was universally agreed without proper preparation). Workers Fight viewed IS as "centrist", i.e. not fully revolutionary, and therefore maintained their own organisation within it. While this gave them a generally "entrist" view of their role in IS—i.e. they saw their task as building their own group within the wider organisation—they attracted a number of members by their emphasis on a clearer political programme and criticism of the narrow "economism" of IS's industrial work.[39] There was a certain ambiguity to Workers Fight's entrism—it claimed it genuinely aimed to reform IS, and some members certainly believed in this—but the decisive factor was the series of disruptive clashes in the branches where Workers Fight existed. Pragmatic splitting of these branches in 1969 was followed by a commission in 1970, whose recommendations formally limited the rights of factions to hold private meetings and to express their disagreements publicly.[40] In 1971, after a lengthy discussion, a Special Conference was held which "dissolved the fusion" between IS and Workers Fight, asking Workers Fight supporters to choose between the two.

The second battle involved an even smaller group, who refused to declare themselves a formal faction but were labelled the "Right" faction because of their emphasis on a propaganda orientation to the Labour Party. This group was particularly concerned with theoretical and programmatic correctness, and their leading figure David Yaffe argued that Kidron's arms economy theory was unmarxist.[41] A series of debates, some of them on technical matters of marxist economics, took place in the internal bulletin in 1972-73. Again it was the apparent disruption of local activity which most concerned the leadership, and led them eventually to expel the leading members of this group.

The legacy of the Workers Fight conflict had been to greatly strengthen the suspicion among the leadership of factional opposition. The "Right faction" affair increased this still further, and seems to have created some difference among the leadership about the amount of patience which should be exercised with "marginal" critics of this kind (the "Rights" never made any serious impact on the membership). But these matters were important, not mainly because the oppositions, including another group, the "Left faction", articulated a little of the unease at IS's workerist politics, but because they coincided with a particularly crucial point in the organisation's development along this line. IS's growth in 1971-73 led the leadership to envisage a major transformation of the organisation into a small party with a significant minority audience in the working class. They looked back to the early British Communist Party as a model, and while one influential perspective was that of a new Minority Movement (a rank and file opposition based on the trade unions), they saw the need to repeat first the "bolshevisation" process which the CP had undergone in 1922-23.[42]

The main single change was the move towards the setting up of factory branches. For the leadership, this was an essential part of IS's transition to a "combat organisation", organised in the class struggle rather than in abstract geographical units. But while the early CP was "almost exclusively proletarian in character",[43] IS was not mainly composed of manual workers, let alone workers in large factories. More than 70 per cent of IS members were white-collar workers, students, unemployed, housewives, etc.[44] The proposal for factory branches was resisted on the grounds that it would split off a minority of manual workers (indeed the section of them most involved in industrial struggle) from the majority of members. The latter would be left in the sort of geographical branches IS had in the late sixties, with no direct links with industrial struggle. Secondly, there was the fear of some critics of IS's economism, that the divorce between industrial struggle and the struggle against wider aspects of oppression would be strengthened. And thirdly, those who noted the growth of the apparatus saw in the move a danger that the leadership, by direct control of the factory branches, would insulate the worker-membership from views emanating from other sections of the members.

There were indeed grounds for these fears. There can be no objection in principle to functional units based on a particular area of struggle, nor to such units playing a direct role in the internal life of a socialist organisation. But if the setting up of branches in factories or indeed in town halls, among teachers, in colleges, etc., was not to result in distortions, a number of things would have been required. There would have needed to be, first, a balanced politics, which placed the particular struggle in the context of wider political struggle; secondly a strong tradition of political discussion, which ensured that members thought about the tasks of the organisation as a whole; and thirdly concrete organisational forms which brought together manual and white-collar workers, students, etc. But in IS, in 1972-73, the first and second were increasingly being weakened, and as for the third, there was no more than lip-service. Non-industrial workers were seen by many of the leadership as having a role within the organisation which was not just different from that of workers, but inferior. Some of them, especially students and those who had been students in the late sixties, were actually suspect, as a layer of members resistant to change, and the main locus of potential opposition. The aim was partly to create a new, dynamic sector of the organisation, the factory branches, not "held back" by the rest.

Factory branches were hotly debated and in fact defeated at the 1972 Conference, and only agreed in March 1973. The perspective adopted spoke only of "at least 10 factory branches" in the following year, and an Organisation Commission was established to pursue the implications of factory branches.[45] Even among the critics of factory branches, there was no general mood of despair; among the majority there was great optimism. The National Secretary, Jim Higgins, wrote in his report that "This conference was the most serious, committed and representative gathering in the history of the group. . . a firmly based springboard for the organisation to make considerable advances in the next 12 months."[46]

IS did indeed grow in that period: to 3,310 members in 195 branches, with 368 of them in 38 factory branches, before the September 1974 Conference.[47] But it was to be the last period of growth until 1977; indeed within four months of the 1973 Conference came the first signs of a crisis which was to tear IS apart. The hectic pace of IS's growth and the impatience of some of the leadership to consolidate a "workers' organisation", free from factional opposition, led in August to what can only be described as a *coup* in the Executive Committee. Cliff's mistrust of "conservative elements" finally caught up with his colleagues in the leadership itself. Arguing that they did not understand the mood of the workers in the factories, he persuaded the National Committee to replace almost all the existing members of the EC with a number of provincial organisers. In one fell swoop, out went Higgins, Protz, Palmer, Hallas—even Nigel Harris—all those who had provided some sort of balance in the leadership. Only Harman remained, with Cliff, and to them were added several comrades based in the North and Midlands, some of them good local organisers, but none of them of national political standing in IS. One of these, Dave Peers, was for the next year the National Secretary; but the most significant addition was that of Jim Nichol, the National Treasurer, who had built up the printshop and IS's finances.

The first noticeable result of this change was that the Internal Bulletin failed to appear for more than six months—which with a previous decision to stop issuing EC and NC minutes, on security grounds, meant that information and discussion on a national scale more or less dried up. Thus for the first time, democracy became an issue for a large section of the membership—a situation exacerbated in some localities, such as Liverpool and Hull, where local organisers created extremely centralist organisations. The new leadership itself, although known as the "leading areas" EC because the provincial members were supposed to represent the experience of major growth areas, was extremely centralised. Cliff was the only source of political initiative left, while organisationally the provincial members could obviously have little day-to-day influence. Peers as National Secretary was new to the centre, and the most important role devolved to Nichol, who before long took over the secretary's post himself.

This ultra-centralised EC was of course responsible to an NC which still included all those who had been pushed out of the leadership. Very soon, its failings and inefficiencies were to require some modifications. But the locus of power had shifted decisively from the collective leadership of the previous five years, to a new and politically unstable axis centred on Cliff and Nichol. Some of the "old guard" were to fight back, but unsuccessfully: the struggle only hastened the consolidation of a much more centralised and undemocratic regime.

III. POLITICAL CRISIS AND CRISIS OF IS, 1974-76

As IS's official historian has noted, while IS was debating factory branches, "events were moving quickly in the world outside also."[48] In fact the struggle against the Heath Government was coming to its climax, the second official miners' strike. It was also, of course, a turning point in the history of the post-war capitalist economy, as the oil crisis precipitated the first world-wide recession for 45 years.

IS's strategy was predicated on a continuation, indeed a further escalation, of the industrial struggle of the previous five years. It argued, correctly, that while there was unlikely to be a catastrophic slump as in 1929, capitalism—especially British capitalism—had no way out of the pattern of deepening recessions and mounting inflation. It argued, too, that the British working class was undefeated (indeed in 1974 it was victorious), and that despite the more serious challenges facing it in the mid-seventies there was unlikely to be a decisive defeat such as that suffered in 1926. The conclusion was, therefore, that there would be more, and bigger, and more political struggles in the coming years.

This assumption was, we can say with the benefit of five years hindsight, fundamentally wrong. True, capitalism has by no means found its way out of its long-term difficulties: the reduction in inflation rates has been no more than would be expected in a cyclical pattern, and unemployment has hardly diminished at all. The working class has not, moreover, suffered historic defeats. But the mass struggles of 1969-74 are a thing of the past. Clearly there has been a whole period of a different character, in which factors to which IS gave little weight have played—for the time being—the decisive part.

As we have seen, there has been a consistent tendency for IS to see politics purely in terms of industrial struggle. And of course it is true that nowhere has the economic class struggle, and the role of workers and trade unions, been of such central political importance as in Britain in the last fifteen years. But IS has failed to understand the impact of politics on industrial struggle itself. In 1970 it tended to underestimate the effect of the Tory victory in escalating the struggle; in 1974 it underestimated the effect of Labour's success in dampening it down.[49] When the new battles failed to appear, it was conceded that the perspective had been "telescoped", but this excuse eventually appeared lame. It is not just that IS underestimated Labour's traditional base, as some trotskyist critics maintain, but that it failed to see how the period of "confrontation" would itself have major political effects.

Throughout much of Europe, the upsurge of student and industrial unrest in the late 1960s and early 1970s has been followed, as the economic crisis has developed, by the consolidation of new reformist politics. The changed expectations, the costs of industrial conflict and the experience of inflation have all had permanent effects on people's attitudes. In countries such as Italy, France and Spain they appear to have produced a fairly radical rise in the position of one or other of the reformist parties— Communist or social-democratic. In Britain, Labour's governmental role has ruled out any such development of left social democracy, while the Communist party has been too weak to offer a focus. The political and ideological changes have therefore been less radical and more diffuse—on the one hand, the "historic compromise" of the trade union leaders with the Labour Government, on the other, the electoral fragmentation which has produced the Nationalists, the Liberal revival of '74, even the National Front's modest but menacing growth. And the underlying pattern has been an ideological swing to the right, with effects not just in the Tory party, but among Labour politicians (both right and left) and the union leadership.

IS's strategy remained formally the same throughout this period: to proceed towards the foundation of a new revolutionary socialist party and rank and file movement. In defiance of the more difficult circumstances in which it found itself, it proclaimed a policy of "steering left" and sticking to its goals. But what this meant, in the new circumstances, was that the distortions and dangers of the previous period were to be exaggerated until the organisation and its goals were radically deformed.

1. *The rank and file movement and the revolutionary party*

By 1973 IS had developed a number of viable rank and file movements, particularly in white collar unions, and had won a small but significant number of bases among manual workers, although these were not generally converted into functioning rank and file bodies. It had long been the intention of the organisation to build these at some stage into a national movement, across industries and unions, which would function as an opposition within the trade union movement as a whole, as the Communist Party's Minority Movement had in the 1920s. Of course, the situation was not quite so simple as that which had faced the early CP, since the modern Communist Party itself possessed a superior base, particularly in major manual workers unions such as the AUEW, EEPTU and TGWU, and in key industrial centres such as Glasgow and Sheffield. What is more, there was a left current in many of these unions, the Broad Left, which was centred on the CP; and the CP possessed a national body, the Liaison Committee for the Defence of Trade Unions, which had played a leading role in mobilising protest strikes against "In Place of Strife" and the Industrial Relations Act. IS had always realistically acknowledged these strengths and appreciated they would not simply disappear.

In the early seventies, however, there were good reasons for noting an improvement in the balance of industrial forces between IS and the CP. In some major white-collar unions, such as the NUT and NALGO, IS had won the leadership of the left, and industrially it had begun to provide some effective competition. More generally, the CP's conflict of loyalties between the rank and file and the left-wing union leaders (such as Jones and Scanlon) seemed to be causing it increasing problems. The Liaison Committee was ceasing to act as an effective focus, and the support mustered by IS and other leftists at its conferences was causing its CP leaders to resort to heavy-handed measures to keep control. Towards the end of 1973, the time seemed ripe to attempt to start an alternative focus for trade union militants. It was decided to organise the first National Rank and File Conference, sponsored by the various rank and file papers, in March 1974.

Although this conference, and the second held later in the year, each attracted around 500 delegates from around 300 sponsoring bodies (mainly union branches, but with some shop stewards committees), a viable movement was not created. Obviously, the early downfall of the Heath government brought about a change in the tempo of class struggle which could hardly have been predicted. But at the same time, the conferences were essentially composed of IS members and their periphery, rather than representative of the militant left-wing of the trade union movement in general. They indicated IS's real and growing influence, but also the still very modest nature of its strength, especially in the manual unions. A determined effort would have been required, to reach out to militants generally, and those influenced by other sections of the left in particular. An exaggerated emphasis on the rank and file movement's independence of IS, and encouragement of others to take their responsibility for it, was needed. In fact, the National Rank and File Organising Committee was established, and quickly became an all-IS body, with hardly any existence independent of IS's Industrial Department. Its initiatives, some of them deliberately modest ones such as support for the families of the imprisoned Shrewsbury pickets, and for Chilean refugees, came effectively from the IS centre. Its real base was quickly reduced to IS itself, and its existence served less to widen support for the individual rank and file movements, than to *narrow* it by placing them much more under central IS control. This was particularly true when in 1975-76 the NR and FOC ran out of steam and was liquidated into the Right to Work Campaign. All the rank and file papers were expected to tie in with the central campaign: indeed for a while some of them appeared to be exclusively concerned with "the right to work." The idea that a rank and file grouping involved a wide layer of trade unionists willing to fight for more militant and socialist policies in their particular union, democratically deciding their own policies, was quickly being lost. Many of the rank and file groups became, and were seen as, little more than extensions of IS, controlled centrally by it. Even the first and strongest, Rank and File Teacher, was the victim of manipulative control by IS; many members of other left-wing groups and independent radicals pulled out and formed a new group, the Socialist Teachers Alliance, which by 1977 clearly possessed a wider base of support in the union.[50]

This decline in support was put down to "the period", which itself was seen as a temporary lull. The period certainly had something to do with it: it was a time when patient, united work might have established a minority in the unions politically opposed to the wage-cutting of the "social contract", but IS now had little time for that. Indeed the rank and file movement itself ceased to be the main preoccupation of the IS leadership, for the launching of IS as the new "revolutionary party" began to be mooted as a short-term aim. The aim of creating a new party had, of course, been a constant one for IS since 1968, and realistically so since a small minority current in the working class, to the left of the Labour Party, was definitely developing. In addition, the aspiration to unity of the far left, repeated unsuccessfully for several years after 1968, had been dropped in 1972. IS had regarded itself as the nucleus of a party, and its own growth as the main means for creating one. But it had always been assumed that a qualitative breakthrough in working-class influence would be necessary; the organisation would need to grow strong roots.

The situation in which "the party" became an immediate issue was in fact one of a downturn in IS's fortunes, not one of major advance. Between 1974 and 1976 membership fell, the factory branches collapsed and the rank and file papers and movement were in many cases reduced to IS rumps. For a considerable period, IS conducted very little activity or propaganda under its own banner, or indeed that of the National Rank and File Movement: everything became the Right to Work Campaign. This campaign was in some ways an imaginative and useful venture: it was for a time virtually the only public protest at the monstrous rise in unemployment, and the only nationally based movement to organise the unemployed. Had it been launched on a wider basis, with a stronger orientation to organised workers, it could have been more successful, with more positive results for IS. As it was, the campaign was narrowly controlled and served mainly as a means of recruiting unemployed youth to the organisation. The effect on IS was to turn it away from serious ongoing work in the trade unions—and the women's and student movements—and from wider political campaigning against the policies of the Labour Government. IS had become a single-issue campaign, but it was clear that once this tactic produced any number of recruits, the real aim of declaring a "revolutionary party" would surface.

The first attempt to float the "Socialist Workers Party"—the name was presented from the start as a *fait accompli,* never put up for discussion by the membership—came at the end of 1975. In a flush of optimism for the Right to Work Campaign, the leadership—still recognising that an IS of fewer than 3,000 members was hardly sufficient for the "revolutionary party"—proposed a massive recruitment of "Socialist Worker supporters." The argument was that a larger number of workers read *Socialist Worker* than were members of IS, and would therefore take out SW cards but not IS ones. These readers were also more working-class than the actual membership, and so would prove the sound basis for the new revolutionary party—the theory of "the conservatism of the membership" was once again rearing its head. The next stage, therefore, would be to merge IS and the SW Supporters into the "SWP."

There was, however, no radical politicisation in this period, and the recruits of unemployed youth did not offset the losses of trade unionists, both manual and white-collar. The "SW Supporters" simply did not materialise, and by the time the 1976 Conference met, six months later, the aim of establishing the SWP was not even in the leadership's perspectives. But by this time, a new issue was rearing its head: racism and the growth of the National Front. IS took to the streets against the Front, and issued a stream of anti-racist propaganda. As the furore over immigration increased in the summer, IS leafleted on a massive scale with the slogan "They're welcome here." The issue was a godsend, since the media (and the membership) were tiring of repeated long-distance marches for the Right to Work.[51] IS's propaganda was undoubtedly effective, enabling some inroads to be made with Asian youth, and even the membership started to rise for the first time since 1974. One feature of the anti-racist campaign, moreover, was a series of campaigns in by-elections against the National Front. The leadership then decided that these negative election campaigns needed to be turned into positive campaigns with Socialist Worker candidates; in this context the "SWP" idea was resurrected. Without a real discussion, without even a founding conference, the Socialist Workers Party was born on 1st January 1977.

2. *"Workerism" and the politics of IS*
   In describing above IS's politics between 1968 and 1973, the term "workerism" was frequently used to describe the leadership's almost exclusive preoccupation with the economic struggles of male manual workers in industry, and its tendency to interpret all other issues in terms of them. This workerism did, however, proceed from a realistic appraisal of the isolation of the revolutionary left from the mass of the manual working class, and a sense of the possibilities in that period of intense industrial struggle. It enabled IS to make major advances—to achieve by far the most serious growth of a revolutionary organisation in the working class since the 1920s. At the same time, it was a major factor which fostered a gap between the leadership, who assumed a special knowledge of workers born of long experience, and the "cadre" of ex-students from the late 1960s. It also helped to undermine the level of politics and discussion in the organisation. In these ways it assisted the degeneration of IS's internal life, and prepared the way for the opportunistic, unrealistic and sectarian politics which IS was to adopt in the new political period which opened in 1974.
   IS's workerism was double-edged: so, therefore, was the development beyond it which occurred from 1973, and particularly from 1975, onwards. Certainly, there were signs of a real recognition of the one-sidedness of IS's politics, and the harm this had done to the organisation's development outside the traditional industries. It began to be seen that, as Birchall tactfully puts it, there had been "an over-emphasis on certain turns."[52] The first sign of this came in 1973-74, when it was realised that the "factory gate" approach was badly affecting IS's intervention in the student movement. A new policy was adopted which gave much more

emphasis to the students' work inside the colleges, and led to the setting up of the National Organisation of International Socialist Societies. But there were still signs of heavy-handed workerism, for example in early 1975 when the Rank and File organisation rejected delegates for a conference of women trade unionists because they came from white-collar union branches! And 1973-75 was the period in which the IS gay group was suppressed.[53]

The most marked movement beyond a narrow workerist approach came after the 1975 Conference, which also marked the turning point in the consolidation of a highly undemocratic internal regime, as described below. There were, of course, good political reasons why crude workerism was no longer viable. For example, racism was becoming an increasingly serious issue, requiring a general political and ideological response, and some black workers were being drawn into activity on a political rather than trade union basis. Similarly, abortion rather than equal pay was becoming the major issue among women; if IS had stuck to its economistic approach, and refused to recognise the wider, non-industrial aspects of women's oppression, it would have been woefully irrelevant to many women. The wider political and ideological crisis which was unfolding under Labour was catching up with IS. But at the same time, in its determination to "build the party", IS was abandoning its emphasis on serious, long-term work at shop-floor and union level. The loss of this valid, indeed vital aspect of IS's "workerism" was the other reason for the wider political stance which IS was adopting.

It was the "build-the-party" approach which determined the application of IS's politics in practice. IS's anti-racist work was very much a propaganda drive aimed at recruitment, and this method applied to black workers led to the rapid exit of the "Black caucus" shortly after it was formed in 1976.[54] IS's support for the National Abortion Campaign was grudging and highly conditional, bringing it into immediate conflict with the majority of the activists, and accompanied by a constant tendency to call demonstrations in opposition to NAC whenever a disagreement on tactics arose. In short, IS showed little concern to build a united anti-racist movement, or to support meaningful black organisations in the localities; let alone to support the women's movement as a whole, or even to unite the socialist feminists within it. IS's work was aimed at recruitment, building the black membership, and building groups around "Women's Voice", its women's paper. Just as with the Right to Work Campaign, the main emphasis was not on building a united movement, and trying to win that movement to IS's distinctive politics, but on counterposing IS and its fronts *organisationally* to the rest of the movement.

IS had indeed ceased to be clearly identified with a distinctive politics. True, it had never had a formal programme, but in the sixties it had developed a coherent analysis of the situation, and as we have seen its practice was partly at least an attempt to influence working-class struggle as a whole in line with its understanding. Even in the early seventies, the rank and file movements were not seen as party fronts, but ways in which militants could be grouped together and the struggle advanced. And despite the workerism of that period, there had been an attempt to draft a political programme for IS (quietly abandoned after 1974).[55] But in the mid-seventies, IS's politics became a function of its particular tactics for recruitment; in 1975-76 IS was content to be identified simply with the "right to work", in 1976-77 with militant anti-racism. The changes of political profile were swift and sharp: the only continuity was the theme of "the party."

The paradoxical relationship between IS's workerism in the early seventies, and the sectarian "party-building" of the later period, undoubtedly confused many IS members who, like the present writer, came to criticise both. Certainly, there was no good reason why a revolutionary socialist organisation should not combine a serious, sustained approach to workers in the factories and the trade union movement, with a principled politics which fights against all forms of oppression. It was a question of general politics, of understanding that socialism is about more than economics, together with the way in which economic, cultural, ideological and political factors are inter-related in the current crisis. It was also a matter of particular analysis, of understanding the real weakness of the far left in the working class, the situation which was developing after 1974, and the need to build up a socialist movement by creating united opposition—within the trade union movement, and other movements such as those of women, black people. But neither of these points were widely grasped in IS in the mid-1970s. In the conflict which developed, opposition to the "party-building" of the new leadership was mainly based on the workerist politics which had played such a contradictory role in the previous period.

3. Internal democracy and the consolidation of the "party"

The "coup" of July 1973 was only the first step in remodelling the leadership of IS so that it would step up the pace of change in the organisation. As we have already noted, the new EC had to contend with an NC which included most of the former leadership. What is more, many of them still occupied crucial posts in the organisation. In particular, Roger Protz was still editor of *Socialist Worker,* which he had built up from a circulation of a few thousands in 1968 to one of 30,000 in 1974 (with a peak of around 50,000 during the miners' strike of that year). *Socialist Worker* was undoubtedly one of the big successes of IS—a popular socialist paper with a genuine audience among rank and file trade unionists, built with the dedicated efforts of a few professional journalists and thousands of IS members and other supporters who sent in local reports as well as selling the paper. Its circulation was twice that of *Tribune,* and roughly equal to the British daily circulation of the *Morning Star* (although *SW* was only a weekly, it lacked the national commercial distribution of the *Star*). Whatever criticisms might be made of the paper, it had real achievements to its credit (and indeed its 1974 circulation has not been surpassed). It had been largely through *SW* that IS had extended its influence over the previous few years.

There was not, so far as we can know, a plan to drastically change the paper and its editorial team, once the new EC had taken over. It was rather the logic of Cliff's belief that the leadership and cadre of IS were too "conservative" to reach out to new layers of workers, which led him next to challenge the paper's editor and its approach. Indeed it was the failure of the EC change—both its inefficiency, due to the removal of key people and their replacement by provincial members who could not play an active role, and the suspicions it aroused among many of the experienced members—which led to this further step. Cliff enlisted the support of Paul Foot, who was the paper's other mainstay (with Protz), to argue that the paper was not a "workers' paper"—it was not written *by* workers. It should include more short articles by workers about their experiences. The assumption was that there was an emerging mass audience for *SW,* beyond the "advanced militants", which the paper was not reaching.

The brief debate which ensued in April 1974 brought out the basic differences which were to divide IS in the next two years. On the one hand, Cliff, who was already writing his study of Lenin, saw IS reaching out to the mass of workers in the factories, and the paper as directly reflecting their daily lives, as Lenin's *Pravda* had tried to do.[56] In his view, and that of his supporters, the decline of the mass reformist party created an opportunity for direct mass influence, and the growth of IS made it poised to achieve this. On the other hand, Roger Protz, and his supporters who included Hallas, Higgins, and Palmer, while not disputing the *relative* decline of reformism and growth of opportunities for IS, did not believe that there was yet a serious mass audience. IS's roots and size were still too weak to enable it to generally influence more than the advanced activists. The mass of workers still supported Labour, and the election of the Labour Government would require a serious political critique to be explained in *Socialist Worker.*[57]

Protz clearly believed that only a modest effort to increase direct workers' involvement in the paper could be made, and that political analysis and features written by "professional journalists" were essential. The real danger was not a "workers' diary", but was indicated in the resolution he proposed. "Any attempt to dilute the politics of the paper, over-simplify arguments and shift the balance of the paper to exposure journalism and over-kill picture display could seriously damage the paper's relationship with [the] key section of the readers", the "politically more advanced sections of workers."[58] This statement was highly prophetic, as *SW* in future was not noted for its workers' contributions, but for its often shrill and sensational journalism, combined with a crude politics. Over the next few years, it was an adjunct to IS's campaigning over the Right to Work and similar issues, rather than a serious "political weekly", as Hallas described it in 1974.[59]

Of course, no one at the time, not even the most cautious, foresaw the extent of the downturn in industrial struggle after 1974, and the decisiveness of the change of period. Set against the advances of the previous few years, Cliff's "two-year perspective of building circulation to 70-80,000"[60] did not seem quite so unrealistic as it does in hindsight. But there is no doubt, in retrospect, who had the surer understanding of the balance of forces in the labour movement, and the problem of the strength of reformism which had to be confronted. And there can be no doubt, too, that IS would have been better to have built surely on the foundations which had been constructed over the previous five years, than to risk them in a pursuit of "change" against the odds of political reality. The costs of this course over the next few years were very great.

The decision on the paper had been taken, as Duncan Hallas and Chris Davison wrote in a critical appraisal, "after a single discussion on the NC without the membership as a whole even knowing about it."[61] The decision was forced through against the wishes of the editor, who in consequence was asked to resign. Jim Higgins, who had moved to *SW* after being replaced as National Secretary, was also sacked. This sudden removal of two long-standing leaders produced "more than 80 resolutions from branches. . . the majority of which expressed concern over the way the dispute had been handled without consultation with the membership."[62] The Industrial Organiser, Andreas Nagliatti, resigned, and Hallas sharply attacked the way decisions were being made. In proposing a series of changes to strengthen democratic decision-making, he insisted that "At the heart of this is the question of democratic centralism. Why are we not in favour of five people running the organisation? Because the whole tradition and experience shows the organisation cannot lead unless it has healthy internal life and there is debate on issues and feedback from that debate."[63] The EC was censured and a new election took place in which Hallas was restored to the leadership.

The effect of this upheaval appeared to be a restoration of internal democracy and a more balanced leadership. An organisation commission was established which was to look into all the problems of organisation which had emerged in the functioning of local and factory branches as well as at a national level. The 1974 Conference, postponed from the late spring until September, finally took place amid a continuing reaction to the arbitrary actions of the EC over the paper. Seven members of the NC, including Higgins and Palmer, produced a critical document for it around a number of issues raised by the dispute. They argued that IS was still a small organisation, which would grow by consistent work rather than "gimmicks and sensations"; that the rank and file movement should grow in the localities, not through central campaigns; that the mass audience of raw young workers was a myth; that the building of white-collar and student branches was a "diversion" from work among manual workers; and that a balanced leadership was necessary, in which "Cliff's great abilities" would be incorporated and "his excesses" disciplined.[64] These ideas had a considerable impact, but Palmer (narrowly) and Higgins failed to get re-elected to the NC (there was no provision now for minorities to be represented, and in any case they had not yet formed a faction). The new leadership was confirmed, and most important of all, the main issues, which centred around problems of organisation, were postponed to the 1975 Conference with the NC given power to take interim decisions.

Events in the next nine months showed that any new "stability" was illusory. The difference of perspectives for rank and file work came to a head in a crucial area, in the AUEW in Birmingham, where IS had its strongest base of engineering workers (who included a number of experienced shop stewards and convenors), organised in several factory branches. The engineering union was not like, say, the teachers' union, where all issues were concentrated in the union branch and it was easy to translate grass-roots support into support in union elections. On the one hand, IS members were heavily involved in some shop stewards' committees. combine committees and industry-based rank and file papers (such as "The Carworker"), but not on a scale to create a real national presence in the union as a whole. On the other, members in Birmingham had worked consistently in the Broad Left electoral organisation and gained some influence there. This had been national policy, but only in Birmingham had IS gained enough strength to make some impact with it. This was one of the problems; indeed in order to give coherence to their scattered AUEW membership the IS leadership proposed to set up their own election organisation, called the "Engineers Charter", to stand an IS member for a National Organiser's post. The pretext was the fact that the Broad Left was beginning to lose ground in AUEW elections, which IS interpreted as creating an opening on the left. (In fact, the ground was being lost mainly to the right, and this swing has culminated in 1978 in the election of a right-wing president to succeed Hugh Scanlon). The Birmingham IS members were not convinced of the reasons for independent candidates, and refused to give up their positions in the Broad Left, which brought them into head-on conflict with the leadership throughout 1975.

The Birmingham engineering workers now became one of the main bulwarks of an opposition led by former EC members such as Higgins and Palmer. The points which had been argued in 1974 were expanded into a fuller "Platform of the IS Opposition." The extreme workerism of the earlier position—the exclusive emphasis on manual workers, and the omission of any reference to women—was moderated. Indeed some of the growing dissatisfaction among IS women, who had been fighting a long battle with the EC for regular publication of *Women's Voice,* was reflected in the platform which called for IS not only to campaign for women's right to work, but also to reject the "narrow perspective that sees women only as workers" and to engage in "non-industrial work." The main points were, however, internal democracy, the independence of the rank and file movement, and a more coherent political approach to the Labour Government, reflected in *SW*.[65]

The issue of internal democracy now came squarely to a head. Indeed, the Organisation Commission report drastically shifted the ground of that discussion, by proposing fundamental changes in the national leadership, local organisation and conference. The NC of 40 was to be replaced as the authoritative body between conferences by a small Central Committee (the old EC) of nine members. There was to be a purely advisory National Council, held infrequently, to which districts would send representatives. The district, made up of a number of branches, was to be the main unit of local organisation. Finally, a conference was to be based on delegates from districts, not branches, with one delegate per thirty instead of one per fifteen, and observers were no longer to be allowed. Most crucial of all, the proposals on districts and conference delegates were to be given *immediate* effect. That is to say, branches were to be amalgamated into districts for the purpose of electing delegates to the 1975 conference. This decision was only taken, by a narrow majority, at an NC meeting in March, barely two months before the Conference, and after the formation of the IS Opposition.

District organisation in itself was not opposed, indeed it was widely accepted that some such organisation was necessary to overcome the distortions likely to arise from the isolation of factory branches from other branches in an area. But some 89 per cent of IS members were not in factory branches,[66] and a large proportion of these were in branches relatively isolated from other areas. To create "districts" everywhere in a couple of months was not only artificial, but amounted in the circumstances to gerrymandering. In a number of areas, branches supporting the ISO and the Left Faction (another opposition group) were combined with other branches to prevent opposition representation. The new 1:30 ratio for delegates was also part of the manoeuvre, and unjustified by any increase in the membership (which was stagnant), since it prevented representation of minority positions in many "districts" which had now only one delegate. By these means, a very large minority, supported probably by at least a third to two-fifths of the membership, was reduced to barely 15 per cent of the delegates. At the same time, a scare was created about "security" which was used to justify excluding all but the 100 delegates (and the full-timers) from the conference. In this atmosphere, the full-time Central Committee was not only approved by conference, but reduced to six members so as to provide an even "stronger" leadership. And at the last minute, a "closed slate" system of election was introduced, which prevented Conference from varying the composition of the CC. Only one slate was proposed.

The 1975 Conference was undoubtedly a turning point for IS. Faced with a strong political challenge, the leadership had changed the rules and made itself into a self-perpetuating, exclusive and virtually monolithic body, whose discussions were not even reported in any detail to the membership. From now on major decisions, such as the launching of the Right to Work Campaign later in 1975 or the move to the "SWP" in 1976, were received by the membership as *faits accomplis*. Discussion took place in the Council, and later in the branches, on implementation of policy, but not generally on policies themselves before they were decided. After 1975 the leadership was, as one long-standing member described it, "unassailable."[67] It was simply not conceivable that the membership could change it in any way, and any alterations would have to come from the top.

By the end of 1975, the CC was moving to force its defeated opponents out of the organisation. First to go, victim of a rule which banned factions from continuing after conference decisions, was the small "Left Faction." Then a number of the Birmingham engineering workers, who refused to accept the decision to stand against the Broad Left in the AUEW, were also expelled. Finally, the steering committee of the IS Opposition were expelled under the same provision against "permanent" factions. The Opposition had decided to re-form after the conference, both to defend their supporters against disciplinary action and to campaign against the turning of IS into the Right to Work Campaign and the proposal to proclaim the "party." Neither of these policies had even been mooted at the conference, and the ban on opposition to them showed the danger of the rule against "permanent" factions which derived from the battles of the early seventies. These policies, as we have noted, took IS further away from a serious and realistic appraisal of the situation in the working class. Without the possibility of effective opposition to them, only outside pressures could change IS's direction.

These pressures were real enough, but for the time being they had little effect on the leadership. As we have noted, the massive increases in IS membership and *SW* circulation proved to be figments of Cliff's imagination; indeed IS's industrial influence was waning. In this situation, with only small, short-term campaigning gains to point to, the CC decided in late 1976 to declare IS with its 3,000 or so members to be "the revolutionary party", the SWP. There was no protest except from isolated individuals.[68] A "Faction for Revolutionary Democracy" had come and gone earlier in the year, its general half-heartedness well summed up by one supporter who explained that with the leadership unassailable, "Whether I or anyone else wants to challenge them at the moment is irrelevant."[69]

CONCLUSION

The degeneration of IS represents, to a considerable extent, a squandering of the potential for a new socialist movement in the generation of students and workers drawn into the upheavals of the late sixties and early seventies. It is precisely because IS achieved real success in mobilising this potential at the time, that its subsequent failures are of such concern. And for the same reason we must reject the explanation that if IS had had some other ready-made politics—be it more "Leninist" or less, more "Trotskyist" or less, or whatever—it would have avoided all these problems. There were other socialist currents: the well established Communist Party, which stagnated throughout this period; and many other small groups, none of which were as successful as IS in breaking out of the sectarian milieu. These alternative standpoints may be able to offer some useful insights into "what went wrong", but none of them can be accepted as a simple "package."

The basic causes were nevertheless political, as I have tried to show. At the most general level of theory and politics, IS's leaders devalued a consistent political response to all forms of oppression, in favour of a one-dimensional "fundamentalist" stress on economic class struggle.[70] More specifically, there were two major features to IS's failure. On the one hand, IS failed to get to grips with some of the "new" features of the situation—the "lessons of May", the women's movement and sexual politics, the changing nature of the working class. On the other hand, there was the fatal underestimate of that very "old" obstacle, the strength of reformist ideas and organisations, and indeed its renewed influence on organised workers as a result of the crisis. It was one thing to know that there was a tendency for Labourism to decline, quite another to understand how and at what pace it would do so.

The most critical of all the political failures, perhaps, was the failure to understand and create the sort of socialist organisation which was required. Formally, IS's critique of stalinism was the most thorough-going of any socialist group's, and IS's break with "orthodox" trotskyism had been over the latter's compromise with stalinism.[71] Throughout the 1950s and 1960s, there had been the object-lesson of the SLL to remind IS of the need for consistent internal democracy and the avoidance of regular expulsions in the building of a socialist organisation. But the looseness of organisation, which was IS's response, proved inadequate to the demands of an enlarged grouping with wider political interventions. There was a period after 1968 in which IS might have consolidated serious democratic organisational forms, and some interesting articles were written on the general theory of the party.[72] Among all the reasons why this did not happen which we have indicated, the leadership of Tony Cliff and his theory of "Leninism" is obviously a crucial factor.

Political criticism on the left is often unnecessarily personal, but there is also a reaction against this which underestimates individuals' roles in favour of abstract political analysis. In the case of IS, it is impossible to ignore the role of Cliff, the acknowledged leader since the foundation of Socialist Review. As the one critical attempt to appraise his influence noted,

> "Cliff has great and probably indispensable strengths, a generosity of his time and considerable talents without any thought of personal reward. The theoretical development of the group is almost entirely his work. Most, but not all, major developments in the group have been the result of his intuition and experience."[73]

But as we have seen, the major turns in IS in the mid-seventies were also very much his work, and their effect was to consolidate him as the indisputable centre of initiative. Not only were most of IS's political weaknesses which we have noted Cliff's weaknesses, but the conception of organisation and leadership was particularly his responsibility.

Since Cliff rediscovered Lenin and the revolutionary party in 1968, he has devoted a good deal of his time to a mammoth biography of Lenin.[74] Critics have noted that he has defined Lenin's political life in terms not of a particular politics, but of a certain gift of understanding the working class and its struggle. Lenin's supreme characteristic in Cliff's eyes was his ability to "bend the stick", to alter course rapidly according to changes in class consciousness. It is this method which Cliff has claimed as his own.[75] His identification with Lenin as leader, rather than with his politics, has been part-motive and part-justification for the catastrophic changes which he initiated in IS in the mid-seventies. It is an identification which is dangerous in principle, not only because Britain in the 1970s is not Russia in the early 1900s, but also because all the experience of the socialist movement since 1917 should have made us all aware of the need for collective responsible leadership and scrupulous observance of socialist democracy within our movement. And of course it is also dangerous in practice since Cliff is no Lenin, and his undoubted talents "are accompanied by a number of less desirable traits."[76]

The process of "intuition", which Peter Sedgwick has noted "is, at its worst, impressionism mingled with emotion,"[77] has marked IS's leadership off very clearly from that of most other trotskyist sects. There is no absolute political dogma, although Cliff tends to draw directly on the Russian Revolution for historical analogy. There is no terrible demonology of revisionists and betrayers, although particular critics have frequently suffered fierce condemnation. There is no general withdrawal from work with other sections of the left, although principled cooperation is frequently refused for more specific opportunist reasons. In all these ways, although it is tempting to compare IS's degeneration to that of the SLL, it fails to conform to the traditional model of the trotskyist sect. The "party" which is left is much more flexible; indeed the growth and well-being of "the party" itself, rather than any fixed ideological position, is the constant principle of the organisation.

The SWP is in fact much more sensibly compared to the CP at various times in its history than to the modern WRP (successor of the SLL). Ideologically, of course, it is still anti-stalinist and revolutionary socialist, but there is a close resemblance to stalinism in the way "the party" itself has become the central ideological reference point for all work. Politically, there is a similarity in the way the SWP works in wider movements—its participation in united campaigns ranging from full participation, through nominal and grudging involvement, to sectarian withdrawal, according to the gains to be made—and its own fronts, where control varies from the very tight to the minimal according to the balance of forces. But it is in organisational terms that the similarities—with the CP today rather than in its classically stalinist days—are the most striking. Central political control, affecting the decisive areas of work, is firmly entrenched in the hands of the small Central Committee. But greater licence is being allowed to members working in less "central" fields—to the women, and now to the intellectuals—although the amount of freedom allowed can naturally be curtailed. This particular combination of organisational hardness and flexibility, together with the political flexibility which is now the SWP's hallmark, seem now to be enabling the organisation to consolidate again its small minority position on the left.

The SWP lacks, of course, the sort of fixed certainties which stalinism gave to British Communism between the thirties and the fifties. There were no world-historic events, like the Hungarian revolution, to precipitate the departure of most of its established membership. If the tragedy of 1956 has been repeated, it has been as pathos—and occasionally as farce. The main IS Opposition group formed, on leaving, a small "anti-sect", the Workers League, whose members have concentrated on deliberately modest, small-scale, work in industry and the community. Although it expected to quickly double its original 150 membership with further refugees from the SWP, it failed to project itself as a political alternative and in fact recruited very few. Its leaders were initially committed to the "workerist" politics of IS in the early '70s, although very slowly as their membership declined a re-valuation of some key questions began to take place.[78] Very many more IS members left as individuals, rather than with the ISO. Among the intellectuals, there were a number who were critical of the organisation's degeneration, but it was here perhaps that there entered an element of farce: there was no concerted protest, and a number left as individuals while others made their peace with the leadership.[79]

The main effects of IS's crisis have, in fact, been to assist the growth of other political currents. The Communist Party has recovered a good deal of the ground among students and intellectuals which it lost in the late 1960s; indeed its "Communist University" and other forums have acted as pace-setters for the far left.[80] The International Marxist Group, which grew mainly among students in the early 1970s, has emerged as the main alternative to the SWP on the revolutionary left, around which other groups such as Big Flame and Workers League have eventually been attracted. This sort of alliance has had significant effects among students, where the Socialist Students Alliance has become the main alternative to the Broad Left leadership, as well as in white collar unions such as the NUT. The IMG and Big Flame have also initiated the Socialist Unity campaign to create a united revolutionary socialist intervention in elections: the first time a significant electoral strategy has been developed by any of the British far left. The SWP have refused to date to join Socialist Unity, preferring to run their own candidates because they see the main aim as direct recruitment of members. Socialist Unity's candidates have had some very modest successes, beating the National Front and (on the left) the Communist Party fairly consistently in a number of local elections.[81] They have also polled more votes than the SWP in every case, but the division has been damaging and the far left has lost a number of opportunities to develop a united presence as a small but serious minority force.

The revolutionary left in 1978 has lost much of the momentum which it possessed before 1974,[82] and there is a slowly growing recognition of the opportunities which have been lost due to our own political immaturity and often senseless divisions. The disorientation which the IS experience has produced among many socialist activists is still far from overcome, but there are some signs of change. Within the SWP, the leadership itself is belatedly recognising that some of the triumphal "we are the party" propaganda has been counter-productive, and has made a "turn" towards "left unity." There is little sign of a real self-criticism, but the change of mood is indicative.[83] Elsewhere on the far left, tentative moves towards a new united organisation are under way.[84] It is undoubtedly the case that a serious core of the far left has survived. Partly because of the weakness of the other sections of the left, the Labour left and the Communist Party, we have a role in British working-class politics that probably exceeds our small numbers. Capitalism has not solved its problems, any more than we have solved ours. There is a long struggle ahead and revolutionary socialists, provided we have a more developed, principled politics and a realistic understanding of the possibilities, have a vital part to play in it.

NOTES

(Place of publication London unless otherwise stated).

1. David Widgery, *The Left in Britain 1956-68*, Harmondsworth, Penguin 1976. p. 47.
2. "Natalia Trotsky breaks with the Fourth International", Appendix to *The Fourth International, Stalinism and the Origins of the International Socialists, Some Documents*, Pluto Press 1971, pp. 100-104.
3. John Walters, "Some Notes on British Trotskyist History", *Marxist Studies*, 2, 1, Winter 1969-70, pp. 45-48. This article, by a participant who was not a supporter of Socialist Review, refutes the commonly repeated accusation that SR "capitulated to anti-Communism" or to "the pressure of imperialism." It is truer to say that the Fourth International, and Healy in particular, capitulated to stalinism in this period.
4. I am preparing a longer companion article, "The Marxism of International Socialism: A Critique", the first part of which deals with Cliff's work.
5. Ian Birchall, "History of the International Socialists", Part I, *International Socialism*, 76, March 1975, p. 18. (Hereafter referred to as Birchall I.)
6. There is a lack of information on this period which Birchall does not fill. (His approach is also ahistorical in some respects—for example, in presenting the "permanent arms economy" theory as an issue in the 1950 split.)
7. The fullest and most accessible presentation of Kidron's argument is in *Western Capitalism since the War*, Weidenfeld & Nicholson 1968; see also my article, "The Marxism of IS."
8. For an excellent critique of the SLL, see Duncan Hallas, "Building the Leadership", *International Socialism* (hereafter *IS*) 40, Oct.-Nov. 1969.
9. Tony Cliff, "Trotsky on Substitutionism", in Cliff et. al., *Party and Class*, Pluto Press n.d. (1971).
10. Birchall I, pp. 18-20, is generally adequate on this.
11. Tony Cliff and Colin Barker, *Incomes Policy, Legislation and Shop Stewards*, London Industrial Shop Stewards Defence Committee, 1966.
12. Birchall I, p. 24. Birchall in fact resigned from IS on this issue at the time: see IS Group Bulletin, Nos. 1 & 2, Feb. and March 1967.
13. Figures in Birchall I, confirmed by internal reports.
14. Cf. Kidron, op. cit., Revised Edition, Harmondsworth, Penguin 1970, ch. 8.
15. Chris Harman, Dave Clark, Andrew Sayers, Richard Kuper, Martin Shaw, *Education, Capitalism and the Student Revolt*, International Socialism 1968. The present writer recalls superimposing an analysis of the political and ideological contradictions on the essentially structural, socio-economic framework of this pamphlet.
16. In this sense, while David Widgery's chapter on the student left ("Make One, Two, Three Balls-Ups") generally understates its impact, his self-consciously messy chapter on 1968 accurately reflects the feel of that year—if it also evades the tricky job of tracing its course in Britain. (Widgery, op. cit.)
17. Birchall I, p. 23. (An example of Birchall's distortion in his suggestion that IS made a "phased withdrawal" from the Labour Party; in reality it was hardly so smooth. Ibid., p. 22.)
18. See Birchall, "History of the International Socialists, Part 2", *IS* 77, April 1975 (hereafter Birchall 2), p. 23, for details of these points. (Characteristically he omits to mention the inflammatory reference to "fascism" in the way these were presented.)
19. Tony Cliff and Ian Birchall, *France: The Struggle Goes On*, International

Socialism 1968. (It is surprising that Birchall, as co-author of this pamphlet, should now fail to stress how much May 1968 changed IS's thinking.)

20. Chris Harman, "Party and Class", *IS* 35, Winter 1968-69, reprinted in Cliff et al. op. cit. There are close similarities between his approach and the more recent article of Norman Geras, "Lenin, Trotsky and the Party", *International* (Theoretical Journal of the IMG), 4, 2, Winter 1977.

21. Kidron, op. cit., ch. 6; for a critique see my article, "The Marxism of IS."

22. This became evident in the debates with David Yaffe et al in 1972-73 (see below). Kidron has now disowned the theory altogether; cf. "Two valid insights don't make a theory", *International Socialism* 100, July 1977.

23. Cliff, *The Employers' Offensive: Productivity deals and how to fight them*, Pluto Press, 1970.

24. Symptomatically, these are not even mentioned in Birchall's "History."

25. Sheila Rowbotham, "The beginnings of Women's Liberation in Britain", in Michelene Wandor, ed., *The Body Politic*, Stage 1, 1972, pp. 91-102.

26. Ibid., p. 99. Sheila Rowbotham was a member of IS in 1968-69, having joined as a result of the unity call, but had left before the women's issues were properly raised in IS.

27. David Widgery, "The Women's Question", *IS Internal Bulletin* (hereafter *IB*), May 1975, p. 53.

28. Widgery, document, *Gay Left* 1, Autumn 1975, p. 14.

29. Bob Cant, "A Grim Tale: The IS Gay Group 1972-75", *Gay Left* 3, Autumn 1976.

30. Jim Higgins, then National Secretary, was particularly responsible for this line; for protests against it at the time, see Martin Shaw, "Which Way for Student Revolutionaries?", *IS* 56, March 1973, and "Intellectuals and Workers: A reply to comrade Trotsky", *IB*, March 1973.

31. Strangely, Birchall 2 fails to mention the ICRSC, althouth it was IS's only serious attempt to build solidarity with the oppressed minority in the North.

32. Birchall 2, pp. 25-26, gives details of what IS actually said on this issue. In general, I accept his account.

33. The IMG had 40 members in 1968, 400 in 1972, and 800 by 1978 (*Socialist Challenge*, 2 Feb. 1978).

34. "Membership Report 1973", presented to 1973 Conference. The same report suggests that only 312 (1972) and 467 (1973) had been members for more than 3 years.

35. See above (and footnote 12).

36. Harman, loc. cit., in Cliff et. al., p. 59.

37. For example, Roger Protz and Peter Sedgwick, "Two views of an election strategy for the left", *IS* 43, April-May 1970; Chris Harman, "The Common Market" and Ian Birchall, "Rejoinder", *IS* 49, Autumn 1971.

38. There was a general absence of theoretical development in IS after 1968, not only on economic matters, but particularly on the new issues which were being posed for marxists. For example, no theoretical writing on women was published, from Hal Draper's imported account of Marx's views (*IS* 44, 1970) until 1977.

39. Two of their more talented recruits have since achieved some fame as spokesmen for a rejection of classical revolutionary ideas: Geoff Hodgson, a Labour candidate and author of *Socialism and Parliamentary Democracy* (Nottingham, Spokesman 1977), and David Purdy, advocate of incomes policy in the CP.

40. Peter Sedgwick resigned from the NC after these proposals were adopted, claiming that they made "a hollow mockery of everything for which IS used to stand" (Letter to NC, 23 May 1970).

41. Some of Yaffe's general views at this time are contained in "The Crisis of Profitability: a Critique of the Glyn-Sutcliffe Thesis", *New Left Review* 80, July-Aug. 1973. Yaffe was a former member of the old propagandist sect, The Socialist Party of Great Britain, and seems to have carried over much of its attitude to theory into his later politics.

42. For a description, see Hugo Dewar, *Communist Politics in Britain*, Pluto Press 1976, ch. 2, "The Party of a New Type."

43. Ibid., p. 35.

44. "Membership Report 1973", op. cit.

45. "Interim Report of the Organisation Commission", *IB* Pre-Conference Issue 1974. This report makes frequent comparison with the "bolshevisation" of the CP.

46. "National Secretary's Report", *IB*, April 1973, p. 2.

47. "Report of the National Committee to Conference", *IB* Conference Issue 1974.

48. Birchall 2, p. 28.

49. A point even Birchall notes, although he fails to draw any more general conclusions (2, p. 28).

50. *Red Weekly*, March and April, 1977, passim.

51. There was a brief moment of transition in which the CC argued for the Right to Work Campaign as the medium for anti-racist work (*IB*, June 1976). Shortly, however, the decline of the RTWC was recognised, and IS campaigned openly on racism.

52. Birchall 2, p. 25.

53. Cant, loc. cit.

54. Independently, this group published a paper for Asian workers, *Samaj in' a Babylon*, for 18 months after they left IS.

55. The fate of the programme, much debated in 1973-74, is a mystery. Although apparently adopted (1974 Conference Report), it has never been heard of since.

56. Cliff, *Lenin* Vol. 1, Pluto Press, 1975, ch. 19 "Pravda".

57. The NC debate on the paper was outlined in the National Secretary's Report, April 1974.

58. Resolution for NC, April 1974.

59. Quoted in National Secretary's Report, April 1974, p. 2.

60. Ibid.

61. Duncan Hallas and Chris Davison, "Reforming the Regime", *IB* n.d. (May 1974), p. 19.

61. National Secretary's Report, April 1974, p. 3.

63. "NC Report", *IB* Pre-Conference Issue, 1974, p. 4.

64. Ken Appleby, Rob Clay, Jim Higgins, Ron Murphy, John Palmer, Wally Preston, Granville Williams, "The International Socialists—Our Traditions", Pre-Conference document, 1974.

65. "The Platform of the IS Opposition", *IS Pre-Conference Documents*, April 1975.

66. "NC Report", *IB* Conference Issue 1974.

67. John Phillips, "Laying the National Committee Ghost", *IB* April 1976, p. 18.

68. Peter Sedgwick, "The SWP Fraud", SWP *IB* 1, Feb. 1977, p. 8; Martin Shaw, "An Open Letter to the CC of the SWP", *Red Weekly* 200, 26 May 1977.

69. Phillips, loc. cit.

70. See my article "The Marxism of IS", forthcoming, and "Back to the Maginot Line: Harman's New Gramsci", *IS* (new series) 1, July 1978.

71. On the need for marxism to go theoretically beyond trotskyism, as well as stalinism, see Martin Shaw, *Marxism and Social Science*, Pluto Press 1975, pp. 117-118.

72. Cliff et al, *Party and Class,* op. cit. Although widely circulated in IS this collection did not stimulate further debate, until the crisis erupted in 1974. The contradictions between the positions of the three IS writers (Cliff, Harman and Hallas) were not brought out at the time.

73. Appleby et al, "The International Socialists—Our Traditions", op. cit.

74. Cliff, *Lenin,* Vols. 1-4, Pluto Press 1975, 1976, 1978 and forthcoming.

75. Ibid., Vol. 1, esp. ch. 14.

76. See Appleby et al, op. cit., for an accurate description.

77. Peter Sedgwick, "The SWP Fraud", SWP *IB* 1, Feb. 1977, p. 8.

78. The Workers League's paper, *Socialist Voice,* has recently shown a welcome awareness of issues such as sexual politics and energy. Some of its earlier leaders, including Jim Higgins, have now withdrawn.

79. Meetings were held in 1976 involving a number of fairly well-known IS academics and writers, but the only outcome was a document written by the present writer together with Richard Kuper, *Political Problems of Revolutionary Socialism Today—The choices facing the International Socialists.* Of those involved, Kuper, Peter Sedgwick, Julian Harber and I eventually left IS, while David Widgery remained.

80. In reaction to IS's theoretical stagnation and the conversion of *IS* into a monthly review, a number of people campaigned in 1975 for a theoretical journal to be set up. This was blocked by the CC, on the ground that it would be a "road out of IS" for a number of intellectuals. In the event, this policy only assisted the flight. Only in 1978 have the leadership, with severely depleted intellectual forces, allowed a theoretical journal (the new series *IS*) to be published.

81. *Socialist Challenge,* 45, 11 May 1978.

82. Cf. David Widgery, "Ten Years for Pandora", *Socialist Review* (new series) 2, May 1978.

83. "The Next Six to Nine Months", CC document 11.1.78.

84. Initiatives towards revolutionary unity have been made by the IMG around *Socialist Challenge* and Socialist Unity. One consequence was a Conference of International Socialists on Revolutionary Unity, partly initiated by the present writer, which has begun to draw together some of those who have left IS/SWP over the years.

Acknowledgements

I have received valuable comments on this paper from Julian Harber, Richard Kuper and Stephen Marks.

REVOLUTIONARY POLITICS: TEN YEARS AFTER 1968

Tariq Ali

Describing the last tortured decade of Trotsky's life, his biographer Isaac Deutscher (paraphrasing Marx) wrote: "This was a time when. . . 'the idea pressed towards reality', but as reality did not tend towards the idea, a gulf was set between them, a gulf narrower yet deeper than ever."[1]

1968 was a year when at least reality began to "tend towards the idea again." The explosions which shook world politics that year are ten years old. They have already become history, but their effects still remain. The French general strike, the Tet offensive of the Vietnamese communists and the brutal crushing of the Prague Spring demonstrated the validity of the central tenets of the revolutionary marxist programme. Revolutions were possible in the West. The working class remained the only agency of social change in the advanced capitalist countries. Prague demonstrated, even more clearly than Hungary in 1956 and East Berlin in 1953, that the spectre of the Soviet bureaucracy could not be exorcised by reforms from within. The battlefields of Vietnam demonstrated that the road to social liberation did not lie through the blind alleys of peaceful co-existence.

The result of all these amazing developments—they all took place within months of each other—was the emergence of a new layer of radicalised militants to the left of the traditional social-democratic and Communist Parties. Tens of thousands of young students and workers waited anxiously for the revolution.

Looking around Western Europe, Japan and North America today, one is confronted by a somewhat bleak political landscape. Virtually all these countries have witnessed important political and economic upheavals. Bourgeois political leaders have fallen prey to a diverse set of convulsions. After May '68 we have witnessed a pre-revolutionary crisis in Portugal and a wave of impetuous workers' strikes in Britain, which led to the fall of the Heath government in 1974. But ten years of struggles have not produced a revolutionary *party*. How can this fact be explained?

The novel experiences of 1968 are indisputable. The fact that the far left grew throughout Europe and emerged as a factor in national politics is undeniable. Ten years have produced a layer of workers inside the factories of Barcelona and Turin, Paris and Birmingham, who are responsive to the initiatives of the far left. True these are only a small minority of the working class. But their very presence marks an important

146

step forward.

But despite all this the sour fact is inescapable: no revolutionary party exists. The masses remain loyal to their traditional organisations. This dilemma continues to confront the "children of 1968." Nor can it be resolved by the invocation of magical political formulae or by Stakhanovesque recruiting drives. Revolutionary parties are born when traditional workers' parties are confronted with a crisis from which no escape is possible. Wars and revolutions have, till now, been the most efficient midwives in this painful process. It took one revolution and two world wars to enable the Italian and French Communist Parties to become hegemonic working class organisations.

But are the reasons for the failure of even one small revolutionary party to emerge rooted in the recalcitrance of objective political conditions or is there an additional factor? Has there been no instance when a correct appreciation of the overall political situation could have enabled a far left group to take a qualitative leap forward? In our opinion there have been at least two instances where the far left failed the test. The extremely favourable situation which opened up in Portugal after the fall of Spinola and which lasted till the ill-fated putschism of the November Days in 1975 was one such period. The prolonged agony of Italian Capital, its institutions and parties was another. And yet it was in both Portugal and Italy that the far left proved incapable of offering a lead which would have an impact on the base of the traditional parties.

The two main ideological poles within the far left since 1968 have been Trotskyism and Maoism as well as mutations of both. The latter current was particularly strong in Italy in 1969. The former had its strength in France, Britain and, more recently, Spain. The developments within the Chinese People's Republic aided in the disintegration of Maoism in the West. Except for a few semi-religious, Maoist sects, the political operas of Peking demoralised a large bulk of its supporters. The direction they went in was a combination of syndicalism and spontaneism. The three largest currents in Italy, Avanguardia Operaia, Lotta Continua and *Il Manifesto* acquired tens of thousands of members. They all produced a daily newspaper and AO had, in addition, two local radio stations. Today Lotta Continua no longer exists as an organisation. The other two have split and different components have merged with each other, but they are still incapable of offering a serious political alternative to the PCI. Their weaknesses and failures to map out a clear and coherent strategy have given rise to the crazy phenomena of the Red Brigades: a grim testimony to the failures of the revolutionary left in Italy. Italian Trotskyism collapsed earlier. Its refusal to grasp the changing political situation in 1967-68 and alter its tactics accordingly had led to it being reduced to a virtual rump. The Italian section of the Fourth International has no more than 400 members in Italy as a whole!

In Portugal the far left had tremendous possibilities. The overthrow of fascism, the enthusiasm of the liberated working masses, the incredible interest in Marxist ideas, the growing awareness of sexual liberation all provided extremely favourable conditions for the far left. And yet, once again, it proved incapable of meeting the challenge posed by the Portuguese events. It allowed itself to be outflanked not just by Cunhal and the Portuguese Communist Party, but also by Mario Soares and the Socialist Party.

The fact that the last decade has not led to any major successes for the working class movement despite the continuing crisis of the capitalist order has led to a number of developments. The rightward shift of the Communist Parties has been seen most dramatically in the turn of the PCI: the "historic compromise" without doubt represents an audacious move away from any form of Marxist politics. Its tragic obverse has been the development of the Red Brigades. In France, Spain and Britain, the continuing impasse has led to the emergence of a "third position" whose most able exponents have been Fernando Claudin, Nicos Poulantzas and Ralph Miliband. But in rejecting the traditional Leninist recipes as well as the opportunistic formulae of Eurocommunism the "third current" has not so far produced any coherent codification of its strategy and tactics for capitalist Europe.

The question which is repeatedly ignored is whether a Leninist strategy has been applied by any of the mass workers parties in Western Europe over the last decade. If it has, and as a consequence has revealed flaws, then clearly there is a basis for trying to develop a "third position." But we would insist that there has been no application of Leninist politics by any of the major Communist Parties in the decade that we are discussing. This can be demonstrated without much difficulty, by briefly discussing three crucial events.

1. French Communism and May '68

How do we characterise the strategy of the French Communist Party in May 1968? Let us first remind readers of how the secretary-general of the PCF saw the situation. Waldeck-Rochet stated after the strike had been dismantled:

> "In reality, the choice to be made in May was the following:
> —Either to act in such a way that the strike would permit the essential demands of the workers to be satisfied, and to pursue at the same time, on the political plane, a policy aimed at making necessary democratic changes by constitutional means. This was our party's position.
> —Or else quite simply to provoke a trial of strength, in other words move towards an insurrection: this would include a recourse to armed struggle aimed at overthrowing the regime by force. This was the adventurist position of certain ultraleft groups.
>
> "But since the military and repressive forces were on the side of the established

authorities, and since the immense mass of people was totally hostile to such an adventure, it is clear that to take such a course meant quite simply to lead the workers to the slaughterhouse, and to wish for the crushing of the working class and its vanguard, the Communist Party.

"Well, we didn't fall into the trap. For that was the real plan of the Gaullist regime."

So the choice for the PCF was immediate economic demands or an insurrection. By no stretch of the imagination could this assessment be described as Leninist. The rhetoric was similar to that employed by Kautsky and the Austro-Marxists. In reality, by excluding all struggles except those related to "immediate demands", the PCF sealed off the road to any socialist transformation. At a time when France witnessed the largest general strike in the history of capitalism, when what was needed was a political focus to the strike, the PCF insisted that no such focus was possible. What was posed by May '68 was the overthrow and dismantling of the Fifth Republic and the establishment of a workers' government based on the mass mobilisations of 10 million workers. The creation of local, regional and national Action Committees was very seriously posed. All the evidence suggests that had such a lead been given it would have been embraced by the French workers. The forces that argued for Leninist politics were not to be found in the factories in 1968 and the PCF marshalls ensured that no student Bolsheviks were allowed into the factories. In reality the PCF leadership was perfectly well aware of the dynamic of the strike. In a recent interview with the French daily *Rouge,* Roger Garaudy has revealed that there was a heated discussion on the party leadership at the time, with some leaders suggesting, albeit cautiously, that the strike could be taken forward, but this was rejected.

The removal of de Gaulle, the disbandment of the CRS, the creation of a new popular Assembly over the grave of the Fifth Republic could have provided the thrust needed to develop organs of power independently of the bourgeois state. But not one single step towards this was taken by the PCF. Instead the PCF leaders accepted the sanctity of Gaullist bourgeois institutions. The general strike was thus defused not by a frontal assault but by the PCF accepting the constraints of the bourgeois state. The historic memory of the French working class took them as far as organising the occupation of the factories (as they had done in 1936), but on their own they could go no further. The only party which could have taken them forward was engaged in constant negotiations with Gaullism to end the strike.

After the successful derailment of May '68 the PCF shifted French working class politics to focus exclusively on the electoral terrain. Its strategy on this front proved to be equally defective. In the months preceding this year's elections it placed its narrow party interests above the interests of the working class as a whole. Its sectarian attacks on the

Socialist Party prevented it from having any impact on the workers influenced by the SP. In 1968 it offered the working class the path of constitutionalism. In 1978 it acted in such a way as to ensure the defeat of the "Union of the Left." The cumulative impact of both events has led to serious division within the party.

The impact of the electoral debacle has led to fissures within the right and left of the party. Jean Ellenstein represents a rightward shifting, PCI-influenced opposition. The distinguished Marxist philosopher, Louis Althusser is the central spokesperson for the left within the party. Ironically enough the debate is taking place not in the pages of *L'Humanité*, but in the columns of the bourgeois daily *Le Monde* and the Trotskyist daily *Rouge!* Althusser's devastating indictment of the PCF leadership was originally published in the former. What was significant was that these debates were not restricted to the party's intellectuals. They had a resonance in the factories. The opposition led by Althusser is making many points similar to the ones made by the Fourth International. Althusser's contention that: "The workers cannot conquer in the class struggle without the CP, but nor can they conquer with the CP as it is" is a clear indication that a political struggle within the party is vital. In fact the comparison between the structures of the PCF and the bourgeois state indicates that the philosopher is prepared for a long haul. The first major debate on the PCF and Eurocommunism took place between representatives of the PCF, the SP and the LCR (Revolutionary Communist League—French section of the Fourth International) at a *fête* organised by the latter's daily paper *Rouge.* This dialogue heard by twelve thousand militants is an indication of the changes that lie ahead. The ability of the French far left to relate to the debates *within* the PCF could well determine the future developments of revolutionary politics in that country.[2]

2. *Chilean Communism 1970-73*

It is not necessary to recount the tragedy of the Chilean development which led to the victory of Pinochet's gorillas in September 1973. This has been done in some detail elsewhere.[3] But the question which is raised yet again is: was the Chilean CP applying a Leninist political strategy? Not even its most ardent defenders have so far put forward that position. The importance of the Chilean events was that it was utilised as the main reason for the "historic compromise" of the PCI.

One of the novel lessons of Chile was that we were able to perceive the functioning of a workers' government within a bourgeois regime. Clearly the significance of this for Europe where the French, Spanish and Italian Communist parties entertained similar hopes was obvious. The lessons learned by the PCI were that the very notion of a workers' government was of itself an ultraleftism which had to be avoided at all costs. What then is the purpose of exercising governmental power? If it is to administer the capitalist state in a more humane fashion while "gaining hegemony" one can say, at the very least, that there is nothing new in this project. It is what Swedish social-democracy carried out for nearly three decades, and what British Labour is doing in this country.

What Chile showed was that the electoral victories of workers' parties created a certain disequilibrium. The existence of a workers' government unleashes a more far-reaching extra-parliamentary mobilisation of all classes than does a strategy of *direct* moves to dual power, short-circuiting the bourgeois-democratic regime. Thus the cordones, the occupation of over 1000 factories, the networks of local supply committees, were more advanced than anything seen in Argentina or Brazil or Uruguay. This situation itself was far more precarious than France in May 1968 insofar as the extra-parliamentary mobilisation of the bourgeoisie was much greater. It understood that the developing working class consciousness posed a real threat to the bourgeois order. Thus the desire of the Chilean CP to avoid the settling of accounts with reaction was a utopia. The offensive of reaction could have been contained much earlier. It was *not* inevitable that the Generals should have the initiative. It was the strategic mistakes embodied in the reformist project of Allende and the Chilean CP which, to use Waldeck-Rochet's phrase, "lead the workers to the slaughter-house."

The weakness of the Chilean MIR lay in the fact that it projected the line of armed struggle without relating it in any meaningful fashion to the evolution of Chilean politics under Popular Unity. The MIR were correct to stress that the state was not neutral, that a test of strength was necessary, etc., but where they failed was to project a political line capable of being understood and assimilated by the broad masses.

3. *Portuguese Communism 1974-75*

If the PCF and its Chilean counterparts applied a political line which was remote from Leninism, was the Portuguese Communist Party closer to the mark? Even a cursory glance at the political tactics of the PCP is sufficient to dispel any such illusions. After the overthrow of Caetano the party was a bedrock of stability for the existing order. It attacked strikes, it raised the slogan of "social peace", it paraded under portraits of General Spinola and it paved the way for the massive growth of social-democracy. Even the *Financial Times* (18 June 1974) saw fit to note that "The Minister of Labour, Avelino Goncalves, (PCP) nevertheless works hard at settling conflicts that seriously affect production, and it is extremely important to note that it is nearly only the Communists who are counselling caution in the use of the strike weapon at this time." This resulted in the Socialist Party being seen as a more combative organisation by many young workers in the early stages of the Portuguese upheaval.

The PCP regained some of its lost prestige by organising together with the SP and the far left the barricades against the attempted right-wing coup of September 27, 1974. It was a united front *par excellence* and was seen as such by the masses. More to the point it succeeded and led to the resignation of Spinola and the collapse of his Bonapartist project for Portugal.

The situation which opened up after Spinola's ouster was tremendously positive from the vantage point of socialism. It ensured that the promised general elections (the first in fifty years) would be held on schedule. The Portuguese ruling class was extremely uneasy about the outcome of the 1975 elections as it feared that the CP and SP would gain an overall majority. Their fears were soon justified: in the April '75 elections the SP-CP popular vote was 56%! It was the highest vote gained by working class parties in any country since the Second World War. The election result was clear proof that the workers wanted their own government. Soares was opposed to having the PCP in a government. He preferred to govern alone on the strength of the SP vote which was 38%. The PCP was shaken by the large SP vote, but instead of mounting an immediate campaign for a workers' government pledged to socialist measures, it sought to develop links with leftists within the MFA. The military Prime Minister Vasco Goncalves was a sympathiser of the PCP. Accordingly the latter attempted to underplay the election results while they cemented their links with Goncalves and sections of the MFA. At the same time the growing split within the army from top to bottom further accelerated the political crisis. Soares now emerged as the main defender of "democracy." With heavy backing from the Central Intelligence Agency a campaign of terror was unleashed against the PCP and its supporters. The only way to reply to both Soares and the right-wing campaign was by recognising the election results and agitating for a workers' government. For there was no other mass alternative. The popular committees did not organise the masses. True, the workers in Lisbon and its environs were for a revolution, but Lisbon was not Portugal and the task of winning the masses still had to be accomplished.

Neither Cunhal nor the largest of the far left groups could reply to the demagogy of Soares. For the social-democratic leader said:

> "What divides us is not Marx or the construction of a classless society. . . what divides us is Stalin, the totalitarian concept of the state, the all-powerful single party, the rights of man (sic) and the problems of freedom. What divides us is not 'nationalisations' or agrarian reforms but how these are to be controlled—by a bureaucracy dependent on centralised power, or by the democratic control of the workers wherever it spontaneously emerges. . ."

This rhetoric was effective precisely because Cunhal could not reply to it except negatively. The largest far left groupings—the MES and the PRP(BR)—thought that the questions raised by Soares were a diversion.

History was soon to teach them that this "diversion" would derail the entire revolutionary process.

It is an interesting paradox that while the French Communist Party diverted the general strike of May '68 by subordinating it to elections, the Portuguese Communist Party showed its contempt for the masses by attempting to bypass the much *more* democratic procedures for a Constituent Assembly in favour of bureaucratic manipulation of sections of the weakened state apparatus. In Portugal the Assembly was, for a period, a more accurate reflection of the overall relationship of forces than in Russia in 1917. It focused the hopes of the majority of Portuguese after five decades of fascism. It produced a constitution which claimed to be both democratic and socialist. Any development of soviets would have to be geared into the contradictions present in the Constituent Assembly and the "unfinished" character of the upheaval that overthrew Caetano. The PCP was remarkably blind to this fact. The far left was intoxicated with the scent of insurrection. A Leninist political strategy was to emerge with the strength of hindsight.

As far as bourgeois democracy is concerned, we have to recognise and grapple with the fact that illusions in it are still extremely strong amongst the overwhelming majority of the working class in Western Europe. We have seen evidence of this fact in France in May '68 (it is worth stressing that the growth of strong oppositions within the PCF emerged in 1978 rather than 1968: in other words after its *electoral* strategy was seen to be extremely counter-productive), in Portugal in 1974-75 and in Spain after the death of Franco.

Does this mean that the bourgeois-democratic leopard has changed its spots? It is the case that there has been a *qualitative* change in the character of bourgeois-democracy since Lenin wrote "The Proletarian Revolution and the Renegade Kautsky"? We would reject any such thesis. Its strength, as far as the working masses are concerned, derives from one basic fact: no other system offers a more democratic alternative. The choice which confronts the working class in relation to existing regimes is not indirect bourgeois democracy versus direct proletarian democracy. It is bourgeois democracy or a bureaucratic and repressive dictatorship. In the above-mentioned text Lenin had been able to utilise his savage invective against Kautsky primarily because of one premise, which, in his own words, was the fact that:

> "Proletarian democracy is *a million times* more democratic than any bourgeois democracy; Soviet power is a million times more democratic than the most democratic bourgeois republic."

Lenin proceeds to explain in his inimitable style why this is so and he explains how in the purest bourgeois democracy the real decisions are made by institutions over which the common people have no control: the banks and the stock exchanges. (One could add, in today's conditions, the International Monetary Fund and the multinational companies to that list.) Through soviet power, argues Lenin, the workers and the oppressed exercise direct power and can recall their representatives on a local, regional or national level if they so desire.

The Soviet Union, China, Eastern Europe are not a *million* times more democratic than the bourgeois republics. As a matter of fact the working class enjoys more *democratic* rights in the West (and in India) than it does in the post-capitalist states. It has been the Stalinist model of "socialism" which has enabled illusions in bourgeois-democracy to persist and even from within the proletariat in the capitalist countries. It is for that reason that the experiments known as the "Prague Spring" which were beginning to democratize Czech society during the first six months of 1968 were viewed with immense interest by the workers' movement in the West. That is why we have always maintained that the future of revolutions in the West is bound up with the overthrow of the bureaucratic regimes in the East. Each will have a profound impact on the other despite the qualitative difference between their respective modes of production.

The fact that proletarian or socialist democracy does not exist in any of the states that have seen the abolition of capitalism whether through popular social revolutions (USSR, China, Yugoslavia, Albania, Cuba, Vietnam) or through the intervention of the Soviet armies in the wake of the Nazi defeats in 1944-45 (Hungary, Poland, Bulgaria, Rumania) or a combination of the two (Czechoslovakia, North Korea) remains a tremendous obstacle for the victory of socialism *in the West*. What this means is that socialist democracy must be institutionalised within the programme of revolutionary marxism. Of course this, in itself, is completely insufficient, but what it will indicate is a serious attempt of those fighting for socialism to learn from the tragedies of the workers' movement. It also has some implications for the sort of revolutionary socialist parties which the far left is currently engaged in building. For rooting these organisations firmly inside the proletarian heartlands of the West will require a mode of functioning which is thoroughly democratic. The experiences of Stalinism have already had a negative impact. However it must be stated that the internal regimes of a whole variety of far left groups in Western Europe (and not excluding those claiming the legacy of Trotsky) are as monolithic as a number of Communist Parties during the heyday of Stalinism; a clear reflection that the long period of Stalinist hegemony of the official communist movement did not leave some of its opponents entirely unscathed!

Nor is it sufficient to say that the writings of classical Marxism are *sufficient* in this regard. While elements of what would constitute socialist democracy are present in the writings of the old Marxist leaders they were never institutionalised. We can take three examples which indicate that Lenin, Luxemburg and Trotsky were, in their different ways, fully conscious of the importance of this problem. In his polemic with Kautsky already cited, Lenin stated that the exclusion of the bourgeoisie from the soviets was not a matter of principle. It was contingent on the concrete situation, i.e. if they were waging a civil war to overthrow the soviet democracy:

> "As I have already pointed out, the disenfranchisement of the bourgeoisie is not a necessary and indispensable feature of the dictatorship of the proletariat. And in Russia, the Bolsheviks, who long before October put forward the slogan of proletarian dictatorship, did not say anything in advance about disenfranchising the exploiters. *This* aspect of the dictatorship did not make its appearance 'according to the plan' of any particular party; it *emerged* of itself in the course of the struggle."

What *emerged* was the fact that the Cadets, the Right Socialist-Revolutionaries and their allies were participating in the Kornilov mutiny! Thus, according to Lenin, they paved the way for their own exclusion. Rosa Luxemburg's criticism of some of the actions of the Bolsheviks were couched within a revolutionary framework, despite the use made of them by reactionaries.[4] She wrote in 1918: "Freedom only for the supporters of the government, only for the members of one party—however numerous they may be—is no freedom at all. Freedom is always and exclusively freedom for the one who thinks differently. Not because of any fanatical concept of 'justice' but because all that is instructive, wholesome and purifying in political freedom depends on this essential characteristic, and its effectiveness vanishes when 'freedom' becomes a special privilege."

Trotsky survived both Luxemburg and Lenin. He could thus observe the functioning of bourgeois democracy from closer quarters and in his writings on Germany, probably the most brilliant analysis by any Marxist of a political conjuncture, he spelt out the tasks that lay ahead if the victory of fascism was to be averted. In the process of doing so he explained that:

> "In a developed capitalist society, during a 'democratic' regime, the bourgeoisie leans for support primarily upon the working classes, which are held in check by the reformists. In its most finished form, this system finds its highest expression in Britain during the administration of a Labour government as well as during that of the Conservatives. In the course of many decades, the workers have built up within the bourgeois democracy, by utilising it, by fighting against it, their own strongholds and bases of *proletarian democracy:* the trade unions, the political parties, the educational and sport clubs, the co-operatives, etc. The proletariat cannot attain power within the formal limits of bourgeois democracy, but can only do so by taking the road to revolution: this has been proved by theory and experience. And these bulwarks of workers democracy within the bourgeois state are absolutely essential for taking the revolutionary road."

We have cited these quotations not in a religious spirit, unfortunately far too common on the left, but to demonstrate that the strands of socialist democracy were present in the writings of all the classical leaders of revolutionary Marxism. The victory of Stalinism in the Soviet Union sealed the fate of proletarian democracy in that country. Equally tragic was the fact that this led to institutionalising monolithism and theoretical absolutism within the Communist Parties for a whole period. And even though the Sino-Soviet split has taken place the mode of functioning of both states, despite their different origins, is not dissimilar.

The "Theses on Socialist Democracy and the Dictatorship of the Proletariat" produced by the Fourth International in May 1977 constituted both a synthesis and systematisation of the strands within classical Marxism on this subject, but also went beyond it in order to take into account the concrete problems posed by fifty years of working class struggles for socialist democracy. The theses presented a revolutionary counterposition to the leading theoreticians of Eurocommunism by arguing that a proletarian pluralism was necessary not just after the victory of socialism, but needed to be institutionalised within the workers' movement today. Moreover it did not require any accommodation of bourgeois democracy. Far from representing an "adaptation to bourgeois democracy" as some far left spokespersons maintain,[5] the theses suggest the best way of overcoming bourgeois democratic illusions within the workers' movement.

As the official Communist Parties in Western Europe continue to take their distance from Lenin and Leninism (the PCE has actually dropped the word Leninist from its constitution) it is essentially the revolutionary left which today defends a Leninist political strategy. We have attempted to indicate that such a strategy was absent from the practice of the Communist Parties in France, Chile and Portugal over the last decades.

Given the developments in some European countries, it is equally necessary to stress that the activities of the Red Army Fraction in West Germany or the Red Brigades in Italy is even further removed from any of the conceptions not just of Lenin, but of classical Marxism. The idea that a revolution will be made by the "heroic actions" of small minorities carrying bombs is not only a disservice to Marxism. Its objective impact is to aid in strengthening the repressive features of the bourgeois state apparatus. Its "theoretical" basis, namely that the more repressive the state becomes, the closer workers will move towards socialism would be amusing if it did not lead to tragic consequences.

The central political lessons of the last ten years can be summed up in a sentence: A socialist revolution in the West will either be made with the consent of the majority of the working masses or it will not be made at all. And unless the revolutionary left recognises this fact and inserts it into its strategic and programmatic aims it will have become a part of the problem rather than the solution.

NOTES

1. I. Deutscher, *The Prophet Outcast: Trotsky 1929-1940*, p. 510.
2. For Althusser's assault on the leadership of the PCF, see *New Left Review*, no. 109. In an interview with the Italian newspaper *Paese Sera*, he extended his attack to the Italian and Spanish Communist Parties. Extracts from the interview were published in *Socialist Challenge*, 1 June, 1978. For a more detailed account of France in May 1968, see Tariq Ali, *1968 and After*, Ch. 2.
3. See Ralph Miliband, "The Coup in Chile", in *The Socialist Register*, 1973; Rojas Sandford, *The Murder of Allende*, and Tariq Ali, op. cit., Ch. 4.
4. This theme is developed by Norman Geras in *The Legacy of Rosa Luxemburg*. Geras's painstaking precision and clarity have rescued Luxemburg from the dubious clutches of liberalism. In another useful text, "Lenin, Trotsky and the Party", *International*, Autumn 1977, Geras discusses the limits and strengths of the portions of the two Russian revolutionaries on the character of the party.
5. A recent example is Duncan Hallas, the chairman of the Socialist Workers Party in a review of one of Ernest Mandel's latest books in *Socialist Review*, no. 3.

CONSTITUTIONALISM AND REVOLUTION: NOTES ON EUROCOMMUNISM

Ralph Miliband

1

The following notes are intended to discuss some of the most important characteristics, tendencies and problems of Eurocommunism; and to do this by reference to three of the books which have been published on the subject recently—Santiago Carillo's *Eurocommunism and the State,* (Lawrence and Wishart, 1977); Fernando Claudin's *Eurocommunism and Socialism,* (New Left Books, 1978) and the discussion between Eric Hobsbawm and Giorgio Napolitano, published under the title *The Italian Road to Socialism,* (The Journeyman Press, 1977). None of them are weighty publications; but they do offer a useful view of the main lines of thought of Eurocommunism and, in Claudin's case, a qualified critique of its strategy. The focus is on Italy, Spain and France; but the discussion is relevant to all advanced capitalist countries. What is at issue is the elaboration of a strategy of socialist advance which, notwithstanding obvious differences, is broadly applicable to all such countries.

Such a discussion is both important and long overdue; and it is of considerable significance that it should now be occurring inside as well as outside Communist parties. Santiago Carillo is the General Secretary of the Communist Party of Spain and Giorgio Napolitano is a member of the Secretariat of the P.C.I. But they write in a style very different from that which has by tradition come to be associated with the pronouncements of high Communist officials, and in a manner which invites comment rather than requiring assent. This reflects pressures which cannot be contained or stifled by the suppressive practices of the past, even the fairly recent past. The same pressures are now at work inside the French Communist Party; and these too are unlikely to be easily neutralised. If this is right, the consequences for the left of all advanced capitalist countries will be very large.

2

As a preliminary, the point needs to be made that Eurocommunism must be sharply distinguished, in theoretical and programmatic terms, from social democracy. There are no doubt definite tendencies towards "social democratisation" in the practice of Eurocommunist parties; and it may be argued that Eurocommunism in the end cannot or will not do more than manage capitalism, if it is given a chance to do so. This is what much of the discussion on the left about Eurocommunism is about. But the Eurocommunist purpose, at any rate, quite clearly goes far beyond that of social democracy. As Carillo puts it, "what is commonly called 'Eurocommunism' proposes to *transform* capitalist society, not to *administer* it; to work out a socialist alternative to the system of state monopoly capitalism, not to integrate in it and become one of its governmental variants." (p. 104) Eurocommunism proceeds from an explicitly socialist purpose. It advocates the thorough transformation of capitalist society; and it proceeds from theoretical premises which social democracy mostly ignores or denies. This is by no means conclusive. But to assimilate Berlinguer to Callaghan, Carillo to Olaf Palme and Marchais to Schmidt is at this point in time sectarian prejudice. As of now, social democracy and Eurocommunism must be taken as basically different enterprises, in the sense in which Carillo defines the latter's purpose. The real question is how the transformation is envisaged; and whether the project is politically viable.

3

The essential and distinguishing feature of Eurocommunism is that it seeks to achieve the transformation of capitalist society in socialist directions by constitutional means, inside the constitutional and legal framework provided by bourgeois democracy; and even though it seeks to effect a great extension of bourgeois democracy itself, the idea is to achieve this also by wholly constitutional and legal means.

There is a sense in which this is an old strategy. After the implantation of the German Social Democratic Party in German political life with the lifting of the anti-socialist laws in 1890, constitutionalism and legality became a major strain in Marxism, and not only in Germany. Carillo quotes at length from Engels's famous Introduction of 1895 in Marx's *The Class Struggles in France, 1848-50;* and it is indeed the case that its reliance on universal suffrage and constitutionalism, though somewhat qualified, is un-mistakable, and may legitimately be used to serve as a justificatory text, if such texts be needed, for the stance adopted by Eurocommunist parties. Nor did Communist parties, after the revolutionary hopes and upheavals following the Bolshevik Revolution and the end of the First World War, seek to operate outside the framework of constitutionalism, at least in bourgeois democratic regimes. In these regimes, and with exceptional episodes that were mainly forced upon them, Communist parties have followed the constitutionalist path of advance, and shunned any other.

One of the most spectacular demonstrations of their willingness—indeed their eagerness—to follow that path was of course provided by their entry, where this was permitted, in bourgeois coalitions at the end of the Second World War, notably in Italy and France, and until their expulsion from office with the onset of the Cold War.

This eagerness to join bourgeois coalitions in this period cannot simply be explained by reference to Russian pressure; or to the craving for office by Communist leaders. There was also at work a view of socialist advance, based precisely on constitutionalist perspectives.

There remained, however, a major ambiguity about this Communist constitutionalism, namely whether it was intended as a means of advance to a point at which an opportunity would offer itself for a revolutionary seizure of power, a "storming of the Winter Palace", to be followed by the proclamation of the dictatorship of the proletariat, meaning in effect the imposition of a "monolithic" one-party dictatorship on a pattern which has long been familiar. Engels's Introduction is itself ambiguous, and can certainly be interpreted to suggest that a period of electoral and parliamentary advances would have to be complemented by a revolutionary upsurge on what he called "the decisive day"; and there is in any case Engels's well-known protests at the emendation of his text in *Vorwärts,* the central organ of the German Social Democratic Party, which was intended, as he put it, to make him appear a "peaceful worshipper of legality" at all costs, a "disgraceful impression" which he wanted wiped out.

One of the main concerns of Eurocommunist pronouncements has been to dissipate any such ambiguity and to insist that the commitment to "normal" politics was total and irrevocable. In this perspective, Communist insertion into the political processes of bourgeois democracy is not the necessary means to an ultimately insurrectionary purpose: there is no such purpose. What is envisaged is the gradual transformation of capitalist society by way of its progressive democratisation in all areas and at all levels. Napolitano speaks of giving "ever newer and richer content to democracy—promoting an effective mass participation in the management of economic, social and political life, transforming economic and social structures, carrying out substantial changes in the power relationship between the classes"; (p. 29) and Carillo discusses in some detail the democratisation of state structures and of economic and social life in general. Neither Carillo nor Napolitano suggests that this process will necessarily be smooth. Carillo evokes the possibility that a government of the left, duly brought to office by constitutional procedures, might "find itself confronted with an attempted coup", in which case it would be necessary "to reduce by force resistance by force". (p. 76) But the intention at least is to proceed by gradual means, and within a strictly constitutional framework.

4

Before taking this further, it is worth asking why Eurocommunism should have come to full flowering now.

An answer to this question would obviously have to take account of the failure of the USSR to "liberalise" or "democratise" in any significant way in the aftermath of the XXth Party Congress in 1956; and of the dramatic demonstration of its opposition to the democratisation of Communist regimes provided by its crushing of the Czech reform movement in 1968. There was, after 1956, a hope in Western Communist Parties that the denunciation of the "cult of personality" and of the crimes associated with it (or at least of some of them) would take care of Stalinism, and usher in a new era which would make it possible for these parties to continue to point to the USSR as an exemplar of socialist democracy in practice, much as they had done previously, and with greater plausibility.

With the passage of time, however, it became ever more obvious that this was a vain hope; that the USSR remained an exceedingly repressive and authoritarian regime, even if it was less repressive than it had been under Stalin; and that to point to it as an exemplar of socialist democracy must discredit both those who were doing the pointing and the notion of socialist democracy itself. In other words, dissociation from the example of the USSR became a condition of political viability let alone success. The process of dissociation was protracted and halting, as is well documented by Claudin; but it was cumulative and irreversible. It also had the advantage of making possible a renewed emphasis by Communist parties on their national vocation, in full freedom from external dictation and in the defence of national sovereignty, independence and so on.

This assertion of independence from the USSR is a feature of Eurocommunism, but it cannot explain its strategic options: after all, the assertion of independence could easily have been allied to an affirmation of a new "revolutionary" purpose, using the word in a sense which Western Communist parties have categorically rejected.

The reason for this rejection has to do with much more than the USSR and reaches out to the very nature of working class politics in advanced capitalist countries, at least under bourgeois democratic conditions. The point is simply that bourgeois democracy imposes certain definite constraints upon parties which seek to achieve mass political and electoral support: by far the most important of these constraints is the acceptance of "normal" politics and the categorical repudiation of insurrectionism. This rejection of insurrectionism is the largest and most important fact about the working class in advanced capitalist countries since 1918; and it has been very greatly reinforced by the experience of Soviet Russia and other Communist regimes.

The point has to be handled carefully. The rejection of insurrectionism must not be taken to signify an enthusiastic endorsement of bourgeois democracy, parliamentarism and representative institutions. On the contrary, there is very deep and widespread scepticism about all of this, and the chances are that it has always been so. For the working class in general, it is probably the case that "politics" has been a term charged with many negative and suspect connotations.

But this scepticism about bourgeois politics has never meant any kind of commitment to its obverse, namely the politics of insurrection and violent revolution. No doubt, there has always been a section of the working class, of different proportions from one country to another and from one period to another, which has found such an option and commitment acceptable. But it has always and everywhere been a small section of the whole; and the overwhelming majority of the working class, not to speak of other classes, has always rejected the politics of revolution. In so far as a proletarian revolution of the classic type requires mass support, the conditions for such a revolution have not been present.

It is of course possible to attribute this to poverty of leadership, to opportunism, or to treachery, or whatever. But this is to put far too much weight upon leadership and much too little upon the structures and circumstances in which leadership operates. Lenin was possible (though not inevitable) in Russia but not in Germany. It is no good saying that the German revolution would have been successful in 1918 if only there had been a well-organised German Bolshevik/Communist Party in existence, with proper leadership. This may well be so. But there are reasons why there was no such party or leadership, which have very little to do with will and persons and a great deal with structures and circumstances. There is a dialectic between leadership and organisation on the one hand, and structures on the other; but that dialectic cannot possibly produce positive results unless there is a minimal "fit" between them. There has been no such "fit" between revolutionary organisation and leadership and the structures and circumstances of advanced capitalism and bourgeois democracy. Another way of saying this is that advanced capitalism and bourgeois democracy have produced a working class politics which has been non-insurrectionary and indeed anti-insurrectionary; and that this is the rock on which revolutionary organisation and politics have been broken.

This is not to say that leaderships of working class movements and parties—in this instance Communist leaderships—could not have done more to further the interests of the working class and the subordinate classes in general, in many different ways. Here the dialectic of leadership and structures does have play, for positive results as well as negative ones. But no leadership, however inspired, and no organisation, however efficient, could have carried mass support for a project whose ultimate purpose was a revolutionary seizure of power.

If failures of leadership are no adequate explanation of this working class rejection of the politics of revolution-as-insurrection, neither is the invocation of a presumed false consciousness on its part leading to an exaggerated regard for the institutions of bourgeois democracy.

Regard for these institutions varies from country to country (higher say in Britain, lower say in Italy), but it is nowhere very high. But in any case, it is not because of an illusory view of bourgeois democracy and of the power which it confers upon the working class that the latter rejects revolution; it is rather because the fruits of revolution, particularly in the political realm, appear so doubtful and indeed so sour that there is acceptance and endorsement of the kind of institutional framework which has been fashioned, not least as a result of working class pressure, in the context of advanced capitalism. Claudin makes the point that after 1919, there developed in what he calls "Comintern ideology" an "essential conflict between council democracy and representative or delegated democracy" with the implication that "only the first was suited to proletarian rule; the second was designed exclusively for bourgeois rule"; and he notes that "the effective workers' democracy of the model was short-circuited (in the Soviet Union—R.M.) by the reality of a system of military, police, economic, administrative, juridical and ideological apparatuses which had escaped all popular control and were now the real power centres—in turn organised and controlled by the central apparatus of the single party." (p. 78) This experience has weighed very heavily upon the socialist project in bourgeois democratic countries; and it is that experience which has helped to legitimate bourgeois democracy, rather than the latter's own intrinsic virtues. It is not these virtues which robbed the working class of a sense of alternatives, but the repulsive character of the actual, existing alternatives. The *idea* of the dictatorship of the proletariat, out of classical Marxism, is not nearly sufficiently compelling to overcome the impact of these alternatives.

In a broader perspective, it is obvious that conditions in advanced capitalist countries would have to become enormously worse, in ways which it is at present difficult to envisage, for the necessary basis of mass support to be engendered which would significantly advance the prospects of a "vanguard party" bent on an ultimate seizure of power. Those groupings which see themselves as embryonic (or actual) "vanguard parties" do in fact work on catastrophist assumptions, and expect that economic collapse, the replacement of bourgeois democracy by some form of authoritarianism and fascism, and even war, will eventually bring about the necessary conditions of revolutionary success and make it possible to repeat the Bolshevik scenario of 1917. On any other basis, the road to power by way of insurrection is blocked. The major difference between Eurocommunists and many—though not all—groupings on the far left which oppose them is that the former believe that it will remain blocked; while the latter believe that it will not. These divergent expectations also naturally produce different strategies: the groupings on the far left do see themselves as potential or actual vanguard parties preparing for the moment of violent confrontation; Eurocommunists for their part see themselves as engaged in what Gramsci called a "war of position" as distinct from a "war of manoeuvre", with the purpose of achieving a gradual and ever-greater implantation in capitalist society and in politics, to the point where the achievement of governmental power by the forces of the left becomes possible, on the basis of a majority registered at the polls.

There is of course no way of knowing whether the catastrophist perspectives are mistaken or not; and they may not be. But they do not seem to afford the basis for an adequate political strategy. It is reasonable to suggest that the bourgeois democratic state, under the pressure of economic, social and political unhingements and crises, may well seek to strengthen further its repressive apparatus and to erode the democratic concessions which it has been forced to make, for instance in the area of labour and trade union law. The process is not uniform: labour may win something inside the factory and lose as much or more on the picket line. The struggle between the forces which seek to constrain and weaken labour and those which seek to reinforce it is a permanent one. But this is obviously a very different perspective from the one advanced by the proponents of the catastrophist thesis. As will be suggested later, Eurocommunism tends to underplay the harsh realities of class struggle. But Eurocommunism's catastrophist critics on the left are forced into far too rigid a mould because of their preconceived view of what socialist transition entails. This, however, should not obscure the problems associated with Eurocommunism.

5

One such problem has to do with the concept of the dictatorship of the proletariat, and with what its rejection by Eurocommunism entails.

The dictatorship of the proletariat may be taken to have three different meanings: firstly, as the "dictatorship" which the proletariat exercises over its enemies in a revolutionary period, with a clear denotation of class violence and repression; secondly, as the hegemony which the proletariat is expected to exercise in society in a post-revolutionary period, in the same sense in which the notion is used in regard to the hegemony of the bourgeoisie in a capitalist society; and thirdly, as an entirely new form of government.

Eurocommunism rejects the dictatorship of the proletariat in the first of these meanings, in so far as it rejects a notion of transition in which revolutionary violence plays a major part. The second meaning presents no great problem, at least in this context, in so far as hegemony, meaning the "domination" of society by the overwhelming majority of the people (an extended version of the working class) is what the whole project is about. The third meaning of the concept, which is also the most important and the one to which Marx was most closely wedded, is much more difficult.

In that meaning, the concept entails an extreme extension of popular rule, almost amounting to direct democracy, with councils and other such institutions as the main form of mediation between people and power; and that mediation was itself expected to be weak and subordinate. The old state was to be "smashed" and replaced by what Lenin called "other institutions of a fundamentally different type." Even though this form of government does involve an element of delegation and representation, the "Comintern ideology", to which Claudin refers in the remark quoted earlier, was right in suggesting an "essential conflict between council democracy and representative or delegated democracy." It is the vision of an all-but-direct democratic form of rule, with a state strictly subordinated to society and in any case in a process of "withering away", which constitutes the essence of classical Marxism's theory of post-revolutionary politics.

I do not believe that this is a viable project in its literal meaning, least of all in a revolutionary period; and that it will not in any case be viable in its literal meaning, under any circumstances, for a long time to come. It represents a leap into a fairly distant future, and leaves the question of the exercise of socialist power unsolved.

But if not the dictatorship of the proletariat in this meaning, what then? The answer which Lenin gave to the question is well known—the dictatorship of the party. Eurocommunism rejects that answer, or at least finds it politically unviable, which is the same thing. What then?

The answer, suggested by Napolitano and Carillo, is a modified, democratised version of parliamentary or representative democracy, but definitely a version of a familiar system. Carillo puts it thus:

"As regards the political system established in Western Europe, based on representative political institutions—parliament, political and philosophical pluralism, the theory of the separation of powers, decentralisation, human rights, etc.—that system is in all essentials valid and it will be still more effective with a socialist, and not a capitalist, economic foundation. In each case it is a question of making that system still more democratic, of bringing power still closer to the people." (p. 105)

The idea is to extend still further and very considerably an already existing democratic system. Napolitano speaks of a "whole series of modifications to be made in the structure and functioning of the state machinery, aiming fundamentally at decentralisation, developing regional and local autonomy, popular participation and control"; (p. 50) and

Carillo similarly speaks of "the bringing of the State apparatus closer to the country, to the people", of "the setting up of regional organs of power", and of "creating a living democracy at all levels throughout the country—a democracy in which effective power will reside in the organs of popular power (i.e. regional organs—R.M.) so that the vitality of that power is such that no groups installed in the central zone of power could wipe it out at a blow." (p. 75)

Carillo concedes very readily that "this conception of the State and of the struggle to democratise it presupposes the renunciation of the idea, in its traditional form, of *a workers' and peasants' State;* of a State, that is, built from scratch, bringing into its offices workers from the factories and peasants from the land, and sending functionaries who had hitherto worked in the offices to occupy their places." This is a very crude characterisation of the Marxist vision and Carillo renounces it all the more readily because, as he goes on to say, "such a State has never really existed, except as an ideal. Even where the revolution triumphed by an act of force, the bureaucracy, with some exceptions, has continued as such and the new functionaries have rapidly acquired many of the bad habits of the old." (p. 76. Italics in text) This being the case, Carillo is content to advocate a democratised version of existing state structures.

What Carillo expresses here is representative of Eurocommunism in general, and is of great importance. He does not accept the idea of the dictatorship of the proletariat which Lenin put forward in *The State and Revolution.* This, I have indicated earlier, seems to be sensible: that idea is not a realistic blueprint for democracy. But having thus given up the dictatorship of the proletariat, Carillo then retreats—and so does Euro-communism in general—to the advocacy of what is in effect another version of radical bourgeois democratic politics.

Of course, Carillo and Napolitano and other Eurocommunists do emphasise the importance they attach to further democratisation, to "participation" and to other features of democratic politics; and the genuineness of their concern is not here in question. But the fact remains—and it is a crucial fact—that this whole perspective amounts, conceptually, theoretically and in practice, to a retreat from the Marxist vision of a dis-alienated politics as a vital part—perhaps the most vital part—of the socialist project. In its sense of an all-but-direct sort of government, the dictatorship of the proletariat was intended to give form to that vision. To stress its "utopian" side—as I do—because of its under-estimation of the role of the state in a post-capitalist society and in any relevant future (and to under-estimate therefore the *problem* of the state) is one thing. To surrender that vision altogether is another and very different one.

This is what Eurocommunism does, for all its democratising concerns and commitments. Its theorists conceive of democratisation as an infinite multiplication of representative bodies at various levels; and this is no doubt required. But they seem remarkably insensitive to the possibilities of enhanced statism and "officialisation" of political life which this *also* opens up. After all, it does not seem unreasonable to think that the multiplication of organs of power, however "representative" they are intended to be, may not do much to dis-alienate politics; and may simply create an enlarged officialdom of "representatives" of one sort or another. But even if this danger is averted or attenuated, the difference is obvious between an elaborate structure of officially sanctioned (and controlled) organs of power, however "representative", and a network of associations, councils, committees and whatever at the grassroots, armed with a genuine measure of power, and operating *alongside* the state and *independently* of it.

The point is a difficult one. It involves breaking with an either/or schema (*either* the dictatorship of the proletariat *or* some version of bourgeois democracy) which has been long firmly fixed, and exceedingly constricting; and it involves breaking with that schema in favour of a search, which is bound to be arduous and problematic, for an adequate relationship between two forms of power—state power and popular power. Marx in *The Civil War in France* and Lenin in *The State and Revolution* made much too light of the former; Eurocommunism is not much interested in the latter where it is not deeply suspicious of it. The socialist project requires a "dialectical" relationship between both.

Claudin has a strong sense of this requirement, though he mainly refers to it in connection with the struggle for hegemony and the achievement of power. He writes that "organs of rank and file democracy should be developed and. . . co-ordinated with the organs of representative democracy." (p. 117) But this is obviously required after the achievement of power as well as before, in the consolidation and extension of a new system as well as in the struggle towards it.

6

Euro-communism is not only based on a working class recoil from violent upheaval in the countries of advanced capitalism and bourgeois democracy. This would hardly constitute the basis for socialist advance of any sort. It proceeds rather from certain assumptions about what the immediate and near future holds for these societies.

The major such assumption, which figures prominently in both Carillo and Napolitano, is that the large majority of the population of advanced capitalist countries now constitutes a potential constituency for socialist transformations; that the "working class" is no longer an isolated and relatively small part of the population but a section of what Marx called the "collective worker" of the capitalist mode of production; and that an alliance between the different parts of this "collective worker", represented by different parties and groupings, is entirely possible, given the massive and growing contradictions of capitalism.

There is nothing inevitable about the coming into being of such an alliance; and neither Carillo nor Napolitano suggests that there is. On the contrary, they both stress that it has to be forged out of a disparate array of social and political forces.

At this point, however, there occurs a very marked difference in approach and emphasis between Eurocommunist party leaders like Carillo and Napolitano on the one hand, and a sympathetic critic of Euro-communism like Claudin. That difference has a number of facets but it essentially consists in the preoccupations of Eurocommunist leaderships with political and electoral gains for their parties; and the preoccupations of their critics on the left with social and political struggles. Neither set of preoccupations need or does exclude the other: but the difference is nevertheless very real.

In effect, Eurocommunist leaders conceive their parties as having a dual vocation—that of both being what Claudin calls "parties of struggle" and "parties of government." In the former role, they want to be the dominant force in the class struggle waged by the subordinate classes. In the latter role, they want to be at the centre of a constellation of forces capable of affirming their hegemony and of translating that hegemony into an effective political presence, whether inside a governmental coalition or outside.

The reconciliation of these two roles is however an exceedingly difficult exercise; and it can easily turn into an impossible one. This is surely the case when a party of the left enters a governmental coalition which is not wholly or predominantly of the left. The following quotation makes the point well:

"A proletarian party which shares power with a capitalist party in any government must share the blame for any acts of subjection of the working class. It thereby invites the hostility of its own supporters, and this in turn causes its capitalist allies to lose confidence and makes any progressive action impossible. No such arrangement can bring any strength to the working class. No capitalist party will permit it to do so. It can only compromise a proletarian party and confuse and split the working class."

The quotation is from Karl Kautsky's *The Road to Power*, which was published in 1909, and it seems apposite today. An "historic compromise" which includes minority participation by the left in an essentially conservative government is most likely to have as its main result the compromising of those on the left who enter into it.

But even where such participation is not involved, the dual vocation of large working class parties with serious socialist purposes is bound to create difficult problems for them in the context of bourgeois democracy; and it is facile for critics on the left to ignore the very real dilemmas which it poses or to pretend that they do not exist or that they can be resolved by the resolute incantation of Marxist-Leninist slogans. On the contrary, the dilemmas are unavoidable and the danger is that party leaders will seek to resolve them by giving in to the pull towards social-democratisation, which also requires the stifling of the criticism which the tendency arouses inside the party. Claudin writes that "between the adventure of extremism and the adventure of the 'historic compromise' (understood as collaboration with the forces that constitute the most fundamental block to the kind of change the present situation demands), space must be found for a realistic policy of advance towards the democratic socialist transformation of Italian society." (p. 119) The point is of wider application. But to find and occupy such a "space" may well require party leaders to forego immediate and apparent political advantage for the sake of a longer-term view of what socialist advance entails; and also the acknowledgement that being a "party of government", in a meaningful and effective sense, is itself a long-term undertaking, which requires not only electoral success but deep and solid popular implantation.

7

Such implantation, and the popular support which it betokens, is the essential (but not the sufficient) condition for the success of the enterprise which ultimately defines Eurocommunism, namely the achievement of constitutional power for the purpose of socialist change.

Unlike social democracy, Eurocommunism has no illusions about the nature of the capitalist state. "The State apparatus as a whole", Carillo notes, "continues to be the instrument of the ruling class." (p. 13) But unlike classical Marxism, Eurocommunism is also founded on the belief that it is possible to transform the various parts of the State and to apply to them the same democratising processes that must be applied to all other parts of the social system. In this instance, what is involved is not the kinds of transformation that were discussed earlier in the representative organs of the state, but in the mechanisms of administration and coercion—the civil service, the judiciary, the military and the police.

This derives very logically from the initial premise that it is possible to conceive of a constitutional transition to socialism. But it is surely enough to note this for the ambitiousness of the whole enterprise to be underlined. To transform this or that aspect of capitalist organisation is bad enough, but to attempt a profound restructuring of the state apparatus, including the military and the police, which the project involves, is much worse, or may well so be taken.

On this subject (and on the project as a whole) Eurocommunist writers such as Carillo and Napolitano leave a strong impression, not of ignoring the difficulties and dangers that are bound to be encountered, but of underestimating them. They repeatedly refer to the internal and external pressures to which a government of the left intent on serious business must expect to be subjected: but what they say about it in no way matches the gravity of the issues.

The reason for this cannot be taken to lie in the personal intellectual merits or political intelligence of either Carillo or Napolitano. The reason for the weakness of exposition lies rather in the basic approach to the whole question of transition. Given their concern to see their parties integrated into the "normal" political process, Eurocommunists are necessarily driven to understate the problems of that transition: to do otherwise would compel them to place much greater emphasis than they deem desirable upon the class struggles which are bound to be part of it; and to discuss with much greater precision their parties' role in these struggles.

8

One of the main features of Eurocommunism is its much reduced claim for the pre-eminence of Communist parties. Thus Carillo on this subject:

> "It continues to be the vanguard party, inasmuch as it truly embodies a creative Marxist attitude. But it no longer regards itself as the *only* representative of the working class, of the working people and the forces of culture. It recognizes, in theory and in practice, that other parties which are socialist in tendency can also be representative of particular sections of the working population, although their theoretical and philosophical positions and their internal structure may not be ours. It regards as normal and stimulating the competition between different policies and solutions to specific problems, and it has no hesitation in accepting, when circumstances warrant, that others may be more accurate than it in analysing a particular situation." (p. 100)

These formulations raise more questions than they solve; and so does Carillo's view of the relation of the Party to the state and society. But there is, in immediate terms, another question relating to the Party which is of great importance and interest, yet which he barely touches upon; and which Napolitano altogether ignores; this is the question of the Party's internal structure and its organizing principle, democratic centralism.

Carillo refers to "organisation as a main component of the effectiveness of political action and unity in action and discipline—once the majority has taken a decision at congresses or in leading bodies between one congress and another—as indispensable weapons." (p. 101) This is code language for two characteristic features of all Communist Parties: the first is a hierarchical organisation which permanently ensures that the leadership carries the day at congresses, and is not therefore much troubled between one congress and another; the second and related feature is the famous ban on factions, which

Lenin imposed on the Xth Bolshevik Party Congress at a point of great crisis in 1921, and which has ever since been used by Communist Party leaderships to disarm and paralyse opposition. There was a time, not so long ago, when the need for discipline was invoked to silence all criticism inside Communist Parties, and to expel the critics. This is no longer the common practice. Criticism is tolerated, so long as the critics do not try to render themselves effective by seeking to come together, and by together pressing their views upon the party.

The simple fact of the matter is that Communist Parties have always been exceedingly undemocratic organisations. In this, they have hardly been unique: all parties are in some degree undemocratic. But the degree matters a good deal; and Communist Parties have been undemocratic to an extreme degree. Not surprisingly, well-entrenched leaders have little reason to want it otherwise, and find it easy to invoke the need for "unity in action" to "protect their supremacy". On the other hand, the contradiction is blatant between Eurocommunist protestations of commitment to democracy on the one hand, and commitment to undemocratic practices inside Communist Parties on the other. That contradiction has now broken surface in the French Communist Party and is a very long way from having played itself out, either in the French or in any other Communist Party. Until it is resolved—and resolved in democratic directions—socialist advance must remain significantly impaired.

CRISIS IN EUROCOMMUNISM: THE FRENCH CASE

George Ross

In the old days the *Parti Communiste Francais* (PCF) was a model of Third International propriety. It was devoted to the Russians, convinced that the Soviet Union was the socialist model to be emulated, enthusiastically accepted the International's theoretical vision, and was internally run along lines very similar to those of the CP-USSR.[1] Of late it has adopted "Eurocommunism." It has become decisively French, abandoned the Soviet model of socialism as a goal, committed itself to democratic norms and adopted a radical reformist United Front strategy for change.[2] Recent events have made it clear, however, that "Eurocommunism" is not a *thing* whose qualities can be listed once and for all, but a complex *process* leading once quite predictable political formations into uncharted waters. What prompts such reflections specifically about the French variant of Eurocommunism is, of course, the French Left's failure in the general elections of 1978. These elections were to be the culmination of more than a decade of PCF devotion to a Eurocommunist United Front strategy.[3] Up to the last minute everything indicated that in March, 1978, a French Left dedicated to serious change would come to power for the first time since Liberation. Hopes, which were very high, were smashed by the results. With the failure of the *Union de la Gauche* a period of reflection, debate and party crisis unprecedented in the entire history of French Communism has begun, a period in which one thing has become obvious. The Eurocommunization of French Communism to the extent which it has occurred, has created new and complex contradictions for the French party. The situation is dramatic and the stakes, not only for the PCF but for the entire European Left, are high.

I. *The Contradictions of PCF Strategy*

At the core of emerging French Eurocommunism lay the PCF's shift towards a new United Front strategy in the 1960's. United Frontism was not an innovation for the PCF, the party having tried it out in both the Popular Front and Resistance-Liberation period. In its earlier manifestations, however, the PCF had always given pride of place to Soviet diplomatic objectives over French domestic goals and this, together with the party's exaggerated reverence for Soviet society and Soviet ways of doing things, made earlier United Front success hard to achieve. Changes in the

172

international communist movement (the effects of "Peaceful Coexistence" and the decline of Soviet leadership) plus changes in the structures of French domestic politics in the Fifth Republic after 1958 (Left-Right polarization which forced the French Socialists to overcome Cold War objections and contemplate collaboration with the PCF) led the PCF back to United Frontism in recent times, but with a new face. Gone was the reverence for the Soviet model and subordination to Soviet diplomacy. In their place were new PCF commitments to the primacy of change in France and a desire to achieve a "socialisme aux couleurs de la France."

The projected dynamics of the PCF's new United Front strategy are easy to describe in the abstract. Initial tactics involved promoting a formal alliance of Left political forces around a programme of structural reform— a step achieved in the present United Front drive with the signature of the Common Programme of June, 1972.[4] The next stage involved promoting the electoral success of this Left alliance. Step three would follow this, consisting of the implementation of the Programme's reforms by a Left government in those ways which the PCF desired.[5] The PCF's strategic hope was that the entire process—mobilization for unity, electoral success and the implementation of a reform programme—would strengthen the Left as a bloc in France while strengthening the PCF within the Left.

In its own mind, the PCF knew that, to achieve the goals, it would have to work simultaneously on two levels of alliance-building. The most obvious level was political. The party had to construct and animate an alliance of the French political Left based on collaboration between Socialists and Communists. The PCF hoped that Socialist-Communist unity would work to rejuvenate French Socialism, pulling the socialist centre of gravity back towards a genuine class struggle orientation away from what the PCF viewed as a bankrupt social democracy primarily interested in unscrupulous coalition-mongering to get political power. The more subtle level of PCF United Frontism was social. The PCF, by virtue of its own historical activity and that of its labour mass organization, the *Confédération Générale du Travail* (CGT) had a strong base of support in the French working class. While this base was constant and substantial, it was not sufficient either in terms of electoral support or to mobilize potential to ensure that the PCF would automatically become hegemonic over a French Left which became a majority in France. As the PCF became aware of this, it began to commit itself to expanding its base outwards towards the "new middle classes", whose rapid growth has been such a notable feature of recent French social change. Here the PCF's Eurocommunist theoretical changes, embodied in the party's official writings on "state monopoly capitalism", provided support. In this perspective, the workings of advanced monopoly capitalism, by squeezing intermediary strata ever more, would make them progressively more willing to join a multi-class, anti-monopoly alliance for change led by the PCF, provided the PCF played its cards properly.[6] Building a cross-class social base for its own positions within a broader United Front with other political forces was, then, the PCF's social alliance goal.

The electoral period of 1977-78 revealed that the PCF had failed in implementing much of this strategic vision. On the political level, the unfolding of the 1970's United Front strayed further and further from the PCF's desired scenario. *Union de la Gauche* was a general success, electorally, after the signature of the Common Programme in 1972. By the Municipal Elections of 1977, it looked very much as if the Left did have the majority which it would need to win governmental power in the 1978 general elections. However, as the *Union's* strength grew, new Left electoral support went disproportionately towards the Socialists. This, in turn, gave the Socialists an ever greater share of political resources relative to the Communists in the alliance. Moreover, as this occurred, the Socialists showed decreasing enthusiasm for moving to the Left in the ways hoped for by the PCF. Rather than shifting away from Social Democracy, the Socialist Party became increasingly dominated by Social Democratic elements around François Mitterrand.

Things turned out even worse for the PCF on the social alliance level. Here, in effect, the PCF was at a loss to find appropriate ways to carry out its desire to broaden its base into "new middle class" areas, despite the fact that, by the mid-1970's, intermediary strata in France were being severely hit by economic crisis. The party attempted a number of publicity-type operations stressing PCF devotion to democracy and liberties (issues which the party knew to be particularly salient to new middle groups) and made all manner of public statements proclaiming Communist support for the difficulties of such groups.[7] Basically, however, none of this successfully translated the PCF's social alliance goals into real politics. A major part of the problem was that the party's own history created reservations in such strata—images of Stalinism and its manichean perspectives on society which gave short shrift to the needs of the middle classes died hard. While things *were* changing in the PCF, the party was unable to convince intermediary social groups that they had changed enough. Beyond this the PCF demonstrated an almost perverse reluctance to broach issues which were obviously salient to new middle class groups in ways which would be favourably received. In the 1970's *autogestion,* feminism and ecology (including the nuclear power issue) all caused great concern in new middle groups. On all of these issues the PCF scorned the arguments which were put forward by the protest groups which raised these issues.[8] The general problem here was not simply that the PCF failed to develop positions which would allow it to build some mass base among new middle strata. Worse still, partly because of this PCF failure, the Socialist Party *was* able to gather such support into its fold.

The shortfall between the PCF's United Front desires and reality was even greater than the facts of renewed Socialist strength and Social Democracy plus the failure of the PCF to broaden its own base indicated. As the Socialists began to feel their new strength, they began to make extravagant public predictions about cutting into the PCF's traditional working class base. François Mitterrand's remark to his Second International colleagues in Vienna in 1972 about the PS reducing the PCF's electorate to 15% was only the first in a long series of such statements by Socialist spokesmen. More important, the party's day-to-day constituency work showed that the Socialist threat was not simply bravado. *Union de la Gauche* legitimated the Socialist Party to the Communist electorate, as Communists themselves ceased attacking the Socialists as class traitors and began to speak of them as loyal comrades. Such legitimation, while absolutely essential for the success of the *Union de la Gauche,* had the effect of opening up parts of the PCF electorate to Socialist raids, as PCF electoral canvassers quickly learned. The PCF's traditional base of support had always included an important group of Left protest voters whose allegiance was less to the PCF *per se* than to Left opposition to the *status quo,* which the PCF had, for decades, represented. With *Union* consecrating the PS as a genuine force of the Left, many such voters began to look to the PS rather than to the PCF. How many such protest voters in the PCF's base there actually were was unclear, perhaps only a few percent. But the loss of even a few percent from the PCF's long-stagnating voter base would have been a major defeat for the party.

That United Frontism was not working the way the PCF wanted it to work was an unpleasant reality for the party, to be sure, but a potentially reversible one as long as there existed no immediate prospect of the Left coming to power. "Union is struggle", as the PCF was wont to observe rather repetitively, and struggle for position between the two major parties in the new United Front was a natural thing.[9] Already, for several months after the PCF's XXIst Congress in 1974, and in response to a series of bye-elections in which the PS gained in relation to the PCF (making serious inroads into the PCF's electorate) the PCF had accentuated the "struggle" side of its *Union* approach, moving with alacrity to strident attacks on the Socialists as "social democrats" uninterested in "real change." The attacks were designed to warn the PS against a "drift to the Right" and against raids on the PCF electorate. Yet the 1974-75 PCF anti-Socialist offensive ended abruptly when the time came to prepare the 1976 cantonal elections (in turn, stepping stones to the all-important 1977 Municipal Elections). From this point until Springtime 1977, comity and entente between the two parties prevailed, even while both jockeyed for position. After the 1977 Municipal Elections, however, a new calculus became inevitable. When events made clear that, other things being equal, the *Union de la Gauche* would win the 1978 general elections, the prospect of power existed. Once the Left formed a government, the relative balance between its major components became a question of political life-or-death involving which party's policies would be legislated and how they would be carried out. It was at this point that the contradictory unfolding of the PCF's United Front strategy became critical. Once countdown towards the 1978 elections began, the PCF had to face the fact that its "strengthen the Left, strengthen the PCF within the Left" strategy had failed. The Left had been strengthened by *Union,* but the Socialists had benefited primarily from this. This meant that, with the Left in power, the Socialists stood to have the clear advantage in resources. And, as the Socialists' advances had become more obvious, the Socialist leadership had moved further to the Right towards more traditional Social Democratic positions. Thus in a Left government, as things stood, the PCF would be faced with the untenable choice between being midwife to a process of social democratic reform or of breaking up the first Left government in France since the 1930's.

By summer 1977 the PCF faced a situation in which it had only unpleasant tactical options from which to choose. It responded by taking the offensive. If increased Socialist electoral strength and PCF strategic failures prompted the Socialist leadership to want to *use* the Communists as a support group for Socialist policies, then what was necessary was to tie down the Socialists *in advance* of the 1978 elections to policies which would be acceptable to the Communists. The opportunity to do this arose when the parties of the Left met to bring the 1972 Common Programme up to date for the electoral campaign. What the PCF leadership decided to do at this point was to use these "actualization" negotiations to *force* the Socialists to espouse the kind of programme which the Communists wanted. To make such tactics credible the PCF had one large threat at its disposal, its ability to break the unity of the Left in the pre-electoral period. This, the Communists reasoned, would be sobering to the PS indeed. Unified, the Left was likely to win in 1978; divided it was likely to lose.

The summer 1977 programme negotiations between the PCF and PS became a session of political Russian roulette. The Socialists refused to update the 1972 Programme in ways which the PCF desired (by adding, for example, the nationalization of the crisis-ridden steel industry to the list of industries to be taken into the public sector). Beyond this, they clearly wanted to water down the existing programme in a number of areas (nationalizations, wealth redistribution.)[10] Socialist responses to PCF programme initiatives confirmed PCF fears that the Socialists wanted to come to power not to work change in France, but to "manage the capitalist crisis." Public statements by many Socialist leaders, in particular by the younger "technocrats" such as Michel Rocard and Jacques Attali (both likely to be in important economic policy-making roles in a Left government) indicated that this was indeed the case. Several weeks of hard bargaining ended in impasse on September 22, when the talks were suspended. Left disunity followed.

II. Left Disunity: The Campaign

The PCF's electoral campaign after September 22 was a response to the contradictory unfolding of its United Front strategy. The party had reasoned that the Socialists would react to the threat of Left disunity by conceding key points in the programme talks. The Socialists did not do so, thus the PCF had to act on the disunity threat, in the hope that the Socialists would, in time, change their positions, as the election drew closer and the electoral costs of Left disunity became more evident. To hasten this end, the PCF launched a brutal and strident campaign against the Socialists, reminiscent of the rhetoric of "class against class" and Cold War attacks on "Right Wing Social Democrats." Communist spokesmen made the Socialists totally responsible for the failure of the programme negotiations and connected this responsibility to a Socialist "turn to the Right" (often, in turn, tied to an alleged rapprochement between the PS and the German Social Democrats). The ultimate logic of such attacks was, of course, to undermine the prospects for Left electoral victory. Although the PCF hoped that this logic would not be followed to its conclusion—perhaps the Socialists would give in—it was obviously prepared to carry it out if need be. Thus it is technically correct to claim—as many observers have done—that the PCF was willing to lose the 1978 elections if one includes the important *caveat* that this will for defeat held true for only *one* of the PCF's tactical scenarios, the one in which the Socialists refused to concede what the Communists wanted.

It was on the social alliance level that the PCF had to face the most unpleasant realities. It had failed to make any real progress towards a cross-class electoral base of its own since 1972. Beyond this, however, Socialist success had actually begun to threaten parts of the PCF's traditional electoral base. The PCF devised an electoral tactic to confront these failures worthy of a Hollywood western film. It decided to draw all of its wagons in a circle around its working class supporters to protect them for the Socialist Indians. This involved pitching the party's electoral appeals to issues felt most strongly by workers and the poor—long discourses on "poverty", the need to "soak the rich", the urgency of raising the minimum wage, preventing evictions, erasing unemployment, and so on. This approach, when coupled with the attacks on the Socialists, was designed to deprive the Socialists of any Left legitimacy which they might have acquired with the PCF's usual electorate in the *Union* period. It had the virtue of making it nearly impossible for the Socialists to touch much of the working PCF vote, given the Socialists' need, at the same time, to concentrate their primary fire on centrist, new middle class segments of the population. It had the fault, however, of rendering the Communist appeal difficult to understand by anyone *but* workers.

The campaign, like the earlier negotiations to update the Common Programme, wound down to a halt. The PCF never stopped brandishing the "Left disunity-electoral failure" club over the Socialists' head. Indeed, as the first round of the elections approached the PCF leadership even hinted that unless PCF electoral support counter-balanced that of the Socialists (the famous "21% is not enough, 25% would be good" remark of Georges Marchais to the January, 1978, PCF National Convention) and/or the Socialists gave in on programme, the Communists might refuse to lend support to Socialist candidates who remained in the second round, a threat which promised total electoral disaster for the Left.[11] The Socialists still refused to budge.[12] Most astonishingly all of this occurred against the background of opinion polls which consistently pointed towards a Left victory, disunity or not. The polls had the effect of removing most of the teeth from the PCF's anti-socialist tactic, for if it seemed that the Left might win despite its internal divisions, there existed no compelling reason for the Socialists to accede to Communist demands. Two contradictory gambles were thus played out to the end. The Communists were banking on the fact that the anticipated electoral effects of Left disunity would force the Socialists to give in on programme. The Socialists believed, in contrast, that Left disunity would not prevent Left success.

When the results of the first round of the election on March 12 were known, it was clear that both Left parties had lost their gambles.[13] The Left had not done badly, if one included the votes of the extreme Left and the Ecologists, in fact it won a plurality of the votes cast. But the parties of the existing Centre-Right majority had done much better than anyone had expected. When projected ahead to the March 19 runoff, the results indicated that the Left's advances were not enough to create a Left majority in parliament. Communist efforts to punish the Socialists for their "turn to the Right" were, however, mildly rewarded. The Socialist vote, which the polls and the Socialists themselves had expected to be 26-27% of the total, stuck at 22.5%. The Socialists had anticipated breakthroughs both on their Right in new middle class groups, and on their Left, in the traditional Communist electorate. Neither breakthrough occurred. The critical 3-4% of new middle class electors in whose hands lay both Socialist success and the election outcome had stayed with the parties of the existing majority, most likely because they had decided, at the last moment, that a divided Left would be unable to govern decisively at a critical juncture of economic crisis. On the Left, the Communists had been quite successful at protecting their own base.

Communist cells and sections talked a great deal about the party's "victory over social democracy" in the week between the two election rounds, by this meaning the party's ability to conserve its usual electoral strength (20.5% of the first round vote) during a difficult period. The talk had an hysterical edge to it, however. Party militants knew from first hand investigation that the party's "soak the rich" campaign had made Communist candidates unpalatable to non-working class voters, a fact which hurt PCF candidates a great deal in constituencies where only a combination of working class and other votes could have led to success (the case in most urban settings, especially Paris). Defeating social democracy seemed even more hollow because the party had clearly failed at its larger gamble, forcing the Socialists to give in on programme by dividing the Left. This failure put the party in a very delicate situation with regard to the second round. Were it to carry out its threats to refuse support to Socialist candidates second round, electoral disaster for the Left and irreparable damage to any future United Front hopes would follow. Yet none of the issues of principle which had led the party to make such threats had been resolved. In this case, principle gave way to shorter-run concerns. On the day following the first round the PCF and PS signed an accord to exchange support without negotiating any new agreements on programme. Party militants were puzzled by this—if the Communist-Socialist rift had not been based on profound disagreements, then why the rift at all, if the split had been based on principle, then why the last minute accord? Such puzzlement did not help in an already difficult situation. Bad blood between Socialists and Communists ran too deep to allow the parties to mount a joint campaign for one week with any enthusiasm. And the outgoing majority, with its positive first round results in hand, was well prepared to move in for the kill. The result was an intense propaganda barrage from the Right in which the crudest kinds of anti-communism had pride of place. By the evening of the second round, March 19, only the size of the majority's victory was a surprise. It turned out much larger than expected in terms of parliamentary seats, even though the real division of votes between the Left and the majority was quite close (only 1%).

III. Contradictions With the Party: Democracy to the Limit. . . For Whom?

Most thoughtful Communists were well aware that the Centre-Right had not won the 1978 elections, rather that the divided Left had lost them. This, in itself, enjoined self-criticism for the PCF. Moreover, the end of the electoral campaign marked the end of nearly a decade of United Front mobilization. Springs which had been tight for years could finally relax. The post-election period would inevitably be a time for reflection, for the analysis of things past. Beyond this, one could sense during the last days of the election period that the PCF rank-and-file needed much debate and discussion in order to put the Left's self-destruction into sensible perspective. The PCF has never been particularly gifted at internal debate and discussion, however. Thus the PCF *Bureau Politique's* post-election version of what had happened was not surprising, on the one hand, but extremely provocative on the other. The party leadership's statement fell into a long and, alas, traditional, line of self-justificatory pronouncements which swept all outstanding issues under the rug. According to the BP the split on the Left which caused the Left's defeat was completely due to the Socialists. The corollary to this was that the PCF had been consistently correct throughout.[14] From this "business as usual" approach, it was clear that the PCF leadership had no idea at all what was going on in its own ranks. By using tired *formulae* whose success depended, in the best of circumstances, on an atmopshere of mobilization, the leadership's remarks were to, as the French so eloquently phrase it, *faire déborder la vase.* An explosion of rank-and-file discontent unprecedented in French Communist history was about to begin.

It was immediately clear at cell and section levels that the PCF's official version of what had happened was not being taken seriously by party activists. Instead a vast amount of questioning began. Had the electoral accord of March 13 been wise? What of the "soak the rich" campaign and its implicit recognition of the PCF's failure to build any cross-class social alliance in the 1970's? The fact that the anti-Socialist campaign of 1977-78 closely resembled that of 1974-75 led some to scrutinize four years of party activity more closely. Would the party be forever stuck in a working class ghetto politically? If this was a danger—and the events of 1977-78 indicated that it was—then how would the party *ever* accumulate enough political resources to be the vanguard of a peaceful transition to socialism? A small minority in the party who actually opposed the split with the Socialists in September 1977 began to speak out (in fact most of the party believed that the split itself had been unavoidable). Another minority in the party, this one even smaller, ventured to suggest that the whole United Front venture had been a mistake. Those who had opposed abandoning the dictatorship of the proletariat at the XXIInd party Congress spoke out. Here there were two schools of thought. One still believed in the dictatorship of the proletariat. The other pointed out that the notion of proletarian dictatorship had been the PCF's theory of the state for the transition to socialism. And, while this theory was indeed unfortunate and out-of-date, its abandonment had left the party without any theory of the state at all. Many in the party who were close to the trade union movement also expressed unhappiness with the ways in which the CGT had been used during the campaign to further PCF goals, at whatever cost to its viability as a labour mass organization.

Rank-and-file discussion was voluminous and many of the issues raised clearly cross-cut one another. At the start questioning was mainly about strategy. What had happened in the course of the recent period to paint the party into the strategic corner of 1977-78, in which it faced nothing but bad options? Focussing on mistakes which had been made led very quickly to focus upon those who had been responsible for such mistakes. And when *militants* looked closely at decision-making in the PCF the first thing which they saw was that something was strange about the internal life of the PCF. Why had the *Bureau Politique* made all of the critical decisions of the electoral campaign without any broad party discussion, a practice which had consistently left the rank-and-file in a position where its only choice was to ratify choices in whose making it had played no role? Why had the party leadership made a one hundred and eighty degree shift on defence policy (towards supporting the *force de frappe* after long years of opposing it) in 1977 without conducting a full debate beforehand?[15] Why had Georges Marchais announced that the XXIInd Congress would abandon the dictatorship of the proletariat on television before any debate had occurred in the party? Why had the leadership decided to make public the minutes of the summer 1972 Central Committee meeting (in which Marchais and others expressed considerable scepticism about the ability of the Socialists to carry out their end of the Common Programme bargain) only in 1975?[16] On quite another plane, why did the Central Committee always act like a rubber stamp for the *Bureau Politique?* Why were major party occasions, Congresses and Conferences, still "grandes messes" in which the proceedings were ritual rather than discussion?[17] And why were delegates to such occasions elected by cooptation from above?

It did not take long for the PCF rank-and-file debate on strategy and inner-party life to rage out of control. Ordinary Communists began to do unheard-of things, such as publishing criticisms in *le Monde* and *Politique-Hebdo* (both rather low on the party leadership's list of favourite reading). The leadership's initial responses to the explosion were like pouring gasoline on an open fire. *Humanité,* the PCF's official paper, refused even to acknowledge that any serious controversy, existed an attitude which involved steadfast refusal to print any but the most orthodox contributions to discussion (all of which, of course, literally forced rank-and-file critics to publish in *le Monde,* despite the fact that doing so violated party rules), or to comment on criticisms when they appeared elsewhere. When the leadership was finally obliged to recognize that something unusual might be going on, it resorted to hackneyed clichés which everyone involved knew to be false. According to the leadership, out of over 600,000 Communists only a handful of malcontents were protesting, and they were the same ones who had protested at the dictatorship of the proletariat affair at the 1976 Congress (an attempt to equate the entire agitation with Louis Althusser and the ever-troublesome Sorbonne section of the party). Moreover, the critics were all "intellectuals" (an attempt to invoke the PCF's tried-and-true "workerist" reflexes).

Such attempts to isolate and repress debate proved inadequate to the task, and tended instead to make the situation worse. While the first round of inner-party discussion was mainly at rank-and-file level, what happened next was the entry of several well-known Communists into the lists. Jacques Frémontier, a Communist writer and editor of *Action* (a party journal) resigned his editorial post in protest over a scandalous and expensive censorship operation carried out by the leadership on an election pamphlet for whose preparation he had been responsible. The pamphlet dealt with the question of civil liberties, and had originally been covered with photographs illustrating political oppression in the USSR and West Germany (the *Berufsverbot*), and had been printed up in more than a million copies before Gaston Plissonier (and old-line member of the BP) and other members of the party Secretariat had ordered it scrapped. A second edition was likewise thrown out before the leadership was finally willing to release a third edition which restricted its pictorial purview to France.[18] At about the same time, Francis Cohen, an astute older militant not known for his risk-taking, published a strongly critical piece on the party's election strategy in one of the party's most prestigious journals (of which he was editor) *la Nouvelle Critique*.[19] Next the PCF's best-known heretics let loose, from Right and Left, in *le Monde*. Jean Elleinstein, the party's most notable "liberal" deviant, were first, three days running, to express some very obvious thoughts: the party's alliance strategy had failed, perhaps the split with the Socialists had been unwise, or at least unnecessary, basic changes towards greater democracy in the party's internal life were long overdue.[20] His predictions for the party's future, should the necessary changes not be made, was gloomy indeed. Next, from the Left, came the thunder of Althusser himself, who, in four very long pieces in *le Monde* (obviously written as a book) left no stones unturned. Everything was wrong with the PCF, its strategy, its organizational life, its ideological stance, its relationship with the masses.[21] Althusser presented his arguments, few of which were new, in an angular and polemical way which angered a good many party activists, even when they agreed with him. Still, the very fact that the PCF's leading Marxist theoretician was willing to put himself completely on the line in this way signalled to everyone, inside and outside the PCF, that the party's crisis was no ordinary one. And at about the same moment two unofficial and highly critical books appeared about life in the PCF written both by respected Communists who clearly had every intention of remaining in the party and fighting the issues they raised through to the end.[22]

The most important rank-and-file rebellion in the history of the PCF was well under way by mid-April, 1978. Discussion was chaotic and un-even, both in its conceptual focus and in its location. Certain party Federations (Federations, the next party level above the sections, are the most important party organizations outside the central apparatus), such as Paris, were totally consumed in controversy, while others (those in the Red Belt around Paris where the party leadership had its local bases) were relatively quiet. Moreover, the debate was carried on almost exclusively in local, as opposed to factory, cells. This was partly because local cells had little to do except be reflective in the aftermath of the elections while factory cells had their daily shop-floor activities to carry on as usual, and partly because factory cell members traditionally protest not in words, but "with their feet", by ceasing to attend meetings and do party work (numbers of factory cells virtually ceased to exist as vital bodies in these weeks). Whatever the reasons for the local vs. factory cell differences, they did provide some ammunition for the leadership in its determined campaign to pin the protest on intellectuals (a word whose vagueness in ordinary PCF usage makes it ideal for pejorative purposes). Leadership attempts to play upon class differences between workers and "intellectuals" did not achieve their objectives, however. Whoever was involved in the debate, and however uneven its geographical incidence, it clearly was very broadly-based. And, no doubt, contributions to the controversy were encouraged by Georges Marchais' declaration—the only one possible given the PCF's bad press after the election—that there would be no expulsions from the party, no matter what happened.

Much of the fracas occurring in the first month after the election was really directed to the party leadership in the hope that it would provide a sensible and comprehensive answer to the issues which were being raised. The leadership had, in fact, an ideal occasion at hand to end the party crisis by making some concessions: the first Central Committee meeting after the elections at the end of April. Here, in a long, magisterial and rather boring report, Georges Marchais gave nothing to protestors, adding insult to injury by labelling the party's critics as potential liquidators of democratic centralism, eliminators of the distinction between the masses and the vanguard party and destroyers of the working class character of party leadership. Beyond this, Marchais' report essentially reiterated the *Bureau Politique's* post-election statement, asserting that the Socialists had been the exclusive villains of the piece and that the PCF had been correct every step of the way.[23] No unusual situation prevailed, Marchais claimed, and no special changes were in order. What Marchais and the leadership wanted was crystal clear. The General Secretary's report was aimed at caricaturing and thereby isolating inner-party protestors, in the hope that, in time, the protest would wither away. Central to this tactic was to get the Central Committee to approve the report unanimously, which it did.

The eagerness with which Central Committee approval was sought tended to undermine this purpose. The CC met for three days, the first of which was used up by Marchais' report, which was adopted on the afternoon of the second day. *After* this, a day of discussion followed.

Few observers failed to note that discussion of Marchais' report occurred only after the report had been adopted, and that therefore the discussion could have had absolutely no effect on the outcome of the Central Committee meeting.

The Central Committee failed to dampen the crisis. Not only did criticism of the party's path not disappear, it intensified. From the exemplary action of several PCF "big guns" (Althusser, Elleinstein *et. al.*), revolt shifted towards long petitions and letters, often in *le Monde,* signed by large numbers of rank-and-file Communists. On 17 May *le Monde* published an open letter from 100 activists demanding a serious and detailed party discussion of the elections, while noting that the Central Committee's deliberations did not fit this description. On May 20 came a similar petition from Aix-en-Provence signed by 300 *militants* (indicating clearly that the revolt was not simply Parisian). Then on May 25 came a petition asking for the party to rethink its relationships to intellectuals, signed by a number of eminent scientists and researchers. The Central Committee's response to the party crisis had turned individual protest into collective action, in overt defiance of the party's rules. In order to counter-act the leadership's attempt to label the protestors as isolated individuals, critics were willing to engage in horizontal communication outside of their cells, in violation of the basic tenets of democratic centralism. Beyond this, the leadership's response had the decisive effect of clarifying one major thrust of the rebellion, anger at the insufficiently responsive and democratic relationships existing between the PCF's leadership and rank-and-file.

By the end of springtime 1978 it was evident that the PCF crisis might take months, perhaps years, to resolve itself. By this point as well the basic issues in the crisis had been clarified. Besides the strategic contra-dictions discussed above, which formed the core of crisis discussions about the party's relationships to the outside world, the other major focus was the profound contradiction between the logic of the PCF's new Euro-communist strategic stance and the arrested state of the party's own internal development. In the last decade the PCF had changed its perspective to recognize that basic social change can come only *democratically* while its own party life had not been sufficiently adapted to reflect this. From a distance, the PCF crisis of 1978 had a certain inevitability about it. In the realm of theory the PCF had come to believe that the expansion of democracy in France was contradictory to the further development of state monopoly capitalism, or, in other words, that French capitalist accumulation could only go on at the expense of democracy. In such a context, the party reasoned, a resolute struggle to defend and expand democracy in France would be profoundly anti-capitalist. Ultimately such a struggle would create the conditions for a transition to socialism which would primarily involve building a newly democratized society in France. The XXIInd Congress of 1976, whose watchword was *la démocratie jusqu'au bout* (democracy to the utmost), was a genuine milestone for the PCF in this respect, fully consecrating, as it did, the "crisis of democracy" logic. However, to the degree to which the PCF clarified its commitment to democratic change it foreordained serious difficulties in its own internal life. The profound strategic changes to a new United Frontism based on struggle for democratic transformations in France had occurred largely in response to exogenous factors (as we have noted, change in the international communist movement and change in the structure of French domestic politics). The party's internal structures, burdened, as they were, by the profound Stalinist legacy of the Maurice Thorez years, changed much more slowly and, even then, only to the degree to which the leadership was willing to allow.[24] And as opportunities for United Front success opened wide in the 1970's, the gap between the party's external commitments and its internal procedures grew steadily. The 1978 crisis was the final outcome of this growing contradiction.

Perhaps the most obvious underlying factor in the explosion of the democratic strategy/internal life contradiction has been the effect of PCF doctrinal changes in the recent period. During the 1960's and early 1970's the party came to accept many of the tenets of parliamentarism. This involved the acceptance of party pluralism in the transition period and in socialism as well, willingness to contemplate a graceful and legal departure from power if the electorate voted out a Left government, and, finally, the momentous abandonment of the party's traditional theory of the state during the transition to socialism (the dictatorship of the proletariat) in 1976. Beginning in the mid-1970's the party also realized the need to affirm its commitment to the spread of liberties—civil, economic and social.[25] Accompanying this realization came a new willingness to denounce the lack of such liberties in the Soviet Union.[26] In general, as the PCF refined its analysis that France had entered a "crisis of democracy" it abandoned the scorn with which it traditionally treated "bourgeois" democratic forms (contrasted, as they usually were in PCF discussions, with the "proletarian democracy" which prevailed in the Socialist bloc) to adopt a perspective which saw the expansion and deepening of just these forms as the road to change. To the degree to which party activists took all of these doctrinal changes seriously they could not help but, in the longer run, subject their own party to the hard democratic critiques which they were being taught, by this very same party, to direct at the rest of French life.

Sociological changes in the PCF reinforced such ideological processes. In the decade between 1968 and 1978, as the party shifted its strategy, and as political prospects for the Left began to look up, the PCF attracted large numbers of new members. Beyond this, as part of the new strategy, beginning in the 1970's, the party leadership decided to transform the party from its earlier hardened *vanguard* nature towards a more Italian-style *mass* party. This change involved more aggressive membership recruitment and a general relaxation in the PCF's once quite stringent recruitment standards. By 1978 the vast majority of PCF members had no political memories other than those of the party's modern United Front thrust. The necessity of Left Union in a "crisis of democracy" to promote a peaceful, democratic transition to a "socialisme aux couleurs de la France" was their political catechism. They knew little of the party's past identifications with Stalinism and had no attachment to the organizational legacies of this past. Moreover, if what few statistics we have on this new membership are reliable, it was relatively less drawn from the traditional working class than the party had once been, reflecting as it did the growth of new middle strata in urban settings.[27] There was an influx of people from the generation and social base of the student movement of May-June 1968, who were likely both to be more involved with traditional democratic forms and the student movement's radical redefinition of them. Newer working class recruits to the party tended to come less and less from the isolated working class sub-society from which the party had traditionally drawn its working class *militants* and more from the modernized, anonymous, consumer culture of France's new working class suburbs. In all this, the generation of older, pro-Soviet, "workerist" party faithful who had long been the backbone of French Communism became a minority. In general, then, the changing structure of generations in the party plus the changing sociology of party membership tended to favour the new stress on democracy.

The ways in which the internal structures of the PCF *had* actually changed paradoxically contributed to the strategy/organization contradiction. Internal de-Stalinization in the PCF started very late (relative to other CP's in Western Europe) and proceeded haltingly. Maurice Thorez, the PCF's long-time General Secretary and its "legislator" of doctrine and structures, only departed the scene in 1963. Until this late date, the party successfully resisted any pressure for change away from its rigid neo-Stalinist internal life. Under Thorez, decision-making was concentrated in the hands of "Maurice" and his immediate coterie, decisions were automatically ratified by obedient Congresses and Central Committees, and then implemented by a core of permanent *apparatchiks* whose primary loyalty was to the Secretary-General himself.[28] After Thorez died, his successors (Waldeck Rochet and Georges Marchais) recognized the need for change away from such a rigid and inefficient party structure; Marchais, in particular, has been a consistent advocate of change. Although not negligible, what has happened has been limited. Collective leadership has come to replace one-man leadership at the top of the party. Very real debate goes on, at the top, between members of the *Bureau Politique,* while Georges Marchais, as General Secretary, is, at best, *primus inter pares.* However, the *Bureau Politique* still decides everything of importance, with little input from below, while the Central Committee and Congress are still rubber stamps for the leadership. Party *permanents* remain the producers of rank-and-file ratification for policies in whose definition they have had no real part (in his series in *le Monde* Althusser called such *permanents* the "prefects" of the PCF). Upper level party leaders, Central Committee members and Congress delegates are still "elected" from lists prepared at the top, limited to the exact number of nominees needed to fill the posts in question, and passed on to the rank-and-file, Soviet style. Yet at the other end of the organizational spectrum considerable care has been lavished to promote open and lively debate on the cell level (and in certain Federations, the section level), a change which the leadership actively encouraged. Thus the Eurocommunization of the PCF has *partially* opened up the party's structures, in ways which, in certain circumstances, could make it extremely difficult for the leadership to control rank-and-file life. As long as the party was totally mobilized in its United Front drive, with cells in constant activity to promote the party's strategic and tactical goals, open discussion at the base tended to focus on the adaptation of the party's line, handed down from the top, to specific local situations. Once the tension of mobilization was released, however, in the Spring of 1978, this new openness on the base level ensured that questioning, then systematic reflection, and, finally, open rebellion had a place inside the party.

In essence, then, Eurocommunist strategic change in the PCF, by stressing democratization as the process whereby socialism would be built, provided the ideological basis for the present strategy/organization contradiction in the PCF. New membership recruitment, on different grounds from the past, created the personnel basis for the contradiction. And the paradoxes of internal Eurocommunist changes in the party made the explosion of the contradiction possible. To the degree to which change has occurred, it has provided inner party space for rebellion in the PCF. Indeed, the major reason why the PCF has never had a crisis of this kind and magnitude before was that there was no space within its Thorezian organization to allow it to emerge, as inner party contradictions were resolved by expulsions, purges and voluntary departures. That this new inner space has contributed to crisis is due to the incompleteness of change on other levels of the PCF's organization. The present leadership has wanted only those changes which it deemed necessary, only on its terms, and only through existing top-down procedures. Little wonder, then, that the PCF runs the risk of an explosion.

Conclusions

How will the PCF resolve its present problems? What will become of French Communism? Logic clearly dictates a return to the United Front strategy pursued by the party in recent years, motivated by a basic concern to "strengthen the Left and strengthen the PCF within the Left." First of all, this would have to involve a renewal of party-to-party alliance with the Socialists, although such a renewal would have to be on other grounds than the 1972 Common Programme, which is now consigned to the archives of the Left's past (a new programme, some kind of tacit general agreement?) Then, for such a party-to-party alliance to work for the PCF's purposes, the party would have to renew its commitment to a social alliance strategy for promoting a broader, cross-class, base for PCF politics. On both strategic levels, however, the electoral months of 1977-78 have made progress immeasurably more difficult. Understandably, the Socialists are considerably more wary of the PCF than they were. Moreover, the PCF's role in the split of Left Union, plus the party's subsequent "workerist" "soak the rich" electoral campaign, not to speak of fallout from the party leadership's actions in the present crisis, have rekindled a substantial amount of anti-communism among the new middle strata to whom the PCF must appeal in order to succeed.

The import of the present party crisis is hard to evaluate. On the one hand, it does involve public display of a good deal of Communist dirty linen, e.g. the contradictions of its strategy and the strategy/organization conflicts. On the other hand, the crisis also proves that the party is still vital, and that processes of Eurocommunist change which the leadership hoped to measure and contain have taken on a powerful life of their own. In this sense, the PCF *needed* a crisis to show how much it had already changed and how deeply its commitment to its new paths was felt. Had things gone on, business as usual, after the 1978 elections, the PCF's credibility would have been damaged for the foreseeable future as a result. All of this said, however, the critical question is how the crisis will be resolved. We know already what the PCF leadership wants to do. And we already know, to a great extent, what the party *contestataires* desire to see. But what the interaction between these two sets of goals will create is unclear.

The Marchais leadership (although far from united on such issues) seemed to have set its course towards some "Italianization" of French communism. It wanted to create a *mass*, as opposed to a *cadre*, party with a degree of openness at rank-and-file level (the PCI's sections are remarkably open), which would be able to appeal to new urban middle strata (the PCI's greatest success). However the leadership did not start with a *tabula rasa*, the PCF had existed for five decades before this "Italianization" project saw the light of day. Thus "Italianization" was designed to proceed without changing the time-honoured and highly-centralized authority structure of the party—the leadership was still to have a complete monopoly of decision-making, things would continue to be run in a top-down way, and a corps of permanent party officials would see that events happened properly. If the leadership had its way, "Eurocommunization" was to have its limits in the PCF.

The leadership has clearly had the upper hand thus far, as the crisis has unfolded, as could be expected in a party in which the leadership has *always* had the upper hand. As conflict moves towards its natural conclusion in the 1979 Party Congress, the leadership will undoubtedly continue to deploy all available tactics against its critics—playing off "intellectuals" vs. workers, local cells vs. factory cells (local cells being where the "intellectuals" live), loyal Leninists vs. "fractionalists" (especially after the response of the leadership to loyal questioning has forced critics to begin breaking party rules), all the while using its control over the apparatus to bring things back into line. The critics, in contrast, are discouraged and confused, with few resources to use except persistence, a willingness to take risks, and the likelihood that discontent within the party runs very deep. For the critics, however, their continuing ability to express themselves and be listened to within the party, which may well last through the next Congress, is a considerable victory. Formal change within the party would be hollow indeed if the habits of controversy and debate among Communists had not had a chance to develop. Thus the continuation of controversy and debate in the party is, in the longer run, much more important than actual organizational change, although one will most likely follow the other. And it is quite likely that the PCF leadership, if faced with continuing opposition to its behaviour, will propose further Eurocommunist organizational change, if only to calm a revolt which nothing else can calm. The leadership will undoubtedly be unwilling to concede many of its present powers, although it may have to concede some. Thus the crisis will probably end—if the leadership's efforts to talk it out of existence and isolate it fail—by trade-offs between the leadership and its critics in which each gets a piece of what it wants. Eurocommunism is a *process,* not a *thing.* The present PCF crisis will certainly establish a precedent for internal controversy among French communists. It is unlikely that in the future things will *ever* be as quiet within the PCF as they have been in most of the party's past. This, plus the likelihood of some actual change in the party's internal structures allowing greater space for open debate, guarantees that the internal Eurocommunization of the PCF will stretch far into the future.

The PCF does not have the leisure, however, to solve its problems at any pace it chooses. Politics waits on no party's pleasure, not even that of the PCF. As we have earlier asserted, the Centre-Right majority did not win the 1978 French elections; a divided Left lost them. The forces confirmed in power in March, 1978 are deeply divided themselves and lack ideological and political *formulae* to mobilize a majority of the French people behind the regime's solutions. Moeover, the regime is condemned to face an intractable economic crisis (for which it is partially responsible) stretching for years to come. Its remedies to France's economic problems, austerity and a "new liberalism" designed to release market mechanisms to the advantage of the monopoly sector, are likely to mobilize strong opposition. Thus despite the Left's 1978 failures, the situation remains propitious for a Left alternative in France. A Presidential election is scheduled for 1981, in which a United Left candidate might well succeed. And if a Left President were elected, he would have the power immediately to dissolve the legislature and call new elections, which a United Left might well win. The opportunity lost by the Left in 1978 is not gone forever, then. It still exists, waiting to be seized, at least through the next round of French elections.

Whether the Left will be able to use its continuing advantage depends directly upon its ability to regroup. And it is here that the present crisis of the PCF looms large. Much depends, of course, on how the Socialist Party ultimately reacts to 1978. But a good deal more depends on the PCF. If the PCF is able to resolve its present troubles by reconstructing a plausible alliance with the Socialists around a platform which can create an electoral majority, if the PCF can develop a successful cross-class base of its own, in short, if it can resolve its major contradictions in the direction of further "Eurocommunization", then future victories may compensate for the defeat of 1978. If the PCF fails, and further opportunities are squandered, then French Communism will deserve the fate which may await it.

NOTES

1. The PCF's history in these years is best found in Jacques Fauvet's *Histoire du PCF* (Paris, Fayard, 1977, 3nd edition). The party's official history, *Histoire du PCF* (Manuel), (Paris, PCF, 1964), gives the party's own version of its positions. Ronald Tiersky, *French Communism, 1922-1972* (New York, Columbia University Press, 1975) is a good English language point of departure.
2. Here see George Ross, "French Communism and the End of the Bolshevik Dream", in David Plotke and Carl Boggs, eds. *Eurocommunism* (Berkeley, University of California Press, forthcoming, 1979).
3. For a more detailed survey of the process leading to the PCF's new United Frontism, see George Ross, "The New French Popular Front" in the *Socialist Register, 1977*, eds. Miliband and Saville (London, Merlin Press, 1977).
4. See *Programme commun pour un gouvernement d'union de gauche*, (Paris, Editions Sociales, 1972).
5. For a less simplified description of all this, see George Ross, in *Socialist Register, 1977*, op. cit.
6. For the official statement of the theory, see PCF, *Traité d'économie Marxiste (le capitalisme monopoliste d'état)*, (Paris, Editions Sociales, 1971, 2 volumes). See also George Ross, "The New Middle Classes: French Marxist Critique", in *Theory and Society,* March 1978.
7. The main substantial PCF and CGT effort to approach these groups in a new way was the foundation and encouragement of UGICT (CFT), a very "modernist" technical and administrative workers' union led by René le Guen,

a PCF Central Committee member. UGICT's magazine *Options*, was for a long time, a model of intelligent and lucid new middle class organizing. The PCF also tried very hard to penetrate intellectuals' unions (teachers', professors', researchers') with some trade union, but less ideological, success.

8. Here there is an interesting paradox. The party's recruitment to membership reflected an important influx of people from new middle class backgrounds. Recruitment to membership and the creation of a mass base are, alas, not the same things. The party has begun to do the former with new middle strata, but failed at doing the latter.

9. See Etienne Fajon, *l'union est un combat*, (Paris, Editions Sociales, 1975).

10. See Pierre Juquin, *l'actualisation à dossiers ouverts*, (Paris, Editions Sociales, 1977).

11. The legislative election procedures in Fifth Republic France involve a two round system. In the first round, which is essentially a primary, all parties—from the largest to the smallest—present candidates. In the second round runoff, which occurs a week later, only those candidates who received over a certain percentage of the votes cast in the first round are allowed to remain. In the second round it has become customary for the less successful candidates of both the Left and majority coalitions to withdraw—even if they might stay technically—and to shift their voting support to the best place candidates. The runoff therefore becomes a Left-Right confrontation. Exceptions to this occur when a single candidate receives a majority of the votes cast in the first round, in which case he is declared elected, and there is no runoff in his constituency.

12. Socialist intentions in all this were less obvious than those of the Communists. The Socialist leaders, impressed with the depth of France's economic problems, were much less willing to confront the task of bold structural reforming than were the Communists. The Socialists were committed to a substantial amount of "welfarist" type change. But their primary goal seemed to be the promotion of a mild degree of new public ownership in France to promote new economic growth, capitalist growth. In any case, the Socialists did not agree with the Communists, and were determined not to give in to Communist pressure. Undoubtedly, Socialist leaders felt that the Communists' posture was a bluff, that the CP really wanted to come to power and would eventually have nowhere to go but back towards unity with the Socialists, a basic misunderstanding of the Communist position. Beyond this calculation, however, lay very real questions about Socialist ideological orientation. The hegemonic leadership group in the Socialist Party *were* social democrats and did not want to be caught up in the logic of change proposed by the Communists. Their position was reinforced by pressure from the powerhouse parties of European Social Democracy (the German SPD, British Labour, the Austrian Social Democrats) against collaboration with the Communists. Socialist electoral projections, which may have been dead wrong, worked in the same directions. It was thought that if the Socialists took their campaign distance from the Communists they would be in a better posture to woo the critical 3-4% of floating "new middle class" voters allegedly intimidated by fear of change and communism. In all this the Socialists replied to Communist attacks in ways which also led them away from concentrating on ousting the Centre-Right majority. Left disunity became a larger campaign issue for the Socialists than attacking the parties in power.

13. For election statistics, see *le Monde*, "les élections legislatives de Mars 1978", *Dossiers et documents du Monde*, March, 1978.

14. *le Monde, Humanité*, March 22, 1978.

15. Almost out of the blue, in May 1978, Jean Kanapa, the PCF's foreign affairs specialist, announced that the party, which had opposed France's nuclear

deterrent from its inception, henceforth supported it, under certain conditions (the main one being that nuclear weapons be targetted *tous azimuts,* against all possible aggressors, and not simply against the USSR). The reasons for this change are still difficult to fathom. Certainly one reason is the desire of the PCF to head the Socialists off at the pass—the Socialists were about to shift on the *force de frappe* themselves, towards a solution which the PCF dreaded, a European nuclear force (along the lines of the dreaded European Defence Community). In order to block this, the PCF decided that an appeal to nationalism, which would unite the party, at least on this issue, with the Gaullists, was the best route. But there may well have been deeper reasons for the change. Since the party engaged in little or no discussion either of the change or of its own reasons for changing, one can only speculate about its motives.

16. See Fajon, *l'union est un combat,* op. cit.

17. The "grande messe" rituals are not difficult to describe. Major party occasions are organized around a "projet de résolution" which the leadership sends out to party members before the occasion is convened. What is prepared in advance, however, is not conflictual discussion about the *projet,* but ritual speeches in support of it to be made from the floor. Then at the Congress (or Central Committee, or Convention) the leadership's spokesman reads a long report which contains or proposes the *projet.* The rest of the time is spent in "discussion" from the floor, which consists essentially in prepared speeches from delegates giving their reasons for believing the leadership's *projet* is correct (. . . "the workers in Renault agree with the report of Georges Marchais for the following reasons" " . . . we have talked long and hard with the municipal employees of Ivry-sur-Seine and it is remarkable how well the lines of action set out in Comrade Marchais' report speak to their needs. . ." and so on). There are, of course, exceptions to this. But the habits of ritual are so deep in the party that the exceptions have to be encoded in the rituals, such that only insiders can understand them.

18. *le Monde,* 21 April, 1978.

19. *la Nouvelle Critique,* April 1978.

20. *le Monde,* 13, 14, 15, April 1978. Elleinstein is, of course, the prolific author of revisionist works on Stalinism and the history of the Soviet Union. He is also vice-director of the PCF's *Centre d'études et recherches marxistes* in Paris.

21. *le Monde,* 25, 26, 27, 28 April 1978. The Althusser pieces were rapidly published in book form, see Louis Althusser, *ce qui ne peut plus durer au PCF,* (Paris, Maspero, 1978).

22. See Gerard Molina and Yves Vargas, *Dialogue à l'interieur du parti Communiste* (Paris, Maspero, 1978), Jean Rony, *trente ans du parti* (Paris, Christian Bourgois, 1978).

23. *Humanité,* 28 April, 1978.

24. The best places to seek understanding of the party under Maurice Thorez are the works of Philippe Robrieux, first his biography of Thorez, which is good on the post-World War II period in particular, *Maurice Thorez,* (Paris, Fayard, 1975), then his own memoirs as a PCF student leader in the critical Algerian War years of the late 1950's up through the *affaire Servin-Casanova* in 1960-61, *notre génération communiste* (Paris, Fayard, 1977).

25. See the party's pamphlet, *Vivre libres,* (Paris, Editions Sociales, 1975).

26. The party shift on civil liberties in the USSR dates from 1975 (immediately prior to this it engaged itself quite fully in an extraordinarily ill-advised campaign to defend the Russians' handling of Solzhenitsyn). Since then it has recognized and condemned the existence of forced labour camps for political

dissidents, moved retrospectively to deplore what happened in the anti-Titoist show trials in Eastern Europe in the early 1950's (and, by implication, to deplore the behaviour of the PCF in this period), and actively criticized the the Russians on a number of issues of civil liberties.

27. Here see François Platone and Françoise Sublieau, "les militants communistes a Paris", in *Revue Francaise de Science Politique*, October, 1975, Jacques Derville, "les communistes dans l'Isère", *Revue Francaise du Science Politique*, February 1975, and Jean-Paul Molinari, "contribution à la sociologie du PCF", in *Cahiers du Communisme*, January 1976. *Cahiers du Communisme* also regularly publishes a statistical breakdown of delegates to PCF Congresses which is revealing about the social composition at least of the delegates. See, for example, *Cahiers*, February-March 1976 for the XXIInd Congress.

28. Again, here see Robrieux, *Maurice Thorez*, op. cit.

HINDESS AND HIRST: A CRITICAL REVIEW

Philip Corrigan and Derek Sayer*

Readers of *Socialist Register* cannot fail to have noted a steady flow of texts by a group of writers in England which has attempted nothing less than the *cleansing* of marxism of all its impurities. From this vast stream, we have chosen to examine one particular current—the work associated with Barry Hindess and Paul Hirst, especially their four book length statements: *Pre-capitalist modes of production* (hereafter *PCMP*), *Mode of production and social formation* (an autocritique of *PCMP*, hereafter *MPSF*), and the two volume work *Marx's "Capital" and capitalism today* (*MCCT, I, II*).[1] The latter, in particular, "intervenes" politically and may be taken to condense the socialism of their project.

Despite our authors' bans and proscriptions, we happen to believe that we are living in a material world which has a history. It is thus, for us, of some moment briefly to stress the location of their work within one wider tradition which has entailed an extraordinary intellectualisation of both marxist theory and the socialist project.[2] The work we are criticising represents perhaps the most notorious example of this. There is thus a similarity in the styles and practices of this kind of work *and* its basic division between mental and manual labour—contributing to the de-skilling of the working class that has accompanied the restructuring of capitalism since the 1950s. These two bases have important implications for the notions of socialism within the texts we are examining.

We begin our critical survey where they begin, with their apriorism, with their commitment to a world which is *only* discursive—the spoken and thought world—a universe of concepts. We show how this, and indeed many of their errors, springs from a misunderstanding of production, of both *what* it is and *how* Marx analysed it. This leads us briefly to consider their claim of "necessary non-correspondence" and the fundamental circularity of their arguments. We conclude by stressing the political and theoretical significance of history as part of the socialist project—that of exposing and overcoming "the Obvious", the many and misleading forms in which Capitalism's relations present themselves "on the surface of society."[3]

---

*We are most grateful to Edward Thompson for his detailed comments on the final draft of this paper. Given our general debt to his work and our *specific* differences it is more than necessary to add the usual statement that the final text is our responsibility alone.

Starting with concepts

Despite their denial of what they misleadingly call the "epistemological project" (Cf. *MPSF; MCCT, I:* 227, 238),[4] their own project has always entailed an epistemology. They have assumed that "Classical marxism" begins with *concepts.* They have argued that we have to cleanse our theoretical and philosophical equipment. Marx fought this fallacy for most of his life. He recognised that it enshrined the most general of all ideological distortions—a metaphysical notion of consciousness—which sustained the seeming vanguard role for intellectuals and recuperated the fundamental division between mental and manual labour. This is *why* our scholars start with concepts. If this seems harsh, consider the following passage.

> Political problems cannot be taken simply as they arise and are specified in political debate. They require critical theoretical evaluation and they may require reconstruction, but they are nevertheless of fundamental importance for the conceptualisation of definite social formations as arenas of political practice. The mode in which political problems are posed and theorised depends on the level of development of both politics and of Marxist theory and on the extent to which they are inscribed one in the other. *Mode of Production and Social Formation* has suggested that one reason for the signal failure of Marxist analyses of modern British capitalism lies in the weakness of the "left" in this country, its doctrinaire gesture politics, its failure to engage major political issues and forces and its consequent failure to generate political problems for theorisation. (*MCCT, I:* 316)

Like so many of the heavy pronouncements of these writers, this finely mixes the trivial but true *and* the novel but erroneous—a reproduction of the obviousness of the world we all live within! The left is weak in England, it seems, because, that is to say, the left is weak... Behind this schema, however, is a set of judgements on the *essentially* nonpolitical "nature" of the working class. This, of course, reinforces their own significance as the theorists who can supply this "lack." Consequent upon this profound "analysis" and their celebration of the separateness and discreteness of the phenomenal forms of capitalist social relations of production, they argue that "it follows"—as Hindess and Hirst text follows Hirst and Hindess text no doubt—

> that the working class is not automatically or essentially socialist, that working-class politics are not automatically progressive. (*MCCT, I:* 242)

This is carried further:

> There is in capitalist social relations no necessary process that subjects this category of agents [that is, economic agents] to tendencies toward homogenization or unification *at the political level. It follows* [N.B.] *that the basis of support for socialist politics must be created by the effects of the political actions of socialists themselves.* (*MCCT, II:* 258)

Behind these unexceptional (and largely Leninist) claims are the most profoundly *anti*-socialist (and un-marxist) commitments which stem from their *beginning* with concepts.

Marx said of the first *Confusius* in 1880—"So many words, so much idiocy"—and we do urge readers to study these texts carefully. Behind the volume of words is a specific commitment. Engels and Marx waged a struggle through their lives against those who thought history comprised only theoretical struggles, who argued that liberation was primarily a mental action. As *The German Ideology* states, such scholars seek to solve "the mystery of theoretical bubble blowing" by:

> resolving the ready-made nonsense into some other freak, i.e. of presupposing that all this nonsense has a special *sense* which can be discovered; while really it is only a question of explaining these theoretical phrases from the actual relations.[5]

Later, in a general argument against idealistic apriorism, Marx and Engels note that for such ideologists "relations become concepts. . . the concepts of the relations also become fixed concepts in their mind." (*Ibid.*, p. 92) Over a decade later—in a work safely on the "scientific" side of the Grand Canyon of the epistemological break, the much abused 1857 "Introduction" to his *Grundrisse*—Marx again discusses that philosophic kind of consciousness:

> for which conceptual thinking is the real human being, and for which the conceptual world as such is the only reality, the movement of the categories appears as the real act of production. . .[6]

He goes on to talk about the "real" subject, and its necessary priority to any thinking ("this holds *for science as well*" he emphasised). Finally, in a famous passage in the 1880 "Notes on Adolph Wagner", which first identified the species *Confusius*, Marx wrote:

> In the first place I do not start out from "concepts". . . What I start out from is the simplest social form in which the labour-product is presented in contemporary society, and this is the commodity. I analyze it, and right from the beginning, in the form in which it appears. . .
> . . . our obscurantist. . . has not noticed that my *analytic* method, which does not start out from man, but from the analytically given social period, has nothing in common with the academic German method of connecting concepts ("with words we can in heat debate/With words a system designate").[7]

Hindess and Hirst, and their co-workers, employ a universalistic and idealistic notion of language. Ominously, in their *autocritique*, they have warned us that "Theoretical discourse, like discourse in general, speaking and writing, is an unlimited process." (*MPSF*, p. 7) Marx's view of language was rather different, indeed he frequently argued against exactly the "mentalization of language" which our obscurantists employ. Apart from the (generally ignored) sustained arguments in *The German Ideology*[8] we find very clear statements in the 1857 "Introduction", for example:

> Production by an isolated individual outside society—a rare exception which may well occur when a civilised person in whom the social forces are already dynamically present is cast by accident into the wilderness—is as much of an absurdity as is the development of language without individuals *living* together and talking to each other.[9]

Against *his Confusius'* idealism, Marx argued that people begin "with taking hold of certain things in the external world in action."[10] Through these extended and specific histories, people:

> will christen these things linguistically, distinguished empirically [*erfahrungsmassig*, i.e. by experience] from the rest of the external world... this linguistic designation only expresses as an idea what repeated corroboration in experience has accomplished... *(Ibid.)*

Our new scholars seem to understand language as did the Left-Hegelians—materiality, specificity, along, of course, with historical experience, have all but disappeared. But, as Marx, Volosinov[11] and many others have established—language is a social phenomenon, patterned and fissured through the modes of its production. Even though, as Rossi-Landi has argued:

> in linguistic production, as in material production, it can happen, and it usually does, that the constant capital takes on a sort of apparently autonomous, monstrous life of its own, subordinating to itself those expenders of linguistic power, without whom it could never have forms nor could it continue to exist.[12]

That is to say, the power of language is not a property inherent in it (language is not a thing), "but comes from the fact that we use it when we speak" (a social relation amongst people). Capitalism transforms the properties of relations (and the power of people) into qualities of things. This is not, however, merely an illusion. As Rubin emphasised:

> in capitalist society the "material" element, the power of capital, dominates. This is not an illusory, erroneous interpretation (in the human mind) of social relations among people, relations of domination and subordination; it is a real, social fact.[13]

When Althusser (and he was by no means the first) argued that there is a difference between an object and the idea of that object, he did it to make possible the eventual emancipation of the working class from the "violence of things", to show, in brief, the potential infinity of the ways that things could be (used and thought). Marx, one might hazard, was also committed to the view that "things could be different." Hindess and Hirst separate ideas, from the things the ideas relate to, as a form of conceptual essentialism; ideas have been so distanced from things that the world is left as it is. This is clear, for example, in their rejection of the idea "of money as a sign and thus money as the measure of value." (*MCCT, II:* 14— the "and thus" as so often—does not follow, but we will let that go). They stress that this means we have to understand "commodities, money, etc" as entities, *as things.* Not, that is, ways of seeing/saying things. Marx frequently noted how an "uncritical idealism" regarding concepts eventuates in an "uncritical positivism" regarding the world. Such concepts are not free-floating, they are "categories for the phenomenal forms of essential relations."[14] These forms may be, and in capitalism frequently are, systematically misleading, thus to begin with "pure" concepts entails the theoretical reproduction of precisely that Obvious, taken-for-granted world which socialists ought to be overcoming.

This systematic reproduction is compounded by what we can only charitably call a partial reading of the "Great Marxists" they constantly invoke. Thus, for a single example, they use a quotation from Lenin's "The discussion of self-determination summed up" at least three times[15] to justify their general argument for the "specificity" (i.e. the non-class-relatedness) of *the political.* There is within this single text—let alone the range of Lenin's work—scope for a different interpretation, and we urge readers to study his whole text. The point is simply that Lenin does not begin with perfect concepts *and then* engage in an analysis, he is enmeshed in a set of struggles. His work is, in fact, riddled with contradictions—as is Bolshevism—because of the extremely complex problems of socialist construction.

A related way in which Hindess and Hirst reproduce "the Obvious" involves their typically Kautskyan (and Leninist in the sense of *What is to be done?*) conception of where correct ideas come from. Certainly, it seems, *not* from political struggles waged by subordinated groups. Our scholars systematically misread the fragility and complexity of historical experience, seeing in poverty—as Marx argued against Proudhon—nothing but poverty. They thus fail to see the ways in which an apparent acceptance of the "powers that be" can accompany a sustained contempt for those powers. Power has to be respected—it can only be treated lightly by those who have never felt, or who no longer feel, its consequences. Mao, in various speeches, has outlined this in a coherent programme: strategically we should despise all our enemies, but tactically we must take them seriously. If we do not despise them strategically, we can easily become opportunist, "all unity and no struggle"; if we refuse to take the all-pervasive problems of capitalism seriously, we shall make adventurist errors, "all struggle and no unity." The work[16] of Edward Thompson has demonstrated how the English working class was made by taking capitalism seriously in each and every particular whilst retaining an extensive contempt for it, manifest in many ways (*several of them theoretical*) as intense resistance. Speaking of an earlier period, Thompson has recently argued how within an apparent "hegemony" the subordinated groups do not accept the definitions forced upon them from above, how, in sum, there is an alternative culture which "constitutes an ever present threat to official descriptions of reality."[17]

*   *   *

"Classical marxism" and production

We should, of course, know better than to talk of *origins*. But when the classical marxism Hindess and Hirst "problematise" as often as not turns out to have been given its phenomenal form in certain seminars which graced the Ecole Normale Supérieure in 1965, there is a point in drawing attention to the fact. For these obscurantists repeatedly write as if classical marxism, in their version, and their own "alternative" exhausted all possibilities. The rhythmic emphasis *"Either. . ." "or. . ."* is one of their favourite devices:

> Either, economism, or the non-correspondence of political forces—that is the choice which faces Marxism.[18]

> *Either* the articulation of relations and forces of production is conceived in terms of some kind of necessity so that the character of one thing [N.B.] the relations or the forces, is deducible from the concept of the other, *or* it must [N.B.] be conceived in terms of the connection between social relations and the forms in which their conditions of existence are secured. (*MCCT, I:* 226)

> *Either* economism: political and cultural means of representation are determined by the economy. *Or* the means of representation are not determined by the economy and there is no necessity for the political and cultural representation of classes and their interests.

> The choice for Marxism is clear. *Either* we effectively reduce political and ideological phenomena to class interests determined elsewhere (basically in the economy). . . *Or* we must face up to the real autonomy of political and ideological phenomena. . .[19]

We shall return to these notions in a later section, we cite the passages to show the form of their discourse—*either* this fictive dogmatically formulated version of classical marxism *or* the latest, sensible cure-all bearing their own brand-name.

This is not to deny that there are problems with the claim—centrally advanced by Marx's 1859 *Preface* (even if taken with Engels' clarifications of the 1890s)[20]—that the economic is determinant in the last instance. Both "ultimate" in "ultimate determination" and "relative" in "relative autonomy" are capacious concepts. Althusser's own solution is well known: any social formation has several distinct "instances", the economic, the political, the ideological, etc. At any given time these are related through a "structure in dominance" in which the economic determines through the combined effectivity of all the instances. We are thus talking, to use Althusser's terms, of a structural rather than a mechanical causality. What matters here is that *this* conception is taken by our luminaries as "classically marxist" (Cf. *MCCT, I:* Ch. 7). And, in their usual pioneering way (the relevant points being made a decade previously, in reviews of *Reading Capital,* by Glucksmann and Poulantzas)[21] they have "discovered" where Ecole Normale marxism went wrong. Teleology, needless to say: Althusser's structural causality entails the clearly teleological claim that "the economy secures its own conditions of existence in the form of suitable political and cultural-ideological levels." (*MCCT, I:* 223) This error it is argued, springs from Althusser's "rationalism":

transposing a relation between concepts, between the concept of an economy on the one hand and those of its conditions of existence on the other, into a relation of determination between objects. . . (*MCCT, I:* 223; Cf. *MCCT, II:* 241f)

To regard concepts as descriptive of real objects in no way necessitates ascribing those objects the power to secure their own conditions. But we will—again—let that (as with many "slippery" features of their logic) pass since what interests us is their ensuing argument.

From the valid point that:

if relations of production presupposes [sic] conditions of existence provided by other social relations they cannot generate those conditions or determine the social relations which provide them. (*MCCT, I:* 227)

a number of critical conclusions are drawn. First, it is argued, any "last instance" thesis must in consequence be abandoned, and the same holds for any postulate of forces/relations correspondence. Second, in the absence of the correspondence postulate and the last instance clause, there remains no good reason for according the mode of production the primacy it has traditionally enjoyed in historical materialism. For them, what results is:

a reduced concept of a mode of production consisting of an economy, a definite combination of relations and forces of production, having definite political, legal and cultural conditions of existence which cannot be secured through the action of the economy itself. (*MCCT, I:* 224)

The primary object of marxist analysis ought to be the social formation understood as "a definite set of relations of production *together with* the economic, cultural and political forms in which these conditions of production are secured." (*MCCT, I:* 222, our emphasis) Third, and more specifically, given this general non-derivability of social formation from mode of production, our authors conclude that:

> political institutions and practices, ideologies and other cultural forms cannot be conceived as classes [sic] or the direct representation of their interests. (*MCCT, I:* 231-2)

Classes are "categories of economic agents", defined by their relations of possession of/exclusion from the means of production, no more. This is the basis, through necessary non-correspondence and massive circularity, for the notorious revisionism of the conclusions to *MCCT, II*

At this point it is pertinent to do something no longer thought worthwhile by many marxists, in their haste to trump the latest cards in the Parisian pack—look at Marx.[22] We will start where so many have before, with the much maligned 1859 *Preface*. This informs us that "social production" entails "definite relations":

> The totality of these relations of production constitutes the economic structure of society—the real foundation, on which legal and political superstructures arise and to which definite forms of social consciousness correspond. The mode of production of material life determines the general character of the social, political and spiritual process of life.[23]

Let us begin with an apparent *lacuna*. Neither here, nor anywhere else within the 1859 *Preface,* does Marx enlighten us as to what *sort* of social relation may or may not be a relation of production. Unlike Hindess and Hirst (and virtually all marxists since Engels) he provides no substantive definition whatsoever. Had Marx's latest revisers troubled to glance back beyond 1965, to those texts of the 1840s which the 1859 *Preface* quite explicitly summarises, this "omission" might have given them pause. *The German Ideology* (a work falling uneasily, in Althusser's fragmented Marx, between the purity of maturity and the danger of youth) explains why Marx could not consistently have given any such specification of the concept:

> definite individuals who are productively active in a definite way enter into these definite social and political relations. *Empirical observation* must *in each separate*

instance bring out *empirically,* and without any mystification and speculation, the connection of the social and political structure with production.[24]

On this premise the *only* general concept of production relations we can develop is precisely the empirically open-ended one implicit in the 1859 *Preface,* viz., any social relation indispensable to any such mode. Since, furthermore, "the economic structure of society" comprises the totality of these production relations, we cannot produce a substantive *a priori* definition of that either. We have, therefore, no grounds for *a priori* inclusion or exclusion of any substantively defined class of relation from "the economy." What *defines* a relation as economic cannot be any innate property which is to be apprehended outside of historical context, but simply its indispensability to a given "way in which people produce their means of subsistence."

If this is the "economic structure", what then of the "superstructure?"[25] The foregoing shows how there can be clearly necessary political, legal and cultural relations of production—relations internal, that is, to the economic structure—which means that the notion of "the political" etc., as distinct, as practices, as levels, as instances, or as institutions within a social formation, is distinctly dubious. Let us return to our text again.

Later in the 1859 *Preface,* Marx writes:

> With the change of the economic foundation the entire immense superstructure is more or less rapidly transformed. In considering such transformations, the distinction should always be made between the material transformation of the economic conditions of production, which can be determined with the precision of natural science, and the legal, political, religious, aesthetic or philosophical— *in short, ideological*—forms in which men become conscious of this conflict [that of forces/relations] and fight it out.[26]

What we suggest is that the base/superstructure metaphor relates to the latter forms of consciousness alone. This has additional warrant from the employment, in *The German Ideology,* of the adjective "idealistic" or "ideological" whenever the metaphor of superstructure is used.[27]

To extend the argument. *Capital,* as a number of recent authors[28] have established, is, *inter alia,* an explanation of ideology. Marx seeks to combat the ways in which the apparent separability of "ideas" actually diminishes the power of human groups. Moreover, when this separation is challenged

> "Morality, religion, metaphysics, all the rest of ideology as well as the forms of consciousness corresponding to these, thus no longer retain the semblance of independence."[29]

That formulation, again, is taken from *The German Ideology.* To return to *Capital:* there Marx explains the illusions of capitalist production in terms of the material experience which sustains them. He distinguishes, specifically, between what he calls *essential relations*, capitalism's "material groundwork or set of conditions of existence,"[30] and the *phenomenal forms* in which these relations manifest themselves in our daily experience. It is the empirically explicable deceptiveness of the latter which accounts for the ideological character of our "spontaneous" conceptions, of "the Obvious." We are arguing that the base/superstructure metaphor can best be understood as a popularised expression of just this distinction. The base is the totality of production relations, in the sense clarified above; the superstructure is not a separate body or kind(s) of relations, but simply the phenomenal forms in which these selfsame relations of production manifest themselves "on the surface of society" and to which everyday conceptions— common sense, in brief—"correspond." Such would include not only the numerous deceptive "economic" forms which Marx analysed in *Capital,* but equally, and from our point of view crucially, the *apparently* independent legal and political "instances" of bourgeois society.[31] It is supremely ironical, therefore, that many marxists have taken the base/superstructure metaphor as an orthodoxy, as a model. Our recent epigones go further—they *celebrate* the separateness and autonomy of all these fetishized appearances, here again they translate qualities of relations into things!

Our reading here, finally, forces us to rethink determination—the "Base" will have much that is "non-economic" *within* it, while links between "base" and "superstructure" cannot be those of external cause, but are internal relations. As MacIntyre argued—before 1965:

> As Marx depicts it the relation between basis and superstructure is fundamentally not only not mechanical, it is not even causal. What may be misleading is Marx's Hegelian vocabulary. Marx certainly talks of the basis "determining" the superstructure and of a "correspondence" between them. But the reader of Hegel's *Logic* will realise that what Marx envisages is something to be understood in terms of the way in which the nature of the concept of a given class, for example may determine the concept of membership of that class. . . The economic basis of a society is not its tools, but the people co-operating using these particular tools in the manner necessary to their use, and the superstructure consists of the social consciousness moulded by and the shape of this cooperation.[32]

Fundamentally—and this they share not only with Ecole Normale marxism but with many others—Hindess and Hirst misunderstood production. This has been the central theme of our writings for some years[33] so we can be brief. Marx included within "the economic structure of society" all social relations entailed in a given mode of production; he sees the "superstructure" as the forms (including the mental concepts and images) in which these relations are presented. The entire Hindess and Hirst project rests upon a fallacious problem. There is *no* question of having to deduce non-deducible conditions of existence from the *concept* of an economy or having to attribute to this economy the power to secure them. First, the relevant concept (if it is to be accurate to reality and not "forcibly abstracted") includes "non-economic" conditions; second, it is not in any case a matter of deduction. What is or is not germane to production is to be ascertained empirically; scientific concepts are *a posteriori* constructs.[34]

Starting with a false problem, employing a conventionalist epistemology and an *a prioristic* methodology, our authors produce not so much false, as redundant solutions. With a more realistic concept of production, one which is fundamentally neither *a prioristic* nor reductionist (but is both materialist and historical) there is no need to expunge the central place which social relations and social forms of production have always had within marxism. As the *Grundrisse* phrases it:

> When we consider. . . society in the long view and as a whole, then the final result of the process of social production always appears as the society itself, i.e. the human being in all its social relations. . . The conditions and objectifications of the process are themselves equally moments of it. . .[35]

Production entails definite social (political, legal, moral, cultural. . .) relations and thus their "superstructural" forms of manifestation; that is (part of) what it *is*. To say this does not entail a claim to the effect that all social relations are "reducible" to production, the question is always an empirical one. Marx held that as a matter of *fact* production relations were the core social relations—establishing the limits of variation for given epochs—in all hitherto existing formations. Indeed, one way in which he conceptualised communist society was in terms of the more conscious and more collective recognition/realisation of the centrality of production relations. In such a social formation politics would become the "administration of things" *because* the "violence of things" would be diminished as the emancipation of labour begins.

*　　　*　　　*

Necessary non-correspondence and circularity

As Stuart Hall has perceptively noticed, what Hirst

> proposes is a *necessary noncorrespondence*—leading, as he quite rigorously understands, to the absolute autonomy of all practices, the impossibility of history and the abandoning of any concept of "complex unity."[36]

In particular, there is a sustained series of arguments (repeated in different texts in almost the same words) to "prove" that class should only refer to categories of *economic agents*. In this perspective class struggle becomes "the struggle of organised bodies of labourers and capitalists" that is "economic class relations" *plus* "the intervention of definite political, legal, and cultural determinations." There are acute tensions here:

> Where there are capitalist relations of production there *must* be conflicting political forces. (our emphasis)[37]

> Where there are economic class-relations there *must* be political and ideological forces having different effects on those classes. (*MCCT, I*: 241, our emphasis)

> A precondition for political programmes adapted to the conditions of struggle is a recognition of basic political realities and *the limits they enforce*. It is toward this end that this book is directed. (*MCCT, II*: 293, our emphasis)

There are problems with the force of the "must" and "limits" in these statements. The second quotation continues:

> But there are no grounds for supposing that these forces are the products of the classes representing themselves and their interests in political and ideological forms. There is no necessity for political and ideological forces to be polarised around the membership of the different classes. (*MCCT, I*: 241-242)

The "grounds" here seems to relate to historical investigations; the "necessity" (like the uses of "automatically" or "essentially" in other quotations) simply caricatures historical materialism. Socialist groups have paid attention to the contradictory nature of political and cultural relations since the 1830s. But, of course, having declared (along with Henry Ford) that history is rubbish, our *Confusiuses* will not discover anything of the real foundations of socialist construction.

In fact, because they do not understand production, they simply split off a thoroughly economistic conception of "the economy" (with, now, "economic agents") from ideational versions of all other production relations. This distinctive methodology has been generalised in Hirst's much quoted analysis of "the classic [N.B.] problem of ideology": this it seems, requires:

> that there be a correspondence (the latter determines the former) and a non-correspondence (the former misrepresents the latter) between ideology and the reality it represents.[38]

This, it must immediately be stressed, presupposes (i) that "corresponding" relations are "determining" relations between *independent* entities, and (ii) that ideology is simply ideational. But, let us follow the vanguard further:

If there is any determining action of the means of representation in constituting what is "represented" by them then these forms of correspondence/non-correspondence are shattered.

There is no necessary relation between the conditions of existence of the means of representation and what is produced by those means, no necessity that they "represent" those conditions. *(Ibid.)*

We do not know any "means of representation" that cannot assist in *constituting* what it represents—whether it is the code of the Hollywood cinema, the materials used by J.M.W. Turner or the language on this page.[39] The second part of the quotation is confused, the point being not that means of representation (sign systems) demonstrate their *own* conditions of existence in what they represent (but it is necessarily the case that their own conditions have to be sustained and reproduced) but that they represent *quite other* realities. That is to say, with Marx, that representations (and images) of the real relations can never totally exhaust concrete reality. Indeed to dogmatize the correctness of "Theory" or "Science" will distort and even prevent human emancipation. For Marx, the task of science was to make possible the accelerated transformation (and not merely understanding) of the realms of stubborn, human-limiting, "objectivity." Thus are the boundaries of necessity to be pushed back! But then Hirst and his colleagues have abandoned scientific socialism in favour of the rule of discourse—a fitting slogan for these authors.

Having sundered production relations, it is to be expected that their texts will be disfigured by a constant circularity which, if we may play their game for a moment, was inscribed in their project from the start. Their claim to found a newly cleansed politics is simply not substantiated. As Putnam has seen, their work argues that concepts "are formed and deployed in the definition and solutions posed by political practice. . . Hindess and Hirst's ground is the constantly shifting one of political practice."[40] But we then have to ask with Graham Burchell "what is this 'politics' of which they speak?"[41] It follows, it seems, that:

Accepting non-correspondence means abandoning the evaluation of political forces in terms of correspondence, and evaluating them instead relative to one's conception of socialist organisation and ideology and relevant to one's conception of the dominant political issues.[42]

Really? *One's* very own judgements? Matters become murkier since evaluating ideologies "always entails political calculation and always takes place from the standpoint of a political position."[43] Whilst politics must be evaluated "in terms of a definite conception of socialist organisation and ideology and an estimation of the dominant political issues of the day." *(MCCT, I:* 238) This is their "solution", vicious circularity: ideologies must be evaluated from a political position *and* political positions must be calculated from a (correct) ideological commitment. The latter entails a notion of "socialism". How is this defined?

> Socialism is a political ideology which bases itself on the objective of constructing a planned and non commodity form of production and distribution. . . (*MCCT, II:* Cf. *MCCT, I:* 49f.)

> If there is no revolutionary conjuncture, the process of socialist construction must first take the form of building the economic and political conditions [N.B.] for a socialist economy. (*Ibid.,* 264)

But there are problems entailed in the more detailed specification.

First—after much rolling of drums and clashing of cymbals—what they revealingly call the "dichotomy between reform and revolution must collapse." (*MCCT, I:* 317)[44] This is:

> Socialist politics can no longer be conceived as necessarily oriented toward the one big push that finally knocks capitalism out of the way and clears the ground for something else. (*Ibid.*)

> An anti-capitalist standpoint need not imply ignorance of the role of management or an inability to intervene with a definite position on questions of capitalist organisation or calculation where there is political debate and a question of public policy. (*MCCT, II:* 260)

Who really operates on the big push theory as a set of tactics? Who does not operate on the basis of being *able* to understand capitalism? The problem is precisely the relation between these two kinds of work—some element of the former's total view, its sustained contempt, *has* to be retained. Or, if the latter alone is extensively practised then precisely that "reformism" they castigate within the leaders of Trades Unions and the Labour Party is what results.

Second, while they correctly support Marx's contention that "planned and co-operative production":

> would overcome the "anarchy" of capitalist production. . . In doing so socialism must deconstruct capitalist forms of economic organisation; breaking up the forms of independence Marx calls socialisation. (*MCCT, :* 151)

They show real restrictions on this "deconstruction." They accept the distorting prism of "national" economy—not as the obvious and elementary starting point, but as the final constraints and conditions of socialist struggle. (*MCCT, II:* 243f.) They also declare:

> Most advanced capitalist societies have removed significant areas of education

from the sphere of commodity forms of distribution and several have done the same for the distribution of medical care. (*MCCT, I:* 317; Cf. *MCCT, II:* 264f., 285f.)

This follows from their reductionist and economistic notion of production (and their decision that "commodities, money, etc." are entities). They—from the same premises—operate with an impoverished notion of power. Hirst has argued:

I would assert that... outside specific institutional forms state power does not exist... Classes do not have "interests" and are not political actors. Only definite organisations, or even individual agents, are political forces...[45]

From this, of course, *it follows:*

State apparatuses *and their powers* have differential degrees of utilisation in the promotion of socialist policies, they do not form "one reactionary mass", any more than the "state" forms a single entity *(except in the constitutional sense).* (*MCCT, II:* 267, our emphases)

We are into the land of "taking power" and not "transforming circumstances and selves." Unless socialist construction is concerned to challenge each and every relation, image and "fact"—and to transform them where they are found to relate to capitalist modes of production or other forms of inhuman constraint, then what is called "socialism" will reproduce domination, subordination and impoverishment. If you take away history—as fictive delusions—then all this dangerous nonsense follows. In fact, State apparatuses condense and represent centuries of bloody formation, always-ever (to sing their tune for a second) against class alternatives and "foreign competition", favouring *particular* forms of capitalist production. This has been well documented in the case of England since the start of the 16th century.[46] Innocently use any of those cultural or political relations of production specifically forged internally in capitalism's long rule and you will reproduce the deformations and crippling agonies of capitalist production and divert, slow-down or even halt (and perhaps reverse) the long struggle for socialist forms of life.

*   *   *

Conclusion: on the political necessity of history

Hindess and Hirst and their co-workers reproduce the Obvious world. They do not provide us with any means of comprehending that world as historically constructed. They do not share Marx's commitment to the fact that *things could be different.* They do not understand that for Marx (and others) socialist construction entails the simultaneous transformation of circumstances (things) *and* people themselves. In this revolution—as Marx defined it *through* his life—all the complicatedly connected relations and forms of capitalist production must be subject to the most comprehensive—because collective, as for once the subordinated can take their destiny into their own hands—scrutiny and change.

What we find in these texts—apart from a general historical ignorance (which does not, of course, stop historical facts from being employed, Cf. *MCCT, II:* 248, 249, 251)—is a failure to come to grips with the ways that socialist practices in the last ten years have challenged and opened what was taken as marxist political theory. For them, for example, Mind is not only all but sexed:

> No one in his right mind would consider that the conditions for a revolutionary seizure of power exist in this country. (*MCCT, II:* 240; Cf. *Ibid.,* p. 260)

The manliness of mind is, as they say, "pertinent in its effects" (does it not also reveal its conditions of existence?).

> The category of economic agents is fissured by numerous divisions with various determinations and effects (differences of income, working conditions, type of occupation, "race", nation and region, *to name the major ones*). (*MCCT, II:* 258)[47]

Their general strategy involves:

> taking seriously issues that may, *superficially,* appear remote from socialism and giving them a high order of priority in the struggle. Issues such as civil rights, the position of women, the control of environment and living space, all involve moving outside the traditional appeals of workerism. (*MCCT, II:* 292, our emphasis)

This is not merely a polemical point either. Lucy Bland, Rachel Harrison, Frank Mort and Christine Weedon have noted:

> it is their initial failure, in the construction of their problematic [in *PCMP*], to reveal that sex and gender relations are *power* relations (involving domination and subordination) which enables Hindess and Hirst to consider the maintenance and reproduction of social relations as relatively unimportant.[48]

> In a sense, the internal consistency of Hindess and Hirst's conceptual framework can remain intact by virtue of the absence of what is perhaps the most significant determinant in those societies, that is, the level of gender politics. What we would question here is not merely an omission from their analysis, but the overall conceptualisation of the political level itself. (*Ibid.,* p. 160)

Although this is said of early pre-capitalist societies (and *PCMP*), things have not progressed. There are many similar absences.

It is as well to remember—since his apostles have clearly forgotten—that Althusser celebrates (in a form and to a degree with which we entirely concur) Marx's theoretical discovery as "the continent of history." In the same text, Althusser also stressed that:

> *There is no such thing as a process except in relations (sous des rapports):* the relations of production (to which *Capital* is restricted) and other (political, ideological relations.[49]

Marx's method cannot be broken into (correct) analytic and (false) historic portions: Marx's notion of a critique *establishes* "the points where historical investigation must enter in."[50] Marx's critique produces concepts which are rational for analytic purposes, as "primary equations. . . which point towards a past lying behind the system" *(Ibid.)*—they expose neither the naturalness nor the logicality of phenomenal forms/concepts, but their historicity. Hindess and Hirst, by contrast, engage in conceptual *reproduction:* handing us back a mystified version of the Obvious, a de-historicized, universalised, mentalized, desocialized world in which the violence of things and the separateness of phenomena are not simply massively evident but positively celebrated.

Hindess and Hirst are part of those whom Marx called the "vulgar mob" who offer us such scraps of bourgeois wisdom as that the study of history is "not only scientifically but also politically valueless." (*PCMP*, p. 312). We call them bourgeois because that is whom their anti-history premises serve. Marx was clear on this very point:

> from the moment that the bourgeois mode of production and the conditions of production and distribution which correspond to it are recognised as historical, the delusion of regarding them as natural laws of production vanishes and the prospect opens up of a new society. . .[51]

To support Marx here is not to deny the difficulty of the struggles for that society. Socialist construction begins long before any convenient benchmark called "The" revolution and has to work within the area of theory because it begins and continues with a commitment to *practical materialism.* We are also stressing that the resources of socialist construction are already here—they are, moreover, the only resources there are—the human beings whose current labour sustains capital's rule and whose images and relations are "stamped and marked" "through and through" as Marx and Lenin agreed, with the restrictions of capitalism. Neither, finally, are we denying that during the long struggle for communism there will have to be struggles (as part of the way that authentic socialist construction is made possible) against forms of domination and restriction not directly generated within, although frequently sustained or utilised by, capitalist relations. We are thinking here of relations constituted as "gender" or "race (skin colour)" or those founded upon the Three Great Differences identified in the history of socialist construction in this century—those between industrial and agrarian production, town and country and—centrally relevant to the texts we have been criticising—between mental and manual labour.

The real emancipation of labour entails a struggle on the broadest front and in that struggle historical materialism—marxist theory understood in terms of accumulated historical experience—remains our only major and fundamental starting point.

NOTES

1. *MPSF* was published by Macmillan in 1977; *PCMP* (1975) and *MCCT, I* (1977) and *II* (1978) all by Routledge. The latter two-volume work was jointly written with Anthony Cutler and Athar Hussain. Other relevant major texts are:*Hirst:* "Economic classes and politics" in A. Hunt (ed.) *Class and class structure,* Lawrence & Wishart, 1977 (cited as "Hirst in Hunt"), "Althusser and the theory of ideology", *Economy and Society* 5(4) 1976; *Hindess:* "The concept of class in Marxist theory and Marxist politics" in J. Bloomfield (ed.) *Class, hegemony and party,* Lawrence & Wishart, 1977 (cited as "Hindess in Bloomfield"), "Classes and politics in Marxist theory" in G. Littlejohn (et. al. eds.) *Power and the State,* Croom Helm, 1978 (cited as "Hindess in Littlejohn"). Major reviews are:
PCMP: J. Taylor, *Critique of Anthropology* (4/5) 1975 and (6) 1976; T. Asad and H. Wolpe, *Economy and Society,* 5(4) 1976; R. Aya, *Theory & Society* 3(4) 1976 and *Monthly Review* 29 (8) 1978; D. Sayer, *Sociology,* 11(1)1977; S. Cook, *Journal of Peasant Studies,* 4(4) 1977.
PCMP and *MPSF:* G. Burchell, *Radical Philosophy* (18) 1977; T. Putnam, *Capital & Class* (4) 1978; R. Johnson, G. McLennan, B. Schwarz: *Economy, culture and concept,* Stencilled Paper no. 50, Birmingham, CCCS, Part III.
MPSF: A. Hussain, *Sociological Review* 26(1) 1978; *MCCT, I:* A. Hunt, *Morning Star,* 17 November 1977; *I* and *II:* D. Sayer, "Cleansing the Temple?" *Sociological Review,* forthcoming; L. Harris "The science of the economy" *Economy & Society* 7(3) 1978. There is one major text which we do not discuss —J. Ennew, P. Hirst, K. Tribe "Peasants as an economic category", *Journal of Peasant Studies,* 4(4), 1977—because of the excellent critique offered in a parallel article to our own—T. Shanin *Defining peasants* (mimeo. Manchester University, 1978) which we hope will enjoy the widest circulation at an early date.

2. For some general observations Cf. Simon Clarke, *Capital and Class* (2) 1977 and his "Althusserian Marxism: a bourgeois disorder" (mimeo. October 1976), plus J. Rancière, *Radical Philosophy* (7) 1974. We should also stress that the increasingly accepted notion that marxism is *ideational*—a project constructed through establishing "Heroes and Icons of the Left"—permeates many journals

and publishing houses, notably *New Left Review* and New Left Books.

3. Cf. N. Geras "Essence and appearance...", *NLR* (65) 1971 (reprinted in R. Blackburn, *Ideology in social science*, Fontana, 1972); J. Mepham "The theory of ideology in 'Capital' ", *Radical Philosophy* (2) 1972, reprinted in *Working Papers in Cultural Studies* (6) 1975; D. Sayer, *Marx's Method*, (Harvester, 1979) Part I.

4. We do not intend to engage in a similar diversion as that of the very project we are criticising, thus we shall not discuss this aspect of their project. It has been well covered, see the *Radical Philosophy* and *Economy and Society* reviews listed in n. 1 above, plus the exceptionally useful text by G. McLennan in *Economy and Society* 7(2) 1978. For general criticism—Sayer "Science as critique" in J. Mepham and D. Ruben (eds.) *Essays in Marxist Philosophy* (Harvester, 1979) and Sayer *Marx's Method*, Ch. 1, which detail Marx's critique of all speculative theorising.

5. *The German Ideology*, Marx/Engels, *Collected Works*, (Lawrence & Wishart, 1976 onwards) Vol. 5, p. 56 (Hereafter simply CW...). Wittgenstein's whole argument against "craving for generality" and "contempt for the particular" needs study in this connection.

6. "Introduction", *Grundrisse*, (Penguin, 1973), p. 101.
   See Sayer *Marx's Method*, Ch. 4, for a detailed discussion of this text.

7. "Notes on Adolph Wagner" (in Marx, *Texts on Method*, ed. T. Carver, Blackwell, Oxford 1975), p. 198, 201. For extended commentary see Sayer, *Marx's Method*.

8. For example *CW*: 5, pp. 43f.

9. "Introduction", *Grundrisse*, p. 84.

10. "Notes on Adolph Wagner", p. 190.

11. V.N. Volosinov, *Marxism and the philosophy of language*, (New York Seminar Press, 1973). This is the 2nd ed., of 1930. See especially pp. 19f., 81f. and C. Woolfson, *Marxism Today*, 21(8) 1977; A. O'Shea, "Multiaccentuality and capitalism", M.A. Course Essay, University of Birmingham, CCCS, 1977; R. Williams, *Marxism and Literature*, Oxford University Press, 1977.

12. R. Rossi-Landi, *Ideologies of linguistic relativity*, Hague, Mouton, 1973, p. 63.

13. I.I. Rubin, *Essays on Marx's theory of value*, (Detroit, Black and Red, 1972), p. 57. Originally published 1928.

14. Marx, *Capital, I* (Moscow, Progress, 1967), p. 537. This can be seen in Marx's whole project—Sayer's work already cited traces this; for early examples in Marx see *CW*: 3, pp. 326-348, and much of *Hegel's Philosophy of Right* and *The German Ideology* (*CW*: 3 and 5 respectively). There is much of value here in Colletti's introduction to Marx, *Early Writings*, (Penguin, 1975).

15. Lenin, *Collected Works*, (Moscow, Progress) Vol. 22, pp. 355f. quoted in "Hirst in Hunt", p. 126; *MCCT, I*: 232f., *MCCT, II*: p. 237. We analyse the contradictory features of Lenin's writing in Corrigan, H. Ramsay and Sayer, *Socialist construction*, cited in n. 22.

16. Thompson's extended discussions will soon be available in his book of essays *The Poverty of Theory* (Merlin, 1978), in the meantime we continue to stress the importance of his fundamentally *theoretical* statement *The Making of the English Working Class*, (Penguin, 1968).

17. E.P. Thompson "Eighteenth century English society", *Social History* 3(2) 1978, p. 164. Cf. Corrigan, Ramsay, Sayer, *For Mao*, (Macmillan, 1979), Part II, Essay 4; Corrigan and Sayer, "Class struggle, moral relations, political economy", *Radical Philosophy* (12) 1975.

18. "Hirst in Hunt", p. 131.

19. "Hindess in Littlejohn", pp. 96-97. Cf. "Hindess in Bloomfield."

20. Engels' letters to Schmidt, August 5 and October 27, 1890; to Bloch, September 21-22, 1890; to Mehring, July 14, 1893; to Borgius, January 25, 1894 (in *Selected Correspondence*, Moscow, Progress, 1975 or *Selected Letters*, Peking, FLPH, 1977) and Engels to Starkenberg, January 25, 1895 in the 1956 ed. of *Selected Correspondence.*

21. A. Glucksmann, "A ventriloquist structuralism", *NLR* (72) 1972, originally published 1967. N. Poulantzas, "Vers une theorie marxiste", *Temps Modernes* (240) 1966.

22. Space limitations mean that we do not develop or document this argument as fully as we wish. For amplification see Sayer, "Method and Dogma in Historical materialism", *Sociological Review* 23(4) 1975; *Marx's Method*, Ch. 4, Section 1; "Science as Critique" and Corrigan, Ramsay, Sayer, *Socialist construction and marxist theory: Bolshevism and its critique* (London, Macmillan; New York, Monthly Review Press, 1978), Ch. 1.

23. Marx, "Preface" in *Selected Writings...* (Bottomore and Rubel edition, Penguin, 1963, p. 67).

24. *CW:* 5, p. 35, our emphases. That this is no youthful aberration can be seen from *Capital, III* (Moscow, Progress, 1971, p. 792) where Marx speaks of the need for "analysis of the empirically given circumstances."

25. This analysis differs from that we have presented earlier (e.g. Sayer, "Method and Dogma"). Although we stand by the criticism of traditional readings given there, we would no longer draw the conclusion that the base/superstructure metaphor should be entirely displaced.

26. Marx, "Preface", (ed. cit., p. 68) our emphasis.

27. e.g. *CW:* 5: 89, 373. The stress on *forms* in some of Engels letters (e.g. to Mehring, July 14, 1893; to Bloch, September 21-22, 1890) is extremely pertinent here. Cf. Marx, "Eighteenth Brumaire", in this light.

28. Cf. the material cited in n. 3 above.

29. *CW:* 5, pp. 26-27. Note the similarity of the language to that of the 1859 *Preface.*

30. *Capital I* (ed. cit., n. 14), p. 80.

31. Nicolaus, in his "Foreword" to the Penguin ed. of the *Grundrisse* (p. 52) suggests this, as does Colletti, op. cit. It is central to recent debates on the State, e.g. in Germany, J. Holloway and S. Picciotto (eds.) *State and Capital,* Arnold, 1978; Cf. Corrigan, Ramsay, Sayer, "The State as a relation of production", paper to B.S.A. 1977 Conference, in revised form as Ch. 1 of P. Corrigan (ed.) *State formation and capitalism,* (Quartet, 1979).

32. A. MacIntyre, "Notes from the Moral Wilderness, 1", *New Reasoner* (7) Winter 1958-59, quoted E.P. Thompson "Open Letter..." *Socialist Register,* 1973, n. 20, p. 97. Cf. B. Ollman, *Alienation...* Cambridge, 1971, "In defence of internal relations", *Radical Philosophy* (13) 1976.

33. This is a central constituent of the two collective volumes already cited— *Socialist construction and marxist theory,* and *For Mao.* Other sketches can be seen in Corrigan, *Journal of Peasant Studies,* 2(3) 1975; Sayer, "Method and Dogma."

34. As we indicated above, n. 4, we are not examining this issue here—for a general analysis see Sayer, "Science as Critique."

35. *Grundrisse,* (ed. cit.), p. 712.

36. S. Hall: "Some problems with the ideology/subject couplet", *Ideology and Consciousness* (3) 1978, p. 120. Cf. his "Culture, the media and the 'Ideological effect'" in J. Curran (et. al. eds.) *Mass communication...* Arnold, 1977; "Re-thinking the 'base-and-superstructure' metaphor" in Bloomfield (op. cit., n. 1 above) and "The 'political' and the 'economic' in Marx's theory of

classes" in A. Hunt (op. cit., n. 1 above).

37. "Hindess in Bloomfield", p. 105. Cf. "Hirst in Hunt" and "Hindess in Littlejohn".

38. Hirst on Althusser (op. cit., n. 1 above), p. 410. Cf. N. Rose "Fetishism and ideology", *Ideology and consciousness* (2) 1977.

39. To think otherwise is essentially "preWittgenstein". Cf. T. Eagleton "Men without language: the novels of William Golding", *Views* (11) 1966, p. 37, and the chapters in M. Barrett, P. Corrigan, A. Kuhn, J. Wolff (eds.) *Representation and cultural production* (Croom Helm, 1979), especially the first.

40. Putnam, op. cit., n. 1 above, p. 153.

41. Burchell, op. cit., n. 1 above, p. 32.

42. "Hirst in Hunt", p. 131.

43. Hirst on Althusser (op. cit., n. 1 above), p. 397.

44. Cf. Corrigan, "Dichotomy is contradiction", *Sociological Review,* 23, 1975.

45. "Hirst in Hunt", p. 152. Their view of power is Left-Weberian in tendency.

46. Marx was clear on this, e.g. *Capital I* (ed. cit.) p. 751. The "systematical combination" that is imperialism which Marx there described shows the dangerous limitations of any marxist analysis of socialist politics founded upon the "prism" of the *national economy.* Cf. P. Corrigan, "Feudal relics. . ." *Sociology,* 11, 1977; *State formation. . .* (op. cit., n. 31 above).

47. Our emphasis. Compare the description in Corrigan, "Politics of Production", *Journal of Peasant Studies,* 1975, p. 346, para 2.

48. *Women take issue. . .* (Hutchinson, 1978), pp. 157-158. The criticism here can be applied to other texts e.g. "Hindess in Bloomfield" or "Hirst in Hunt."

49. L. Althusser, "Marx's relation to Hegel", (1968) in his *Politics and history* (NL Books, 1971), p. 186. We do not accept his impoverished view of what *Capital* contains.

50. *Grundrisse,* ed. cit., p. 429. Cf. Sayer, *Marx's Method,* Ch. 6.

51. Marx, *Theories of Surplus Value, III* (Moscow, Progress, 1972), p. 429. Cf. Sayer, "Science as Critique." Meillassoux makes a similar point in his criticism of *PCMP:* Hindess and Hirst's denial of the significance of "historical social and political context" "throws doubt on their claim to be working within historical materialism." Meillassoux, as we do, sees their "point of view" as "a strict codification of the idealist-judicial approach of bourgeois science under the guise of Marxism." C. Meillassoux, *Economy & Society* 7(3) 1978, p. 329.

C.B. MACPHERSON: LIBERALISM, AND THE TASK OF SOCIALIST POLITICAL THEORY

Ellen Meiksins Wood

Just as Marxist political theory or the "theory of the state" has begun to flourish, there has been a revival of formal political philosophy on the intellectual right. Whether or not these trends are directly related, it is not surprising that left and right should diverge into two modes of theorizing about politics so opposed in both substance and method. If Marxist political theory is intended to penetrate the realities of class power, academic political philosophy has often had the effect not simply of justifying those realities but of mystifying them in a cloud of philosophic formalism and abstraction. Particularly in the English-speaking world, conservatives have found in the discipline of political philosophy an academic home that suits them especially well; and with the recent general upsurge of intellectual activity on the political right in Europe and America, the discipline has been given a new lease of life.

The legacy of minor 20th century "classics" in the field of political philosophy has been dominated by various shades of conservatism: for example, the works of Leo Strauss and Hannah Arendt in America or Michael Oakeshott in Britain. Their efforts have been abetted, at least indirectly, by analytic and linguistic philosophy, which have served the cause of political conservatism simply by denaturing, depoliticizing political theory, depriving it of any capacity for social criticism. These traditions have now been extended by a variety of apologies—usually abstract and formalistic—for inequality, bourgeois individualism, property rights, and free enterprise, by writers such as John Rawls, Robert Nozick, and Oakeshott's disciple, Kenneth Minogue. On the other hand, the field has been virtually abandoned by the left, no doubt partly because of the devaluation of the "political" as "epiphenomenon" which has so long characterized Marxist theory, but also because the conventions of political philosophy have tended to depoliticize the political by abstracting it from its socio-historical substance.

C.B. Macpherson has for many years been the single major voice from the left in the traditional disciplines of political philosophy and the history of political thought. His work, especially his classic *The Political Theory of Possessive Individualism* published in 1962, has been groundbreaking. Above all, it has done much to repoliticize political philosophy, giving it some

215

foundation in history and revealing its ideological function. Macpherson's theory and method are not, however, Marxist; and questions can be raised about what his standpoint actually is. Certainly he writes from a perspective that rejects the consequences of capitalism, but the rejection of capitalism is not consistently grounded in a commensurate *analysis* of capitalist social relations. Often Macpherson's analysis of capitalism appears to accept that system at its own valuation. At such times, the effect of his argument is not so different from the very theories he criticizes—pluralist political science, marginal utility economics, the "market model" of man and society; and he ends by confirming their ideological mystifications.

What makes it especially difficult to characterize Macpherson's standpoint is that it seems to vary. There is no doubt that throughout his career he has vigorously attacked modern political theory for obscuring social realities and the nature of capitalism, particularly for neglecting the consequences of class relations. Nevertheless, there is a continuity between his more critical works and those in which he most closely approximates the conceptual framework of his adversaries. Even in his criticisms there are theoretical ambiguities which open the way for a convergence with his opponents.

Macpherson's ambiguous theoretical approach and its programmatic implications are most visible in his latest book, *The Life and Times of Liberal Democracy,*[1] the culmination of the work on liberalism which has occupied him since *Possessive Individualism.* If his political philosophy as outlined in *The Life and Times* is intended to embody a socialist programme, that programme is contradicted by its theoretical underpinnings. Most significantly, he seems particularly unwilling here to pursue the implications of *class,* with all this entails—even when, in the analysis of liberalism, he appears to characterize that doctrine as a class ideology. This reluctance to deal with class reflects a more fundamental methodological problem. Macpherson's work, despite its historical foundations, still remains to a considerable extent within the methodological conventions of traditional political philosophy, abstracting political theory from the social realities that underlie it. Even if Macpherson explicitly proposes a programme of social and political changes that go beyond the mere reform of capitalism, considerable importance must be attached to the fact that his account of capitalism differs very little from conventional portraits by apologists for capitalism. His approach compels one to ask how an essentially liberal-pluralist *theory* can produce, or even be compatible with, a socialist *practice.*

A critical examination of *The Life and Times of Liberal Democracy* can, therefore, be instructive, especially if it is contrasted to what a Marxist theory might do with an analysis of liberalism. There are two major ways in which a study of liberal democratic principles can play a useful part in a socialist political theory. First, an examination of the meaning of liberalism and its historic role in the evolution of bourgeois society may be a useful adjunct to an interpretation of class power in capitalist society and the nature of the capitalist state in its principal contemporary form. Secondly, a consideration of liberal democracy and the "bourgeois liberties" which it has codified may serve as a means of confronting the problem of the *political* in a *socialist* society: how and why—or whether—the "political" question persists in a classless society, and to what extent and in what ways the organization and administration of a classless society still require "bourgeois" legalism as a protection against arbitrary power. How a theory situates itself with respect to these two issues must have important strategic and programmatic implications.

If Macpherson's view of the world, with all its contradictions, were idiosyncratic, it would be enough to expose the contradictions and propose an alternative approach to his analysis of liberalism. Since, however, he is in many ways typical of a certain kind of "socialism" particularly characteristic of Britain and North America, something important can be learned from an effort to explain the very existence of a political theory such as his. It could conceivably be argued that the contradictions in his position result merely from tactical considerations. He does often write as if his primary object were to persuade liberals that some kind of socialism follows naturally from their convictions, by representing his own brand of socialism as an extension of liberalism. He often appears to be self-consciously addressing an audience that needs to be persuaded that socialism—a doctrine which, apparently, must parade in sheep's clothing as something called "participatory democracy"—is the last and best form of liberal democracy, preserving what is essential and valuable in the liberal tradition and devoid of its evils. Such a conspiratorial interpretation of Macpherson's argument would suggest that he *intentionally* obscures as much as he reveals about the nature of both capitalism and liberalism.

It is more likely, however, that Macpherson's approach is not merely a tactical ploy, and that his failure to produce an analysis commensurate with his apparent ethical commitment to socialism is part of a political and intellectual tradition which has been seduced by liberalism itself, in theory and practice. This is a tradition—particularly characteristic of Britain and North America—which has produced a form of socialism riddled with contradictions between its moral indignation at capitalism and its inadequate understanding of the social phenomenon that provokes that indignation. The tradition seems also to be part of a more general intellectual tendency which abstracts political theory from social analysis. These same factors may also help to account for the particular usefulness of abstract political philosophy as an instrument of bourgeois hegemony precisely in those countries where the liberal tradition has been strongest.

Macpherson's Argument

The Life and Times of Liberal Democracy is an account of changes in liberal democratic theory presented as a series of historically successive "models" which represent several major doctrinal shifts since the foundation of modern liberalism in the utilitarianism of Bentham and James Mill. The purpose of this schematic history is, writes Macpherson, "to examine the limits and possibilities of liberal democracy"; (2) that is, not merely to examine the nature and development of the liberal tradition up to now, but to explore its future possibilities. The book, then, is meant to be not only an intellectual history, but also—and, it seems, primarily—a political programme.

Although Macpherson proposes an explicit political programme, which he chooses to describe as an extension of liberal democracy, the concern here will not be primarily with that. The programme is far too sketchy to sustain close analysis. More significant is the project implicit in his analysis of liberal democratic theory, what that analysis says and fails to say about the nature of the society that spawned the doctrine and what it implies about the conditions and possibilities for transforming that society. It will be argued that Macpherson's characterization of liberal democracy—and his suggestion that his own programme is an extension of that tradition—may obscure the realities of capitalist society and one of its hegemonic doctrines in ways which have serious programmatic consequences. Secondly, Macpherson puts his stress in the wrong place and has missed the chance to illuminate those aspects of the liberal legacy which may be of greatest relevance to a socialist programme.

Macpherson begins by isolating what for him is the essential meaning of liberal democracy: it is the principle of "a society striving to ensure that all its members are equally free to realize their capabilities", (3) as that principle was enunciated, according to Macpherson, by J.S. Mill and the "ethical-liberal democrats" who followed him. This meaning of liberal democracy can, he argues, be dissociated from liberal democracy in its more general sense, "the democracy of a capitalist market society (no matter how modified that society appears to be by the rise of the welfare state)." (3) Up to now, Macpherson suggests, the two meanings have been combined; but "a liberal position need not be taken to depend forever on an acceptance of capitalist assumptions, although historically it has been so taken." (4)

What Macpherson calls liberal democracy is carefully distinguished both from undemocratic liberalism—such as that of John Locke—and non-liberal, or more accurately, pre-liberal democracy, such as that of Rousseau or Jefferson. The distinctions are important. Liberal democracy is specifically associated with a class-divided society; the doctrine pre-supposes and accepts the division of society into classes, and merely seeks to "fit a democratic structure" to a class-divided society." (10) This foundation in class divisions distinguishes liberal democracy from those pre-19th century utopian democratic theories which were intended as reactions *against* class societies: for example, Winstanley's programme for a classless democracy grounded in communal property, or Rousseau's "one-class" society based on a community of independent small producers who are in a position neither to exploit nor to be exploited. Liberal democratic theory is a doctrine which emerged only in the late 18th or early 19th century precisely because it was only then that some—albeit limited—form of political democracy no longer appeared incompatible with class divisions and the security of property. (Although Macpherson does not explain why this was so, an explanation grounded in Marx's account of capitalism would serve very well here: with the increasing separation of producers from the means of production, what Marx calls "other than economic" modes of exploitation are increasingly replaced by "economic", and the role of the "political" in the relations of production accordingly changes. As we shall see, however, Macpherson avoids any language or mode of analysis which suggests a Marxist conception of productive relations and class domination.) Liberal democracy could now become the doctrine of those wedded to the prevailing system of property and class relations. In the 17th and 18th centuries, democracy had been perceived by the upper classes as class-rule by the wrong class, the poor, and hence as a threat. The main tradition was undemocratic or anti-democratic, until historical circumstances were such that a limited form of political democracy no longer appeared as a threat to property and class-domination. (10) Pre-liberal democracy, then, did not presuppose capitalist market relations; non-democratic liberalism did assume some form of capitalist market relations but regarded democracy as a threat to those relations. It is the unique characteristic of liberal democracy that it no longer assumes the incompatibility of political "democracy" with class divisions generally and capitalist market relations in particular.

Macpherson's ultimate theme concerns the future prospects of liberal democracy *without* capitalist market assumptions. "Liberalism", he writes, "had always meant freeing the individual from outdated restraints of old established institutions. By the time liberalism emerged as liberal democracy this became a claim to free all individuals equally, and to free them to use and develop their human capacities fully." (21) The linkage of liberal democracy with capitalist market assumptions was based, he argues, on an economy of scarcity which persuaded liberal democrats that only the productivity of free enterprise capitalism could achieve the ethical goal of freeing all individuals "to use and develop their human capacities fully." If we can now assume, continues Macpherson, that the technological limitations on the possibility of a good life for everyone have been surpassed, the linkage of liberal democratic ends with market society is no longer necessary.

The argument is an interesting one. It is certainly crucial to an understanding of liberal democracy to recognize the extent to which it is grounded in the assumption of class divisions and capitalist relations. And though Macpherson is sometimes a bit coy and cryptic about this, there can be little doubt that at the outset of the argument, liberal democratic doctrine is meant to be seen not as essentially and principally democratic but as the ideology of a dominant class, the bourgeoisie, whose commitment even to a limited political democracy is conditional, determined by its own changing needs in a particular historic situation.

This account of the foundation of liberal democracy as a class ideology makes the rest of the argument rather puzzling. If the doctrine is based on class-division, one must question Macpherson's characterization of its ethical position as a commitment to the free and equal development of all individuals. For that matter, one might wonder why he chooses to single out liberal democracy as the embodiment of this cherished principle when a doctrine opposed to the class-nature of liberal democracy—that is, Marxism—is more centrally and genuinely concerned with this ethical commitment than is liberalism in any of its forms. More importantly, one must ask whether Macpherson is telling us what we really need to know about the linkage of liberal democracy to "market assumptions" and capitalist relations. Is it, for example, so easy to dissociate the doctrine from its foundations in capitalism by simply assuming away the "economy of scarcity" (even leaving aside questions which may arise about the usefulness and precision of the notion of "scarcity" and the "surpassing" of scarcity)? It is typical of Macpherson's approach that he is often able to treat capitalism as if it were merely the (temporary) instrument of liberal democracy, or even of liberal democratic thinkers and their ethical goal. A very different picture emerges—as will be suggested later—from an approach that grounds the analysis of ideas and institutions firmly in social realities, making it possible to examine the foundations of liberal democracy in capitalist relations of production.

Macpherson's Four "Models" of Liberal Democracy

The four models of liberal democracy are designated as "Protective Democracy", "Developmental Democracy", "Equilibrium Democracy", and "Participatory Democracy." The first, which makes its case for democracy on the grounds that it alone can protect the governed from oppression, is found in the utilitarianism of Bentham and James Mill, reluctant democrats who simply felt that the needs of an essentially capitalist economy in the then prevailing conditions demanded such political reforms as the extension of the franchise. The "developmental" model, which Macpherson divides into two stages, is a more humanistic one. The model is best represented by J.S. Mill (although Macpherson recognizes the anti-democratic elements in Mill) who first articulated the principle which for Macpherson is the essence of the tradition, that aspect of it he wants to preserve: the commitment to the self-development of all individuals equally. In the 20th century, this developmental model, represented by philosophical idealists like Barker or Lindsay, pragmatists like Dewey or "modified utilitarians" like Hobhouse, while retaining Mill's ethical commitment lost some of his realism concerning the obstacles to the fulfillment of the liberal goal posed by the realities of class and exploitation. They simply assumed that the regulatory and welfare state would suffice to bring about the desired end. The third model, the currently prevalent one, is that of modern social scientists, the "pluralist elitist equilibrium model" inaugurated by Schumpeter and developed by political scientists like Robert Dahl. This model, argues Macpherson, lacks the ethical dimension of the previous one and offers a description, and a justification, of stable democracy as a "competition between elites which produces equilibrium without much popular participation." (22) Democracy according to this model is "simply a mechanism for choosing and authorizing governments, not a kind of society or a set of moral ends. . ." (78) Having critically examined each of these models in turn, explaining the reasons for their successive failures and eventual replacement by a new model, Macpherson finally turns to the emerging model of "Participatory Democracy", which began as a slogan of the New Left student movement. He proposes to develop this into a complete model to supersede earlier ones, embodying a specific political programme and some suggestions about the kinds of social and ideological changes which would be needed to make the political programme workable.

Macpherson's analysis of the first two models is the best part of the book. More could certainly have been said about the ways in which the doctrine expressed the realities and structural needs of capitalism at a particular stage of development. One might like to hear something about how the particular nature of capitalism at that stage and in those places which produced this version of liberal doctrine affected the nature and demands of the working class. And no doubt a good deal needs to be said here about the ways in which the liberal bourgeois state has both conducted and contained class conflict and how the dominant class has maintained hegemony, not least by means of liberal-democratic theory and practice. Still, there is at least no doubt that both models in various ways responded to the practical demands of capitalism and were imbued with its assumptions, values, and contradictions; and one essential point is still relatively clear at this stage of Macpherson's analysis: liberal democracy—whatever disinterested moral commitments he may attribute to it—is still the ideology of a class-divided society, still an ideology expressing the needs of a class committed to the prevailing capitalist relations.

Much of the value of Macpherson's analysis is lost, however, in what follows. His account of Model 3 is by far the weakest—and the weakness is particularly serious since this model is the currently prevailing one and is meant to be understood as reflecting the realities of capitalism today. Moreover, it is in his analysis of this model that the shortcomings of Macpherson's whole approach become most obvious.

Macpherson discusses this model as, in turn, a description, an explanation, and sometimes a justification of the actual political system in Western democracies, while conceding that these theoretical functions cannot always be kept distinct. Democracy in this case is "simply a mechanism for choosing and authorizing governments. . .", consisting of "a competition between two or more self-chosen politicians (elites). . ." (78) "Democracy is simply a market mechanism: the voters are consumers, the politicians are the entrepreneurs." (79) Macpherson's first and most extraordinary judgement on this model, however, is as follows: "As a description of the actual system now prevailing in Western liberal-democratic nations, Model 3 must be adjudged as substantially accurate." (83)

With this apparent acceptance of the pluralist-elitist democratic description of politics in capitalist society, Macpherson effectively sweeps away most of what it is important to know about capitalism as a system of *class*-relations, about class power in capitalist society, about political power as a means of maintaining class dominance, and about the liberal bourgeois state as a class state. All the apparently useful insights about liberal democracy as a class ideology, suggested in his earlier discussion, are thus also called into question. Indeed, his analysis now appears to have practically conceptualized out of of existence both *class* and *state.* At best, the analysis—at least implicitly—replaces them with the ideological mystifications of "elites" and "political system" and their version of the issues raised by an analysis of society in terms of class and state. Pluralists like Robert Dahl—and, apparently, Macpherson—do recognize that there are inequalities of political power and differences in access to the instrumentalities of government. There are "elites" of various kinds, but these elites compete for power and no dominant and consistent concentrations of power exist. What this means, then, is that there is no such thing as *class* power, or at least not in any sense that is politically relevant, and certainly that there is no *ruling* class. Above all, there is no conception of the state as an institution whose function is to sustain a particular social order, that is, a particular set of productive relations and a particular system of class dominance.[2]

Macpherson and the Mystifications of Capitalist Ideology

Macpherson's apparent acceptance of what can only be called the ideological mystifications of the pluralist democratic model must raise questions about his whole enterprise. Indeed, his very criticisms of the model only serve to confirm that he shares its most fundamental premises and is unable—or unwilling—to confront in more than the most superficial ways the consequences of class power and the nature of the state in a class society. On the face of it, his criticism of the model seems at first to address itself to the problem of class:

> I want now to show that the Model 3 political market system is not nearly as democratic as it is made out to be: that the equilibrium it produces is an equilibrium in inequality; that the consumer sovereignty it claims to provide is to a large extent an illusion; and that, to the extent that the consumer sovereignty is real, it is a contradiction of the central democratic tenet of equality of individual entitlement to the use and enjoyment of one's capacities. The claims for optimum equilibrium and consumer sovereignty are virtually the same claim—two sides of the same coin—and so may be treated together as a single claim. (86-87)

When Macpherson begins to specify the nature of the inequality which concerns him, however, the issue of *class* and *class power* recedes:

> In so far as the political purchasing power is money, we can scarcely say that the equilibrating process is democratic in any society, like ours, in which there is substantial inequality of wealth and of chances of acquiring wealth. We may still call it consumer sovereignty if we wish. But the sovereignty of such unequal consumers is not evidently democratic. (87)
> ... The political market system *is* competitive enough to do the job of equilibrating the supply of and demand for political goods—in so far, that is, as it *does* actually respond to demands which are very unequally effective. Some demands are more effective than others because, where the demand is expressed in human energy output, one person's energy input cannot get the same return per unit as another person's. And the class of political demands that have the most money to back them is largely the same as the class of those that have the larger pay-off per unit of human energy input. In both cases, it is the demands of the higher socio-economic classes which are the most effective. So the lower classes are apathetic. (89)

The question of "unequal" political power is thus reduced to a matter of unequal "purchasing power"; and *class* has become, at best, the bogus "socio-economic class" of conventional "stratification" theory: "income groups", "inequality of wealth and of chances of acquiring wealth"—anything but a *relation* of domination and exploitation. This is a concept of inequality (*inequality*, not *class*) entirely consistent with the pluralist-democratic view and often, indeed usually, conceded by theorists whose arguments, far from recognizing the existence of class and class power, are designed to *deny* them. It is here simply a question of *individuals*, meeting indirectly in the market-place—in this case, particularly the political market-place—and competing for valued goods and services, all in possession of some purchasing power, but some simply equipped with more than others. The political relationship among these individuals appears to be little more than the superficial relationship of relative advantage or disadvantage in the market-place, not a relation of power or domination. Indeed, it now seems likely that Macpherson's concept of *class* generally, even when he seems most conscious of its importance, may not be a concept of class at all. It may, in retrospect, be significant that throughout the book he consistently speaks of "capitalist market relations" rather than capitalist relations of production.

On this score, it may be useful to refer to the example of Max Weber, whose legacy so often serves those who want to evade the issues posed by Marx. Weber in his own definition of class quite deliberately and painstakingly avoids the implication of class as a *relation*, a direct relation of domination; and in particular, he carefully obscures the nature of capitalist exploitation by reducing capitalist social relations of production to the "competition" of "market relations." According to Weber, people belong to classes insofar as their "fates" are "determined by the chance of using goods or services, for themselves on the market." All goods and services, all commodities, including labour, are conflated. The difference, and the relation, between those whose "market situation" gives them control of the means of production and those who have only their labour-power to sell are reduced to the vague and neutral terms of their relative advantages in market competition for goods and services. The one thing that is conspicuously absent in this definition is the idea of class as a *relation*. The only "relation" between classes that is encompassed by this definition is their competition for valued goods and services; they come together by "meeting competitively in the market for the purpose of exchange." Nothing is said of the direct relation which is the essential consequence of an "exchange" in which human labour-power is one of the commodities. The most that Weber is usually prepared to say about the "property" and "lack of property" which are the "basic categories" of class situation is that "the mode of distribution, in accord with the law of marginal utility, excludes the non-wealthy from competing for highly valued goods; it favours the owners and, in fact, gives to them a monopoly to acquire such goods." Class struggles, then, seem to amount to little more than extensions of this competition for goods and services.[3]

Macpherson appears to be operating with a very similar conception of class, not only in his latest book, but in his earlier works. *Possessive Individualism,* for all its ground-breaking analysis of political theory as ideology—apparently *class* ideology—is actually remarkable for its lack of a concept of class. More recently, (and in an article selected as the first in Robin Blackburn's collection of essays by "radical scholars" on *Ideology in Social Science*), Macpherson—ostensibly attacking the mystifications of contemporary economics—defines capitalist as follows:

Are we in an era of post-capitalism? I do not think we are. The change is not as great as some would suggest. It all depends, of course, on how you prefer to define capitalism. If you define it as a system of free enterprise with no government interference, then of course our present heavily regulated system is not capitalism. But I find it very unhistorical to equate capitalism with *laissez-faire.* I think it preferable to define capitalism as the system in which production is carried out without authoritative allocation of work or rewards, but by contractual relations between free individuals (each possessing some resource be it only his own labour-power) who calculate their most profitable courses of action and employ their resources as that calculation dictates.

... What the state does [by its interference] is to alter the terms of the equation which each man makes when he is calculating his most profitable course of action. Some of the data for the calculation are changed, but this need not affect the mainspring of the system, which is that men do act as their calculation of net gain dictates. As long as prices still move in response to these calculated decisions, and as long as prices still elicit the production of goods and determine their allocation, we may say that the essential nature of the system has not changed.[4]

Although this passage purports to be an attack on the ideological mystifications of conventional social sciences, there is nothing in it which is incompatible with either pluralist political science or bourgeois economics and their typical obfuscations of the nature of capitalism. Indeed, Macpherson's characterization of capitalism is significant precisely because of the extent to which it shares the fundamental premises of modern economics: the reduction of relations of production to market relations, the transformation of social to individual relations and relations of exploitation to relations among equally free and sovereign individuals, and even an acceptance of the marginal utility theory of value. All these premises have the effect of obscuring the ways in which the mode of production structures the "free" choices of individuals; concealing the special social meaning of the "free" exchange in which one party sells his labour-power; depriving the concept of class of any significance; and reducing the "factors of production"—notably capital and labour—to a sameness which, above all, divests the relation between them of its exploitative nature and justifies the "rewards" of capital. Furthermore, there is nothing in Macpherson's account of state intervention in capitalism that suggests an appreciation of its role in "reproducing" capitalist relations of production or maintaining the structure of class domination characteristic of that mode of production. Here, as in *The Life and Times of Liberal Democracy,* Macpherson's conception of political power and inequalities of political power is either devoid of any concept of class or is based on a concept of class which carries with it no suggestion of a social relation, of power and domination, rooted in and constitutive of a particular set of exploitative relations of production.

The temptation is very strong at this point to dismiss Macpherson's extension of liberal democratic theory as little more than another version—albeit unusually critical—of the pluralist democratic apology for fundamentally capitalist relations of production. And yet, his own programme as outlined in the discussion of Model 4, "Participatory Democracy", suggests—however schematically, cautiously, superficially, and often naively—something beyond a merely reformed bourgeois-liberal state grounded in capitalist relations of production. Although he adopts for his programme the somewhat innocuous term "participatory democracy" (which, for example, the Liberal Prime Minister of Canada, Pierre Trudeau, at one point quite comfortably appropriated for his own political programme), Macpherson seems to have something rather more radical in mind. I have already suggested that these explicit proposals seem to me less significant than the programmatic principles implicit in his analysis of liberal democracy; and that I do not intend to comment on the explicit programme in detail. Still, it is only fair to say that Macpherson's programme does at least appear to take for granted that social conditions must be radically transformed if "participatory democracy" is to work; and that the bourgeois state apparatus must not simply be appropriated by the right people but must be replaced by radically different political forms. In language more reminiscent of Luxemburg than liberalism, he proposes what he calls a "responsible pyramidal councils system", with competitive parties; and he argues that such a political system would not work in the presence of class divisions and oppositions. His account of how this transformation might be achieved places considerable—though far from unbounded—faith in some of the currently fashionable expressions of social protest: environmentalism, neighbourhood organizations, and movements for "decision-making" in the work-place, and in general, growing doubts about "the ability of corporate capitalism to meet consumer expectations in the old way. . ." (105) Nevertheless, the programme is not simply reducible to a call for the reform of capitalism. In any case, the essential problem is that Macpherson's very sketchy programme is less significant even programmatically than the analysis of liberalism which occupies most of the book. That analysis does, after all, represent Macpherson's conception of the society which needs to be transformed and thus establishes the conditions, the possibilities and limitations, of the desired transformation. However radical the explicit programme may be, the analysis essentially contradicts it by accepting capitalism on its own terms.

Liberal Democracy and Capitalism

Macpherson argues that there has been an historic linkage between democratic liberalism and "market assumptions." The link between liberalism and capitalism, however, seems to hinge largely upon the ideals and perceptions of particular thinkers; and capitalism almost appears as an instrument of liberalism, whose commitment to the capitalist system is secondary, contingent, and temporary. He does acknowledge that certain historical developments had to take place before even the limited political democracy of advanced liberalism could prove acceptable to the propertied classes and compatible with capitalist "market relations"; but he never explains these developments, and his mode of analysis actually discourages an understanding of them. Above all, his argument provides no means of explaining what it is in the fundamental nature of capitalist relations of production that made their linkage with liberal democracy possible and, if not actually necessary, at least very convenient under given historic conditions. There is no suggestion in Macpherson's argument—and no methodological or theoretical possibility of suggesting—that liberal democracy, though not a necessary and universal consequence of capitalist productive relations, is nevertheless firmly grounded in these relations. To put it another way, Macpherson's mode of analysis cannot explain how and why capitalist relations of production have historically been a necessary if not sufficient condition for the development of liberal democracy, and conversely, to what extent and in what ways liberal democracy has sustained those productive relations.

How, then, should one assess the relation between liberalism and capitalism? Two problems are of major importance to socialist theory and practice: the first concerns liberal democracy in the present, its role in capitalist society; the other concerns liberal democratic principles in the future and whether liberalism has produced a legacy that will still be useful to a socialist society.

The first question which should be raised deals with the nature of capitalist relations of production and the sense in which they form the kernel of liberal democratic principles. This question has important strategic implications. One could, for example, begin by assuming not only that the relation of liberal democracy to capitalism is tangential and contingent, but even that liberal democratic "freedom" and "equality" are somehow *antithetical* to capitalist domination and inequality. Such an assumption is at least implicit in Macpherson's analysis; and Social Democratic revisionism seems to have been based on a similar view, with its strategy of "patchwork reform" and passive faith in some "peaceful process of dissolution"[5] which would eventually and more or less automatically transform capitalism into socialism. This strategy seems to have been based on the assumption that the liberty and equality of bourgeois democracy were so antithetical to capitalism that the mere maintenance of bourgeois juridical and political institutions, assisted by reform, would produce a tension between freedom and equality at this level and unfreedom and inequality at other levels of society.[6] This tension would in a sense replace class struggle as the motor of social transformation. At the other extreme might be a position that regards liberal democracy as so completely a mere reflection of capitalism that it must be regarded as simply a deception, a mystification. This is roughly the position of various ultra-left groups. Liberal democratic capitalist states, according to this view, are not substantially different from authoritarian or even fascist forms of capitalism. If such radically divergent programmes are associated with different assessments of liberalism and its relation to capitalism, an attempt to situate liberalism in the capitalist mode of production cannot be an insignificant task for socialist political theory.

To determine the relation between liberalism and capitalism, one might begin with Marx's own account of juridical equality and freedom as an integral part of capitalist relations of production. Equality and freedom—of a particular kind—are, suggests Marx, inherent in exchange based on exchange values. The relation between subjects of exchange is a relationship of formal equality; moreover, it is a relationship in which the parties, recognizing each other as proprietors, "as persons whose will penetrates their commodities"[7] and who appropriate each other's property not by force, are *free*. Capitalism, as a *generalized* system of commodity exchange, then, is the perfection of this form of juridical equality and freedom; but here, of course, freedom and equality acquire a rather special meaning since the particular exchange which constitutes the essence of capitalism is that between capital and labour, in which one party (juridically free and "free" from the means of his labour) has only his labour-power to sell. This means that the very object of the "free" exchange between "equals" is precisely the establishment of a particular social relation, a relation of unfreedom and domination which nevertheless retains, indeed is based on, the formal and juridical freedom and equality of the exchange relationship. Thus, wage-slavery, based on the commodification of labour-power, is characterized by a kind of "freedom" and "equality" that distinguishes this form of exploitation from all other relations between exploiter and exploited—master and slave, lord and serf—in which surplus-extraction relies more directly on relations of juridical or political domination and dependence.

Marx goes on to comment on the "foolishness" of those socialists (specifically the French and in particular Proudhon, though he might just as well be commenting on any number of modern social democrats, revisionists, and Labourites—perhaps even Macpherson himself?) ". . .who want to depict socialism as the realization of the ideals of *bourgeois* society"[8] and argue that the freedom and equality characteristic of that society have simply been *perverted* by money, capital, etc. For Marx, the unfreedom and inequality of capitalist relations are, of course, not perversions but *realizations* of the form of freedom and equality implied by simpler forms of commodity exchange. Thus while bourgeois freedom and equality represent an advance over preceding forms, it is a mistake to regard them as antithetical to capitalist inequality and domination.

The equality and freedom of capitalist productive relations can, therefore, be regarded as the kernel of liberal democracy, insofar as the latter is the most complete form of *merely* legal and political equality and freedom. As Marx suggests, the "constitutional republic" is as much the juridical principle of capitalist exploitation as brute force is the juridical principle of other modes of exploitation; and both express the right of the stronger:

> All the bourgeois economists are aware of is that production can be carried on better under the modern police than e.g. on the principle of might makes right. They forget only that this principle is also a legal relation, and that the right of the stronger prevails in their "constitutional republics" as well, only in another form.[9]

A proper evaluation of liberal democracy, then, implies an analysis of the ways in which the capitalist state is an active agent in class struggle, the ways in which political powers are deployed in the interests of the dominant class, how the state enters directly into the relations of production—not only on the higher planes of *class* struggle, but in the immediate confrontation between capital and labour in the work place itself; the ways in which, for example the legal apparatus and police functions of the state are the necessary foundations of the contractual relation among "equals" which constitutes the domination of the working class by the capitalists. An analysis of the link between liberalism and capitalism must recognize that the "autonomy" and "universality" of the capitalist state are precisely the essence of its perfection as a *class* state; that this "autonomy" and "universality" (which are not merely apparent but to a significant extent real), the appearance of class-neutrality which is the special characteristic of the capitalist state, are all made possible and necessary by precisely that condition which also makes capitalism the most perfect form of class exploitation: the complete separation of the producers from the means of production and the concentration in private hands of the capacity for direct surplus-extraction. It must be acknowledged that the clear separation of class and state in capitalism—expressed, for example, in the state's monopoly of force, which can be turned against the dominant class itself—is not merely a separation but a more perfect symbiosis, in effect a cooperative division of labour between class and state which allocates to them separately the essential functions of an exploiting class: surplus-extraction and the coercive power that sustains it.

At the same time, liberal democracy, while grounded in the juridical principles of capitalist productive relations, cannot be reduced to them. The minimal form of freedom and equality intrinsic to capitalism *need* not give rise to the most developed form. If equality and freedom of a very limited and ambiguous kind are essential and common to *all* capitalist social formations, liberal-democratic political institutions have *not* been equally common and are certainly not essential to capitalism—even if they have been most conducive to capitalist development under certain historic conditions. The nature of the relation between capitalism and liberal democracy must, therefore, be further specified with due consideration not only to general structural links but to the particular realities of history. One must go beyond the function of juridical and political freedom and equality in sustaining capitalist relations of production and the position of the dominant class, and take account of the value liberal democratic political forms have had for subordinate classes, indeed, the degree to which these political and legal forms are the legacy of historic struggles by subordinate classes. The role of liberal democracy in civilizing capitalist exploitation must be acknowledged; and this acknowledgement entails a recognition of the crucial differences among forms of capitalist state. It should no longer be necessary—although it clearly often is—to point out that there is a massive difference between capitalism with a liberal face and capitalism in a fascist guise. Not the least difference concerns the position of subordinate classes, their freedom to organize and to resist. The seduction of working class movements by liberal-democratic political forms cannot be lightly dismissed as a failure of class-consciousness or a betrayal of the revolution. The attractions of these institutions have been very real in countries where the tradition has been strongest. In those countries where the tradition has been weak, recent history has surely demonstrated as dramatically as possible that the absence of these forms has serious consequences and that their acquisition and retention are worthy goals for a working class movement. Any socialist strategy ignores at its peril the hold exercised by these political principles and institutions or underestimates the legitimacy of their claims.[10]

To sum up: Liberal democracy can neither be completely separated from nor reduced to the principles of capitalist exploitation. Any reasonable analysis must consider both the foundations of liberal democracy in capitalist relations of production and its historic role in checking the excesses of capitalism. A just appreciation of liberalism and its role in capitalism must, therefore, be founded on both structural and socio-historical analysis, taking into account not only the fundamental structure of capitalist productive relations in general but also the specificities of particular capitalist societies and the historic struggles that have produced them.

The second major question that a socialist theory should raise about liberal democracy also concerns its association with capitalism, but from a different point of view. If liberal democracy was born out of capitalist relations of production, should it also die with them? If liberal democratic institutions have acted to *civilize* as well as to support capitalism, is the need for such institutions dependent on the persistence of capitalist relations of production, or might a socialist society be faced with problems that demand similar solutions? In other words, has liberalism produced a legacy that can and ought to be adopted by socialism?

Liberalism and the Socialist State

Macpherson tries to establish a link between liberalism and socialism by arguing that the essence of liberal democracy is an ethical commitment to individual self-development for all, a commitment that issues logically in socialism. This is a rather empty formula, however. To extract this "ethical commitment" from liberal democracy as its essential principle is to evacuate its socio-historical substance and to forget the association of liberal individualism with capitalist exploitation and class domination. If any system of ideas is fundamentally concerned with this ethical commitment, it is socialism—specifically Marxism—which attacks those very relations of exploitation and domination obstructing the free development of the individual; but, while it may be true to say that socialism could not have existed without liberalism, our understanding of either is not advanced by regarding one as a mere extension of the other and ignoring the fundamental ways in which they are diametrically opposed. Liberalism and socialism can be conflated in this way only by means of an empty formalism which voids them of their social content.

Instead of attempting to abstract from liberal democratic doctrine an ethical meaning contradicted by the social reality embodied in liberal theory and practice, it would be more useful to look at the concrete political principles and institutions of liberal democracies to see whether there is in them a legacy worth preserving. This requires a consideration of the social needs served by these principles and institutions, and a judgement about whether similar social needs persist in a socialist society. From this point of view, it can be argued that if liberalism is about anything worth preserving, it is about certain ways of dealing with political authority: the rule of law, civil liberties, checks on arbitrary power. This function of liberalism must be conceded even if the status of "bourgeois liberties" is at best ambiguous in a class-divided society where they may not only obscure class oppositions with a false equality but actively serve as instruments of class power and hegemony. It is not here a question of how *democratic* "bourgeois democracy" may or may not be. In fact, one ought perhaps to begin by again separating the "liberal" from the "democratic." It may be that the most important lesson of liberalism has little to do with democracy but is concerned with controlling state power— and here, the earlier *anti*-democratic forms of liberalism may have as much to say as does liberal democracy.

To say that liberalism has a lesson for socialism in this respect is, of course, to make a highly contentious assumption, namely that the state will persist as a problem in classless society and that the most democratic society may continue to be faced with a *political* problem analogous to that of undemocratic societies. Much of socialist doctrine is based on the assumption that, if the state will not actually wither away in a classless society, state power will at least no longer constitute a *problem*. Social democrats who have unbounded faith in the efficacy of bourgeois democratic forms seem not to regard the state as a problem even in capitalist society. Indeed, they treat it as an instrument of salvation. More interesting questions are raised by socialists who are convinced that the state apparatus of bourgeois democracy must be "smashed" and replaced by something radically different. As Ralph Miliband has argued, those who speak of the "smashing" of the bourgeois state have not squarely faced the fact that they will—indeed must—replace the smashed state with yet another, perhaps temporarily even strengthened, state; that the smashing of the bourgeois state and its replacement by a revolutionary state do *not* in themselves mean the "dictatorship of the proletariat" if that concept still carries its original democratic implications; that there is always a tension between the necessity of "direction" and "democracy", between state power and popular power, which has been consistently evaded.[11] So serious is the problem, suggests Miliband, that democracy can be preserved only by a system of "dual power" in which state power is *complemented* by widespread democratic organizations of various kinds throughout civil society.

It must be added, however, that the problem is not likely to be confined to some awkward "transitional" phase during which a strong state will undertake to fulfill the promise of the revolution by transforming society. If, for example, as Marx suggests, the central organizational problem of *all* societies is the allocation of social labour, then there is a sense in which the *political* question will be particularly important *after* the complete overthrow of capitalism. Capitalism is, after all, a system in which that central social problem is not dealt with "politically", a system uniquely characterized by the absence of an "authoritative allocation" of social labour. It is a system with what Marx calls an "anarchic" social division of labour not dictated by political authority, tradition, or communal deliberation but by the mechanisms of commodity-exchange. One might say that it is capitalism, then, which in this very particular sense involves the "administration of things and not people"—or, perhaps the administration of people by things; while the new society will be faced with a new and substantial organizational problem which very much involves the administration of people.

Marxist theory has not done much to clarify the issues at stake, let alone resolve the problem of the state under socialism. Marx and Engels had little to say on the subject of the state in future society, and what they did say is often ambiguous. In particular the debate has been plagued by a vagueness and inconsistency in the use of the term "state." We are told that the *state* will "wither away" in classless society. If (as it usually but not always the case) the state is defined as a system of class domination, it is a mere tautology to say that the state will "wither away" once classes are abolished. The definition of the state as synonymous with class domination resolves nothing. It simply evades the issue. On the other hand, if the "state" refers to *any* form of public power, it is not at all clear that the state will disappear with class—nor is it clear that Marx or Engels thought it would.

Whatever Marx and Engels may have thought about the future of the state, the real question is not whether a public power will be needed in a classless society, but whether that public power will constitute a problem. In other words, are there certain problems inherent in public power itself whether or not it is *class* power? I take it for granted that it is hopelessly naive to believe in an advanced socialist society administered by simple forms of direct and spontaneous democracy. It is difficult to avoid the conviction that even classless society will require some form of *representation,* and hence *authority* and even *subordination* of some people to others. That premise granted, it must be added that, whether or not one uses the term "state" to describe political and administrative power in a classless society, it seems unduly optimistic to believe that there can ever be a case in which power exercised by some people on behalf of others does not constitute a problem. Socialist political theory must, therefore, face the problems posed by representation, authority, and subordination, and the fact that their very existence makes possible the misappropriation of power.

These problems cannot be dismissed by the mere assertion that representation, authority, and subordination will present no danger in the absence of class. Among other things, it is necessary to consider the possibility (hinted at by Marx himself, for example in his discussions of the Asiatic mode of production and other pre-capitalist formations) that public power may be, and historically often has been, itself the *source* of differentiation between appropriators and direct producers. There is good reason to believe that public power, instituted to undertake socially necessary functions—warfare, distribution, direction of communal labour, the construction of vital public works—has often been the original basis of the right to and capacity for surplus-appropriation. In other words, the state—in the broad sense—has not emerged from class divisions but has, on the contrary, *produced* class divisions and hence also produced the state in the narrow sense. It does not seem wise to assume that no constant and institutionalized protection will be needed in the future to prevent the similar transmutation of "political" authority into "economic" power, public power into something like class domination.

However much Marx or Engels may have tended toward political utopianism, the view that public power in classless society will still be a problem requiring conscious and institutionalized control is entirely consistent with the fundamental Marxist view of the world and the meaning of the socialist revolution. Marx's belief in the complete transformation of society once class domination disappears does not imply that all problems associated with class domination will automatically and forever dissolve of themselves. On the contrary, the essence of the transformation itself is that socio-historical forces will for the first time be consciously controlled and directed instead of left to chance. This is what Marx means when he speaks of man's history before the revolution as "pre-history" and thereafter as "human history." The planned direction of social forces certainly does not refer simply to "economic" planning in the narrow sense—the planning of production quotas, and so on. The "economic" is itself a *social relation,* and the social relations of production themselves must be "planned." Furthermore, if "economic" power, the power to extract surplus labour, consists in a relationship of domination and coercion, then it is also and above all *political* power; and the planning of the social relations of production must include "political" planning at every level of society, institutional measures to prevent the re-emergence of domination and exploitative relations.

Even in a classless society there will probably have to be organizations whose conscious and explicit object is not simply to complement but to *check* power and prevent its misappropriation. There will have to be on-going institutions, not simply emergency measures such as the power of recall, to act to this specific end, and equally important, to maintain a *consciousness* of the problem. Assuming that the political form of socialism will be a *representative* system, with some kind of administrative apparatus, there will still be tension between state power and popular power. Representation is itself a problem; and to the extent that the political problem cannot be practically resolved by replacing representation with direct democracy, by further democratizing the system of political organization, the problem must still be faced on another plane. In other words, the very existence of a state—however democratically representative—necessarily places a special task on the agenda: not simply democratic organization throughout civil society, but—and this may not be the same thing—what Marx calls the *subordination* of the state to society.[12]

The debate on the future of the state ought not to be reduced to a matter of textual interpretation; but discussions of the question are bound to return to the sketchy comments made by Marx and Engels on the subject. Since it is probably easier to demonstrate that they were optimistic about the disappearances of politics than to prove that they saw the state as a continuing problem, a few remarks in support of the latter interpretation should be added here. Particularly interesting is what they have to say—or at least imply—about the legacy of bourgeois liberalism and its possible application to post-revolutionary society.

It must be said, first, that both Marx and Engels may have clouded the issue by asserting that in a classless society the *state* will disappear or that the "public power will lose its political character."[13] This is not the same as saying that there will *be* no public power, or even that the public power will cease to be a problem. Engels, who most often and explicitly repeated the assertion that the state "in the proper sense of the word" would disappear, is also the man who, in attacking the Anarchists, stressed the continuing need for *authority* and *subordination* and mocked the Anarchists for believing that by changing the name of the public authority they had changed the thing itself. Even if, as Engels writes, "public functions will lose their political character and be transformed into the simple administrative functions of watching over the true interests of society,"[14] the problem is not self-evidently resolved. Is it not possible that—even in Engels' own view—institutionalized measures will be required precisely to *ensure* that the public power, vested with authority over others and subordinating others to it, will maintain its purely "administrative" character and continue to act in the true interests of society? In a class society, such a humane and "unpolitical" public power would be impossible; but, if it becomes *possible* only in a classless society, it does not necessarily become inevitable.

That Marx, too, may have perceived the state as a continuing problem is suggested by the very formula, "the subordination of the state to society." Note, first, that he does not here speak of the *absorption* of the state by society, as he appears to do in his very early work,[15] nor does he refer to the state's dissolution. What, then, is meant by the subordination of the state to society? Other texts—for example, *The Civil War in France* where Marx discusses the Paris Commune—suggest it means that the public power will consist of officials who are the "responsible agents of society", not "superior to society." The problem, however, only *begins* here. How is society to ensure that its officials will remain "responsible" and not "superior" to it? Marx may seem to dismiss the problem too lightly and optimistically, since he has little to say about it except to speak of the subjection of officials to instant recall. It cannot, however, be taken for granted that he failed to see the problem or to recognize its magnitude.

In the "Critique of the Gotha Programme" where the "subordination of the state" appears, Marx hints not only that the problem of the state will persist in communist society, but that the restrictions on state power instituted by the most "liberal" of bourgeois societies may have something to teach on the score of dealing with that problem:

> Freedom consists in converting the state from an organ superimposed upon society into one completely subordinate to it, and today, too, the forms of state are more free or less free to the extent that they restrict the "freedom of the state."[16]

"Freedom" in bourgeois society is, of course, something very different from the complete "subordination of the state to society" which can occur only in the absence of class domination. On the other hand, Marx appears to see some kind of connection between freedom in the bourgeois state and the subordination of the communist state to society, a connection that has something to do with the establishment of checks on state power, institutionalized restrictions on the "freedom of the state." He goes on to ask: "What transformations will the state undergo in communist society? In other words, what social functions will remain in existence that are analogous to the present functions of the state?" Marx undoubtedly contributed to the optimistic notion that the state will eventually wither away; but he is here apparently suggesting that the state will persist, that it probably will have certain functions analogous to its present ones, and that it may even pose analogous problems. Furthermore, the precise nature of these analogies can only be determined "scientifically", and ". . . one does not get a flea-hop nearer to the problem by a thousand-fold combination of the word people with the word state." This may mean that a democratic state is still a *state,* and will require conscious and institutional efforts to restrict its "freedom"—which, among other things, appears to mean to restrict bureaucratization—if it is to be subordinated to society. Insofar as the most "liberal" forms of the capitalist state represent the hitherto most advanced modes of restricting the freedom of the state, it is possible that socialists have something to learn from "liberalism" in this regard.

What particular kinds of restrictions on the state's "freedom" Marx had in mind is perhaps suggested by Engels' comments on the Gotha Programme—and his remarks are somewhat surprising:

> ". . . a heap of rather confused *purely democratic demands* [figures] in the programme, of which several are a mere matter of fashion, as for instance, the "legislation by the people" which exists in Switzerland and does more harm than good if it does anything at all. *Administration* by the people, that would be something. Equally lacking is the first condition of all freedom: that all officials should be responsible for all their official acts to every citizen before the ordinary courts and according to common law."[17]

The implication here is, again, that freedom lies in restricting the freedom of the state; and it is clear that this is not simply a matter of establishing more democratic legislative or representative institutions, but concerns above all the administrative apparatus. Particularly striking is the importance Engels attaches to the law and the court system in restricting the freedom of the state. There is a suggestion that certain legal systems represent a kind of *opposition* to the state—perhaps even an organization "in society"—rather than a mere instrument of the state. The common law system, the "independent" judiciary, judges who are not part of the administrative apparatus, the jury system, the recourse of citizens to "ordinary courts" against state officials—characteristics more typical of the English legal tradition and of those legal systems which emanate from it—are being implicitly opposed to the continental tradition and in particular, its system of administrative law. In short, Engels appears to be suggesting—in what may seem an excessively optimistic echo of English bourgeois ideology—that the "rule of law" in the particular English sense can play an essential role in restricting the state's freedom. And if the efficacy of "liberalism" in this form as a real check on the bourgeois state can certainly be questioned, such a view cannot simply be dismissed. While Engels goes on to repeat the optimistic conviction that the advent of socialism will mean the dissolution of the state "in the proper sense of the word", it is not at all clear that for him—or for Marx—this means the disappearance of public power as a problem. It might be useful, then, to consider bourgeois legalism and other "liberal" restrictions on the freedom of the state and what these institutions may have to teach about the modalities of subordinating the state to society even under communism.

Liberalism and Revolution

In any case, whether or not liberalism can teach socialism anything about the post-revolutionary state, it can at least reveal something about the seductiveness of a particular political tradition, which has more immediate strategic implications. It is significant that countries in which the liberal—not necessarily *democratic*—tradition has been strongest, working class movements have been least revolutionary and have most consistently placed their faith in the political institutions of bourgeois democracy. Socialist movements in other countries may have *acquired* that faith; but the English, for example, have had a mainstream labour movement with an unbroken tradition of loyalty to these institutions. It seems also to be true that where liberalism has been strongest, socialist theory has been least Marxist. Even Marx himself was affected by this political tradition. He did, after all, suggest in 1872 that Britain and the United States were the countries most likely to achieve the transition to socialism by peaceful means. Addressing a meeting in Amsterdam, he said:

> You know that the institutions, mores, and traditions of various countries must be taken into consideration, and we do not deny that there are countries— such as America, England, and if I were more familiar with your institutions, I would perhaps also add Holland—where the workers can attain their goal by peaceful means. This being the case, we must also recognize the fact that in most countries on the Continent the lever of our revolution must be force. . .[18]

Without speculating on the accuracy of this judgement, it is instructive to consider why Marx made it, what factors he found operating in England and America that distinguished them from other countries which would more probably require violent revolution to achieve the transformation of society. No doubt England was the most proletarian country in the world; and Marx seems to have expected America to become "the workers' continent par excellence', as he suggests later in the Amsterdam speech. In the relevant paragraph, however, Marx does not refer to the *class* configurations of different countries, but to their "institutions, mores, and traditions." As for which institutions and traditions he particularly had in mind, it seems unlikely that the crucial "variable" for Marx was the degree of *democracy* by itself. England in 1872 was still 13 years away from universal manhood suffrage (and even further removed from a system of one man—one vote, or any kind of universal adult suffrage), and had a far from democratic political tradition; while France had already experimented with universal manhood suffrage and other politically democratic institutions long before, was on the eve of establishing a bourgeois democratic republic, and had provided the world with its most influential democratic tradition. Considered in the context of other statements by Marx—for example, in the "Critique of the Gotha Programme", the "18th Brumaire", and the letter to Kugelmann of April 12, 1871—the judgement of the Amsterdam speech appears to be singling out not so much the democratic elements of English and American political institutions, but their "liberalism", particularly the degree to which they restrict the "freedom of the state", in contrast to the more strongly bureaucratic and police states of the major capitalist countries on the Continent, which would almost certainly require violent revolution to "smash" their rigid state apparatus.[19] In other words, the apparently less rigid British and American forms of capitalist state at least created the impression that the structure of domination, at the pinnacle of which stood the state, could more easily be shifted by peaceful, parliamentary means.

If Marx allowed himself a certain optimism concerning the political forms and traditions of liberalism, it is not so difficult to understand how such a large proportion of the working classes which experienced them directly could be so tenaciously faithful to a political tradition that has not been notably democratic. The recourse subordinate classes have had to judicial and political institutions in their relations with dominant classes, together with the restrictions on the "freedom" of the state itself, have created a faith in the efficacy of legal and political forms; and this faith cannot be dismissed as unreasonable, especially in the British case. A similar tradition may in part account for the peculiarities of American social movements—which the prosperity of American capitalism is not sufficient to explain. Even in the face of a state in which the working class is the most inadequately represented of any major capitalist country, and where the state has often exhibited its hostility to the working class and to expressions of social protest, the Americans have, of course, been notable for their failure to produce a serious labour movement; and equally significant, for the tendency to reduce social issues to *constitutional* questions and social protest to *civil rights* movements of various kinds.

One is always struck by the extent to which grievances are addressed to the state and the constitution, or alternatively the source of the evil is attributed to the state's overstepping its proper bounds, while the underlying social relations of capitalism are seldom called into question. It may even be significant that more immediately "constitutional" crises like Watergate seem in their effects on the public consciousness to overshadow more fundamental expressions of the *social* contradictions endemic to capitalism. In contrast, French students and workers in May, 1968, for example, seemed much more inclined to look to the social foundations for the source of their grievance—even though the student protest began over such apparently superficial issues as the size of university classes. Perhaps the nature of the French state—with a tradition progressing from absolutism to Bonapartism to rigid bureaucratism—has something to do with this different perception of the social world and the place of the state within it.

The same factors which produce an apparently unshakeable faith in the efficacy of the political and legal forms of bourgeois democracy may also help to explain the relative scarcity (at least until recently) of Marxist analysis among intellectuals in precisely those countries where the liberal tradition has been strongest. C.B. Macpherson himself is a significant case in point, an example made the more striking precisely because his commitments often appear to be radical. Although in his own analysis of liberal democracy he does not single out that aspect of the tradition which seems to have been most seductive, it can be argued that the inadequacies of his analysis—regarding class and state, the nature of capitalism, the organic link between liberalism and capitalism, his abstraction of liberalism from its social foundations—can probably be explained by the fact that he is part of that Anglo-American tradition of political thought and of socialism which for understandable historic reasons has fallen under the spell of liberalism. Again, this is an intellectual tradition which, while expressing a moral indignation at capitalism, fails to ground that indignation in a commensurate analysis of capitalism and the bourgeois state which goes substantially beyond capitalism's own evaluation of itself. This tradition begins at least with J.S. Mill; and for all Macpherson's perception of the contradictions between Mill's ethical position and his analysis of captalism, it cannot be said that his own argument is much less plagued by the same contradictions.

It is also significant that where the liberal political tradition has been most captivating—and most plausible—"pure" *political* theory, abstracted from social analysis, has been a particularly well-developed intellectual genre; and this medium has had a special attraction for theorists whose object is to justify existing social relations. A Marxist theory of the state, therefore, is an absolutely necessary corrective to the mystifications of that political and intellectual tradition. At the same time, if Marxist political theory is to have the desired counter-hegemonic effects, it ought not to confine itself to the "theory of the state" as it is now understood, but should meet these ideological mystifications on their own ground. Political philosophy must be firmly grounded in its socio-historical context. It is noteworthy, for example, that no socialist history of political theory has yet been written to counteract the innumerable more or less abstract and ahistorical textbooks in the "history" of political thought. Macpherson has certainly broken ground in this respect, but much more needs to be done. Particularly where the abstractly "political" tradition has been so strong in theory and in practice, socialists ought not to leave unchallenged an intellectual tradition which in its very nature, in both content and form, has been a huge mystification.

NOTES

1. C.B. Macpherson, *The Life and Times of Liberal Democracy* (Oxford: Oxford University Press, 1977). Page references of quotations from this book will be indicated by numbers in brackets in the text.
2. Cf. Ralph Miliband, *The State in Capitalist Society* (London: Weidenfeld & Nicholson, 1969), pp. 2-4.
3. Max Weber, *Economy and Society* (New York: Bedminster Press, 1968), pp. 927-8.
4. C.B. Macpherson, "Politics: Post-Liberal Democracy?" in R. Blackburn, ed., *Ideology in Social Science* (London: Fontana/Collins, 1972), pp. 29-30.
5. This is how Marx describes the principles of German Social Democracy in his circular Letter to Bebel, Liebknecht, Brache et. al. of September 17-18, 1879.
6. Cf. Lucio Colletti, "Bernstein and the Marxism of the Second International", in *From Rousseau to Lenin* (London: New Left Books, 1972), pp. 92-97.
7. Marx, *Grundrisse*, ed. M. Nicolaus (Harmondsworth: Penguin Books, 1972), p. 243.
8. Ibid., p. 248.
9. Ibid., p. 88.
10. E.P. Thompson has shown very effectively how the "rule of law" and the principles of constitutionalism in England have both served and modified the dominance of the ruling class. See, for example, *Whigs and Hunters*.
11. Ralph Miliband, *Marxism and Politics* (Oxford: Oxford University Press, 1977), pp. 180-90.
12. Marx, "Critique of the Gotha Programme", *Selected Works* (Moscow: Foreign Languages Publishing House, 1962), Vol. II, p. 32.
13. *Communist Manifesto, Selected Works,* op. cit., vol. I, p. 54.
14. Engels, "On Authority".
15. For example, in "On the Jewish Question", or the *Economic and Philosophic Manuscripts of 1844.*
16. "Critique of the Gotha Programme", op. cit.
17. Engels, Letter to Bebel, March 18-28, 1875, *Marx and Engels: Selected Correspondence* (Moscow: Progress Publishers, 2nd ed., 1965), p. 293.
18. Marx, "Amsterdam speech", September 8, 1872.
19. Engels later shows less confidence in the flexibility of the American state. In his 1891 introduction to Marx's *The Civil War in France,* he cites the U.S. as the country in which the state power has most successfully made itself "independent in relation to society", rendering the nation powerless against politicians who take possession of and exploit that power—despite the absence of a standing army and a rigid bureaucracy.

CAPITAL ACCUMULATION, CLASS FORMATION AND DEPENDENCY—THE SIGNIFICANCE OF THE KENYAN CASE

Colin Leys

The aim of this paper is to clarify some of the issues that have been posed in the theoretical debate about "dependency" and to reconsider the evidence from Kenya in the light of this clarification—if possible, carrying the discussion a small step further in the process.[1]

I. *Theoretical questions*

The most important question of all those which are at stake in the debate about "dependency" is whether or not there are theoretical reasons for thinking that the ex-colonies cannot (as Marx put it) "adopt the bourgeois mode of production" and develop their productive forces within it.[2] The underdevelopment or dependency school in general argues that the patterns of subordinate development established at the periphery of imperialism before and during the colonial phase are self-perpetuating. Frank, for instance, identified a historical sequence of mechanisms (the "contradiction of continuity in change") through which metropolitan capital secured monopolies enabling it to appropriate the surplus generated at the periphery and largely transfer it to the metropoles, the latest and apparently most invulnerable mechanism being the monopoly of techno-logy possessed by the leading multinational corporations.[3] Warren, in his well-known critique of the underdevelopment school, argued that the patterns of underdevelopment are self-eliminating because decolonisation gives rise to regimes in the ex-colonies which need, and have some power to obtain, a measure of industrial development.[4] Admittedly this develop-ment is carried out by multinational industrial companies within the frame-work of imperialism but the multinationals as such, and the imperialist states, put no obstacles in the way of this development leading to further stages of industrialisation and hence to a general process of capitalist development; and as a result, Warren argues, the industrialisation of the Third World, and the spread of capitalist relations of production there, has in fact been going ahead rapidly.

Against Warren, Emmanuel argued that underdevelopment is indeed self-perpetuating, but not because it is the nature of multinational manu-facturing capital to operate in the periphery precisely for the purpose of plundering the locally-generated surpluses for the benefit of its owners in the metropoles, as the underdevelopment theorists proposed; but because its very presence at the periphery is always exceptional, all capital being drawn in general not to the periphery but to the areas of its greatest existing concentration, where demand is highest. And Emmanuel, supported by Petras and others, rather convincingly challenged Warren's general evidence for holding that industrialisation and capitalist relations of production had actually spread rapidly at the periphery.[5] On the contrary, Emmanuel showed that much of the statistical evidence related to the growth of very small-scale craft production, with very low levels of productivity, and largely pre-capitalist or non-capitalist in character; that industrialisation had not been accompanied by a rise of agricultural productivity, which is essential for sustaining any long-term development of capitalist industry; and that, in consequence, industrial output per head of population in the Third World had risen much more slowly than in the metropoles, so that the prospects of capital being drawn towards the periphery on an increasing scale, as Warren expected, were not increasing but diminishing.[6]

The bearing of this debate on the case of Kenya, and *vice versa,* can be approached in a preliminary way by looking at an aspect of the debate that was treated by the participants—mistakenly, I think—as a side-issue. Warren illustrated part of his case by citing data from twenty-two countries identified by Chenery as having the fastest-growing economies in the Third World. Petras and his colleagues criticised this on the grounds that all of these countries were in different ways *exceptional.*[7] Five had specially heavy inflows of foreign capital "for reasons that are largely political" (Taiwan, Jordan, Puerto Rico, South Korea, Panama) and all of these except Taiwan were small. Nine others had enjoyed exceptionally rapid growth of primary exports and "no marxist scholar with whom we are familiar has ever argued that underdeveloped countries with rapidly developing primary export sectors cannot industrialise at least through the stage of light import substitution."[8] The remaining eight also enjoyed unusually high levels of capital inflow and most of them also exhibited certain specially favourable features—Singapore and Costa Rica were "tiny" countries and their industries, and those of the Phillipines, were based on assembly operations so that their growth depended on low wages. Mexico had "extraordinary" advantages derived from its tourist attractions and its proximity to the USA. Brazil's and Turkey's growth depended on a repressive redistribution of income from the poor to the rich.

The conclusion which Warren's critics drew from all this was that the manufacturing growth rates of these countries were not evidence of "autonomous industrial growth" in the Third World, as Warren believed. But this is a case of too much zeal. Britain, too, was once an "exceptional" case. This is an important part of the burden of the eighth section of

Volume I of *Capital*. On the one hand, domestically,

> "The money capital formed by means of usury and commerce was prevented from turning into industrial capital by the feudal organization of the countryside and the guild association of the towns. These fetters vanished with the dissolution of the feudal bands of retainers, and the expropriation and partial eviction of the rural population."

On the other, there was primitive accumulation abroad:

> "The discovery of gold and silver in America, the extirpation, enslavement and entombment of mines of the indigenous population of that continent, the beginnings of the conquest and plunder of India, and the conversion of Africa into a preserve for the commercial hunting of blackskins, are all things which characterise the dawn of the era of capitalist production. These idyllic proceedings are the chief moments of primitive accumulation. Hard on their heels follows the commercial war of the European nations, which has the globe as its battlefield. . ."

For the transition to the capitalist mode of production to occur, however, all these developments had to come together *somewhere:*

> "The different moments of primitive accumulation can be assigned in particular to Spain, Portugal, Holland, France and England, more or less in chronological order. These different moments are systematically combined together at the end of the seventeenth century in England; the combination embraces the colonies, the national debt, the modern tax system, and the system of protection. These methods depend in part on brute force, for instance the colonial system. But they all employ the power of the State."[9]

How else, but through such "systematically combined moments" occurring in some particular place, could capitalist development—the progressive transformation of relations of production into capitalist ones through the expanded reproduction of industrial capital—ever occur? This is not to say that such "combinations" can and eventually must occur everywhere, as Marx's earlier writings sometimes implied. But it does suggest the curiousness of the argument of Petras and his colleagues in this instance, which proceeds by "removing" and "subtracting" from Warren's list of rapidly industrialising countries in the Third World any which can be shown to have "special" reasons for rapid industrialisation. Behind this mode of reasoning one detects the straw man of a utopian conception of capitalist development, similar to the one which Warren rightly discerned as underlying much "left" discussion of these questions: this time, a conception of capitalism developing evenly and universally throughout the Third World, without help from low wages based on repression, imperialist military expenditure, etc.

Even Emmanuel dismisses the rather complex issues involved here with the remark that "certain marginal movements of capital, concentrated for various reasons in some small country, such as Greece, Taiwan, or the Ivory Coast, may enable such a country to cross the threshold of development", adding—not altogether plausibly, it seems to me—that "it is *because* the other countries do not follow this path of ultra-liberal opening to international capital, that the few countries that do follow it have a chance, however, slight, of succeeding with it."[10] Apart from anything else, it is not obvious why *movements* of capital, even marginal ones, should be considered decisive, unless what is meant is that most of the capital formed at the periphery presently flows to the metropoles; on this assumption, capitalist production relations certainly cannot develop at the periphery, and what is needed is to *stop* the movements of capital that are generally occurring (though on Emmanuel's own data, the evidence actually suggests a modest net flow of capital to the periphery considered as a whole). But then, we cannot lightly dismiss the "various reasons" why, in a significant number of cases, the flow of capital from the centre to the periphery has actually been sufficiently large to sustain capitalist development there.

To summarise: the debate about dependency and underdevelopment has not shown either that capitalist development cannot occur at the periphery (or "in the Third World"), or that it is eventually bound to. What it demonstrates is, rather, the need to study and theorise the conditions under which other periphery countries have, and others have not, experienced significant measures of such growth. Broadly speaking, there seem to be three principal levels at which this work needs to be conducted: the level of the "logic of capital", the level of capitalist geo-politics (imperialism), and the level of class relations and class struggles in particular social formations, each level determining and being determined by the others. By the "logic of capital" I am referring both to the international logic of capital in general—so-called "capital-logic"—and to its implications for the investment decisions of particular capitals in particular sectors in particular countries. The level of "capitalist geo-politics" refers to the forces which determine that, for instance, exceptionally large flows of "official" capital (bilateral or multilateral) occur for certain countries, materially affecting the logic of "private" capital flows, while comparable efforts of "technical assistance", civil and military, and corresponding ideological and cultural efforts, equally determine the conditions for the reproduction of capital in those countries.

The rest of this paper, however, will be concerned only with the last of the three levels, that of class relations and class struggles in a particular social formation, and furthermore, it will be largely concerned with the process of domestic capital accumulation which has formed the basis for the constitution of one particular class, rather than with classes and class struggles in general. This is doubly one-sided, and the result has at most the status of a working paper, subject to correction in the light of work at other levels, and on other aspects of the level of class relations and class struggles, which mostly remains to be done. Some justification for these limitations can be found, perhaps, in the fact that a focus on relations between classes constituted out of the pre-existing relations of production has been conspicuously missing from much of the previous discussion of the problem of development, and notably from the discussion of the idea of the "articulation of modes of production" by means of which several influential writers have attempted to theorise the issues involved.[11]

This is a point forcibly made by Robert Brenner in his recent critique of Frank, Wallerstein and other "neo-Smithian" theorists who—to over-simplify—have conceived of capitalist production relations developing in particular places, or not, according to the dictates of market forces, neglecting the particular presuppositions about the social structure which underlay the role assigned to the market by Smith in his account of the development of capitalism.[12] Brenner, correctly in my view, stresses instead the centrality of the class relations which Smith took as given. On this view, what is decisive for the development of capitalist production relations is the prior configuration and character of classes—for instance, the availability or otherwise of "free" labour, the respective political power of non-landed and landed classes affecting the possibility of capital investment in land, and so on. The *dependentistas*

> failed to focus centrally on the productivity of labour as the essence and key to economic development. They did not see the degree to which the latter was, in turn, centrally bound up with historically specific class structures of production and surplus extraction, themselves the product of determinations beyond the market. Hence, they did not see the degree to which patterns of development or underdevelopment for an entire epoch might hinge upon the outcome of specific processes of class formation, of class struggle.[13]

What produces *under*development is not the "transfer of surplus" appropriated by metropolitan capital from the periphery of the metropole, significant though this may be. Rather, such a transfer should be seen as an *effect* of structures at the periphery which militate against the productive investment of the surplus at the periphery. Speaking generally, these are class structures which permit absolute surplus labour to be appropriated, but prevent the realisation of relative surplus value:

> "in other words, the development of underdevelopment was rooted in the class structure of production based on the extension of absolute surplus labour, which determined a sharp *disjuncture* between the requirements for the development of the productive forces (productivity of labour) and the structure of profitability of the economy as a whole."[14]

Brenner's discussion may be open to the criticism that the class structures of the periphery tend to figure in it as determined by *past* struggles but appear relatively immune to determination by class struggles initiated by imperialism itself—thus tending to avoid the question which is central to theorists of the "articulation of modes of production" (notably Rey), namely: what prevents capitalists, once capitalism has become dominant on a world scale, from removing such obstacles to its valorisation as inhospitable or recalcitrant class structures in particular countries or regions? Brenner's answer would seem to be that nothing prevents this in general: it is a historical and conjunctural question whether the interests of the bourgeoisie require these obstacles to be overcome in a given case; and secondly, whether this is outweighed by the relative strength or weight of the class interests opposed to this.[15] While this seems to me correct, analysing the general nature of these relationships does seem to be an important task which needs to be undertaken, on the basis of a range of studies of which the Kenyan case reviewed here is at most a suggestive example.

II. *Precolonial and colonial indigenous accumulation in Kenya*

The chief way in which the Kenyan experience is relevant to the theoretical questions discussed above may be simply stated. While several aspects of Kenya's development may at first sight seem to be illuminated by means of the concepts of underdevelopment and dependency, the process of domestic capital accumulation since the early 1940s does not lend itself so easily to analysis from this perspective.

This is particularly apparent in the period since independence. Once the uncertainties of the transition had been resolved, the high overall growth rate of the 1940s and '50s was resumed (an absolute annual average rate of growth of 6½%, or about 3% per annum per capita in real terms), with an all round increase in productivity, a steady decline in the non-monetary share of output, (from 25% of GNP in 1964 to 19% in 1973) and some growth—its true extent is not known—in the share of wage and salary employment in total employment. In other words, the relatively high and sustained level of capital accumulation was accompanied by an extension of capitalist relations of production. A growing proportion of households came to depend on wage labour, and the reproduction of labour power was increasingly commercialised. By 1974-75 64% of the median small farm's household consumption was purchased for cash and 19% of its income was derived from wage labour (small farms accounted for approximately 75% of all Kenyan households, the remainder being more or less wholly dependent on wage employment or on income from capital).[16] In manufacturing, labour productivity rose (in large scale firms the gross product per employee rose just under 20% between 1969 and 1973, and in relation to total labour costs, the gross product rose just under 23%), though in agriculture productivity appeared to stagnate in the 1970s, after rising in the 1960s.[17]

These developments attracted and were in turn reinforced by a net inflow of capital from abroad. Private capital inflows began to exceed profit outflows after 1970 and while the various measures taken after 1970 to curb hidden transfers to surplus (via overinvoicing, management and patent fee payments, etc.) could only be partially successful, covert outflows seem rather unlikely to have equalled, let alone exceeded the real rate of total net capital inflows, which ran at an annual average of K£ 42m for the period 1968-75.[18] In any case, as Emmanuel has pointed out, the historic cost of the technology transferred to Kenya under management contracts and patent fees was far higher than the cost of these arrangements to Kenya.[19] Meanwhile the level of foreign indebtedness remained low, and was still further reduced in real terms by inflation.[20]

At this stage in the discussion, the general theoretical implications of all this for underdevelopment and dependency as explanatory concepts may be put to one side, permitting us to focus instead on the question: what is the explanation of the Kenyan growth process, and what significance does the explanation have for the prospects of capitalist development in Kenya in the future?

Kenya has not been in receipt of exceptionally large flows of official capital or technical assistance, nor has it had any exceptional growth of primary commodity exports or, in general, any major advantage in terms of endowment or location over neighbouring countries.[21] Nor, on the other hand, has its overall rate of growth been due to exceptional growth rates in one or two "enclave" sectors unrelated to the rest of the economy. While some marked geographic and sectoral imbalances exist, growth has been more or less equally pronounced both in agriculture and outside it, in small and large scale farming, in manufacturing and in commerce, in the private and the public sectors, etc.

A more plausible explanation of Kenyan economic growth since the 1940s lies, rather, in the specific social relations of production developed before, during and since the colonial period, and particularly—but in no sense exclusively, as will be seen—in the key role of the class formed out of the process of indigenous capital accumulation.

This process has been the subject of a highly original and complex analysis by M.P. Cowen, of which only a few central themes are essential here.[22] Cowen established that before the colonisation of East Africa the relations of production existing in what is now Central Province—the most populous, productive and economically strategic area of Kenya—determined the formation of a class of accumulators of the principal means of production—land and livestock—through migration onto new land, raiding, and long-distance trade. The tendency of this accumulation, which was in large measure "primitive", was to concentrate the means of production more and more in a few hands, excluding others from access to them, a tendency which those threatened with exclusion could overcome, by and large, only through migrating themselves (usually as labourers clearing land for others in return for stock and a share of the new land). Colonial settlement closed off further migration, by alienating land to white settlers. On the other hand the colonial state launched some, at least, of the pre-colonial accumulators on a fresh path of accumulation by appointing them "chiefs" who were enabled to loot their new "subjects" by means of unregulated taxes and fines, and to further accumulate land within the now restricted African land areas by engaging in costly litigation.

The transformation of this class into a class of agrarian capitalists (appropriating surplus value through wage labour proper) was, however, thwarted by (a) the settler farmers' monopoly, enforced by the colonial state, over most of the available African surplus labour; (b) parallel settler monopolies over the production of most of the agricultural commodities (notably coffee) or over markets (e.g. for maize), on which capitalist agriculture could be based; (c) the intervention of international capital—as opposed to small and medium settler capital—in commodity production, either through plantation production (in the case of wattle), or through permitting the still existing mass of smallholders to produce commodities under the supervision of large scale foreign capital. This permitted the smallholdings to survive as units of production (a situation confirmed by the universal issue of freehold land titles from 1955 onwards) and deprived the indigenous class of capital of the opportunity to further enlarge their landholdings and exploit the labour of those who became proletarianised.

Meanwhile, the route of entry to the "accumulator" class, and the basis of further accumulation for the individual agents within it, had necessarily shifted from the old forms of primitive accumulation to wage income, increasingly based on education; and to the sphere of commerce, the avenues for which were gradually widened by political pressure brought to bear on the colonial state by new organisations such as the Kikuyu Central Association and the Kavirondo Taxpayers Welfare Association—whose ascendancy also signified the displacement of the older, "primitive" accumulating element within the indigenous class of capital, by the "modern", educated element. Although these efforts preserved and even permitted some enlargement of the accumulated capital of this class, it was wholly confined to the sphere of circulation and hence to the limited share of surplus value to be obtained there, in face of unremitting pressure both from Asian merchant capital and from the growing weight of international productive capital.

By the end of World War II a direct challenge to this limitation was finally articulated by the militant wing of the Kenya African Union, leading in 1952 to the declaration of emergency. Meanwhile international capital had moved into Kenya on a much larger scale, and in the context of Britain's interest in expanding colonial commodity production as a contribution to the solution of the dollar shortage, the colonial state also began to dismantle the barriers to indigenous capital accumulation. African exclusion from the "white highlands", the ban on African-grown coffee, restriction on credit for Africans and opposition to the issue of individual land titles all disappeared. Finally, white settler capital was largely removed from the configuration of class forces by the independence settlement agreed in outline in 1961.

Cowen's object in tracing these developments is precisely to establish the specificity of the transition from precapitalist to capitalist relations of production, a transition seen as governed by the complex interaction of the forms and "periods" of indigenous and foreign capital over the past 100 years—a question central to the theme of this paper. For the moment, however, let us focus on the more limited question of the light which this perspective throws on the current role of indigenous capital accumulation in Kenya.

III. *Contemporary indigenous capital accumulation*

When negotiations for independence were begun in 1960, the economic and political weight of the indigenous owners of capital was already decisive.

The often-cited expansion of smallholder farm output that occurred in the decade 1955 to 1964, for example—from K£5.2m to K£14.0m per annum—is remarkable not least for the capital investment it implies, especially when we consider that down to 1964 the cumulative total of government and bank lending to smallholders was only K£1.7m.[23] The size distribution of the output tells the same story. In Murang'a in 1970-71 14% of the members of one coffee cooperative studied by Lamb (i.e. all the growers of a given area in Kikuyu country) supplied 64% of the crop, and in the same season in two tea-growing locations of the neighbouring Nyeri District, studied by Cowen, 20% of the growers supplied 55% of the crop (in 1965 20% had supplied 64% of the total;[24] in other words, the initial impetus came even more markedly from those with the capital to make the necessary investment and pay the necessary wages). Similar reflections are prompted by the fact that from 1959, when Africans became eligible to buy land in the former white highlands, down to 1970, at least K£7m and perhaps as much as K£10m of privately-owned capital, mostly from Central Province, was invested in large-farm purchase. Bearing in mind the degree of concentration involved in both the expansion of smallholder production, and the purchase of large farms from white settlers, these figures serve as useful if very rough indicators of the scale of accumulation which had been achieved during the colonial period by the indigenous class of capital, in spite of massive competition from foreign capital of all kinds, and with very little support from the colonial state.

Besides the scale of their capital, the indigenous class of capital—which after the reforms of the 1950s we can increasingly term an indigenous capitalist class—had a further highly significant asset. It was heavily concentrated in not only the largest ethnic group—composing with closely related neighbouring people about 25% of the total population, but also in the economic and political centre of the country. Combined with its strong representation in the state apparatus (due to its heavy investment in education) the indigenous bourgeoisie was exceptionally well placed to convert its natural dominance in the nationalist movement into a position of strategic control over the post-colonial political re-alignments needed for the next phase of accumulation. By mid-1966—2½ years after independence—these realignments had been completed and the framework of an effective "power bloc" under the hegemony of the Kikuyu bourgeoisie was clearly established.

From this time onward the state apparatus superintended a series of measures which rapidly enlarged the sphere and the rate of indigenous capital accumulation. The principle measures used were trade licensing, state monopolies, state finance capital, state direction of private credit, and state capitalist enterprise.

These measures have been discussed elsewhere and need not be re-capitulated here.[25] Their effects may be seen in a broadly sequential pattern whereby in one sector after another, according to the relative difficulties posed for indigenous capital by varying technical and capital requirements, African capital became first significant, and then preponderant. The movement into the former white highlands began in 1959. By 1977 it was estimated that only 5% of the mixed farm area within the former "white highlands" remained in expatriate hands. The transfer to African owners of expatriate-owned ranches and coffee plantations was well advanced and the transfer of the much more concentrated tea estates was no longer impossible to envisage. By 1974 the Development Plan claimed that most "small commercial firms have already been transferred to citizen owner-ship" and that "larger and more intricate" firms still in foreign hands would be Kenyanised by 1978:[26] by 1977 the evidence suggested that this target would be substantially met. The transfer to African capital of urban real estate, already well advanced by 1976, received a fresh impetus from the sudden rise in liquidity due to the exceptional coffee sales of that year, and led to a rush to purchase the remaining foreign owned large office blocks in central Nairobi, suggesting that the complete African occupation of this sector was no longer a distant prospect.

Information on the diverse range of activities comprised under "services" is largely insufficient to disclose the rate of penetration by African capital. Passenger road transportation was largely in African hands by 1977 as were tour companies, laundries and dry cleaning, and a rapidly growing share of the hotel and restaurant sectors. Sectors still substantially in foreign or at least non-African hands were those still protected against African entry by a combination of technical and capital barriers, often reinforced by a degree of monopoly: e.g. construction, financial services, insurance, mining, and manufacturing. But in each of these fields a significant degree of penetration had already begun, and in manufacturing, the most important of all, a new phase of African entry seemed to be beginning by 1977.

Except for 1975 and 1976, the rate of growth in each of the sectors progressively occupied by African capital remained high, and a conservative estimate suggests that the share of the total operating surplus accruing to African private capital by 1975 was of the order of a third, or about K£180m, sufficient to permit very substantial further movement into new sectors and subsectors (especially when one takes into consideration the limitations of the data, which tend to understate the output of African enterprise).[27] (Table 1) The essential function of the state was to displace monopolies enjoyed by foreign capital and substitute monopolies for African capital, and also to supplement individual African capitals with state-finance capital and state-secured technology, to enable them to occupy the space created for them in the newly-accessible economic sectors.

In noting the important role of the state in facilitating this movement of African capital out of circulation and into production, we must avoid the mistake of attributing to it an independent role. Its initiatives reflected the existing class power of the indigenous bourgeoisie, based on the accumulation of capital they had already achieved.

This is not a merely academic point. Unless the exercise of state power after 1963 is grasped as a manifestation of the class power already achieved by the indigenous bourgeoisie, it can lead to serious mystification. The most common form of this is to see the state's economic role as expressing the "modernising" vision of the state bureaucracy (the "elite"). On this view the whole process of the appropriation of surplus value by the exploiting classes disappears behind an ideological conception of "development" in the interests of "the people of Kenya." Alternatively, one version of the dependency school sees the state as a more or less independent *mediator* between foreign capital and local capital according to some conception of a "balance" which, since foreign capital is evidently much stronger, can only provide minor gains and compensations for local ("dependent") capital.[28]

Some such conception was at times implicit if not explicit in my own earlier work on Kenya. Instead of seeing the strength of the historical tendency lying behind the emergence of the African bourgeoisie I tended to see only the relatively small size and technical weakness of African

TABLE 1

Monetary Economy	Percentage growth of GDP at constant prices				Operating surplus 1975* K£m (5)	Estimated share of African private capital % of Col. 5 (6)	K£m (7)
	Annual average 1964-1972 (1)	1973-1974 (2)	1974-1975 (3)	1975-1976 (4)			
Agriculture	6.5	− 0.6	0.1	6.9	94.52	50%	47.26
Forestry	6.3	12.4	0.2	4.3	1.80	25%	0.45
Fishing	3.6	− 5.1	—	4.5	1.27	50%	0.64
Mining & Quarrying	6.7	− 9.9	2.8	10.1	1.62	0	0.0
Manufacturing & repairing	8.1	8.9	2.6	12.5	73.57	5%	3.68
Building & Construction	9.5	− 9.7	− 3.6	2.8	8.50	10%	0.85
Electricity & Water	7.8	9.4	10.9	11.8	9.08	0	0.00
Transport, Storage & Communication	7.6	− 1.0	− 3.0	6.0	24.34	50%	12.17
Wholesale & Retail Trade	6.1	− 3.1	− 7.6	8.2	65.54	70%	45.88
Banking, Insurance & Real Estate	10.6	18.3	5.9	2.7	31.19	5%	1.56
Ownership of dwellings	1.5	2.7	1.0	2.0	46.01	50%	23.0
Other services	10.5	13.2	6.8	3.1	7.65	10%	0.77
Total enterprise	7.2	2.5	− 0.1	7.2	365.09*	37%	136.26

*Provisional figures (*Statistical Abstract 1976*). *The Economic Survey 1977* shows a revised total of K£257.17m. The provisional total for 1976 was K£482.22m. Since a large part of this increase was coffee revenues, the effect would be to raise the African share of the total substantially for 1976.

(Sources: *Development Plan 1974-78, Statistical Abstract 1976, Economic Survey 1977*)

capital in face of international capital, and to envisage the state as little more than a register of this general imbalance; rather than seeing the barriers of capital scale and technology as relative, and the state as the register of the leading edge of indigenous capital in its assault on those barriers.

The general theoretical error involved here needs no further emphasis, but it is worth while illustrating one of its many effects from another, related angle—the significance of contemporary forms of "primitive" accumulation in countries like Kenya.

In Kenya the spectacular phase of accumulation through modern forms of plunder was probably the years from 1971 to 1975, commemorated in a celebrated series of pseudonymous articles in the *Sunday Times* in August 1975.[29] However, such practices as the commandeering of state-owned land and livestock or the semi-forcible take-over of expatriate farms or businesses, were not unknown earlier, and liberal observers were apt to be very preoccupied with these on moral grounds. But what needs to be considered about such practices, however, is not only their distributive effects, but their effects on production, inasmuch as they may contribute significantly to a concentration of capital in indigenous hands sufficient to overcome specific barriers of scale. The part played by primitive accumulation in the development of European capitalism is so well known that we should at least be ready to recognize its possible significance in a periphery country like Kenya today.[30] Some forms of such accumulation have probably been pursued on quite a broad scale, moreover, such as the importation or export of goods whose import or export is supposed to be banned.[31] A spectacular special case which occurred in 1976-77 reinforces the general point. When the world price of coffee had risen to ten times the average price for 1975 it was estimated that between 10% and 30% of the entire Ugandan coffee crop, worth between K£20m and K£60m, was being smuggled through Kenya rather than sold to the Ugandan Coffee Board. So valuable was coffee at this time that two "robberies" of Ugandan coffee in transit on Kenya Railways in one week of August 1977 accounted for coffee worth K£400,000.[32]

Clearly, the scale of capital concentration which may be achieved through these forms of modern "primitive" accumulation does not guarantee that such capital will be invested productively. Much of the capital accumulated in African hands in the last ten years will have been unproductively invested and much of what has been productively invested has involved the acquisition of existing assets, resulting in the transfer of capital into other sectors or out of the country. Nonetheless the significance of these transactions for the long-run potential for further accumulation by indigenous capital remains profound. A striking example comes from the expatriate-owned coffee plantations. In 1974 the capital value of plantations, and also foreign-owned ranches, was still considered a major barrier to their purchase by Africans.[33] But starting in 1973 and developing into a rush by 1975, about half of the total hectarage of foreign-owned coffee was bought by Africans; by the end of 1977, 57.3% of the total had changed hands, i.e. nearly 18,000 hectares, worth about K£18m at 1975 prices.[34] Most of this undoubtedly came from various sources of finance capital, but the funds in question were also largely the result of the previous phase of accumulation by Africans. And the process was already well advanced when the coffee boom began. By 1977 a high proportion of the new owners had paid off their loans and were actively searching for new investment opportunities. Speaking generally, and bearing in mind the concentration of coffee output in a few hands within the small-holder areas, rising from the earlier phases of capital accumulation, the effects of the coffee boom would be to put a large part of the K£200m realised from coffee sales in 1976-77 alone (the equivalent figure for 1974-75 was K£33m) into the hands of the indigenous capitalist class.[35] (It must be borne in mind that the coffee estates which changed hands in 1973-77 rarely afforded the new purchasers much land for household cultivation of other crops. They belonged to the realm of capitalist, not pre-capitalist relations of production.)

These reflections are relevant to the highly significant contemporary movement of African capital into manufacturing production. In commerce, returns are quick and the capital outlay is relatively small, but in the long run profits are liable to be forced down by competition from other commercial capitals and by industrial capital, in relation to a share of surplus value the total of which is determined at the point of production. In Kenya, this was experienced by the leading African capitalists as a rapidly narrowing scope for further displacement of foreign capital from the sphere of circulation, coupled with a growing awareness of the limitations of that sphere. These themes recurred in discussions with those concerned with industrial investment, such as the following:[36]

> In 15 years, if the political climate of Kenya and the world economy stay stable, 90% of manufacturing will be Kenyan owned. Where else is there for people to go? Agricultural land is finished—all the big farms are sold and divided up. Distribution is all taken up. Africans don't want to go into tourism, it is too risky—politically. And very tight [sc. competitive]. So they will go into manufacturing. As the market is narrow, this means they will buy into existing businesses. The public ones will go quietly by purchase. The price will rise till foreign owners, considering the risk, sell. Private ones will take longer but will gradually go. New ones will start with parastatal or local control.

This analysis (not all of it indisputable) reflected the viewpoint of a state official. The (African) manager of a major multinational conglomerate, himself also an active independent capitalist, said:

> In the early independence years, people lacked capital. Smallholdings under consolidation [the pooling of land fragments carried out in the 1950s when freehold titles were issued] generated a bit, then people moved into the Rift Valley schemes [in the former white highlands] and most of them did quite well. Then the Africanisation of trade generated more—if you had the Breweries franchise at 3½% it was a monopoly and people came to you [i.e. you didn't have to work to get customers]. In general, retail trade isn't hard and people learned to do it well. Now a point has been reached where people have some capital and want to know how to preserve it against inflation. Also they are starting to come into the income tax net and above a certain income, they realise income is not so important. What they want is to secure the future for their families and so on; and this means you must own productive assets—that is the only way you can make capital grow. . .

It was also interesting to note how the shift from the sphere of circulation to that of production was reflected in a shift of class imagery, as evidenced in several interviews:

> People think they must be a manufacturer to be someone. If you have a beer distributorship, that's nothing to be.

> The challenge of industrial investment is that you must wait for a return, but when it comes, it is higher.

> Local people don't want just to put their money in; they want control.

It would be misleading to say that by 1977 African capital was moving primarily into manufacturing production. There was still considerable scope for movement in the sphere of distribution and services. But the movement into manufacturing was under way, with the following specific features:

a) Capital was being *concentrated* in sufficient volume and in *appropriate forms* for industrial investment. Five specific forms were in evidence. Most common (especially in new investments), and perhaps in the long run most significant, there were *syndicates*, usually of 4 or 5 individual capitalists, formed to make one or sometimes several investments in manufacture, usually taking 25%-30% of the equity together with a state investment corporation and a foreign manufacturer, but sometimes with a controlling interest. Recent new projects involving such groups were plants to manufacture drugs, tea, shoes, soap, furfural, pipe-fitting, plastic sacks for agriculture, etc., etc. Secondly, *cooperatives* of various types had begun investing in manufacturing; usually these were agricultural (producer) co-operatives, moving into a project connected with farming (e.g. to produce fertiliser) but other types of cooperative were also increasingly moving along the now familiar path from agricultural through commercial to manufacturing investment. This was particularly likely to happen to some land-purchase cooperatives which had invested in coffee plantations. Third, there were *mass investment companies,* of which the prototype was Gema Holdings Corporation, an offshoot of the Gikuyu, Embu and Meru Association, formed in 1971. Gema Holdings, formed in 1973, went public in 1976. It was controlled by a group of leading Kikuyu capitalists, with an original issued capital of K£1m. In August 1977 it offered GEMA members K£2½m in new K£5 shares, an issue which was quickly taken up. Its non-agricultural investments already included a roofing tile factory and a new truck assembly plant, co-owned with Fiat. Other "ethnic" investment companies were planning to follow this example. An earlier example, with different origins, was the ICDC Investment Company, an offshoot of the state-owned Industrial and Commercial Development Corporation. Set up in 1967 with initial funding and continuing management provided by the parent ICDC, its shares were sold to Africans. By 1970 its total capital value was K£100,000. By 1976 this had risen to K£700,000, with investments valued at K£1m. Fourth, a variety of *state economic institutions* had begun to act as industrial investment companies, in addition to the longer-established investment corporations (the ICDC and the Development Finance Company of Kenya, in which the state was a minority shareholder). This was particularly true of some of the large number of agricultural parastatals, which were beginning to invest in the processing of agricultural commodities: cashew nuts, vegetable dehydration, maize cob by-products, etc. The Agricultural Development Corporation (originally a state-farm management organisation) alone had invested in the manufacture of sugar, processed fruit, cattle feed, vegetable oils and the factory production of poultry, often in association with a private investor or syndicate. Finally, there had been a notable growth of *merchant and industrial banks,* some of them tapping new sources of foreign capital. This was true of the state-owned Industrial Development Bank, established in 1973, which by 1976 had increased its original capital by about 200% by drawing on World Bank funds.

b) Skills and knowhow had been accumulated. One of the most striking changes in Kenya since 1971 was the coming "on stream" of a new generation of technically trained state economic functionaries. The Industrial Development Bank staff were a leading example of this, combining advanced technical (economic and accounting) qualifications with considerable specialised experience, but the pattern was being repeated in other organisations. Some of these new economic functionaries were themselves spearheading the entry of private African capital into manufacturing, under the freedom given to officials in 1971 to engage in private enterprise. The financial controller of one large parastatal had, thus, also established three manufacturing companies in which he had a controlling interest, the largest of which had assets worth K£1.7m.

A very important skill is that of taking over an established company. In the late 1960s a land-purchase cooperative wishing to buy a farm from a white settler was almost wholly dependent on advice from political patrons. By the late 1970s such organisations generally knew most of what was needed in order to buy, manage or subdivide a large farm, and some of them were learning how to buy and manage other kinds of asset. An extreme case of the acquisition of take-over skills was the takeover in 1975 of Mackenzie (Kenya) Ltd., a foreign trading conglomerate with assets of some K£2.7m., by a syndicate, one of whose two shareholders was the African chairman of the company, appointed three years previously. According to Swainson, this was only the first and so far most important of a number of similar takeovers which obviously depended largely on the inside knowledge of the leading figures involved.[37]

Swainson, the leading authority on corporate development in Kenya, considers that African advance into the manufacturing sector will be slow, and given the capital requirements of much manufacturing industry, this judgment seems reasonable. Nonetheless the rate of return in this sector is relatively high (Langdon found that 20% on assets employed was the norm for foreign-owned subsidiaries) and there seems to be no obvious reason why the initial rate of African penetration achieved by 1977 should not gradually accelerate in the following decade.

IV. *Formation of an indigenous bourgeoisie*

To examine properly the process of class formation associated with indigenous capital accumulation—a process occurring at several levels (social, political and ideological as well as economic) and involving complex interactions between the events in the distinct "historical times" of the different levels—would be a separate study in itself, far beyond the scope of this paper. Here we can simply note certain rather obvious indicators of this process, which do little more than testify to its existence (even that little, however, has some bearing on the theoretical significance of the Kenyan case to which we must return in the final section):

a) An increasingly evident differentiation during the decade in which the accumulators had spread out of their original base in circulation. Distinct fractions of African capital—primarily merchant, agricultural and industrial, but also financial (e.g. stockbroking) and rentier (e.g. real estate), and within the first two of these, large-scale/modern and small or medium scale/archaic—had begun to crystallise around various recurrent issues: for instance, the scope and level of protection afforded to manufacturing (merchant capital favouring more limited protection), wage controls (more important for smaller, more archaic forms of capital, with lower levels of productivity), and so on.[38] Besides the formation of these class fractions the formation of certain significant strata (determined by political and ideological practices) could also be discerned: in particular, a small, older political stratum, heavily involved in the various forms of modern primitive accumulation, increasingly giving way to a younger generation more equipped to dispense with primitive forms of accumulation and oriented strongly towards fully capitalist valorisation of the inherited family capital: the higher-level "straddlers", i.e. holders of salaried positions, state, parastatal and corporate, using their salaries and their privileged access to credit to create independent basis of accumulation: and a stratum of low-profile entrepreneurs, in the classical mould, with sometimes surprisingly large capitals invested in relatively advanced fields of production, a stratum destined to assume greater importance through the long run growth and deepening of its investments.

b) A notable development of adjutant, auxiliary ranks immediately subordinate to and serving the African bourgeoisie: lawyers, accountants, stockbrokers, insurers, heart specialists and psychiatrists, as well as a layer of ideologists, including academics and journalists.

c) A parallel development of bourgeois culture: increasing resort to private schooling, followed by university education at the family's expense in Britain or the USA (bourgeois parents increasingly regarded the University of Nairobi as intellectually and socially inferior, as well as unsafe, given its periodic encounters with the paramilitary police);[39] a distinctive bourgeois life-style in terms of housing, entertainment, etc.; a bourgeois marriage circuit with a manifestly dynastic aspect; the growth of a weekly and monthly magazine culture which reflected these tastes and interests, but also some of the more political concerns of its younger, more sophisticated elements for institutional reform and for the establishment of civil rights seen as essential in creating stable and reliable conditions for economic life.

d) A progressive development of bourgeois class consciousness through a series of struggles with other classes and fractions. The decisive years here were 1965-69, during which the political challenge of the petty-bourgeois/urban trade union/rural landless alliance led by Odinga and Kaggia was outmanoeuvred and finally destroyed in the banning of the Kenya Peoples Union in 1969. In the course of these struggles, the unionised working class was brought effectively under control of the state, first through a state-controlled union central organisation, and subsequently by a ban on strike action and an effective system of wage controls. The petty-bourgeoisie was also decisively neutralised as an independent political force. The populist tendency maintained, after the breakup of the KPU, by a group of parliamentary backbenchers, was ultimately curbed through the murder of J.M. Kariuki and the subsequent detention (or exemplary jailing on conviction for offences) of his most effective successors; while the middle and poor peasants were as far as possible organised as clients under the patronage of the bourgeoisie through a comprehensive system of ethnic organisations with their associated "self-help" movements, rival ethnic colleges of technology, ethnic investment holding companies, etc.[40] These organisations and their offshoots, ostensibly trans-class, must be understood as class organisations of the bourgeoisie in its relations with the peasantry, just as much as the Federation of Kenyan Employers was the principal class organisation of the bourgeoisie in relation to the organised working class; and as KANU—through its very lack of organisation and effectiveness—was the class organisation of the bourgeoisie in relation to all other classes, perpetuating their disorganisation, their under-determined condition, *vis-à-vis* the bourgeoisie which "led" it (superintending its endless factional struggles, and the repeated campaigns for party revitalisation and reorganisation, apparently preparing for an exercise in mass democracy which never came).[41]

V. *Kenya and the dependency debate*

The role of the indigenous bourgeoisie has been stressed virtually to the exclusion of that of any other class, partly to redress an obvious shortcoming in my own earlier work. The decolonisation process in Kenya, lasting roughly from the mid-1950s to the mid-1960s, was governed primarily by the neo-colonial "class project" of international capital, but the subsequent period was determined primarily by the class project of the indigenous bourgeoisie, and the failure to grasp and interpret the nature of this dialectical shift was a serious one, due mainly to an inadequate historical analysis of the material bases of the different fractions of capital in Kenya.

But besides the need for historical reparation, it is equally important to put the indigenous bourgeoisie at the centre of any discussion of the bearing of the Kenyan case on the theoretical issues discussed at the beginning of this paper. Put in its most general terms, the point seems to be that there were two distinctive (and indeed exceptional) circumstances affecting the development of the relations of production in Kenya. First, the existence of an indigenous process of capital accumulation in central Kenya which was sufficiently advanced at the moment of colonisation for the accumulated capital, and the class places formed in the process of its accumulation, to be *transmitted*—albeit transformed in various ways—through the colonial period into the moment of decolonisation: and second, the installation under colonialism of a foreign but *resident* bourgeoisie (the settler fraction) which, through the colonial state, appropriated a large part of the means of production (land and livestock) and secured the partial proletarianisation of most of the population) and the complete proletarianisation of a significant minority) while at the same time establishing (again largely by means of state intervention) the infrastructural and other conditions for the domestic accumulation of capital.

International capital played a part, too, intervening in particular to reduce the value of labour power by raising productivity in the staple food-producing sector, (i.e. reducing the exchange value of maize), advancing the large amounts of capital needed to extend commodity production (e.g. tea, tourism), etc. But in a typical "colonial trade economy" international capital (merchant, industrial or state) appropriates surplus value partly through unequal exchange, and partly through direct controls over household commodity production, in ways which, broadly speaking, leave largely intact the forms and much of the substance of pre-capitalist relations of production (in particular the household ownership of the means of production and often limited dependence on commodity production for reproduction of the household as a productive unit); whereas in Kenya, this relationship between international capital and peasant households was established relatively late in the colonial period, and not before settler capital had made considerable inroads into the economic independence of the peasant household throughout large parts of the country. Moreover, the hegemony of settler capital created other conditions favourable to the *local* valorisation of capital. The colonial state, in the era of settler hegemony, secured access to the whole East African market, which together with a common currency facilitated the realisation of productive capital in Kenya and so opened the way to relatively early industrialisation initiatives, simultaneously enabling merchant and finance capital located in Kenya to appropriate a significant share of the surplus value generated in Uganda and Tanganyika.

The dialectics of capital accumulation in Kenya thus involved (a) the subordination of indigenous capital to settler capital, but not its *destruction;* (b) the assertion by settler capital of claims on labour power and the means of production which greatly limited the scope for international capital to enter into direct relations of exploitation with peasant commodity producers, and undermined much more radically than in most African countries the precapitalist relations of production: and (c) the ability of the indigenous class of capital not only to substitute itself effectively for the settler fraction of capital at independence—i.e. as an internal bourgeois, not a petty-bourgeois, class—but also to set about recovering from international capital a good part of the field of accumulation which it had succeeded in occupying. In effect, the indigenous capitalist class assumed the hegemonic place in a new "power bloc" (i.e. alongside international capital and elements of non-indigenous local capital), in the context of an economy which was already capitalist in more than the usual sense: i.e. not merely one in which the still preponderant precapitalist relations of production (peasant household commodity production in particular) were subjected to the laws of the capitalist mode of production, in both direct and indirect ways; but also one in which for some important sectors, and to some extent for the "economy as a whole", the "structure of profitability" no longer depended simply on extending relations of exploitation based on absolute surplus labour (intensifying labour in various ways) but increasingly on raising labour productivity.

In less abstract terms, Kenya appears, from this analysis, as a modest example of a "systematical combination of moments" conducive to the transition to the capitalist mode of production. This does *not* imply that no further obstacles remain in Kenya to the uninterrupted domestic accumulation of capital, i.e. the uninterrupted development of the productive forces through the extension of capitalist production relations progressively throughout the entire economy. Nor does it imply that the indigenous bourgeoisie is "progressive" in the anti-imperialist sense ascribed to it by the theorists of the Comintern, still less that it is preparing a bourgeois-democratic revolution for Kenya, in the nineteenth century sense of *that* term. Nor, finally, does it imply a "menshevik" political position of support for capitalism in Kenya as the necessary preliminary to communism. What it says is that capitalist production relations may be considerably extended in a periphery social formation, and the productive forces may be considerably expanded within and through them, for reasons having primarily to do with the configuration of class forces preceding and during the colonial period: and that the limits of such development cannot be determined from the sort of general considerations advanced by underdevelopment and dependency theory.

In the case of Kenya, while the extension of capitalist production relations has been extremely rapid since independence, the process is threatened by multiple contradictions. One is the well-known limitation of the internal market, which presses Kenyan industrial capital both towards the search for export markets—in which it has had some success, especially in 1977 after the loss of the Tanzanian market following the border closure—and towards foreign policies aimed at re-establishing a new *internal* market within the East African region.[42] These initiatives, which probably hold considerably more promise than the apparently more "radical" alternative, proposed by the ILO, of internal income redistribution (in addition to being politically more acceptable to the bourgeoisie), should not be underestimated. However, the limitation remains a critical one for any economy not capable of producing, ultimately, for the *world* market: the question of how and in what terms a country such as Kenya may be enabled to transcend that limitation is all-important, even though it still lies somewhat in the future as far as Kenya is concerned, and certainly cannot be usefully speculated about here.

A more immediate and severe contradiction lies, I think, in the powerful place of "middle" peasant household production in agriculture, which may be approaching the limits of its expansion.[43] Current policy thinking within the Kenyan state bureaucracy favours the extension of this form of production, based on high labour inputs per hectare, even though with apparently declining labour productivity (agricultural output per head of population seems to have declined steadily since 1970).[44] While this would serve the interests of international capital which appropriates surplus value more or less directly from such production, it would hardly serve the interests of the indigenous bourgeoisie who, however, would confront a major political problem in any attempt to raise the productivity of labour and their own appropriation of surplus value by trying to extend capitalist relations of production in agriculture (e.g. by policies designed to polarise the smallholder areas towards kulak and capitalist farming on the one hand, and proletarianisation on the other). Yet without an increase in agricultural productivity, it seems doubtful if the momentum of capitalist production can be maintained in industry in the longer run. Here again, the limitations of the analysis of this paper do not permit useful speculations about the development of this contradiction: though it too should not be attributed any absolute character.

As for the political character of the indigenous bourgeoisie, its interests are partly coincident with those of the international bourgeoisie, and partly in contradiction with them. If it is "progressive", it is progressive in relation to the petty-bourgeoisie which seeks to defend, in general, relations of production—especially smallholding and petty trade—in which the exploitation of the workers does not expand the forces of production (however much that defence is couched in the rhetoric of populism and petty-bourgeois socialism). In relation to the workers, the indigenous bourgeoisie is exploitative and oppressive, and the bourgeois freedoms which a section of it increasingly desires—such as freedom from the disruption of production by unrestrained and unpredictable forms of primitive accumulation, freedom from political threats to the security of personal fortunes, freedom from low-quality and politically dependent judicial officials—are for itself, not for workers; furthermore this wish is in contradiction with the equally strong wish for a state capable of repressing both worker and petty-bourgeois attempts to organise industrial and political class struggle. To recognise the important role of the indigenous bourgeoisie in the combination of "moments" giving rise to the development of capitalism in Kenya is, therefore, not to succumb to ideological illusions about its historic mission or its current political character.

In conclusion, the foregoing discussion can perhaps be linked to the broad theoretical issues raised at the beginning of this paper, in the following way: the Kenya case seems to lend useful support to the general position adopted by Brenner, and may even help to put in somewhat clearer perspective the question which is at issue in the debate between Frank, Warren and Emmanuel. Frank, following Baran, located the primary mechanism of underdevelopment in processes of "surplus transfer" ("loot", in Baran's paradigm case of India) from periphery to metropole by individual capitals. Warren, seeing no theoretical reason for attributing to individual capitals (at least after the decolonisation process had ended in independence) any general motive to transfer surplus in this way, concluded that it would henceforward not do so, and so that capital formed at the periphery would not be accumulated there too. Emmanuel, rejecting the alleged evidence that this was happening, proposed instead that capital is drawn towards the poles of its own existing accumulation.

The point of view suggested by this paper is that all of these positions are mistaken insofar as they propose tendencies inherent in "capitalism in general"; whereas that each of them may, on the other hand, be correct and illuminating considered as an explanation of the movement of capital, and its consequences for the development of capitalist production relations and capital accumulation, in particular historical circumstances. Thus Baran's paradigm case of India had two significant features. One was the nature of the pre-existing relations of production in India, let us call them quasi-feudal, which, as Marx eventually noted, proved highly resistant to displacement by capitalist ones. The other was the character of British capital at the period in question—still largely family capitals, still competitive, focussed strongly on the necessity to expand constant capital within the existing production unit in order to maintain market shares. In these circumstances it was understandable that the original process of looting India in order to establish capitalist production in Britain should continue as a process of repatriation of profits earned from sales in India in order to expand capitalist production in Britain. The capitals which primarily figure in the work of Warren and Emmanuel, however, are corporate monopoly capitals, with the organisational capacity and political freedom to select their points of accumulation according to a global rationality. In this very different situation, the total combination of "moments" at any given place in the "periphery" (even this term must be increasingly questioned) becomes decisive, in relation to the corresponding combinations at the relevant places in the "centre." This of course is an excessively mechanical formulation. However, it is evident that—precisely in certain "exceptional" instances—capital has flowed to, or simply been rapidly accumulated at, strategic points in the so-called periphery, where the relations of production and the balance of class forces have produced conditions permitting the realisation of "surplus profits";[45] while at the same time—precisely in certain similarly "exceptional" countries in the so-called *centre*—there have been parallel processes of declining rates of accumulation, where the balance of class forces has given rise to conditions which have seemed hostile to the interests of capital, e.g. Britain.

NOTES

1. This paper is based on a short visit to Kenya in the summer of 1977 financed by the Canada Council, and generously assisted by Dr. David Court. Its intellectual debts, especially to Mike Cowen, should be obvious.
2. Cf. the recent contribution to the debate by Robert Brenner, who poses the same basic question ("The Origins of Capitalist Development: A Critique of Neo-Smithian Marxism", *New Left Review* 104, July-August 1977, pp. 25-92).
3. A.G. Frank, *Capitalism and Underdevelopment in Latin America*, Monthly Review Press, New York, 1969.
4. Bill Warren, "Imperialism and Capitalist Industrialisation", *New Left Review* 81, September-October, 1973.
5. Arghiri Emmanuel, "Myths of Development versus Myths of Underdevelopment". *New Left Review* 85, May-June 1974, and P. McMichael, J. Petras and R. Rhodes, "Imperialism and the Contradictions of Development", ibid.
6. The same general point is argued from different theoretical premises by Geoffrey Kay in *Development and Underdevelopment: A Marxist Analysis*, Macmillan, London, 1975.
7. McMichael et. al., op. cit., p. 96.
8. Ibid.
9. *Capital* Vol. I, Penguin Books, London 1976, pp. 915-16.
10. Op. cit., p. 78, italics in the original.
11. The same point was argued, very cursorily, in my "Underdevelopment and Dependency: Critical Notes", *Journal of Contemporary Asia* Vol. 7, No. 1, 1977, p. 105. See also A. Foster-Carter, "The Modes of Production Controversy", *New Left Review* 107, January-February, 1978.
12. See note 3 above.
13. Op. cit., p. 91.
14. Op. cit., p. 85.
15. See Brenner, pp. 91-2 where he speculates on the possibility that industrial capital in the metropoles, eager for new markets and cheaper labour, may now lend new strength to the class interests behind industrialisation at the periphery, enabling them to "force the class structural shifts that would open the way to profitable investment." By contrast Emmanuel, writing in 1974, considered the advanced countries "nowadays too rich not to be able to absorb themselves, without difficulty, all the new capital that is formed in them", (Emmanuel, op. cit., p. 77).
16. Central Bureau of Statistics, *Integrated Rural Survey 1974-75*, Nairobi, 1977, Tables 8.13 and 8.9.
17. Calculated from *Statistical Abstract 1976*, Government Printer, Nairobi, 1977, Tables 109(a) and (b), 235 and 82(d). While these are very crude indicators, the tendencies seem large enough to be accepted as broadly valid for present purposes.
18. The real rate of net capital inflows is taken to be the inverse of the trade balance. Emmanuel (op. cit., pp. 75-7) argues convincingly that this is the best measure. The main measures taken against hidden transfers were withholding tax on licence, patent and management fee payments, and a system of inspection of all imports in the country of origin.
19. Op. cit., p. 63.
20. Debt service charges as a percentage of the value of exports, fell from 3.5% in 1971 to 2.5% in 1976. See *Economic Survey 1977*, Government Printer, Nairobi 1977, pp. 61-2.
21. Kenya's receipts of official capital aid per capita have been approximately equal to the average level for the continent as a whole. Moreover, a third of the largest

single component of bilateral aid (the British) has been payments for land purchase from British nationals who repatriated about 60% of it to Britain again.

22. M. Cowen, "Differentiation in a Kenya Location", East African Universities Social Science Council, 8th Annual Conference, Nairobi 1972; "Notes on Agricultural Wage Labour in a Kenya Location" (with F. Murage); "Concentration of Sales and Assets: Dairy Cattle and Tea in Magutu, 1964-71", IDS Working Paper 146; Nairobi 1974; "Patterns of Cattle Ownership and Dairy Production: 1900-1965" mimeo 1974; "Wattle Production in the Central Province: Capital and Household Commodity Production, 1903-1964"; "Real Wages in Central Kenya, 1924-1974", mimeo 1976 (with P. Newman); "Capital and Peasant Households", July 1976, mimeo; "Notes on Capital, Class and Household Production", mimeo, n.d.; "Some Problems of Income Distribution in Kenya" (with K. Kinyanjui), Institute for Development Studies, Nairobi, March 1977. The following section is almost wholly based on Cowen's work though it is in no way a summary or overview of it.

23. Leys, *Underdevelopment in Kenya*, Heinemann, London 1975, pp. 53 and 100.

24. The data from Lamb and Cowen are cited in J. Heyer, et. al., Agricultural *Development in Kenya*, Oxford University Press, Nairobi 1976, pp. 195-97. Heyer notes (p. 18) that the controls applied to new growers of such crops in the 1950s were such that only the relatively rich could comply with them.

25. See Leys, *Underdevelopment in Kenya*, Ch. 5, and N. Swainson, "The Rise of a National Bourgeoisie in Kenya", *Review of African Political Economy* No. 8, 1977, for fuller details.

26. *Development Plan 1974-78*, Government Printer, Nairobi, 1974, p. 366. "Citizens" includes non-Africans, mainly Asians. However the takeover by African capital of "larger and more intricate firms", was well advanced by 1977, with 1500 quit notices issued to Asian traders in 1973 alone (Economist Intelligence Unit report on Kenya, Uganda, Ethiopia and Somalia, No. 3, 1973). In 1974 69 large trading companies in Nairobi, including at least one major one owned by non-African Kenyan citizens, were accused of illegal importation and closed down until such times as, in practice, they agreed to sell the businesses to Africans (see Swainson, op. cit.).

27. In Table I the estimated African share of "wholesale and retail trade" is set at 70% because this item in the national accounts includes hotels and restaurants where international and non-African domestic capital is still relatively strongly entrenched. "Operating surplus" represents the value of total output less the cost of intermediate inputs and labour but includes consumption of fixed capital (i.e. depreciation) and is not equivalent to profits.

28. e.g. S. Langdon, "Multinational firms and the State in Kenya", *IDS Bulletin* Vol. 9, No. 1, July 1977, pp. 36-41.

29. John Barry, "Kenya on the Brink", *Sunday Times,* August 10, 17 and 24, 1975.

30. E. Mandel concluded from the historical evidence for Britain that "for the period 1760-1780 the profits from India and the West Indies alone [i.e. from plunder and slavery] *more than doubled* the accumulation of money available from rising industry alone" (*Marxist Economic Theory*, Merlin Press, London 1968, p. 445).

31. Six licences for supposedly banned imports of basmati rice in 1971 were worth approximately K£3 million (see *Underdevelopment in Kenya*, p. 158). At the end of 1977 one of Kenya's biggest textile companies failed, apparently because of competition from illegal imports.

32. *Weekly Review*, August 22, 1977.

33. *Development Plan 1974-78*, Pt. I, p. 216.

34. Annual Report of the Coffee Board of Kenya of 1977, reported in *Weekly Review*, May 5, 1978.

35. For comparison, total GNP in current prices was K£1,253 million in 1976. In Nairobi in mid-1977 one heard many stories recounting the amazing windfalls of the new coffee estate owners, all of which had essentially the same features: an estate containing 100 acres of coffee trees was purchased for K£50,000 in 1974 with a down payment of K£10,000, the balance being borrowed from the Agricultural Finance Corporation. In 1976-77 the average price of a ton of coffee was about K£2,000, so the value of the crop at a ton per acre would be about K£220,000. Even if, as was common, the estate was fully managed for the owners after tax would still be at least K£100,000 for the season.

36. The following extracts are from interviews with state, parastatal and private company officials in Nairobi in 1977.

37. N. Swainson, "Foreign Corporations and Economic Growth in Kenya", Ph.D. Thesis, London University, 1977, p. 249. This pathbreaking study will be published by Heinemann in 1979.

38. In identifying these fractions and their mutual relations, it is more than ever necessary to distinguish between "places" in the relations of production, which are determined by the historical processes of development, and the agents who occupy the places, some of them occupying more places than one.

39. I owe this point to M.P. Cowen. It was strikingly borne out in interviews.

40. The middle and poor peasantry thus constituted a typical "supporting" class for the bloc of classes in power, a class kept "underdetermined" through the ideology of tribalism, in particular.

41. The real significance of the often intense factional struggles within local branches of the party, a party without a real function, would seem to be to serve as partly ritual periodic indicators of the relative strengths of bourgeois and petty bourgeois class fractions. It should perhaps be added that the state apparatus also served as the class organisation of the indigenous bourgeoisie in relation to the international bourgeoisie, and the Presidency, with its surrounding apparatus, also served as the class organisation of the indigenous bourgeoisie in relation to the non-indigenous domestic bourgeoisie.

42. In 1976 Kenyan exports to Tanzania were worth K£33m. or roughly 13% of all Kenyan exports, offset by imports from Tanzania worth K£12m. The loss of this market through Tanzania's closure of the border in February 1977 was serious but was offset by the domestic market expansion resulting from the coffee boom, and to a lesser but significant extent by expanding exports to other regional markets. Kenya's handling of relations with Tanzania, which contributed to the border closure, is difficult to explain in terms of the interests of Kenyan capital, and an explanation should perhaps be sought in the excessively confident pursuit of those interests by the Kenyan state apparatus.

43. "Now, within the contemporary period of expanded household production, the reproduction of households out of produced commodities is reaching the limits of existing commodity forms of production" (Cowen, "Some Problems of Income Distribution in Kenya", op. cit., Section 3, p. 36).

44. The quantity index of monetary sector agriculture rose from 100 in 1972 to 101.8 in 1975, and monetary agricultural GDP rose from K£94.3m to K£95.2m in the same period. This was before the impact of the better weather and prices of 1976-77, but suggests that per capita agricultural output is tending to decline in the medium run.

45. In the sense proposed by Ernest Mandel in *Late Capitalism*, New Left Books, London 1976, Ch. 3.